Making Diplomacy Work

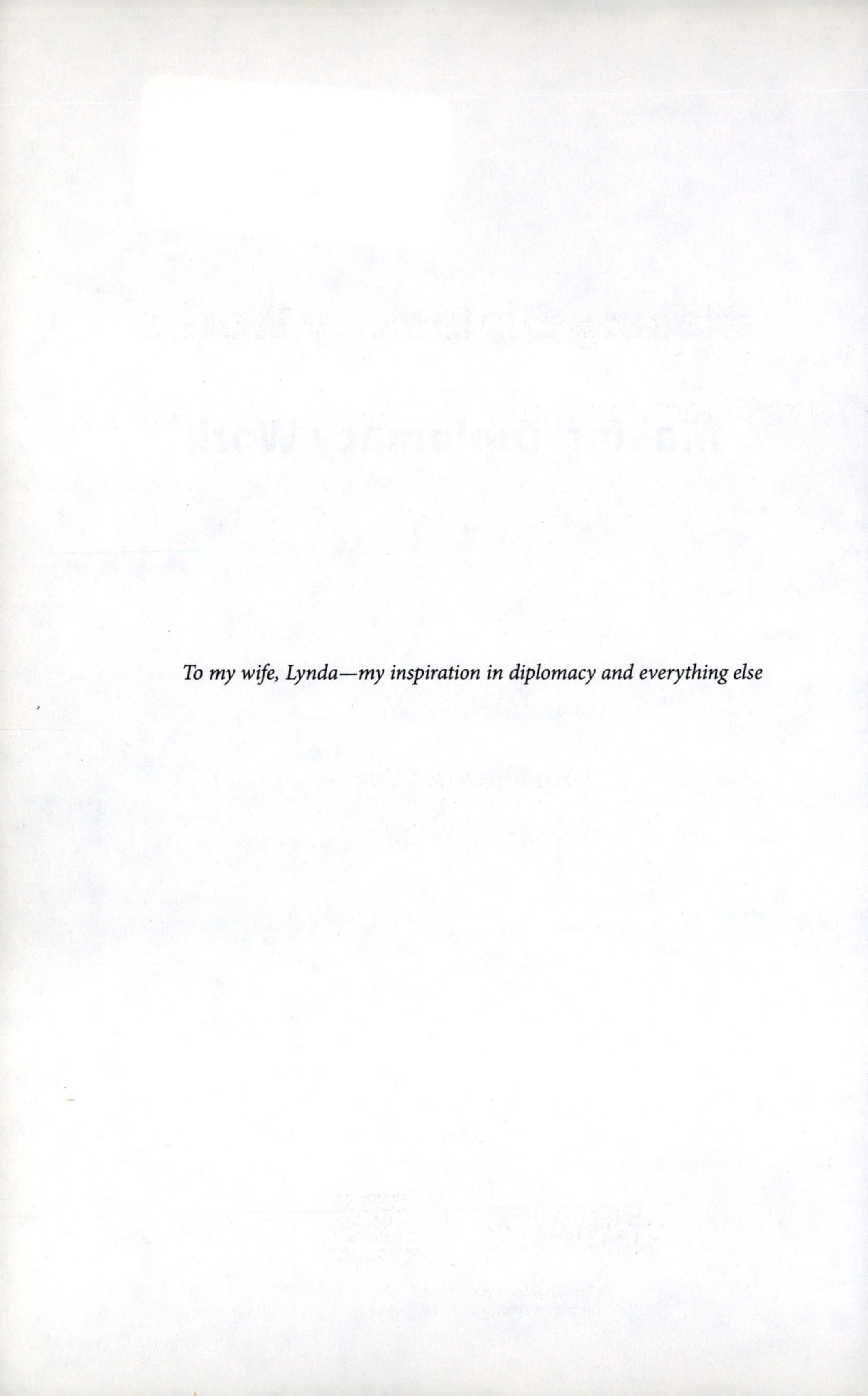

To my wife, Lynda—my inspiration in diplomacy and everything else

Making Diplomacy Work

Intelligent Innovation for the Modern World

Paul Webster Hare

Boston University

Los Angeles | London | New Delhi
Singapore | Washington DC | Boston

Los Angeles | London | New Delhi
Singapore | Washington DC | Boston

FOR INFORMATION:

CQ Press
An Imprint of SAGE Publications, Inc.
2455 Teller Road
Thousand Oaks, California 91320
E-mail: order@sagepub.com

SAGE Publications Ltd.
1 Oliver's Yard
55 City Road
London EC1Y 1SP
United Kingdom

SAGE Publications India Pvt. Ltd.
B 1/I 1 Mohan Cooperative Industrial Area
Mathura Road, New Delhi 110 044
India

SAGE Publications Asia-Pacific Pte. Ltd.
3 Church Street
#10-04 Samsung Hub
Singapore 049483

Acquisitions Editor: Sarah Calabi
Associate Editor: Nancy Loh
Editorial Assistant: Raquel Christie
Production Editors: Natalie Cannon and Veronica Stapleton Hooper
Copy Editor: Cathy Kottwitz
Typesetter: C&M Digitals (P) Ltd.
Proofreader: Dennis W. Webb
Indexer: Molly Hall
Cover Designer: Karine Hovsepian
Marketing Manager: Amy Whitaker

Printed in the United States of America

A catalog record of this book is available at the Library of Congress.

ISBN: 9781452276489

This book is printed on acid-free paper.

15 16 17 18 19 10 9 8 7 6 5 4 3 2 1

TABLE OF CONTENTS

PREFACE

There are fewer than one million career diplomats in the world in a population of over seven billion. Diplomacy is something most people read about rather than do. I practiced it for thirty years but seldom read about it—its origins, development, flaws, and achievements. I worked for what is generally regarded as one of the best-resourced and influential diplomatic services but never thought too much about diplomacy as a global activity. My brief was different—to represent the United Kingdom and its interests.

Why then write a book?

When I started teaching American and international students at Boston University, I found that most of the available literature, though not misleading, did not convey the practical aspects of what diplomats do. It generally was written from a Western perspective while the practicing diplomat soon recognizes that the objectives and methods of diplomacy are far from universal. And the literature was overly deferential. It did not question how far diplomacy needed to catch up with the world. There was little analysis of the reasons for the successes diplomacy achieved, only rare acknowledgment of its regular failures, and scant questioning of its ritualistic elements, which occupy much diplomatic time. I have tried to fill this gap and provide a comprehensive survey of modern diplomacy, its institutions and challenges. I hope that students in universities and in diplomatic academies will find the book stimulating enough to pursue their interests and practice diplomacy in some part of the world.

The second reason for the book was selfish. I became fascinated in what I was teaching. The global breadth of diplomacy is astounding, and the extent to which it lives every day beyond the desk of the bureaucratic toilers was rarely noted. But this fascination was soon tinged with frustration. Could it be that global—not national—diplomacy was a human endeavor that had no lobby, no advocates, and no resourcing? Who genuinely wanted to build on the ancient cornerstones—the Vienna Convention, the UN Charter—that were framed to improve it? Would academic specialists produce a new blueprint, or would ambitious undersecretaries in foreign ministries strive to perfect the system?

And what of the retired ambassadors like me? Generally, they have devoted themselves to producing memoires and tales of hidden triumphs and secrets betrayed. Beyond these, where were the innovators?

Building on this, the third motivation was to encourage work on diplomatic innovation. It is alarming to think that this is currently solely an issue for seminars and doctoral theses. If methods and framework determine outputs, then the inadequacies of the diplomatic process might in some way account for diplomacy's high failure rate. To both the specialist and the casual observer, the future of diplomacy looks bleak. And the future is what most of diplomacy is about. Only rarely does world governance acknowledge its responsibility to future generations—Articles 225 of the Brazilian Constitution and 20a of the German Basic Law do so in relation to natural resources. I did, however, find some encouragement in the past capacity of diplomacy to renew itself. And I saw urgency in the new waves that are crashing on diplomacy's shore—the exponential growth in the number of countries participating in the diplomatic system since 1945, the rise and capacity of globalized nonstate actors, and the myriad opportunities and vulnerabilities for diplomacy in the accelerating information and communications revolution.

The fourth objective of my discussion of diplomatic innovation was to provide diplomacy with a means to look at practical reform. There is a need to identify some instruments to limit the nonpeaceful, nondiplomatic means that now have greater capacity to hurt and weaken diplomacy. But no book is needed to state the obvious—that not all leaders in the world are anxious to explore the benefits of better diplomacy. Many would prefer to use military or economic muscle to get their way. The problem is that the world can no longer rely on such instruments to settle disputes or create a new world order. In short, diplomacy matters more because states individually are becoming weaker. Yet they share a collective interest in improvements because, as in all team games, the results demand combined efforts.

As for diplomatic reform, most current discussions center on which countries should have permanent seats on the United Nations Security Council or which might attend the next summit on whatever issue. Leaders acquiesce in the undemanding round of private conversations and photo opportunities because they have little time or inclination to probe deeper into international relations. So a major obstacle that all reformers have to overcome is to present some ideas that are not only workable and beneficial for diplomacy but that would also fit with the domestic agenda of those who must agree to them. No leader will commit diplomatic suicide, and any proposals made in this book for changes in and additions to current diplomatic practice try to recognize this.

The diplomatic examples given in the text reflect events that at the time of reading may seem in the distant past. But obviously, diplomacy throws up innumerable examples from which to quote every day. Major events are often assumed to be game changers for diplomacy. But in reality they seldom are. As I write this, Ukraine, Gaza, and the Islamic State (IS) are the focus of intense activity at United Nations, in capitals, and in the media. I hope that this book will prove its applicability to formulate diplomacy, no matter what the issue. Diplomacy is poor at predicting problems or outcomes, and I am no psychic. So in every class I teach, I try to review what new issues are arriving in diplomatic inboxes and their relevance for what diplomats do.

The book's title reflects my view that diplomacy can work better in the modern world but must also be made to work harder to justify itself. It is also important to differentiate one country's diplomatic expertise from the overall activity. The core of diplomacy is that it should not be a zero-sum activity. If it doesn't prove its worth, then its influence will gradually erode. The book looks at diplomatic practice through an unsentimental prism, offers some reflections from my own life as a diplomat, and attempts to point to paths that might make it more productive for all involved and for all affected by it. It is also intended to nourish the thinking of those interested in the way the world is run, how it functions internationally, and how diplomacy can seize new opportunities and guard against new threats.

If it fails in these tasks the fault is mine, not because such a book cannot be written.

ACKNOWLEDGMENTS

A diplomat's family members have to accept much in their own lives to support a career they did not choose. Yes, of course, there is enjoyment and adventure, but the price of movement, change, fear, and insecurity is often high. It is character building but also regularly gives the diplomat pause for thought. Is it really worth the disruption to the lives of others?

So my love and thanks go to my family for allowing me to have a career that gave enormous variety and interest and ultimately led to this book. Without my wife, Lynda, my life would never have taken the diplomatic path. She had a diplomatic career before mine, often working at the highest levels of the British government. So she knew all about it before I did and encouraged me to try it. Becoming a diplomatic spouse, she put warmth and love into our homes in numerous houses and countries. At the same time, she tried to help the underprivileged in the countries where we were posted. She did a lot of good and made the most of whatever assets diplomats have. She also bit her tongue many times and is relieved it's over. Our children, Antonia, Victoria, Andrew, Matthew, Alexander, and Marina all cheerfully (mostly) endured the changes and partings that diplomacy brings. Our family has continued to grow since we left the service. And I would like to thank the spouses of our children and our five grandchildren, none of whom complain about the regular re-airing of tedious diplomatic anecdotes.

Our children all proudly spent parts of their lives at remarkable international schools that often make diplomacy bearable for children. In their cases, these were the Escuela Campo Alegre in Caracas and The International School of Havana. Students from over fifty countries were their classmates. Throughout the world, the work of thousands of international school teachers means children of diplomats are no longer automatically shipped off to boarding school. The teachers also have lives of adventure, but they often endure tough conditions without the apparatus that gives diplomats support. My thanks go to them.

Beyond family and teachers, I owe a debt of gratitude to the many diplomats I have met, liked, and admired. They were mostly interesting and cordial colleagues. Some were lazy, some super energetic, some gave terrible advice, but all usually enjoyed what they did and saw the value of building friendships and common interests in an edgy world. Without such a cadre, no book like this would be worth writing.

If I had not had the opportunity to teach, none of this would have been written. I would like to thank my students and colleagues in my new cameo career at Boston University. Though a novice at teaching, I have been welcomed into the sanctuary of learning. My students have given me their attention and ideas, and it was because of them that I thought this book worth writing. At Boston University, I have been nurtured by numerous colleagues, especially Andrew Bacevich, Susan Eckstein, Erik Goldstein, William Keylor, Adil Najam, Scott Palmer, and Vivien Schmidt. In 2004, the United Kingdom's Foreign Office sent me for a year to Harvard University's Weatherhead Center and I saw the positive impact of academic study on diplomacy. The directors of the center, Jorge Dominguez and Kathleen Moloney, showed me how effective the best universities are in reaching out to the world.

There is no shortage of good ideas for intelligent innovation in diplomacy and I am grateful to all those who have contributed to the final chapter of this book.

Finally, of immense importance to what I hope you will read, has been the support and encouragement of the team at CQ Press. In particular I would like to thank Sarah Calabi, Raquel Christie, Cathy Kottwitz, and Veronica Stapleton Hooper. They were immensely patient and helpful.

PUBLISHER'S ACKNOWLEDGMENTS

CQ Press gratefully acknowledges the contributions of the following reviewers:
Marcus Holmes, Fordham University–Rose Hill
Aaron Zack, CUNY–Baruch College

INTRODUCTION

Diplomacy is an unusual activity.

It is often undertaken with no perceivable results and engaged in by individuals sometimes with little or no common interest and with no common approach to the process. There are no international auditing standards, no internationally recognized training qualifications, and few final successes. Diplomats are widely perceived as privileged (due to their immunities and tax-free status) and prone to talk rather than act. Yet hundreds of thousands of people are paid to work as diplomats. The activity happens continuously throughout the world. In every minute of every day, someone somewhere will be engaged in diplomacy. Contemporary diplomats serve sovereign states but also increasingly look for allies in nonstate sectors. Many of the governments that employ them are weak, seen as increasingly responsible for the world's problems but significantly handicapped in their capacity and in their resources to respond. There is no global lobby for better diplomacy. Many ponder the direction of the world and the forces that appear to govern it. Few if any solutions receive high-level consideration. Meanwhile, in a world more interconnected and more interdependent than ever, diplomacy struggles to find the shared solutions that match the shared interests states have. The diplomatic bottom line is that we live on the same planet. And all recognize that diplomacy is still the most effective way of setting an agenda to deal with the world's issues.

Diplomacy is not easy to define. Communication between groups and societies is a constant theme and is seen as a common good. But this is done in so many different ways it is often not clear what is happening and when. Nor is it clear that all that purports to be diplomacy and uses resources assigned to diplomatic activity has any point at all. Ernest Satow, in his classic *Guide to Diplomatic Practice*, wrote that diplomacy is "the application of intelligence and tact to the conduct of official relations between the governments of independent states and between governments and international institutions."[1] In practice, diplomacy is defined by its functions more than by its institutions. Diplomacy is an activity performed by distinct groups that has evolved into a permanent activity with content, partners, and measurable results. Much of its evolution to what we see today has been haphazard, with states agreeing to the codification of immunities and privileges and what functions of diplomacy are permitted but little else since. Yet governments do not frame the tasks of their diplomats in identical terms, nor do the roles of professional diplomats fit into government systems in the same way. Their status and influence over political and economic power differ greatly.

The roles of diplomats in the modern world appear clear. They have evolved through history, and states show a strong capacity to mimic each other. Diplomats gather information, report on international events using overt and covert sources, compete for commercial opportunities for their national companies, and offer consular services to their nationals. Diplomats need to be versatile, confident, and competitive. They vie for attention, and little attention is paid to whether the methods they use are productive for the contemporary world. Collective reforms seem less and less likely, even though in the century since Satow produced his guide diplomacy has been radically transformed through technology, revolutions, and wars. As Sir Ivor Roberts explained in the preface to his new edition of Satow in 2009, older editions needed "radical surgery" to make modern sense: "Diplomacy has changed too much in its practice if not its essentials. Satow would find much to amaze him in the conduct of diplomacy but not its underlying purpose."[2]

Satow's formula has been used with variants over many years. The most important operative words in it are *intelligent* and *tact*, both of which suggest the need for a strong aptitude to adapt to the needs of the time. These aspects are generally unchanging, but experts writing later have highlighted other elements. Sir Harold Nicolson, whose book *Diplomacy* first appeared in 1939, focused on the universality of the activity to every system of governance known to man: "Diplomacy is neither the invention nor the pastime of some particular political system, but is an essential element in any reasonable relation between man and man and between nation and nation."[3] Henry Kissinger stressed the element of striving for agreement through peaceful means, describing diplomacy as "the art of relating states to each other by agreement rather than by the exercise of force."[4]

WHY DIPLOMACY? THE KEY ELEMENTS

Rather than strive for a perfect definition, it is perhaps more helpful to examine some of the key elements that influence the activity of diplomacy. Six features distinguish what we are seeking to identify. The first is the parties involved in diplomacy do not represent themselves. They are engaged in their work as representatives of sovereign states. Second, diplomacy requires two or more parties, and these parties do not represent the same entity or government. Third, there needs to be a willingness and means to communicate between the parties. This creates a relationship that will be built up through trust and will be seen as valuable. Fourth, the nature of the relationship is normally continuous, not spasmodic, and requires round-the-clock access. There is no end point, no final victory, no diplomatic World Series. Whatever happens, however much blood has been spilled, you can safely bet that diplomatic methods will sooner or later be resurrected. Fifth, the content of the relationship is not limited by any universal definition of what is permitted. Each party defines what it sees as its interests in engaging in diplomacy. Sixth, all parties may seek to involve other actors in their diplomacy who may or may not be state entities.

If these are the features that define diplomacy, it is also instructive to differentiate diplomacy from related activities. Diplomacy is applied to international relations and foreign policy. It is not identical to either but is a process that has a strong input into both. Theories of international relations are not given much attention among professional diplomats, and this book is not intended to discuss such theories. Yet the academic study of international relations can assist our understanding of diplomatic practice. The theorists try to dissect and rationalize why diplomats act in certain ways on behalf of sovereign states and believe that some universal conclusions can be drawn.

The first group of theorists, known as the realists, sees states as the center of diplomatic activity and the purpose of diplomats they employ to promote the national interest. National interest and power are nearly always synonymous. The state is unitary, rational, and gives priority to security issues. The nonstate actor is a minor player who does not influence outcomes. Writers who have favored this approach include Niccolo Machiavelli, Thomas Hobbes, and Hans Morgenthau. Kenneth Waltz stressed the importance of institutions and practice in influencing realism and has been called a structural realist. Waltz attempted to use theories to analyze the causes of war and whether individuals, states, or international institutions were their prime cause. The second tradition, known as the liberal tradition, sees many more influences in play and suggests that diplomacy is a major contributor toward the positive development of international understanding. Nonstate actors and international organizations share with sovereign states the central roles in diplomacy. All, to some extent, are mutually dependent. This suggests a forward movement dependent on the relative influence of different actors in this pluralistic system. Writers who favored this approach, which places universal humanitarian values at the center of international relations, include the Dutch legal scholar Hugo Grotius and the German philosopher Immanuel Kant. The third group is sometimes called the economic structuralists and sees all international actors as defined by the contemporary world economic order. In particular, they see the capitalist system as promoting divisions between states and regions creating dominant and dependent relations. Karl Marx argued that the international nature of capitalism was a major determinant of relations between states. Fourth, the English School of theorists draws on a mixture of approaches and sees the world of international relations and diplomacy as influenced by many competing forces. They also recognize an international society as a rational concept where individuals, not just states, matter and where international institutions, rules, and norms can become accepted as in the self-interest of states. In their view, states are multifaceted, not unitary actors. Writers who have developed this hybrid approach include Martin Wight and E. H. Carr.

Another field of study has focused on how diplomats operate in the context of society. Do diplomats add something to the evolution of international relations, or does their own behavior in practice set the parameters for what diplomacy can achieve? The theory developed by Paul Sharp in his book *Diplomatic Theory of International Relations* suggests that the content of diplomacy and the way its practitioners behave does in practice influence international relations. Diplomats, Sharp argues, generally have mixed motives for their actions. Like Machiavelli, they prioritize survival for themselves and their states. They also try to maximize the interests and rights of their countries, and then they try to increase the state's power. In Sharp's view, diplomats think diplomatically and try to build trust in diplomacy and smooth the edges of disputes. They put a premium on the maintenance of relations. Yet whatever their motives, Sharp believes that diplomats cannot depart from their essential separateness from each other and the groups they represent. There can never be a complete convergence or merging of interest. The fact that the groups of diplomats represent states does not mean that they will be any more successful in promoting convergence than groups based on other common allegiances, such as science or religion. The degree of separateness inherent in diplomacy also implies that groups are unlikely to have much interest in diplomatic interchange with countries that can do them little good and cause them little harm. Diplomats have to be selective in a world of over 190 national groups and many thousand more issue groups.[5]

John Dryzek believes that any deliberative governance depends on building consensuses. And diplomacy is an important part of international deliberation. If diplomacy is to work at all, as in all deliberative fora, there must exist one or more of the different types of consensus: first, the normative consensus, where values are agreed; second, the epistemic consensus, where there is agreement on what impact policies will have; and third, a preference consensus, where there is actual agreement on what should be done. Dryzek recognizes the difficulty of achieving any or all of these in discussion, but the key element for diplomacy is the acceptance of metaconsensus—acceptance of differences in discourse—which he sees as necessary for progress in all forms of deliberative discussion.[6]

Whichever theory one favors, the results of diplomacy are impressive. In the last century or so, diplomats have achieved great success through institution building, settlement of disputes, international rule making, agenda setting, and in preserving peace when war seemed a more likely outcome. Equally, failures are not hard to identify. Some countries, despite having extensive diplomatic relations and having employed skilled diplomats, do not succeed in surviving. Many countries in history have failed even though they had the benefits of modern diplomacy. Yugoslavia and Sudan provide recent examples of disintegration. And the veneer of peaceful coexistence on the planet does not reflect reality for many. Conflicts—interstate and intrastate—have caused over twenty million deaths since World War II, and since 1990 over 90 percent of the deaths have been of civilians. In 1992 alone, UNICEF estimated that 500,000 children under five years old died as a result of armed conflicts.

The report card of diplomacy is not easy to grade. Diplomacy is a complex system, and the variety of tasks assigned to diplomats, and not sought by anyone else, reflects its growing complexity. Governments pay the budget so their interests as they perceive them will govern the results they hope to achieve. Inevitably governments want to implement a diplomacy that will appeal to a domestic electorate or will achieve nationalist benefits. But the achievement of enduring results depends increasingly on rapid international choreography, with quick coordinated responses, tapping into expertise and resources from many sectors. As states with declining resources become conscious of the need to partner with other actors to ensure their survival and capacity to influence international events, diplomacy breaks out of its separateness in different directions. Nonstate actors and individuals such as Bill Gates or Mo Ibrahim operate in different ways from interstate diplomacy.

Box I-1 **International Relations Theory**

International relations theory is part of society's attempt to rationalize how human groups interact. Diplomacy, of course, affects international relations, and may follow some of the same rules. But equally, it may simply reflect the type of institution the world chose to create or the natural habit of all states to copy each other in a search for status.

International relations theory also sets itself different tasks from a study of diplomacy. It seeks to predict how states will behave and how rules govern the conduct of relations between states. Diplomacy is now conducted by so many actors, and with such varying degrees of skill and success, it would be surprising if patterns of activity were predictable.

And the issue of ethics? Diplomacy, whether for promotion of state interest or for collective activity, is not governed by a moral code but, rather, by what suits best the interests of the actors.

Few dispute that diplomacy matters. It is rooted in common existence on one planet and the collective benefits all countries derive. The world needs diplomats and their activities. They are just as necessary when governments are strong or weak. Diplomacy does not have an electoral cycle and diplomatic history may matter little in the context of current crises. Many of the existing diplomatic institutions were conceived in an era when governments and their diplomats were revered and commanded authority beyond the possibilities of most governments today. The world is now less deferential to every human activity, including diplomacy. Yet part of the rationale of international agreements on diplomacy like the Vienna Convention on Diplomatic Relations is that well-executed diplomatic relations are beneficial to every country's international relations. Like other sociological movements, diplomacy's influence has expanded and contracted through history. Some generations have bequeathed much; others little. Diplomacy's core functions remain valid in any era. The world's problems are diminished if diplomacy takes all its opportunities and the mechanisms work well. This does not mean that all countries will or need to relinquish their national interest. But it is central to the themes of this book that better diplomacy, more intelligent diplomacy, is not a zero-sum game. It is in everyone's interests, whether they are states or nonstates, that global issues are treated with smart diplomacy. And it is in everyone's interests that diplomatic failures are recognized and that sovereign states collectively try to improve diplomacy rather than acquiesce in old, stale habits.

ABOUT THE AUTHOR

Ambassador Paul Webster Hare is currently a lecturer at Boston University where he teaches classes on Diplomatic Practice, Arms Control and Nonproliferation, and on Cuba in Transition. Ambassador Hare was the British ambassador to Cuba from 2001 to 2004. He has been designated a Lieutenant of the Royal Victorian Order by Her Majesty Queen Elizabeth II.

Hare graduated with first class honors in politics and economics from Oxford University in 1972 and from the College of Law in London in 1976. He worked for five years in the private sector, in law and investment banking, before serving for thirty years in the British Diplomatic Service. Hare served overseas in Portugal, New York, at the U.K. Representation at the European Union in Brussels, and in Venezuela as Deputy Head of Mission. He was Head of the Foreign Office's Non-Proliferation Department and the first project director for the United Kingdom's presence at the Shanghai World Expo in 2010.

Hare is a fellow of the Weatherhead Center for International Affairs at Harvard University and was a member of the Brookings Institution Core Group on Cuba. His novel, *Moncada: A Cuban Story*, set in modern Cuba, was published in May 2010.

SAGE
50
YEARS

chapter 1

Diplomacy in History

There was no rule book agreed upon when diplomacy was created. Practitioners made it up as they went along. Diplomacy began through practice in stages of human history where contacts between strangers—those outside family units—were systematized. Harold Nicholson noted that there has been no smooth development of diplomacy and that it has suffered repeated setbacks.

The word *diplomat* derives from the Greek word for an official document, *diploma*, meaning "I fold" or "fold double." Those who organized such diplomas were the first to be called diplomats, the name eventually passing to the holder of the document that conferred privilege, formality, and status in the diplomatic system. The Medieval Latin *diplomaticus*, which means "related to documents and texts," is also related to the vocabulary of the activity. Yet the practice of diplomacy predates countries and indeed the word itself. The word *diplomacy* has been in common usage in the English language for a little over two centuries.

Diplomacy in the form we would recognize today developed when permanent contact and dialogues between governing entities such as city-states came to be seen as mutually advantageous. States had evolved and their functions required contact. The content of the contact was of course determined by the agenda and customs of the times. In Mesopotamia, there are letters dating from the third millennium BCE between Egyptian dynasties and other political leaders and entities in the region. In China, military strategy influenced Chinese views of the world and trade with the outside world was not encouraged. The Chinese also favored a tribute system, which committed regional powers such as Korea and Vietnam to back the regional order. And the Chinese view of foreign policy partially depended upon the concept of *te* or virtue. The Chinese emperor's *te* was respected by others and military force was held in reserve. The Greek city-states like Athens, Sparta, Thebes, and Corinth were sufficiently refined in relations to ascribe names to those performing different diplomatic functions—the *angelos* or *presbys*, the *keryx* and the *proxenos*. A *proxenos* represented another state while remaining resident in his own state.

Diplomacy's role as the principal messenger between governing entities depended of course on the capacity of the technology of the time to deliver those messages and the content of the relations that developed. Those diplomats who were appointed often benefited from some existing connections, either through families, marriages, or by common faith in God (as in Byzantium) or the pope (Rome). Both empires saw diplomacy more as a way of consolidating their influence rather than as a forum for dialogue. Rome did not instigate international agreements nor indeed pay much attention to the drawing of boundaries between Roman and non-Roman lands. Yet some surprising diplomatic practices developed. In the Roman Empire, foreign nations, but not Rome, handed over high-ranking hostages as a way of guaranteeing their promises. In the early history of Islam, the Prophet Mohammed received a delegation of Christians in Medina in 631 CE and signed the Treaty of Najran. Even in times of extreme conflict in history, diplomacy surfaced with some success. During the Crusades, the liberation of Jerusalem in 1228 was achieved through diplomacy. And Christians tried to enlist Mongols to fight against Muslims through persuasion and bribery.

The key consideration in nominating the first diplomats was that a person of trust and discretion should be appointed to act as a go-between. There were no prescribed patterns of behavior. Trade was an early global issue, but the most common feature of early diplomacy was the weakness of the states. In the sixteenth century, European states were generally weak in comparison with Ming China or Ottoman Turkey. The envoys appointed were usually unsalaried, seldom in contact with their employers, and were left to build a private network of contacts. The pace of diplomacy was slow, its content and objectives limited. But practice and utility of diplomacy borrowed from numerous sources.

THE BUILDING BLOCKS OF MODERN DIPLOMACY

Many of the features familiar to contemporary diplomacy can be identified in events in history. Nicolson suggests that the conference of Sparta in 432 BCE was the first example of a diplomatic meeting.[1] This conference was called by the Spartans to decide whether to go to war with Athens, and an Athenian delegation was invited to stay and address the Spartan assembly. Ivor Roberts notes that the Byzantines sought to compensate for their reduced military power by enhancing the role of the diplomat from simply being a "herald or an orator" to a more flexible and results-oriented intermediary.

The Italian states were small, generally without territorial ambitions and were dependent on trade for their wealth. So the advantages of a permanent diplomatic presence increasingly made sense. Thus in the 1450s, Francesco Sforza, ruler of Milan, sent Nicodemo Trincadini as his confidential agent to Cosimo de' Medici, the most powerful citizen of Florence. The Italian Wars from 1494 to 1559 ironically gave a boost to the business of diplomacy with the Italian states becoming the focus of regional rivalries. At that time, diplomatic representation outside their region was of more interest to the Italian states than to the larger powers. Before 1500, Milan, Naples, Venice, and Florence had all sent envoys to France or Spain and the papacy followed by appointing resident nuncios in the major courts of Europe. The first appointment of a British ambassador is generally considered that of John Sherwood as ambassador to Rome in 1479. By the time of Queen Elizabeth I (1558–1603), resident ambassadors had also been appointed to the Ottoman Empire, the Venetian Republic, the Holy Roman Empire, and the Kingdom of France. In 1585, the first book was published on diplomatic law, written by Alberico Gentili, who escaped from the Italian inquisition to take up a position at All Souls College, Oxford. His book *De Legationibus Libri Tres* discussed the inviolability of ambassadors and the rules governing the operation of diplomatic missions. So the practice and code of conduct of diplomacy preceded the establishment of strong sovereign states.

The next milestone in diplomacy's development was the recognition of the value of diplomacy in consolidating the sovereign state. There is no precise date in history when the sovereign state began to be recognized under international law as an entity with legal rights and obligations. Rather, a state assumed sovereignty when it exercised effective control over a population within a defined territory. And it had long been established under customary international law that heads of state, when present in the territory and at the invitation of another sovereign, were entitled to privileges, honors, and full immunity from civil and administrative jurisdiction. The rise of the state also gradually shifted the emphasis of diplomacy away from its former binding influences like the papacy, the Holy Roman Empire, and Islam. States gave and still give diplomacy its most comfortable home.

The power of the growing state gave rise to analysis of the use of nonmilitary methods in international relations. Machiavelli has lent his name to this aspect of diplomacy—the raison d'état or ends justifying the means. Though the recognition of state interest and survival is essential in diplomacy, Machiavelli's concentration on the zero-sum nature of diplomacy disguises the shared interests that lie at the heart of its conduct. Machiavelli's Prince was advised that "it is much safer to be feared than loved, if one must choose."[2] And Machiavelli suggested that ambassadors should be accompanied by military officers disguised as valets. The idea of using diplomacy to smooth edges of relationships was far removed from his thoughts. Cardinal Richelieu was an early example of a powerful political leader who saw the role diplomacy could play in consolidating the power of the state. He saw it as important enough to dedicate units of government and officials to its pursuit. Richelieu's contribution to the creation of diplomatic institutions is described in Chapter 3. Once states incorporated diplomacy into long-term strategy, diplomats needed continuity of operations, particularly in the art of negotiation. In his *Testament Politique*, written in 1638 for private use by Louis XIII, Richelieu advised "it is vitally important to negotiate continuously . . . even if one will make no present gain."[3] He allied Catholic France with the Protestant cause during the Thirty Years' War and his strategy toward the Holy Roman Empire helped engineer a balance of power in Europe, the first collective representation of which was at the Peace of Westphalia in 1648.

If Richelieu and Machiavelli influenced the evolution of diplomatic strategy, then a book in the 18th century by a Swiss lawyer, Emerich de Vattel, titled *Le Droit des Gens* had a strong influence of the evolution of diplomatic practice. Vattel formulated the international approach to diplomatic representation and rights of every state.

> Every sovereign state then has a right to send and to receive public ministers; for they are necessary instruments in the management of those affairs which sovereigns have to transact with each other and the channels of that correspondence which they have a right to carry on.[4]

Vattel discussed the role of various ministers serving a state but designated the role of ambassador as "the minister of the first rank." And his book assigned a distinct role to embassies, which had "a special purpose" so that "each Nation possesses both the right to negotiate and have intercourse with the others, and the reciprocal obligation to lend itself to such intercourse."[5] In Vattel's writings, widely admired by America's founding fathers, we can see many of the core principles of diplomatic privileges and immunities, later codified in the Vienna Convention on Diplomatic Relations (see Chapter 2).

The Congress of Vienna in 1815 was the nineteenth century's monument to a new order in Europe after years of devastating wars. One of the problems that the growing use of ambassadors had produced was the question of recognition of titles assumed by sovereign states. Some were reluctant to recognize the Dutch monarchy. And the title of emperor used by Peter the Great of Russia was not recognized for years by most European powers. As diplomatic ritual grew at courts, so did the struggle for precedence between envoys. Particularly acerbic rivalries over precedence developed between France and Spain over the status of their envoys. In an early example of diplomatic versatility, in 1661 the Spanish envoy in London cut loose the horse pulling the French ambassador's coach to deprive him of his position in a parade. The Congress of Vienna, as well as settling a peace, also concluded a formal arrangement on diplomatic precedence. Its "Regulation Concerning the Precedence of Diplomatic Agents" of 1815 established an agreed basis for diplomatic representation, including precedence, and such predictability and stability greatly assisted the development of diplomacy in the nineteenth century.

The second half of the 19th century saw significant growth in the numbers and role of diplomatic missions. The British still had only five full embassies and nineteen legations in the late 1860s. These numbers are, however, deceptive because there were also many representatives of the British Empire elsewhere in Asia, Africa, and the Middle East. The India office was and remained a force in U.K. diplomacy for decades to come. After two wars with China, both the United Kingdom and France established resident missions in Beijing. In 1871, China and Japan exchanged missions. By 1878, China had envoys in London, Washington, St. Petersburg, and Tokyo and legations in Berlin, Paris, and Madrid. That did not remove tensions in the conduct of diplomacy. In 1900, there was a prolonged siege of diplomatic missions in Beijing in the midst of the Boxer Rebellion.

DIPLOMACY AND COLLECTIVE ACTION

After the carnage of World War I and the military alliances that governed most diplomatic calculations, the new post-1918 diplomacy had to react to failure. New forces emerged, such as the power of the press, the power of the governed, and the decline of elites; there was also the emergence of mass ideologies such as communism and fascism. A leader with a soaring vision and a high sense of morality was keen to offer new ideas to fill the diplomatic vacuum. Woodrow Wilson seemed to have the ear of the world in his ambitious plans for new collective diplomacy, promoting transparency, self-determination, and universal values. But Wilson's own style of diplomacy at Versailles was in reality highly selective, and he did not listen to the ideas of others. Germany and its allies were largely excluded from decisions, which in the analysis of many diplomatic historians sowed the seeds of the disintegration of the Versailles peace.

The major innovation that Wilson and his generation of diplomats bequeathed was the League of Nations. This was the creation of a permanent diplomatic conference. Though the League eventually achieved nearly universal membership, reflecting disgust with a failed system of diplomatic deadlock, it collapsed because of actions of key sovereign states: the failure of the United States to ratify, the nonparticipation of Germany, and the absence—except for five years—of the Soviet Union. Nevertheless, the League of Nations proved a diplomatic learning experience, and after the Second World War diplomacy made another attempt at establishing a permanent conference. The Charter of the United Nations made what were seen as crucial improvements to the League as diplomacy reasserted itself after 1945. Again, collectively diplomacy was seen to have failed, and collectively new fora were established and objectives were set. The objectives of the movement that created the United Nations and the way it functions today are discussed further in Chapter 4.

As Ivor Roberts notes, these collective movements did not destroy the power of states. "The shape of the post-war world was . . . not set by a world forum but by a series of summit meetings of the three Allied leaders, Roosevelt, Stalin and Churchill at Tehran, Yalta and of Truman, Stalin, and Churchill then Atlee at Potsdam."[6] Spheres of influence dominated diplomacy between 1945 and 1990, and the West's approach to the Soviet Empire and Communist China was a policy of containment. Though the United Nations influence on diplomacy for much of these forty years was peripheral, it did evolve in other ways. Meanwhile, the Cold War provided predictability and strong states, which assisted the functioning of diplomacy in key respects.

The Cold War years produced diplomatic innovation in other ways. Two competing states, the United States and the Soviet Union, negotiated a series of arms control treaties as a framework for shared interests. The U.S. Secretary of

State Henry Kissinger showed that diplomacy of imagination and skillful linkages of issues were possible even in a developed, bureaucratic democracy. Kissinger saw that that the United States could develop a relationship with China, even after the appalling turmoil of the Cultural Revolution was still fresh in the memory. It was realpolitik but also showed a belief that diplomacy between leaders using modern technology was better than a static, rudderless, bureaucratic machine.

The complex global issues that have arisen after the Cold War—such as nonproliferation, terrorism, and climate security—have not generally lent themselves to such leader-driven strategic diplomacy, and the search for a formula to deal with crises and shared issues has not progressed much beyond multilateral conferences of states. This is a formula that has been practiced in many eras. Examples are the Congress of Berlin in 1878, the London Maritime Conference in 1956, the UN Conferences of Law of the Sea in the 1980s, and the climate change conferences in the 1990s and the twenty-first century. But the degree of innovation and the extent to which the sovereign state model can make progress on global issues has been limited. Summitry between leaders—such as the G20 and G8—is seen by some as a method of making the sovereign state a more effective decision maker and promoting the possibilities of convergence between opposing views. Even when conferences are unsuccessful, Satow advised that diplomacy must use whatever event or meeting is arranged for its own purposes. He saw them as opportunities to buttress the authority and influence of diplomats.

Collective action and addressing global issues have generally been secondary activities in the history of diplomacy. Sovereign states have seen the prime function of diplomatic negotiations to enhance the security and viability of sovereign states. Where security was perceived as shared, diplomats cemented the perception through treaties or through marriages between royal families. Both reduced the separateness of diplomatic activity. The consolidation and viability of the sovereign state was achieved successfully for many in Europe and diplomacy played its part. Expansion into other territory, such as throughout Africa during the 19th century, provided a convenient outlet for ambition or, in the case of the United States, expansion to its open frontier in the West. Diplomacy was often seen as an extension of such aggressive intent, less expensive than war perhaps but ultimately with similar goals. But these frontiers became exhausted, and conflicts between economic and political forces were increasingly concentrated within existing territorial sovereignty. Diplomacy now had more and different work to do.

Diplomacy in history therefore shows that while there are common threads in the way diplomats have behaved since the creation of the recognized functions of the dedicated envoy, much has evolved due to major developments in societies, governance, and economic systems in the last five centuries. It is instructive to look at past seismic shifts in factors affecting diplomacy. Such shifts are still occurring, and diplomacy must continuously demonstrate the capacity to react and refresh its operations.

REVOLUTIONS, WARS, AND THE CHANGING WORLD

Political revolutions have greatly affected the development of diplomacy and the raw material of dialogue. The French and American Revolutions changed fundamentally the blueprints for society and the way states would operate without the glue of feudalism or aristocracy. The concept of accountability to the governed took hold. Power vested in the people cut across the concept of the sovereign state belonging to the ruler. A casual reading of history may suggest that the democratic principles gained sway very quickly after such revolutions. This was far from the truth. Though the U.S. Founding Fathers had a radically different vision of society from many government leaders in Europe, they were by no means enthusiastic about the democracy as we would recognize it today. They did not abolish slavery or give women the right to vote. What was seen as forward-looking and intelligent in 1776—the Satow principle of effective diplomacy—would attract different views today.

Words on Democracy

Remember, democracy never lasts long. It soon wastes, exhausts, and murders itself. There was never a democracy that did not commit suicide.

—*John Adams*

Democracies have ever been spectacles of turbulence and contention; have ever been found incompatible with personal security or the rights of property; and have in general been as short in their lives as they have been violent in their deaths.

—*James Madison*

Radicalism is anything that presents a new challenge to diplomacy. Indeed some revolutions confront conventional diplomacy as part of the old order that needs to be overthrown. The Bolshevik Revolution of 1917 proselytized by force and diplomatic ardor. The Soviet Union was not even recognized as a state by many for several years. The United Kingdom led the way in 1924, but the United States did not establish diplomatic relations until 1933. The Islamic Revolution in Iran in 1979 changed the whole context of Iranian diplomacy, and the power structure in the Middle East and its effects are still being felt in regional alliances. Such revolutions lead to diplomatic countermeasures until the results are assimilated.

Just as a commercial organization will adjust its strategies to a change in the environment in which it operates, so does diplomacy. Diplomacy reacts to failures, remembers undesirable precedents, and makes the best of bad circumstances. It seldom sees perfection as practicable. Not all diplomacy favors peaceful outcomes. Diplomacy has played its part in preparing for wars, winning time through deception, and convincing other states to lend support or join alliances. And in some cases, this has been a regular focus of diplomatic activity. France and Germany fought each other three times between 1870 and 1940, and Russia and Germany fought twice. Across the world, Japan and China were in frequent conflict in the same period. Wars were expensive and destructive, and they weakened victors in different ways from the defeated. Wars of course redrew boundaries and served up new issues to the diplomatic agenda. Few countries have invested more in their diplomatic relations since 1945 than France and Germany. But events of the 1940s between China and Japan—such as the use of chemical weapons and the treatment of captured Chinese—still fester and cause diplomatic tensions today. Between 2011 and 2014, Syria used skillful diplomacy to stall and avoid international intervention in a civil conflict.

Another obvious factor that has changed diplomacy is the number of parties claiming the rights of a sovereign state. Revolutions and wars both played their part post-1945 in making self-determination a preferred solution to handle the territorial conflicts. Diplomacy showed its capacity to invent state creation as an outcome, even if the path to independence was seldom bloodless. The principles of self-determination had long been an aspiration of U.S. foreign policy. President Wilson addressed this issue in a speech to Congress in February 1918: "National aspirations must be respected; people may now be dominated and governed only by their own consent. 'Self-determination' is not a mere phrase; it is an imperative principle of action."[7] The Atlantic Charter of 1941, setting out Allied goals for the postwar world, referred to it. The United Nations Charter highlighted self-determination in its preamble, and the United Nations General Assembly in December 1960, with its resolution *Declaration on the Granting of Independence to Colonial Countries and Peoples,* provided for the legal linkage between self-determination and its goal of decolonization. With the implementation of this principle, the activity and agenda of diplomacy was changed forever. Diplomacy agreed to invite many new participants and has produced scores of new countries in a nonlinear growth.

TABLE 1.1 **Member states of the United Nations**

Year	*Number of States*
1945	51
1955	80
1965	117
1975	144
1985	159
1995	184
2005	191
2013	193

Source: United Nations, Member States, available online at http://www.un.org/en/members/growth.shtml.

Diplomacy more than tripled its family of states in nearly seventy years (as shown in Table 1.1) and simultaneously had to tackle the new global issues that emerged. Some of course were familiar. The eternal task of diplomacy to avoid war had already produced global treaties in The Hague and Geneva Conventions. Older issues like slavery had already been discussed and produced a global response. The world had devised means of regulating the prices of international commodities and controlling sea and air traffic. Postal treaties and a Universal Postal Union had been created to facilitate communication. But the distinctive feature of diplomatic activity in the nineteenth and twentieth centuries was that governments were the dominant actors and, though they licensed entities such as the East India Company to engage in business, the influence of nonstate actors on global issue diplomacy was limited. The extent to which this has changed in modern diplomacy is discussed in Chapter 10.

Another distinctive feature of the world post-1945 is the enormous growth in international trade and investment. Some of this trade is carried out by state-owned entities, but the majority by the private sector. Successful diplomacy has facilitated the communications involved in building trust, stability, and the rules of law that underpin such buying and selling. Figure 1.1 shows that the percentage of world GDP accounted for by trade grew from barely 3 percent in 1960 to almost 50 percent fifty years later. The interdependence and interaction involved in this accelerating process is unimaginable without diplomacy though the outcome has made individual sovereign states much less capable of determining their own outcomes.

The extent to which overseas entities commit funds to other states also reflects a diminishing of the power of sovereign states. Foreign Direct Investment (FDI) and capital flows again have transformed the world since World War II. According to the World Trade Organization, FDI, which had accounted for only 5.2 percent of global GDP between 1953 and 1973, increased to 25.3 percent between 1973 and 2007.

These developments have equally influenced diplomacy itself. As the United Nations' Trade and Development Report of 2011 states, "economic integration and interdependence in the world today have reached an unprecedented level."[8] And the overall growth masks other important trends that have impacted how diplomacy functions. Trade and investment have always been currencies of diplomacy, but in recent years, regional patterns have shown a peaceful revolution. During the period from 1995 to 2010, developed countries noticed a substantial decrease in their share of the world merchandise trade as developing countries increased their share from 29 to 41 percent. During this time, China's share alone increased to more than 10 percent, Latin America and the Caribbean rose to 5.9 percent, and Africa's share increased to 3.2 percent. Additionally, the trade between developing countries is booming. In 2010, foreign direct investment flows from developing countries were 29 percent of the global total.[9]

The speed and intensity of communications have always been a major influence on how diplomacy has developed. The greater the distance of diplomats from their home base, the greater was their freedom to decide. This was

Figure 1.1 **World Merchandise Trade, 1960–2011**

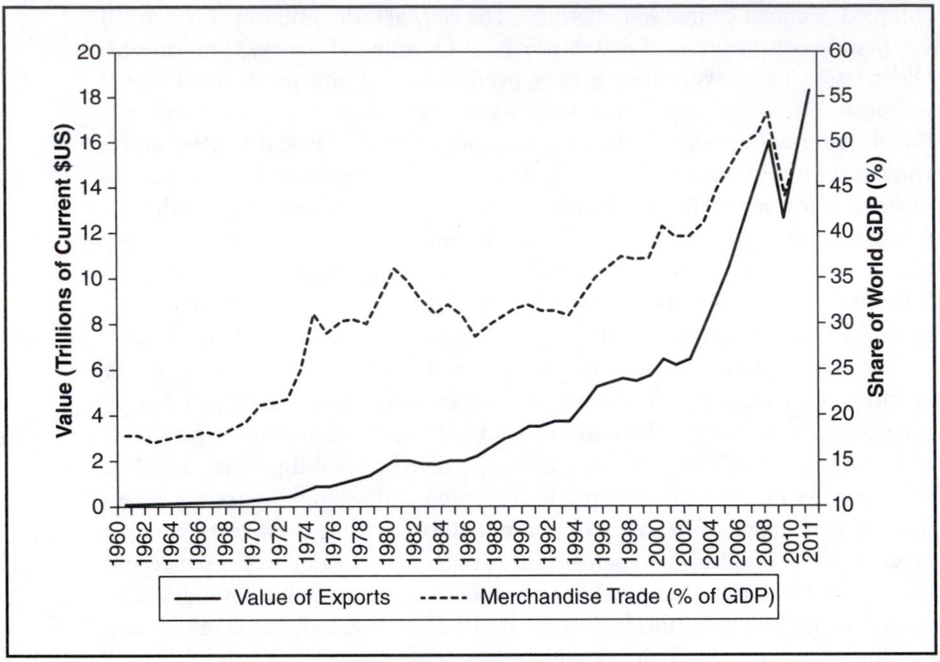

Source: Dr. Jean-Paul Rodrigue, "The Geography of Transport Systems," http://people.hofstra.edu/geotrans/eng/ch5en/conc5en/worldexports.html.

for long the reality of the life of envoys. A dispatch could take almost two months to reach America from Europe in the early nineteenth century, and in 1822 the record time for an urgent dispatch from London to Vienna was a week. In 1829, Claude Chappe's semaphore system, invented in 1792, began to be employed to speed up diplomatic communication time. Messages could then be sent from St. Petersburg to Berlin in just fifty hours. By 1853, telegraph cables linked Berlin, Paris, and London. Yet, even in 1914, a letter took six days to get from St. Petersburg to Paris. Adverse weather conditions regularly intervened to extend the time. Some thought that cables and mechanized transport would signal the demise of envoys. In 1876, when asked to approve the upgrading of the British legation at Rome to the status of an embassy, Queen Victoria suggested that "the time for Ambassadors and their pretensions [was] past."[10]

Both Presidents Wilson and Truman traveled to Europe by sea for the Paris and Potsdam conferences in 1918 and 1945 respectively. Franklin Roosevelt was the first U.S. president to fly in an airplane on official business in 1943. Digitalization has meant that distance involved in diplomatic communications no longer matters. The volume of communications also is now unlimited. In previous eras, correspondence was frequent but took time to arrive. It was, however, carefully preserved, much more so than one suspects in the digital age. In the 1820s, the United Kingdom published its first Blue Book of diplomatic correspondence. Others followed this example.

Now the absence of physical constraints on communication is not an unmitigated benefit for diplomacy. Diplomacy's successes can be built more easily but its vulnerability exposed ever more rapidly. U.S. Army Private Manning needed only a few blank CDs to wreak instantaneous havoc on the world's largest diplomatic system with the click of a switch. The impact of the information and communications revolution is discussed in detail in Chapter 11.

STATES AND LEADERS DECLINE

The major revolutions discussed have in many ways enhanced the importance of diplomacy and magnified its failures. The participation of more states would, one might assume, put more of a premium on nimble diplomatic footwork. Yet over 75 percent of the state actors in the world have fewer than twenty million inhabitants. These state actors, though represented equally in the United Nations General Assembly, have very diverse diplomatic capacities and are at different phases of their history. They are affected in different ways by forces that determine how international relations evolve.

At the same time, as more countries are investing in the sovereign state model, the communications across national boundaries have eroded many of the barriers that have been traditional and predictable features of the sovereign states. Unlike the changes in technology and their influences on the history of diplomacy in the past, the changes the modern world is experiencing are occurring at breathtaking speed. The accessibility of information, its speed of transmission, and the blurring of differences between domestic and overseas issues have undermined the influence of states over diplomatic processes and increased the influence of nonstate actors. The term *nonstate actor* does little justice to their activities or influence in the modern world. As Clay Shirky has said, talking about nonstate actors is like calling an automobile a horseless carriage.[11] The expanding role of nonstate actors in diplomacy is discussed in detail in Chapter 10.

Increasingly, funding is available from sources outside government for global causes. Tapping into cross-border technology, money can be transferred to any corner of the world, using the global commercial infrastructure that itself feeds off this diplomatic activity. Global commercial corporations are, of course, familiar with negotiating, persuasion, and public communications, and they use such diplomatic skills in global markets for energy, minerals, or where access to new consumers is promised. Both states and nonstate actors are now applying resources and strategies to a whole range of global issues, sometimes working in tandem, sometimes in competition. The capacity of nonstate actors both as agenda steerers and also problem solvers and creators has been vastly enhanced. Diplomatic practice has struggled to adapt. For political leaders of diplomatic machines, the complexity of actors, the scarcity of taxpayer-derived resources and declining impact of state actions means that public scrutiny, accountability, and electoral cycles steer international relations to short-term perceived advantage. Days of quick fixes and emergency reactions leave little space for grand visions or the thoughtful framework laying of past diplomatic eras.

Today, diplomacy is accessible and influenced by a multiplicity of players. It is a skill applied with differing degrees of success by entities of vastly different capabilities. While some objectives of states may be shared—for example, preserving peace in the interest of self-preservation—this does not mean that the outcomes they derive from achieving such peace will be identical. The overall context of a country's diplomacy varies according to the country's vision of the world order. Does the state see the world order evolving in a direction where cooperation with others in collective diplomacy serves its interests and, if so, in what areas? Does the state aim to use overseas relations to enhance its power to counter the influence of others? Does it apply its diplomacy as a medium for balancing power with others? Does it see threats to its current status or see opportunities for advancement?

The conventions of diplomacy and the statutes governing diplomatic institutions reflect the nature and form of sovereign state interactions at the time they were created. Nothing has yet been framed in the same guise to facilitate interaction between transnational commercial forces or the increasing activism, positive and negative, of civic societies. Diplomacy has not yet defined its working methods with nonstate actors. Because of the modern proliferation of states, and the decline in individual state power the process of diplomacy assumes more importance. How diplomacy performs increasingly determines whether and how problems are addressed.

One category of actors that are often discounted as a constant in diplomacy is political leaders. They now have infinitely greater capacity to engage in diplomacy themselves because of technological changes. Their physical location or their preoccupations with domestic politics does not constrain forays into diplomacy. Yet they themselves differ in their working methods and motivations from leaders of even fifty years ago. As Kissinger commented in his book *Diplomacy*, it is wrong to assume political leaders have any aptitude for diplomacy. They have little in common, often reject the multistate model of Western diplomacy, and are preoccupied with other things. They run

> bureaucracies of such complexity that, often, the energy of these statesmen is more consumed with serving the administrative machinery than with defining a purpose. They rise to eminence by means of qualities that are not necessarily needed to govern and even less suited to building an international order.[12]

If we look, therefore, to a new generation of world leaders to pull the world together to solve its problems through skillful diplomacy we are likely to be disappointed. Most contemporary leaders seem to acquiesce in the institutions and mechanisms they have inherited. They have little time or interest in exploring diplomatic innovation.

DIPLOMACY AND FOREIGN POLICY

Diplomacy is an instrument and a part of foreign policy. It fits alongside other elements such as military alliances, trade, and overseas development assistance, and it plays a part in producing outcomes of foreign policy. But it is not the policy itself. The processes diplomats use to achieve similar foreign policy objectives differ greatly in their content and sophistication. Diplomacy is also not the same concept as international governance. There are again areas of overlap. Certainly governance is assisted and defined by good diplomatic process. But diplomacy is more the plumbing and the wiring of the international system of institutions and governing guidelines. Diplomacy has operated over centuries, during which many concepts of world order have been used by diplomats to frame their behavior and objectives. In the modern era, two broad views of how the world order functions still color diplomatic activity.

The first concept sees the objective of diplomacy as creating and maintaining a balance of power. Endorsed by the realist theorists of international relations, balance of power proponents argue that sovereign states use their diplomacy to maximize their individual power. They work with other countries in alliances but ultimately take all responsibility for their security. The advantages perceived for this framework are that it mirrors the natural Darwinian order where the strongest survive and a country, relying primarily on its own military and economic assets, can predict the outcomes. Its supporters believe it produces periods of stability because countries know where they stand. Kissinger points to the policies and philosophy of Theodore Roosevelt as reflecting the overt use of the balance of power in U.S. history. Under his approach, the United States chose to behave as a crusader and project its strength through decisive national interventions such as in the Panama Canal and in brokering a peace settlement between Japan and Russia.

The second approach is one in which diplomacy is used to implement a foreign policy that favors collective security. A country gives priority to cooperation with other countries because it recognizes its interdependence. The big issues of diplomacy are global and require collective solutions. Using the state's diplomacy to lock in cooperation through global laws, norms, and alliances is necessary to produce results in critical issues like nonproliferation of weapons of mass destruction, climate security, and terrorism. Similarly, a state favoring collective approaches is likely to see the promotion of common values in such areas as human rights and government transparency as being important diplomatic activities. Supporters of collective security argue that the moral beacon of diplomacy or example setting can be effective in influencing the behavior of others rather than the crude projection of power. Kissinger identifies Woodrow Wilson as an example of a strong advocate of collective security. In his view, power alone could not determine the conduct of international relations.

Diplomacy that favors such collective actions seeks to share resources, responsibilities, and believes that problems require a collective effort, perhaps led by international institutions, to produce enduring solutions. This offers a different, more optimistic vision of the world than one where shifting power structures, as in the balance of power, determine outcomes. In his *Peace Without Victory* speech of 1918, Wilson summarized how his views differed from the alternative approach to foreign policy: "There must be, not a balance of power, but a community of power; not organized rivalries, but an organized, common peace."[13]

Both elements—balance of power and collective security—are present in the diplomatic strategies of the major diplomatic actors. The advantage of the collective security approach to states of limited resources is obvious. Sharing resources and relying on military protection helps pay other bills. But it is often no easy matter to arrive at practical consensus on differing issues and therefore to take any meaningful action. Few states would welcome having to depend on the protection of others in all circumstances. Sovereignty must ultimately mean something.

The history of diplomacy is instructive in identifying the major influences on how diplomacy has developed. Diplomacy does evolve, and its methods have had to adapt. It is true that some form of communications have always existed in diplomatic history, nonstate actors have long encroached on the domain of sovereign states, and commercial interests have been important issues throughout its existence. But history does demonstrate that the terrain of diplomacy shifts. It remains a cosmopolitan activity with a belief in common interests. It may appear that a lot happens in the world but little changes, so a shoulder shrug may be the natural response. However, history may also suggest that risks of making diplomats complacent and finding comfort in traditional methods are surely more dangerous. We now turn to how the diplomatic services we see today have evolved and the key characteristics of modern diplomatic behavior.

SUGGESTIONS FOR FURTHER READING

1. Black, Jeremy. *The History of Diplomacy*. London: Reaktion Books, 2010.
2. Roberts, Sir Ivor, ed. *Satow's Diplomatic Practice*, 6th ed. New York: Oxford University Press, 2009.
3. Hamilton, Keith, and Richard Langhorne. *The Practice of Diplomacy: Its Evolution, Theory, and Administration*. London: Routledge, 2011.
4. Kissinger, Henry. *Diplomacy*. New York: Simon & Schuster, 1994.
5. Sharp, Paul. *Diplomatic Theory of International Relations*. New York: Cambridge University Press, 2009.

chapter 2

Who Are the Diplomats and How Do They Operate?

Having learned something of how the history of diplomacy has evolved, we now look at how the profession of diplomat has developed, the methods used to recruit them, and how a common way of treating diplomats has been formulated.

THE EVOLUTION OF THE DIPLOMATIC CADRE

Diplomatic systems evolved with the creation of an organizational structure to institutionalize the functions and resources of diplomacy. For the career of a diplomat to develop, the role of diplomacy within a system of government had to be recognized. And for this to happen, the skills of diplomacy had to be seen as worth teaching. They could not simply be acquired through breeding, money, or both.

Early appointments of diplomats, as we have seen in the case of the Italian city states, were of well-connected and well-heeled envoys. Increasingly, these were seen as not undesirable qualifications but something less than a complete resume. States needed communicators who were schooled in what were seen as diplomatic skills. Writers like François de Callières (1645–1717), an advisor to the King Louis XIV of France, recognized the distinctive talents required. His book, *De la Manière de Négocier avec les Souverains,* became an early guide to diplomatic practice and recommended rules that could be applied in diplomatic negotiation.

Box 2-1 Diplomatic Recognition

Diplomats are usually deployed only in states with which their countries have diplomatic relations. And a normal first step in this process is the recognition under international law of one state by another. Recognition is usually a written acknowledgment, but diplomatic relations do not follow automatically. The United States recognizes the state of North Korea (Japan and South Korea do not), but has never established diplomatic relations with it. Western Sahara is a territory where sovereignty has been disputed for decades between Morocco and Sahrawi Arab Democratic Republic (SADR), also known as the Polisario Front. Over eighty countries recognize the SADR as the legitimate ruler of Western Sahara, while the Arab League recognizes Morocco. The world is also divided over recognition of Kosovo. Recognition of governments may also be an issue. In the early stages in the Syrian Civil War, the EU, Saudi Arabia, Libya, and Qatar—and eventually the United States—recognized the Syrian National Council as the legitimate representative of the Syrian people.

Callières, who had himself negotiated treaties, thought diplomacy of such importance that its practitioners required special skills and knowledge and that a professional cadre was required. He argued that if it were

> a firm and lasting maxim in France, not to employ any persons in public negotiations, except those that have gone through this kind of apprenticeship, and these sorts of studies . . . the King would be better served in his negotiations.[1]

De Callières also saw the need to give advice on drinking. A diplomat "should drink in such a manner as not to lose control of his own faculties while endeavoring to loosen the self-control of others."[2] And he noted that patience, calmness, and a willingness to be bored were essential attributes of the professional diplomat: "One should avoid bitter and obstinate discussions with Princes and their ministers but reason with them without passion and without always wanting to have the last word."[3] Sound advice in many other contexts as well!

Progress toward the diplomatic system we recognize today has been gradual. The type of career that developed has changed according to technology of the time and the functions seen as appropriate for diplomats. In that process, two divisions were commonly observed until recent times. First, officers who served overseas did not serve at home. Second, the political and consular specialties were treated as different careers.

Maintaining separate careers for those serving in the home ministry or department from those in the overseas service persisted until well into the twentieth century in many diplomatic services. Though the U.K. Foreign Department, later named the Foreign Office, was established in 1782, it was only in 1919 that its staff in London and the Diplomatic Service overseas were merged. In 1943, they were both merged with the Consular Service. The Foreign and Commonwealth Office that exists today was itself a merger of the Commonwealth and Foreign Offices in 1968. Social stratification also played its part in developments as the belief persisted that higher social echelons should represent the country abroad, while others should remain at home. It was not until after the Wriston Report of 1954 that the U.S. Foreign Service was fully integrated in career terms with the U.S. State Department, which had been responsible for home service officers.

The division between diplomatic and consular functions also continued until well into the twentieth century. The United States had a small diplomatic service throughout the nineteenth century. Yet the consular service—including consuls, consular agents, and commercial agents who protected American ships and crews abroad and promoted American commerce—had become an important instrument in the search for export markets. There were already 480 U.S. consulates in 1860, including the commercial agencies, and by 1890 the number had risen to 760. In 1895, President Cleveland started the practice of filling consular vacancies on the basis of written examinations, including language tests. Other measures regulated the payment of salaries and inspections of consular posts. Today, ease of travel and communication has greatly reduced the need for so many consular posts.

Commerce was already a mainstay of foreign policy and diplomacy in the eighteenth century. Yet the British Foreign Office did not acquire a commercial department until 1865. In 1880, a commercial secretary was nominated to the British embassy in Paris with consular status. Until 1856, most American consuls were unsalaried, even though international influence was increasingly exerted through business. In the nineteenth century, foreign investment became a major component of foreign relations. Germany invested in Romanian railways, France in the Ottoman Empire, and the United Kingdom in Egypt. The Russian government borrowed on the French financial markets, and the U.S. government worked for business interests to build the Panama Canal.

Along with organizational changes, diplomatic systems instituted entrance exams, open to all, and stressed the need for language training. The Prussian foreign ministry had been established soon after the Napoleonic era and in 1827 was one of the first in the world to require entrance examinations and formal university qualifications. The French stuck longer to old traditions and had no systematic recruitment beyond accepting the social elite who displayed the beautiful manners of the era. The French ministry moved to its purpose-built premises on the Quai d'Orsay in 1853, but no entrance exam was instituted in France until 1877. The Russian foreign service began an entrance exam for diplomats, including language proficiency, in 1859.

After World War I, the United States remodeled its diplomatic service to reflect its growing interests and presence overseas. The small U.S. diplomatic service, which in 1924 numbered 122 men serving mostly in Europe, was an exclusive group. It was paid little and was highly elitist, drawn from rich and high society. In contrast, the 511 members (in 1924) of the consular service served in 256 overseas posts under professional regulations and enjoyed a generous pay scale. The State Department oversaw the consular service but had little real control over the diplomatic service. The Foreign Service Act of 1924, known after its congressional sponsor as the Rogers Act, merged the diplomatic and consular services into a new Foreign Service. It established pay and retirement to make the service attractive and accessible to more and professionalized the oversight, recruitment, and training of officers. The act also instituted interchangeability between diplomatic and consular assignments and between assignments abroad and at home in the State Department. The Rogers Act also formally enacted a system of promotion on merit and retirement at sixty-five years old. The first women and African Americans were recruited into the Foreign Service in the 1920s. Until 1972, the British Foreign Office still required women who married to resign from the service. Conditions of employment have changed: in 2014, there are spouses who have job share postings—four months on, four months off.

Even after the passing of the Rogers Act, the resistance of the traditionalists to admit consular officials to embassies persisted. It resulted in the appointment of Wilbur Carr, who started his career as a clerk in the State Department and rose to director of the U.S. consular service, as Chairman of State's personnel board. The State Department also tried to resist attempts of the Agriculture and Commerce Departments to appoint their own attachés. The establishment of the Foreign Service opened the way for the appointment of career officers as chiefs of mission. But the importance of political appointments to such positions persisted for the remainder of the twentieth century and into the twenty-first. Career officers rarely make up more than half of the total of U.S. chiefs of mission.

After World War II, the United States expanded its service again. Diplomacy was seen as a vital support for the new U.S. outreach. From only 840 officers in 1940, the service grew to more than 1,300 in 1953. By 1957, there were 3,400 officers after the integration of many home civil service officers into the Foreign Service. In 2013, the United States had 270 posts. In June 2011, according to a Government Accountability Office (GAO) report, the State Department employed 13,385 Foreign Service officers and 44,256 locally engaged staff. The comparable figures in 2011 for France were 5,988 and 5,177 with 271 missions; the United Kingdom had 4,580 and 8,659 with 245 missions; and Estonia had 539 diplomats in 46 missions. Not all countries favor large numbers of diplomats. In 2012, there were reported to be more staff at the U.S. embassy in New Delhi than the whole of the Indian diplomatic service. The comparative sizes of staff and uses countries make of them will be discussed in Chapter 9.

THE USE OF INTELLIGENCE

International relations after World War II did not only give a boost to diplomatic staff. The expectation of long-term hostility resulting from political and ideological divisions of the Cold War gave a major impetus to the budgets and recruitment of agencies concerned with intelligence gathering. This was a continuation of long-standing practice of using nondiplomats, such as military attachés, in missions. The French diplomat Marquis de Noailles noted in 1901 that intelligence and espionage had been "the besetting sin of the attachés wearing epaulettes."[4] The British Foreign Office assumed responsibility for the Secret Intelligence Service and the Government Code and Cypher School after World War I. But the U.S. Central Intelligence Agency was established only in 1947 to consolidate foreign intelligence gathering. The Soviet Union saw intelligence as one of the major functions of its diplomatic service, and the representatives of state security (KGB) and Soviet Military Intelligence (GRU) were strongly represented in embassies. Counterintelligence operations grew to defend conventional diplomatic activity from this new growth industry. Diplomatic missions could, of course, be goldmines of information. British intelligence with assistance from the eavesdropping Government Communication Headquarters (GCHQ) is alleged to have broken the cipher codes of the French embassy for three years during the United Kingdom's negotiations for accession to the European Economic Community (EEC) and had full access to cables sent by the embassy to the French foreign ministry.

The use of diplomatic cover for intelligence operations is obviously invaluable, but it challenges the separateness of diplomats and the basis of trust of overseas missions, which we shall examine later in this chapter when discussing immunities and privileges. And the boundary between reporting and intelligence gathering is impossible to draw. Intelligence activities in a practical sense are a manifestation of the intelligent use of diplomacy recommended by Satow. And some of the intelligence officers included in diplomatic missions are liaison points with the host country's intelligence community. Intelligence is widely shared among states in areas such as international criminal investigations and nonproliferation of weapons of mass destruction, so like diplomacy it has a peace-promoting purpose. Intelligence challenges the boundaries of diplomacy, but in many practical ways, it complements it. In any case, given the history of international contacts, the amount of data now digitalized, and the venal nature of some human conduct, intelligence has to be incorporated in any survey of how diplomacy functions and the opportunities that are presented.

PROFESSIONALS OR POLITICIANS?

Chapter 9 will discuss how far national organizational reforms see consolidation, centralization, professionalization, perfecting of diplomatic functions, and greater efficiency as the keys to better diplomacy. The professionalizing of the diplomatic service means that cadres have been created. Such cadres, following the German sociologist Max Weber's view of society, may behave like occupational groups and promote professionalization as means of securing rewards and ensuring a monopoly in the provision of their services. A career structure, with entrance requirements and promotions, breeds an institutional culture where organizational strategies and institutional survival in the face of rivalries assume an importance of their own beyond the activity of diplomacy. As Sir Ivor Roberts wrote in his final dispatch to the British Foreign Secretary in 2006, "Wading through, the plethora of business plans, capability reviews, skill audits . . . we have forgotten what diplomacy is all about."[5] The establishment of a professional diplomatic career has influenced the acceptance of practices of where and how diplomats operate and has promoted a fierce determination to defend the monopoly of such status.

Yet this process of professionalizing has now raised other questions because of the changes in skill sets that governments perceive they need for diplomats. The British Foreign Office no longer promises a career for life and is recruiting personnel from a wide variety of career paths. Previous careers in the military, with non-government organizations (NGOs), in business, and in academic life are now seen as offering a good basis for entrance into foreign services. In many countries, there has been a trend toward deprofessionalizing the cadre with the employment of outside contractors and consultants. Specialists in finance and human resources now figure on boards of major diplomatic services. We have already seen how many local staff the major diplomatic services employ. The progress made in refining the efficiency of the services has paralleled business methods and the introduction and integration into diplomacy of new technologies. All diplomatic services, as will be examined in Chapter 3, have to compete for resources with other parts of government, many of which have now assumed prominent roles in international relations on issues such as education, the environment, and overseas development assistance.

Throughout history, the skill set of a diplomat has been a search for a mixture of qualities. Many systems have included political and business figures whose skills have been seen as appropriate for diplomacy. The results that are sought will vary according to the governing system. Is the diplomat to be an extension of the political master? How is the work of the diplomat to be measured? Is it important that he or she be well liked by the host government? Would this result in favors? Is the main function to be a source of confidential information from the host government? Is it necessary to be a political associate of the sending government? How far is the diplomat just another bureaucrat or is the main task to master strategy and deploy Machiavelli's wiliness? Is the professional to be a party animal, with a capacity to stimulate unguarded comments and pick up valuable information? Should the diplomat be a businessperson with managerial skills, or an issues person, perhaps an expert on defense or environmental issues? Or rather a facilitator, a stimulator of others, a team builder? What languages are necessary for the job?

Whatever the relative merits of career versus politician, many diplomatic systems have appointed political figures as ambassadors. Examples have been Benjamin Franklin (U.S. ambassador to France), Sir Christopher Soames (U.K. ambassador to France), and Adan Chavez (brother of the President of Venezuela and Venezuelan ambassador to Cuba). All have served in lieu of professional diplomats. The political figure, well connected at home, will be seen as an individual of weight and influence in the country where he or she serves and someone who will have direct lines of communication to the head of government. A politician may feel that a professional cadre of diplomats will try to implement their own favored policies. The state may not appear as the unitary actor that some theories promote. An individual of trust whose position is owed to head of government may do the job better. But the individual may lack any background in diplomacy or knowledge of the language or culture of the country to which he is accredited. For many years, Pakistan had a tradition of sending retired senior military figures as envoys, reflecting the long periods of military control of the government. President Obama continued the tradition in the United States of naming trusted allies from outside the career of diplomacy as heads of mission to major U.S. posts. The former CEO of the Henson Company, Charles Rivkin, a Democratic Party fund-raiser in California, was U.S. ambassador to Paris. The former head of Goldman Sachs in Germany, Philip Murphy, was ambassador to Germany, and as U.S. ambassador to China the former U.S. Secretary of Commerce, Gary Locke, succeeded the former Republican governor of Utah, John Huntsman. The status and title of ambassador clearly matters to attract such individuals to the job, which is probably a good thing for diplomacy!

The time of service of the envoy in a diplomatic post can also be an important consideration. The old model of a personal envoy sent by a ruler meant that a representative would spend years in one post. The U.K. Viceroy John Lawrence spent a total of sixteen years in India, preceded by two years language training. In smaller countries, the practice is still to rely on trusted individuals for long periods. Their connections and knowledge of a posting outweigh all arguments for rotation. Such is the case with the long-serving representative of the Republic of Djibouti to the United Nations and to the United States, Roble Olhaye, who as of mid-2014 had been in his posts since 1988 and in 1989 was appointed as nonresident ambassador to Canada.

Overall, the personality and ability of the head of mission is important. He or she must represent the state in circumstances that may be routine but may also have no precedents. The head must be versatile, capable of making decisions with little or no guidance but must also follow wider foreign policy considerations of his or her government, which the envoy may not personally support. The ambassador must be contactable by the receiving state at all times. I recall being summoned by the Cuban Foreign Minister at three o'clock one morning to talk about U.K. assistance in evacuating Hugo Chavez from Caracas, during his brief removal from power in 2002. Overall, the head of mission's behavior and performance matters in diplomacy. As Sir Jeremy Greenstock has written, "It is surprisingly easy to make an ass of yourself. Yet the influence of a small power can be enlarged, and that of a great power can be diminished, by the personal effectiveness or ineffectiveness of its representative."[6]

DIPLOMATIC PRIVILEGES AND IMMUNITIES

Whether diplomats deserve special treatment because of the nature of their jobs compared, for example, to traveling merchants and businessmen has exercised legal systems in states and experts for centuries. How to enforce implementation of such special provisions—called immunities and privileges—and limit abuses has also been a preoccupation. The practice has only been codified in international law since 1961.

Box 2-2 **Diplomatic Privilege**

The words *diplomats* and *privileges* are often seen as closely associated. Sales of cars promoted for UN diplomats in New York City gives the flavor: "BMW of Manhattan, Inc. recognizes the invaluable role played by the Diplomatic Community worldwide. It is for this reason that BMW of Manhattan has introduced the Diplomatic Privilege Program, created exclusively for Diplomats and Members of International Organizations."

Source: BMWNYC.com, http://www.bmwnyc.com/WebSiteSurvey.

Many traditions of immunities and privileges go back to ancient times. As we have seen, the word diplomacy derives from the Greek and Latin, indicating a special status of holding a document. Equally, the Islamic world used the concept of *aman*, or safe conduct, accorded the diplomat a status outside ordinary citizens. As late as 1400, most of the Western world still thought of itself as one undivided society and the Roman Catholic Church's Christianity was a fundamental influence on medieval thinking and activity. Roman law gave some legal basis for diplomatic immunity, but it sometimes found itself in conflict with canon law of the church. The latter dealt in detail with key diplomatic concepts like sovereignty, the preservation of peace, and the rules of war.

Certain words came to be used to identify the individuals who enjoyed the special status of diplomats. The *nuntius*, who in the medieval world was charged with preparing for meetings between principals, was granted special recognition and immunities. And the *procurator* who performed specific functions such as the delivery of documents, the payment of debts, and conclusion of treaties was also treated in ways distinct from ordinary citizens where he performed his functions. As diplomats came to assume distinctive roles, which began to intrude on preciously protected areas of sovereignty, then they needed themselves to acquire special status. Following the customary conventions that heads of state enjoyed for immunities and privileges, it was a natural extension of such customs to accord similar privileges to the diplomatic staff who represented them.

Because of slowness of communication and the time it took to deliver messages, guarantee of safety of envoys in their journeys to their posts was seen as the first prerequisite. Once in a post, the envoy was in practical terms isolated with little support day to day and much leeway in terms of how diplomatic functions were fulfilled. This stress on protecting the individual, rather than the government that was represented, is one reason why the issue of immunities and privileges has long and durable roots in diplomatic history. The role of the church in diplomacy and usefulness of diplomacy to the papacy also gave diplomats a special status. There was recognition that the ambassador had a noble calling, and this was supported by senior church figures.

Bernard Du Rosier, Archbishop of Toulouse, described in the fifteenth century what protection diplomats needed in the performance of their functions. He stressed practical measures like freedom of access, transit, safety from violence and exemption from local taxes, tolls, and custom duties. Du Rosier produced a first guidebook for diplomatic practice, his *Short Treatise about Ambassadors*, in 1436 when he himself was serving at the court of the King of Castile. His book throws invaluable light on the diplomatic practice of its time. His writings concentrated on diplomatic practice before the establishment of the resident embassy. In his day, payment of per diem rates for ambassadors was often delayed, and it became normal practice for the receiving state to pay the living expenses for ambassadors. So this was one way that the treatment of ambassadors began to differ from the treatment of heralds and simple messengers.

New attention was given to the status of envoys when permanent missions came to be the norm. Many got into financial difficulties and had to be protected from creditors. There was general acceptance that ambassadors did not have immunity from crimes but recognition that if they did transgress, they should be punished by the sending state. It was in this way that the powers of the receiving state to expel offending diplomats emerged. Important concepts of declaring a head of mission persona non grata developed and Hugo Grotius, the renowned Dutch jurist (1583–1645), argued for setting out the full legal basis for immunities and privileges. Gradually, the practice developed that, even though an ambassador could be expelled, he could not be detained or tried. And immunity of an ambassador from civil liability was established in the seventeenth century, protecting those who fell into debt.

By the middle of the eighteenth century, Vattel's work, *Le Droit des Gens,* had established key elements of the customary privileges and immunities of diplomats, their premises, property, and communications. Vattel and Grotius (who served himself as Sweden's ambassador to France, having been sent into exile by the Dutch authorities) both saw the diplomat's status as being tied to the concept of extraterritoriality. They were separate from the jurisdiction of the territory in which they served. It is, however, generally accepted that the foreign mission's premises are not deemed to be foreign territory. Crimes occurring within diplomatic premises are governed by the law in the host state.

After centuries of acceptance of customary status and long debates by international jurists, it took until the second half of the twentieth century for the modern practice of diplomatic and consular immunities and privileges to be codified. The Vienna Convention on Diplomatic Relations of 1961 (VCDR) was the result of five years of work within the UN's International Law Commission. It sought to codify what had arisen over past centuries and made clear that anything that was not expressly covered in the document might still be a valid immunity or privilege under customary law. In drafting the VCDR, the UN was recognizing old problems and anticipating new ones. The Cold War had created a hostile environment for diplomats, and the process of the decolonization underway in the 1950s and 1960s anticipated the creation of many new states, most of which would be small and whose diplomats would be vulnerable and short of resources to establish genuinely independent diplomatic services. They needed to have certainty in status.

Like many international treaties and conventions, the VCDR has been subject to lack of enforceability and created tensions when its provisions have been ignored. Communist China treated it and diplomatic missions in Beijing with contempt. At different periods in history, the U.S. and U.K. embassies in Tehran have been invaded and ransacked. Yet norms have been established that most states have been loath to contravene, even under provocative acts. Attacks on the premises of embassies and residences of diplomatic staff, because they are symbolic and vulnerable targets, have occurred frequently throughout history. Yet the convention still stands and has been supplemented by a Vienna Convention on Consular Relations of 1963 (VCCR). Together the two conventions are some of the most widely ratified conventions in the world. As of 2013, 189 states had ratified the VCDR and 176 the VCCR.

THE VCDR AND VCCR

What then does the VCDR contain and how far is it still relevant to how diplomats behave?

The VCDR is based on reciprocity—every state in the system plays the role of both a sending and receiving state. The first important concept is that international relations are a public good and that friendly relations greatly enhance the value of international discourse. So the rationale is that diplomats function better and achieve better results if they operate within a predictable and reciprocally enforced legal framework. The preamble to the VCDR makes clear the immunities and privileges are not for the personal benefit of the diplomat, but "to ensure the efficient performance of the functions of diplomatic missions as representing states."[7] The VCDR aims to make diplomacy more efficient not to facilitate agreeable lifestyles for diplomats.

Article 2 of the convention establishes the principle of mutuality: "The establishment of diplomatic relations between States, and of permanent diplomatic missions, takes place by mutual consent."[8] This is diplomacy in its purest form. International relations must be noncoercive, and the VCDR establishes a level playing field and does not permit any discrimination. In diplomatic relations there can be no second or third class partners.

The third important provision of the VCDR is Article 3, which defines inter alia the recognized functions of a diplomatic mission. These functions are the closest the modern diplomatic system has come to defining its own practice. First, the mission is to represent the sending country. Second, it is authorized to protect the interests of the sending state in the receiving state, which includes the protection of nationals. Third, the mission may negotiate with the government of the receiving state. Fourth, the mission can ascertain, by all lawful means, conditions and developments in the receiving state and report thereon. Fifth—and the widest provision of all—the mission may engage in promoting friendly relations between the sending and receiving state, which is stated to include developing their economic, cultural, and scientific relations.

In order to benefit from the provisions of the VCDR and VCCR, the diplomat has to show he is operating within these parameters. If he or she chooses to engage in activities that are not permitted by the VCDR, then the immunities and privileges granted do not apply.

What else does the VCDR preserve of the immunities that have been recognized, as the VCDR notes, "from ancient times"? The VCDR makes no stipulation as to who should be appointed as head of mission but does state that "members of the diplomatic staff of the mission should in principle be of the nationality of the sending State."[9] The value of having diplomatic staff is enhanced if they have the trust of the receiving state. In the case of the head of mission, the prior approval of the receiving state must be sought—the French term *agrément* is used to describe this. The VCDR states that, apart from the head of mission, all other staff may be freely appointed by the sending state. The persona non grata provision of Article 9 balances this and gives the receiving state the ultimate power to expel any diplomatic agent.

It is clear, therefore, that appointing heads of a diplomatic mission itself involves diplomacy. A formal approach proposing a candidate is made by the sending state to the receiving state. If diplomatic relations are to flourish, then the head of mission should be a figure that is acceptable to the receiving state. Agréments are refused, and under the VCDR no reasons need be given. For all other members of the mission, the receiving state has no influence on appointments but the names of military attachés can be required in advance. In other respects, the VCDR tries to make diplomatic relations flexible. The expenses of representation are high and remain a concern to smaller countries. So the accreditation of one ambassador to several countries is a way to alleviate this. Similarly, the provisions that locally engaged employees of missions are acceptable have added great flexibility and practicality to employment, as such employees are generally excluded from the immunities and privileges granted to the diplomatic staff.

Once accepted as a head of mission, the diplomat must present his credentials to the receiving state and from the date and hour of this credentials ceremony, his or her status as head of mission begins. The VCDR states, "The head of the mission is considered as having taken up his functions in the receiving state either when he has presented his credentials or when he has notified his arrival."[10] But the privileges will normally begin on arrival; in some cases the presentation of credentials will not be arranged for several days or weeks.

Generally, the VCDR does not discriminate between a head of mission and other diplomatic staff. All are treated the same. Some reduced level of immunities and privileges may be accorded to administrative and technical staff and service staff who are not nationals of the receiving state. The VCDR is specific that the immunities and privileges shall only apply to acts of such staff performed in their official duties.

The VCDR goes on to grant significant immunities and privileges to diplomatic staff, their premises, and their archives. The concept of inviolability is central to how they are treated and reinforces the sense of separateness and protection that diplomacy enjoys. Article 22 states that "the premises of the mission shall be inviolable."[11] No part of diplomatic premises or property can be entered by the security agents or other officials of the receiving state without the consent of the head of mission. There is no exception to this rule even when under Article 41 the receiving state believes that the premises are being used for "purposes incompatible with the functions of the mission."[12] Important for today's functions, this inviolability includes vehicles, archives and documents (which cover computers and other devices containing official material such as smart phones), and also the communications equipment of all embassies. Inviolability has also been important to the development of the practice of diplomatic asylum, which is not mentioned in the VCDR and has been treated on an ad hoc basis by sovereign states. The presence of inviolable buildings within a country has created a unique separateness of space and functions outside of the normal rules of law operating within that country.

In an age of ready identification of a diplomatic mission as a target for attack, the receiving state must in all circumstances protect the premises of the sending state. Article 22.2 of the VCDR states that the "receiving state is under a special duty to take all appropriate steps to protect the premises of the mission against any intrusion or damage and to prevent any disturbance of the peace of the mission or impairment of its dignity."[13]

Among the most important personal privileges accorded to a diplomat is the exemption from taxation. Article 34 of the VCDR provides that a diplomatic agent should be exempt from all dues and taxes. There are exceptions to this rule if the taxes, like sales taxes and value-added tax (VAT), are included in everyday prices. Second, where the taxes are levied in activities unrelated to the diplomatic activities, such as property taxes on personal purchases of, for example, a holiday home for the diplomat. A third exception where tax must be paid is a diplomat's obligation to pay estate tax. And a final category where there is no tax exemption is in relation to charges for services rendered. So taxes on municipal services like road cleaning or road and bridge tolls must be paid. These exemptions in the VCDR are designed to preserve the separation of diplomatic staff of the sending state from the receiving state and thus avoid any blurring of their status with those of nationals who pay taxes to fund the government services of the receiving state.

The VCDR also recognizes that even with inviolability and nonliability for taxes on property and income the diplomat could still be effectively controlled by the receiving state to limit his or her effectiveness. So the VCDR provides that the receiving state may not restrict the travel of diplomats, nor interfere with their communications. And an important revenue source for many countries—visa and passport fees—cannot be taxed by the host country, again reinforcing the separateness of all financial transactions.

A diplomat is also immune from prosecution for a crime committed in a country to which he or she is accredited. Under Article 31 of the VCDR, there are no exceptions to this at all. As early as 1571, when Scotland was independent, the Bishop of Ross, the representative of Mary Queen of Scots, was held captive by Queen Elizabeth of England. English lawyers had given their opinion that an ambassador who incited an uprising against a ruler to whom he was accredited could be tried. However, the customary law of not treating ambassadors like common citizens suggested the opposite, and the Bishop was held for only a short time before being expelled. This provision for immunity from criminal jurisdiction is obviously an extraordinary measure given that diplomats, if this is enforced to the letter, could literally get away with murder. The VCDR saw the need to protect diplomatic agents against a receiving state wishing to harass them through its own judicial system by making certain offenses criminal and using these to restrict freedom of diplomatic activity. The crime of blasphemy might be one. So instead of limiting the criminal immunity they included the pragmatic provision that in cases where the activity was indeed criminal and outside official functions, the sending state could waive the immunity of those concerned (Article 32). This is indeed an important provision that limits the scope for diplomats to go rogue and abuse their privileges.

Box 2-3 Limitations of the VCDR

The tragic case in 1982 of the Austrian ambassador to Yugoslavia accidentally but fatally shooting the French ambassador on a hunting trip in Yugoslavia shows that the VCDR had not covered all eventualities. There was no possibility of diplomacy simply washing its hands of this incident. Instead the matter was settled in the Austrian courts, which determined that though the hunting party was hosted by the Yugoslav government and was therefore part of the ambassador's official duties, the Austrian government was not liable for its diplomat's actions.

Modern examples of diplomatic immunity being claimed for prima facie criminal acts are the Libyan diplomats involved in the murder of policewoman Yvonne Fletcher outside the Libyan embassy in London in 1984 and the case of Raymond Davies, the U.S. attaché, who shot two Pakistani motorcyclists in 2010. In neither case did the sending country waive diplomatic immunity. In the case of the deputy head of mission of the Republic of Georgia who was arrested in 1997 for vehicular homicide and driving under the influence in the United States, the diplomat's immunity was waived.

The VCDR is specific in granting diplomatic agents the necessary freedoms to perform their functions without restrictions. Article 26 guarantees their freedom to travel and Article 27 their freedom to communicate with the sending state for all official purposes. The same article provides that "official correspondence of the mission shall be inviolable."[14] This covers the treatment of the diplomatic bag. It does, of course, also now cover encrypted digital communications. None of these can be intercepted, inspected, or interfered with. On the surveillance of, rather than interference with, free communications, the VCDR is silent, and if there were negotiations to revise the convention, this matter would certainly be seen as a clarification that was needed. Likewise, the prominence afforded by the VCDR to diplomatic bags seems partly outdated, though still relevant. In modern diplomacy, the regular arrival of diplomatic couriers, often former military officers traveling in the first class cabin with the diplomatic bag in the adjoining seat, is now an infrequent event. But the importance of the diplomatic bag remains, particularly in the transporting of equipment. Parts for communication equipment, security doors, and new construction components are all normally shipped to the site of diplomatic missions. Armored cars for ambassadors would similarly constitute cargo in a diplomatic bag, which cannot be inspected.

If the number and variety of privileges and immunities are impressive, there are some important balancing provisions that give to the receiving state significant powers to prevent abuse and to protect the sovereignty of the state. First, the general power of declaring "any member of the diplomatic staff of the mission persona non grata"[15] is absolute and requires no reason. So, even though the appointment of diplomatic staff is not restricted under the VCDR, any unwelcome nominees could be easily removed. The VCDR also provides that the size of the diplomatic mission must be what is regarded as reasonable and normal in all the circumstances (Article 11). Thus, a proposal by the embassy of North Korea to appoint another twenty commercial officers to serve in London could be rejected on VCDR grounds alone.

Article 41 is another key balancing provision of the VCDR. Nowhere does the document mention espionage but this has long been an integral part of diplomacy. In this respect, again the VCDR has been realistic and permitted diplomatic activity is framed in terms of noninterference. Article 41 provides that "without prejudice to their privileges and immunities, it is the duty of all persons enjoying such privileges and immunities to respect the laws and regulations of the receiving State. They also have a duty not to interfere in the internal affairs of that State."[16] As we have seen, if the receiving state decides there has been such interference, there are provisions for expelling any diplomat as not acceptable. This declaration of persona non grata is unlimited and no reason for the expulsion is required. Indeed, the VCDR even allows persona non grata to be declared against a diplomat who has yet to enter the country.

How closely are these important provisions followed? In the annals of diplomacy there are many instances where the provisions of the VCDR have been disregarded or have led to complex disagreements between sending and receiving states. There are many known instances of agrément being refused for the appointment of a head of mission and many others that have not come to light. In the recent history of U.K. relations with Iran, the nomination for British ambassador of David Reddaway was refused by the Iranian authorities. This was, of course, Iran's right under the VCDR. An infamous flouting of the duty to protect of the receiving state also involves Iran. In November 1979, the United States embassy in Tehran was invaded by students. For over fifteen months, the staff was held hostage with the receiving state taking no action to give effect to their duty to protect the mission or the immunity of the diplomats. In more recent times, diplomatic missions in Syria have been attacked and the missions closed.

Interpretation of the VCDR is also sometimes disputed. Even the issue of what constitutes a tax, and therefore from which diplomatic staff is exempt, has been subject to argument. Many embassies in London have long refused to pay the congestion charge imposed on all vehicles entering central London. The embassies that refuse to pay say that it is a tax. The British government says it is a law, similar to a toll on a road that diplomats, as we have seen, must pay. As of mid-2012, the Foreign Office listed the unpaid charges by leading embassies as follows:

- USA: £6,146,640
- Russia: £4,653,960
- Japan: £4,160,280
- Germany: £3,641,170
- Nigeria: £3,129,030[17]

Use of the persona non grata provisions is still frequent and the reasons given reflect the changing nature of diplomatic activities. In September 2012, Russia demanded U.S. Agency for International Development (USAID) officials leave the country, accusing the United States of using their programs on such issues as good governance to interfere in Russian internal affairs. In the words of the Russian Foreign Ministry statement, "We are talking about attempts through the issuing of grants to affect the course of political processes, including elections on various levels, and institutions of civil society."[18] The United States and Venezuela also had reciprocal expulsion of diplomats in 2013. The tit-for-tat reactions are also common. Indeed, in the VCDR itself, there appears to be recognition of this practice in Article 47, which recognizes an exception to the principle of nondiscrimination:

1. In the application of the provisions of the present Convention, the receiving State shall not discriminate as between States.
2. However, discrimination shall not be regarded as taking place . . . where the receiving State applies any of the provisions of the present Convention restrictively because of a restrictive application of that provision to its mission in the sending State.[19]

Even in countries with close economic ties, diplomats are often used as pawns to show disapproval of behavior. The United Kingdom was a major aid donor to Malawi in 2011, but it did not prevent Malawi from declaring the British High Commissioner persona non grata when his cable describing the President of Malawi as "becoming ever more autocratic and intolerant of criticism"[20] was leaked. The British immediately expelled the Malawian acting High Commissioner in London. What diplomats say in private as part of their reporting on developments in the country is part of the game that all play under the VCDR. Carlos Pascual, the U.S. ambassador to Mexico in 2010, was only doing his job in reporting what he saw as the shortcomings of the Mexican police. Wikileaks published what he reported alongside thousands of other U.S. cables they had harvested from the U.S. digital system and the Mexicans spotted it. Diplomats are regularly used as a vent for sovereign state anger, frustration, and hurt pride. In this way, the VCDR provides sensitive states with an outlet that avoids anything more violent—an undervalued service to international relations.

Other abuses concern the freedom of communications granted to diplomatic missions. Diplomatic bags have been used for arms and drugs trafficking. Yet a case occurring at a London airport in 1984 was unusual. It was not in fact a case, more a crate. A customs officer became suspicious that two large crates with air holes in them were perhaps not normal diplomatic cargo, even though they were labeled as emanating from the Nigerian High Commission. Because the cartons did not have lead or wax seals they did not constitute a diplomatic bag, so the U.K. authorities checked the contents, knowing that a former Nigerian foreign minister, Mr. Umaru Dikko, had been abducted earlier that day. Mr. Dikko was found drugged and unconscious in this diplomatic cargo. The Nigerian diplomats involved were declared persona non grata.

The Vienna Convention on Consular Relations is two years younger than the VCDR (drafted in 1963) and almost double the length. It is beyond the scope of this book to review in detail the differences and provisions of this document, but there are many overlaps and some important new features. The roles of the consular officer are defined in great detail, unlike the parallel provisions in the VCDR. Article 5 sets out consular functions with the first one defined as "protecting in the receiving State the interests of the sending State and of its nationals, both individuals and bodies corporate, within the limits permitted by international law."[21] Specific consular roles are identified, such as appearing before tribunals, looking after the interests of minors, transmitting judicial and other documents, performing duties of a notary, and assisting merchant ships and aircraft registered in the name of the sending state. These functions, long the stock in trade of consular officers throughout history, are codified in the VCCR.

Consular services have been provided by states for centuries and, as we have seen, many consular officers figured in international relations in the nineteenth century. The word *consul* seems to have had its origins as signifying an arbitrator in commercial disputes. Consular officials also figured in a system of extraterritorial rights, which were established in the nineteenth century between western powers and Asian countries—China, Japan, and Siam. These officials were not subject to national laws but to those of their home state. And the VCCR built on the large number of bilateral conventions governing consular immunities and privileges and a few regional agreements such as the Havana Convention of 1928.

What then are provisions that merit attention as establishing different provisions between consular and diplomatic officials? First, consular officials are divided in two broad categories: career and honorary consuls. Career consuls themselves are divided into three classes: consuls general, consuls, and vice-consuls. The honorary consul is an appointment of great flexibility and continues to be widely used. He or she is usually a local resident in the receiving state with a private business or active in some profession. There is no requirement that such honorary consuls should be citizens of the sending state and may indeed be of any nationality, including that of the receiving state. The honorary consuls perform only limited duties and are usually paid an honorarium. Most deal with providing local assistance to distressed subjects—those that have been robbed, may need emergency medical care, or are in trouble with the local authorities for whatever reason. They visit citizens of the states they represent in jail and are a cost-effective way of handling local issues with an experienced resident of the country. They know the local authorities and can apply common sense with a dollop of official clout.

The head of a consular post does not present credentials; rather, he or she will hold an exequatur that confirms the appointment. No advance approval is required for such appointments. A consul, unlike a diplomatic agent, can be required to give evidence in a court of law in the receiving state. Consular premises were generally not treated as inviolable before the VCCR, and customary law provided only limited immunities and no privileges to consular posts and consuls. This status was seen as unsatisfactory as states began to merge their consular and diplomatic services after World War II. States therefore concluded consular conventions and gave some inviolability to consular premises as well as extensive tax and customs privileges to career consuls. This practice is followed in the VCCR, and the status of career consuls on immunities and privileges has many similar, though not always identical, features to those of the VCDR for diplomatic staff. Under Articles 40 and 41 of the VCCR, the career consul enjoys some personal inviolability. The receiving state is under a duty to protect his or her "person, freedom and dignity."[22] A consular officer enjoys some immunity from criminal charges, and he or she may be arrested or detained only in the case of a grave crime. In such an event, the head of the consular post must be notified. All these immunities are stated to apply only "in respect of acts performed in the exercise of consular functions."[23] This was the subject of the dispute between the U.S. police in New York City and the deputy consul general of India in 2013, when the official was arrested on charges of giving false information on a visa application of an employee.

Rules on waiver of immunities by the sending state are similar in the VCCR to those of the VCDR. An honorary consul has very limited personal immunity or privileges, and if he or she is a national of the receiving state, then the only immunity would be to the official files kept in a separate part of a work office.

One important provision of the VCCR, which recognizes the central role of consular officers in protecting their nationals, is Article 36. This provides that

> a. consular officers shall be free to communicate with nationals of the sending State and to have access to them. Nationals of the sending

State shall have the same freedom with respect to communication with and access to consular officers of the sending State;

b. if he so requests, the competent authorities of the receiving State shall, without delay, inform the consular post of the sending State if, within its consular district, a national of that State is arrested or committed to prison or to custody pending trial or is detained in any other manner.[24]

This of course is essential to enable the fulfillment of the protecting function, central to the VCDR, and requires close liaison between officials of the sending and receiving states.

WHAT IS CHANGING IN DIPLOMATS' BEHAVIOR?

The establishment of the common immunities and privileges is one of diplomacy's successes and preserves a system of continuity, respect, and common aspiration for diplomacy. It is one of the clearest illustrations of treating diplomacy and its officials as a public international good. What reforms of the VCDR and VCCR does modern diplomacy suggest may be appropriate to take account of the expanding functions of modern diplomacy?

Diplomats now negotiate on issues far removed from territorial boundaries and tariff levels, which may have seemed the standard fare of former times. Double taxation, prisoner exchange, education protocols, and environmental cooperation are among those that have become the common currency of modern diplomacy. The vast growth in tourism, education exchanges, and business travel means more work for diplomats dealing with nationals in trouble, injured by natural disasters, or charged with crimes. Diplomats talk to local media and NGOs. Yet they are living in an environment where the government may control many aspects of governance—parts of the economy, communications, media, and the judiciary. The spirit of the VCDR and VCCR is that it is in no state's interests to create an overtly hostile environment where diplomats resent their treatment.

Diplomats and their consular equivalents are also in touch digitally with their own nationals and with citizens of the receiving country in ways that were unimaginable twenty years ago. Protecting citizens or communicating with protecting powers is a more demanding job because cell phone calls, texting, and social media allow more possibilities. The diplomat and the consul are always contactable and are usually the helpers of first or last resort. As will be discussed further in Chapter 9, the increase in foreign travel has highlighted the differences in law between states—for example, in policies on gender and sexuality issues, dress codes, and drugs and alcohol availability—and the demand for consular services has increased greatly. From 2011 to 2012, British consular services handled nearly 280,000 face-to-face inquiries and helped in over 97,000 assistance cases, including those cases involving deaths or murders, forced marriage, or child abduction. Between February 2011 and February 2012, there were nearly 10.5 million visits to the travel and living abroad pages of the U.K. Foreign Office website.

The principles of the VCDR and VCCR remain sound, but the growing intrusiveness, globalization, and footprint of communications, together with the interaction of diplomatic and consular officials with nonstate actors, mean that diplomatic functions are expanding. They mean that the boundaries of activities of sending and receiving states are no longer as clear. Through social media, missions can now contact direct citizens of the receiving state without the knowledge or permission of its government. How far, for example, does freedom to communicate and freedom to report on a country extend to using diplomatic staff and facilities to debate issues with the nationals of the country? How far do the conventions cover active promotion of trade and investment opportunities by the sending state, which may reduce the business and income of those in the receiving state? How far can a mission use public diplomacy programs to promote a more favorable view of the sending state among the receiving state's public? And is the use of all forms of surveillance equipment from a diplomatic mission totally unlawful or is merely an extension of the reporting function under the VCDR?

DIPLOMATIC ASYLUM

One consequence of the diplomatic inviolability provisions of the VCDR and VCCR is the capacity of a mission to offer diplomatic asylum. This by its nature is never without controversy. Diplomatic asylum is sought when a person or persons uses the inviolability provisions of the VCDR and VCCR to seek refuge in a diplomatic mission. There is no reference in the VCDR to this, and nations have never agreed to a worldwide convention or treaty that codifies the practice. In Latin America, where Atle Grahl-Madsen described the effects of decades of political turmoil as leading to situations "where today's government officials may be tomorrow's refugees, and vice versa,"[25] there are several conventions related to the right of asylum. The most recent is the Organization of American States (OAS) Caracas Convention of 1954, drafted in response to the mass invasions of embassies in the aftermath of the coup against President Arbenz in Guatemala. Though it does provide for guidelines on when diplomatic asylum may be granted, only fourteen of the thirty-five members of the OAS have so far ratified the convention.

Most countries are extremely cautious about the granting of asylum because it is likely to become a lasting irritant to diplomatic relations. The missions granting such asylum requests generally mark themselves out as doing something that may displease or embarrass the receiving state. On several occasions, Fidel Castro reacted with fury to embassies in Havana giving asylum to Cuban dissidents by bombarding the same missions—Peru in 1980, Mexico in 2003—with hundreds of other supposed dissidents. Nevertheless, asylum is widely perceived as a legitimate use of diplomatic missions. Tensions in civil society and the global media attention to several high-profile cases suggest that its use in on the rise. Nevertheless, the International Law Commission, charged with drafting the provisions of the VCCR and VCDR, agreed that the issue of diplomatic asylum should be set aside, and so it is reasonable to assume, as the preamble of the VCDR states, that the "rules of customary international law"[26] still govern how it is treated.

Under general international law, asylum is regarded as a matter of humanitarian practice rather than a legal right, and the UN has stated that the right to grant asylum is a right of a sovereign state. The Declaration on Territorial Asylum adopted by the UNGA in 1967 affirms that "the grant of asylum is a peaceful and humanitarian act, a normal exercise of state sovereignty, and that it shall be respected by all other states."[27] Asylum requests are stimulated by knowledge of the world outside and the rights others enjoy. Indeed the concept of virtual asylum, meaning a request based on denial of Internet access, is now being mooted. The case studies of diplomatic asylum discussed below illustrate the complex mixture of factors that apply. The granting of asylum is seldom a final solution in diplomacy.

Case Study

The case of former President of Honduras Manuel Zelaya shows the granting of asylum in Latin America has a recent high-profile example. Manuel Zelaya was rumored to be planning a referendum to change the constitution to permit himself multiple terms as president. Hondurans in other parts of government reacted with alarm. They removed Zelaya from power, arresting him in his pajamas, and sent him to exile in Costa Rica in June 2009—a combined action by the Honduran Assembly, opposition, and Supreme Court. Zelaya resurfaced in September 2009 in the Brazilian embassy in Tegucigalpa. The former president had been smuggled into Honduras in the trunk of a Brazilian diplomat's car. The Honduran government originally gave the embassy a deadline of ten days to surrender Zelaya and then surrounded the building with troops, threatening to cut off water and electricity. This was certainly far from the spirit and letter of the VCDR. Article 22 states that

> the receiving State is under a special duty to take all appropriate steps to protect the premises of the mission against any intrusion or damage and to prevent any disturbance of the peace of the mission or impairment of its dignity."[28]

The Honduran government said that Zelaya's activities were in any case incompatible with asylum as he was using his presence in the Brazilian mission to campaign politically for his reinstatement as president.

Eventually Zelaya negotiated another exile—this time in the Dominican Republic. In 2011, he signed an agreement with the new president of Honduras permitting his return.

Zelaya's case was unusual, both in content and solution, as strong political elements were involved, and most OAS governments, including the United States, did not recognize Zelaya's removal from power. But Brazil's solution, frustrated at the affront to a democratically elected president, was to use the VCDR provisions for an overtly political purpose. The inviolability of their premises and property—a diplomatic vehicle—was used to reintroduce Zelaya back into the country. It was a misuse of the VCDR to use the premises to protect a political figure however unjust his removal from office might have been. It is hard to see Brazil's action as anything other than an interference in internal affairs. Second, by permitting Zelaya to campaign from within the embassy, it was in contravention of Article 41.3 of the VCDR, which states that "the premise of the mission must not be used in any manner incompatible with the functions of the mission."[29]

The next example shows another type of diplomatic asylum, where a political activist uses a diplomatic mission in the country to draw attention to his treatment in the receiving state. In April 2012, Chinese dissident Chen Guangcheng arrived at the U.S. embassy in Beijing following a dramatic escape from house arrest. The blind dissident had scaled a high wall and was driven hundreds of kilometers to Beijing. Unlike Zelaya, this example is of an ordinary citizen, who had found living in his own country uncomfortable but, while not actually in jail, was restricted in movements. He timed his arrival at the U.S. embassy to make maximum diplomatic impact as the U.S. Secretary of State was about to visit China. He knew that the attention he would receive would be direct and swift. Negotiations began, and the United States proposed that an educational visa be obtained for Mr. Chen to leave China. Diplomatic negotiations were used to provide an acceptable outcome and to supplement successfully the provisions of inviolability of the VCDR, which gave the time that was needed for a solution. Neither the United States nor China wanted to make a lasting issue of the case.

The VCDR provisions were used successfully in the independence struggle of one of the world's newest states—East Timor. In 1999, the East Timorese leader Xanana Gusmão was housed for two weeks in the British embassy compound in Jakarta and then successfully transported out of Indonesia through use of the British ambassador's car. Indonesia's initial plan was to fly Gusmão to Dili and hand him over to the UN mission in East Timor. But this would have been dangerous because of the warring militias who had taken over. The cause of a new sovereign state was well served by the VCDR.

The lives of several U.S. embassy personnel were also protected by the Canadian mission in the aftermath of the invasion of the U.S. embassy in Tehran in 1979. The Canadian ambassador Ken Taylor, working with a CIA agent who had arrived in Tehran pretending to be a movie director, issued false Canadian passports to them with authority issued by a special Canadian Government Order in Council. This showed a diplomatic intelligence of which Satow might have approved, and the story was the basis of the compelling movies *Argo* and *Canadian Caper*.

In June 2012, Julian Assange, the founder of Wikileaks, an organization that had leaked thousands of U.S. diplomatic cables to the international media, took refuge in the

(Continued)

(Continued)

embassy of Ecuador in London. Mr. Assange had been on bail granted by British courts pending his appeal against extradition proceedings to Sweden on sexual assault charges. That appeal was lost. Mr. Assange was familiar with diplomatic practice, including of course the use of missions to make communications to the sending state. Article 27 of the VCDR states that the mission may employ all appropriate means for such communications, including diplomatic couriers and "messages in code or cipher."[30] A disgruntled U.S. government employee at a U.S. military facility in Iraq contacted them with diplomatic material of interest.

Few have done so much in modern times as Mr. Assange to give the administrators of diplomatic services pause for thought. The function of reporting from the receiving state requires more of diplomats than mere repetition of what is in newspapers. Mr. Assange, however, associated the centuries-long practice of confidential reporting and communicating with the host government as a betrayal of transparency in government. His Wikileaks organization had for several years sought to reveal details of documents that illustrated the secrecy of government, business, and organizations and that, in its view, deserved to have the whistle blown on their activities.

Mr. Assange, an Australian national, had not been charged with an offense in relation to Wikileaks' operation in the United Kingdom or Sweden, but once inside the embassy of Ecuador stated he would remain there indefinitely. Having shown contempt for one part of the VCDR, he now availed himself of another. It is interesting to note that Ecuador did ratify the OAS Convention of 1954 on Diplomatic Asylum, which in Article III states, "It is not lawful to grant asylum to persons who, at the time of requesting it, are under Indictment or on trial for common offenses or have been convicted by competent regular courts and have not served the respective sentence."[31]

Despite the apparent inconsistency with Ecuador's obligations, British police have, at the time of writing, continued to respect the inviolability of the embassy. This case has again reminded diplomats that asylum is easier granted than ended. During his stay in the embassy, Mr. Assange attempted to orchestrate the granting of further asylum status for the U.S. National Security Agency (NSA) contractor Edward Snowden who, though not in a diplomatic mission, applied with Wikileaks' guidance for asylum to fifteen countries, including Ecuador. The British newspaper *The Independent* reported in July 2013 that relations between Ecuador and Mr. Assange were becoming "incredibly strained," information they stated they obtained from a source in Quito—at least respecting diplomatic confidentiality![32]

AND PERSONALLY

My own experiences give examples of the importance of the VCDR for maintaining diplomatic activity. In Venezuela, I served as deputy head of mission of the British embassy from 1994 to 1997. In late 1994, Hugo Chavez, a military officer, was pardoned for his role in a 1992 coup against former President

Carlos Andres Perez and released from jail. Chavez's plans quickly became the talk of political classes in Venezuela and its press pundits, and we picked up a new nervousness from our contacts with the police. I discussed with my ambassador, John Flynn, the interest of the United Kingdom in contacting Chavez to assess whether he was a credible political figure and, if so, how he might launch his campaign. The United Kingdom had considerable commercial interests in Venezuela, not least in the oil industry. Our Chilean-born press attaché, Carlos Villalobos, had good contacts with everyone in politics and duly arranged a lunch meeting in February 1995, which we fixed for a well-known Caracas restaurant. I attended with Villalobos, and Chavez came with his then senior advisor, Luis Miquilena. We realized what we were doing was unusual, as we did not know of any other embassy that had contacted Chavez for a meeting. We did, of course, maintain regular contacts with all parts of the Venezuelan political system. So we took the precaution of informing the Venezuelan security service (DISIP) in advance of the purpose of our meeting, knowing that what we did would be in public view.

The content of our talks proved that Chavez did indeed have interests in a political career, and we reported duly to London as one of our many meetings in Venezuela that year. However, all was not well with our hosts. We had been seen in the restaurant as the police were tracking Chavez's moves. The following day, officers came to the embassy and said they wanted to arrest Villalobos and me for interference in Venezuelan internal affairs. Clearly, this was a reference to Article 41 of the VCDR; in their view, we were exceeding our diplomatic functions. It was more serious in any case for Villalobos, who did not have full diplomatic immunity. Diplomatically, we turned to another recognized function of missions—negotiation. The ambassador made our case to the minister of the interior—we did not take sides, we talked to everyone, and, if anything, a chat with a representative of a Western democracy should be good for Chavez's initiation to political life. We were perhaps vindicated in diplomatic reporting responsibility when, in 1998, Hugo Chavez was elected as President of Venezuela, and remained in office until his death in 2013.

SUGGESTIONS FOR FURTHER READING

1. Berridge, G. R. *Diplomacy: Theory and Practice*, 4th ed. New York: Palgrave Macmillan, 2010.

2. Sharp, Paul. "Diplomacy in International Relations: Theory and Other Disciplinary Perspectives." In *Diplomacy in a Globalizing World: Theories and Practices*, ed. Pauline Kerr and Geoffrey Wiseman. New York: Oxford University Press, 2012.

chapter 3

The Institutions of Bilateral Diplomacy

Precedence, Protocol, Ministries, Embassies

We have looked so far at the way diplomatic services developed and the reasons for their consolidation into their present from. We have also looked at the origins of immunities and privileges of diplomatic and consular staff and the codification of these provisions in the Vienna Conventions.

The Vienna Convention on Diplomatic Relations (VCDR) provides a framework within which diplomatic missions are expected to operate. But it does not define or prescribe in any detail in what daily activities diplomatic machines should engage. Understanding diplomatic practice in the contemporary world means analyzing contributing features like the use of a common language, the formal methods of communication employed by diplomats, the use of precedence, and the development of diplomatic institutions to conduct diplomacy. Of these institutions, we will discuss the bilateral machinery in this chapter—the ministry of foreign affairs and bilateral embassies. In Chapter 4, we will discuss multilateral institutions.

We have seen that what we would now recognize as diplomats have existed for centuries. But to progress beyond random representations, overseas order had to be imposed and the institutions of bilateral diplomacy established. Before establishing institutions of diplomacy, the activity itself had to be formally recognized. This in itself is relatively recent. And it is believed that *diplomacy* as a term was first applied to the conduct of international relations in 1796 by Edmund Burke. The ministries of foreign affairs in the world generally predate the widespread establishment of embassies, and their functions multiplied once there were overseas missions to manage. But there is surprisingly little in international agreements that even refer to the ministry, let alone to what it should do. This is because ministries are a matter for the sending state and are fashioned to fit into domestic political systems, which have infinite variety and surprisingly little in common.

MINISTRIES

Departments of government specializing in foreign affairs were established once the practice of diplomacy became an activity to which governments dedicated attention and resources. In ambition and centralization of diplomatic effort, France led the way. Cardinal Richelieu had a unique perspective on the value of diplomacy; he combined senior positions in the Catholic Church with being chief minister of Louis XIII from 1624 until his death in 1642. He used the two to craft an overarching theme to his foreign policy, recognizing that France was vying for supremacy with the Holy Roman Empire. Maintaining equilibrium in Europe was central to French ambitions. And to achieve that, diplomacy needed to play a constant role in structuring his foreign policy—the négociation continuelle of the diplomatic process. Richelieu's skill in theory and practice were both notable, but his most lasting legacy to diplomacy is the institution of the foreign ministry.

Cardinal Richelieu's foreign ministry was the first of its kind; it was consciously created in 1626 to respond to the demands placed on French domestic political institutions. Permanent ambassadors overseas were the natural corollary of a strong central ministry because he believed that negotiating everywhere would increase the reputation and prestige of Louis XIII and France. And, as Berridge observes, "More diplomacy multiplied the possibilities of inconsistency in both the formulation and execution of foreign policy."[1] Therefore, a domestic bureaucratic apparatus was needed to coordinate efforts and manage communication and appointments. Richelieu was meticulous in applying the terms of the agreements he negotiated with other states, recognizing the overriding importance of trust and confidence in the development of diplomacy. And the more diplomacy was undertaken, the more documents and materials were accumulated. A collective memory was established, with future diplomats able to refer to past reports and letters.

Until 1626, the French government had managed foreign affairs according to the different secretaries of state created in 1547, with responsibility divided according to geographical area. There were also separate departments involved with war and dealing with the military outside France. Richelieu saw that one department and one minister were needed to speak and correspond in the name of France. There needed to be a unit of government that would do nothing but diplomacy and foreign policy. The creation of the British Foreign Office in 1782 and the U.S. State Department in 1789 were examples of a general trend to bring the administration of diplomacy under the jurisdiction of a single ministry. By the early nineteenth century, the "Diplomatic Services of the [European] nations," argued Nicolson, "had been recognised as a distinct branch of the public service in each country."[2]

Another element that facilitated the growth of direction and purpose of diplomacy was the use of a common language. Here, the role of France was central as well. The Ordinance of Villers-Cotterêts, passed in 1539, decreed that all French administrative documents must be in the French language. Until then, the use of Latin and regional dialects were common in France. As France became the dominant European power, the French language came to be associated with power and influence. It became chic but also useful to speak it.

French was the lingua franca—a language for communication between groups like diplomats not sharing a common tongue. By the seventeenth century, French was recognized as the language of diplomacy and international relations throughout the world. French expressions have endured in diplomatic usage such as *agrément*, *démarche*, *note verbale*, *aide-mémoire*, and *chargé d'affaires*, and in the traditions of precedence and protocol. Another major step had been taken to institutionalize the practice of diplomacy.

The issue of precedence took a major step forward in 1815 at the Congress of Vienna. This was the first area of diplomatic law to be codified, and the Vienna Regulation was signed by the biggest powers of the day—Austria, Spain, France, Great Britain, Portugal, Prussia, Russia, and Sweden. The previous system of precedence was established by the pope in 1504, and the new regulation showed the growing secularization of diplomacy. Henceforth, seniority in precedence would be based on the official date of presentation of credentials, with the longest serving diplomat being accorded the highest seniority. The Vienna Regulation also reduced the number of titles assigned to diplomatic heads of mission to three. These were confirmed in the VCDR of 1961.

The use of the French language also reflected the declining influence of the church. The king of France had begun using French frequently in diplomatic matters by the end of the sixteenth century. Despite resistance, the French language gradually usurped Latin as the language of choice, and the Congress of Vienna in 1815 and the Congress of Paris in 1856 were conducted in French throughout. By this time, English was also gaining ground. In 1800, Lord Glenville started using English for all his communications to diplomats at the Court of St. James. And as the globalization of diplomacy proceeded apace with globalization of business and culture, the English language has increasingly been used as the highest common denominator for international discourse. Today, some 40 percent of those under thirty years old in the EU claim to speak some form of English.

If language developed to ensure ease of communication and avoidance of misunderstanding, common methods of written communication have also provided common standards to diplomats. One such format is the note verbale, a customary vehicle for communication between an embassy and a ministry of foreign affairs. It usually opens in the third person: "The . . . Embassy presents its compliments to the Ministry of Foreign Affairs and has the honor to inform them that . . ." The notes are numbered, but not the paragraphs. The ending of the note, after the substantive matter is completed, is also a third-person salutation. Other formal notes, sometimes called a *speaking note* or a *non-paper*, may be left with an official of the ministry when a diplomat calls, so there is less scope for misinterpretation of what a diplomat might say. Not all diplomats organize their thoughts well, and in many cases, their fluency in the local language will not be all it should be. So putting things in writing, usually prepared in the embassy by a native speaker of the language, is a sensible precaution.

Another important public good that diplomacy aspired to give the world was the value of honesty. To flourish and achieve its objectives, diplomacy had to demonstrate that it produced worthwhile exchanges in international relations and that what was said and written could be counted on. With regular deception being practiced, no weight would be given to its proceedings. De Callières, as a founding father of diplomacy, had recognized the indispensability of honesty,

> no doubt the art of lying has been practised with success in diplomacy; but unlike that honesty which here as elsewhere is the best policy, a lie always leaves a drop of poison behind, and even the most dazzling diplomatic success gained by dishonesty stands on an insecure foundation.[3]

That diplomacy did progress in areas like precedence, language, and forms of address suggests that most practitioners took their jobs seriously. All diplomats and all states share an interest in maintaining the observance of these key tenets of global diplomacy.

THE MODERN MINISTRY OF FOREIGN AFFAIRS

In several respects, the VCDR and Vienna Convention on Consular Relations (VCCR) give formal recognition to the role of ministries of foreign affairs and embassies in a way that had not been formalized hitherto. There are references in the conventions to the central role of the ministry of foreign affairs, particularly in the receiving state as a point of contact for the permitted activities of diplomatic missions and their staff. One example is in Article 19 of the VCDR on the obligation to notify the ministry when a charge d'affaires is appointed:

> If the post of head of the mission is vacant, or if the head of the mission is unable to perform his functions a chargé d'affaires ad interim shall act provisionally as head of the mission. The name of the chargé d'affaires ad interim shall be notified, either by the head of the mission or, in case he is unable to do so, by the Ministry for Foreign Affairs of the sending State to the Ministry for Foreign Affairs of the receiving State or such other ministry as may be agreed.[4]

In many other respects the ministry is the one-stop shop for communications between embassies and the receiving state.

The early foreign ministries were not institutions that we would recognize today. The British Foreign Secretary Charles James Fox's budget in 1782 was £14,178, which equates to approximately £20 million today. In practice, it was much less than that, since more than a third was swallowed up in his own salary. His Foreign Office had a total of eleven staff: seven clerks, one chief clerk, two undersecretaries, and one female employee known as the "necessary woman." Ministries were small, full of aristocrats who were largely deskbound. George Canning's Foreign Office in 1822 only had twenty-two staff. In 1861, there were still only fifty-two. The British government started to depoliticize the diplomatic service and make it similar to the civil service. Lord Cowley in the 1850s and, to a greater degree, Lord Lyons in the 1860s were the first senior diplomats to owe their appointments to their professional abilities rather than political considerations.

Prior to 1856, the only qualifications required of British diplomats to be admitted to the Foreign Office were a private income of not less than £400 per year, two months' probation in the Foreign Office, and nomination by the foreign secretary. Between 1815 and 1860, 60 percent of attachés appointed by the British Foreign Office to British missions were drawn from the aristocracy and out of twenty-three ambassadors appointed in this period, only three were commoners. Beginning with Lord Clarendon's introduction of an entrance examination in 1856, a candidate's quality of handwriting and grasp of foreign languages assumed importance. Only in 1905 was the Foreign Office exam assimilated with that of the wider civil service. And diplomats did not need to have graduated from university. Between 1871 and 1907, only 37 percent of them were graduates. The MacDonnell Committee of 1914 abolished the income qualification of the British diplomatic service, improving the chances of those without private means to have a diplomatic career. The institution of the foreign ministry had taken strides to be a full professional institution. The pattern was the same elsewhere. Even as late as the outbreak of World War I, it was estimated that some two-thirds of Austria-Hungary's diplomats came from the landed gentry. Yet in other ways, modernization was taking effect. The Austro-Hungarian foreign ministry appointed commercial directors to embassies in London, Paris, Berlin, and St. Petersburg.

Training and on the job experience in different situations also became a feature of how foreign ministries prepared their staff. The normal way of supplementing the staff of the embassy was through unpaid attachés. However, Russia under Peter the Great was the exception; the czar sent groups of young nobles to Venice, the Dutch Republic, and England for training, and Russians of lower social standing were sponsored by the government to study languages abroad. A college of training for the Russian foreign ministry was established in the 1720s. The Habsburgs had provided systematic diplomatic training in the sixteenth and early seventeenth centuries, and the Orientalische Akademie was established in 1754 to train consular and diplomatic staff for the Near East. In 1724, with the founding of the Oxford and Cambridge Universities' regius chairs of modern history, the British government stated the aim was to avoid the necessity of employing foreign nationals in the civil and diplomatic services. Yet it was not until the mid-nineteenth century that systematic training of all diplomatic staff developed in Europe. The United Kingdom had trained administrators for the East India Company from 1806 and established a professional civil service for home departments following the Northcote-Trevelyan Report of 1854. The U.S. Federal Civil Service was established in 1871.

Now diplomatic services worldwide offer distinctive in-house training to their intake, with full-time courses at different stages of a diplomatic career and some designating the training centers as academies. Thus, the Bangladeshi Foreign Service Academy was established in 1996 for enabling foreign service officers to become "effective diplomats in a changing world scenario."[5] The academy runs sixteen specialized courses and organizes "Training Seminars, Short Courses and Round Table Discussions on various subjects relating to Diplomacy, Foreign Policy and important current Topics."[6] In 2013, a new language center opened in the heart of British Foreign Office main building, training over one thousand students per year, and aiming to increase the number of Arabic and Mandarin speakers in British missions by 40 percent over 2010 levels.

EXAMPLES OF MINISTRIES OF FOREIGN AFFAIRS IN ACTION

In Chapter 1, we saw that the size of the foreign service for the U.S. State Department was 13,354 U.S.-based staff and over 44,000 locally engaged staff (2011 figures). Yet the number of employees of the State Department was among the smallest of U.S. federal departments. The Department of Energy employed over 16,000 federal officials and 93,000 contractors. The U.S. Department of Commerce employed 23,000. The U.S. Department of Homeland Security employed at least 200,000, and the U.S. military had in full-time service over one million personnel. The distribution of the State Department employees is, unsurprisingly, constantly adjusted to meet changing priorities. Figure 3.1, from the 2012 GAO report, shows how the State Department moves its resources across the regions.

The Department of State is at the center of diplomacy in the U.S. system of government, but in the contemporary world, it struggles to maintain its distinctive role of managing international relations. Increasingly, other departments of state conduct direct diplomacy with other countries. Its political affairs department would in its early history have been the predominant influence for U.S. foreign policy. Now geographical bureaus in the Department of State sit alongside those dealing with global issues that are not country specific. Energy resources, environmental affairs, arms control, public diplomacy, democracy, and human rights all have dedicated undersecretaries. The offices that report directly to the secretary of state reflect the importance of women's rights, the global AIDS coordinator, the inspector general, and the Office of the Special Representatives and Envoys. In recent years, special advisors to the secretary of state have been appointed for civic engagement, outreach to youth, and diplomatic innovation. The protocol department is the point of contact for information and legal issues connected with the conduct of diplomatic missions. Its Bureau of Management is central to administration, command of budgets, and the delivery of diplomatic functions.

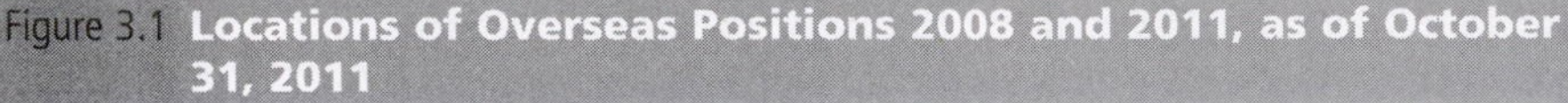
Figure 3.1 Locations of Overseas Positions 2008 and 2011, as of October 31, 2011

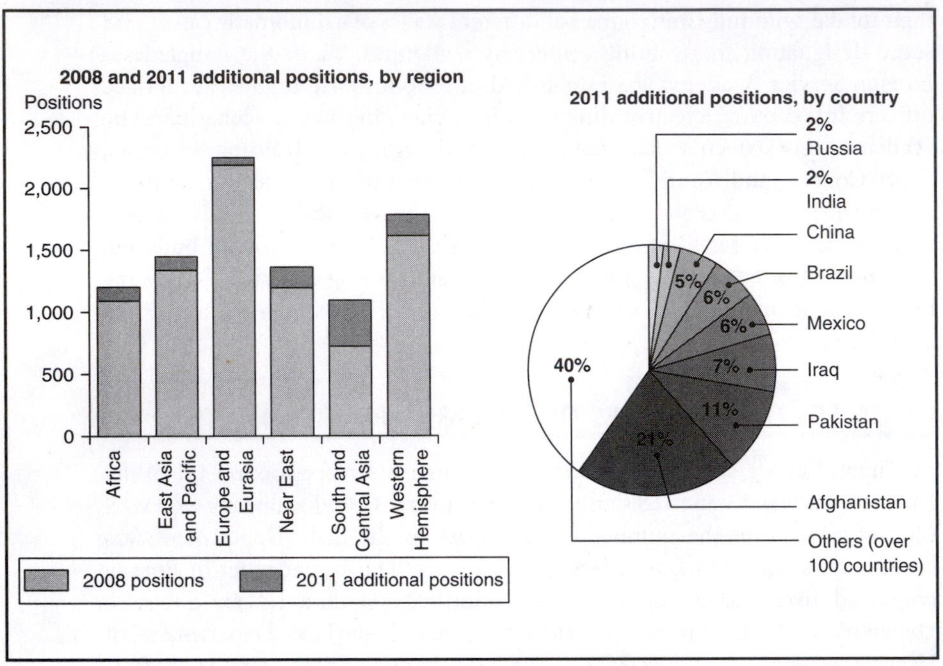

Source: Government Accountability Office, "Foreign Service Midlevel Staffing Gaps Persist Despite Significant Increases in Hiring," June 2012, http://www.gao.gov/assets/600/591595.pdf.

One role that the Department of State still retains is as a repository of knowledge on diplomacy. The collective memory of past relations used to be in paper files and metal cabinets, accessible with difficulty, and shredded after a designated period of years or made accessible to academic researchers. The Department of State's archives are the most frequently sought in the U.S. administration. Under U.S. law, the review of classified records is required after twenty-five years, and additional requests for the releases of earlier documents can be made under Freedom of Information Act, dating from 1966. An important benefit of the digitalization of data is in streamlining internal use of such data in the ministry. Now, U.S. missions and interested bureaus can access data instantaneously and contribute seamlessly to internal policy reviews or problem-solving processes. See Chapter 11 for discussion of the information and communications technologies revolution.

A globalized world has made diplomacy a common feature of government business, going beyond the designation as foreign. Many other departments of state now have regular, often daily, contacts with overseas officials and organizations. Departments like defense, development, education, and environment are negotiating international agreements directly with overseas countries. In

Japan, for example, the Ministry of International Trade and Industry is seen as the lead department on exports and imports, alongside organizations like Japan External Trade Organization (JETRO). Far from controlling policy issues in increasingly complex areas involving scientific, computing, and environmental expertise, the ministry of foreign affairs may have a peripheral role in problem solving compared to state and nonstate contracted experts. Indeed, to ensure the foreign ministry still keeps its own authoritative voice, the heads of the foreign ministries have come to appoint their own specialist advisers in areas like economics and climate security.

Budgets of other departments have also come to dwarf expenditure on diplomatic services. The budget of the U.S. State Department in 2013 was approximately $16 billion, plus the additional expenditures that constituted foreign assistance and contributions to international organizations. In the same year, the U.S. Department of Defense budget was over $700 billion. Even the U.S. intelligences agencies, which input many key issues of diplomacy, have a combined budget of over $40 billion—the CIA alone employs over 21,000. In 2014, the United States maintained over 700 military bases or offices overseas, compared to 278 embassies and consulates. The budget for the United Kingdom's Foreign and Commonwealth Office (FCO) was in 2011 £2.35 billion and was described by the foreign secretary William Hague as representing "0.65% of all government departments' combined resource."[7] Hague went on to say, "the entire spending of the Foreign Office, including the World Service, the British Council, international subscriptions and everything else, is less than the spending of Kent County Council"[8]—an administrative region in England with a population of 1.4 million. By comparison, the U.K. Department for International Development (DFID) took 1.65 percent of total government expenditure and the Ministry of Defence (MOD) had 8.62 percent of the total. Beyond these figures, it is common for foreign ministry budgets to make contributions to international organizations like the United Nations and weather the vagaries of currency fluctuations, which impact heavily what is spent on a foreign service.

Given the peacemaking objective of diplomacy, it may be surprising that the major diplomatic services in the world operate in countries that are among the largest military spenders. Even countries that have shunned overseas military operations—like India, Japan, and Germany—spend far more on their militaries than on their diplomatic services. Figure 3.3 shows the extent of the "outgunning" of diplomacy.

It would be wrong to assume that many ministries of foreign affairs have the stature they retain in governments like the United States and United Kingdom. In many countries, they are far removed from the formation of key strategic decisions in the system of government. Their status will be reflected in the role of the foreign minister, the position of the minister in the cabinet or council of state, its relative budget, and the attention that is devoted to providing a comprehensive foreign service. Fragmented systems of power are a regular challenge to diplomats serving overseas and reinforce the arguments for having a permanent professional cadre who can get under the skin of who really runs a country.

Figure 3.2 **U.S. Department of State Organization Chart**

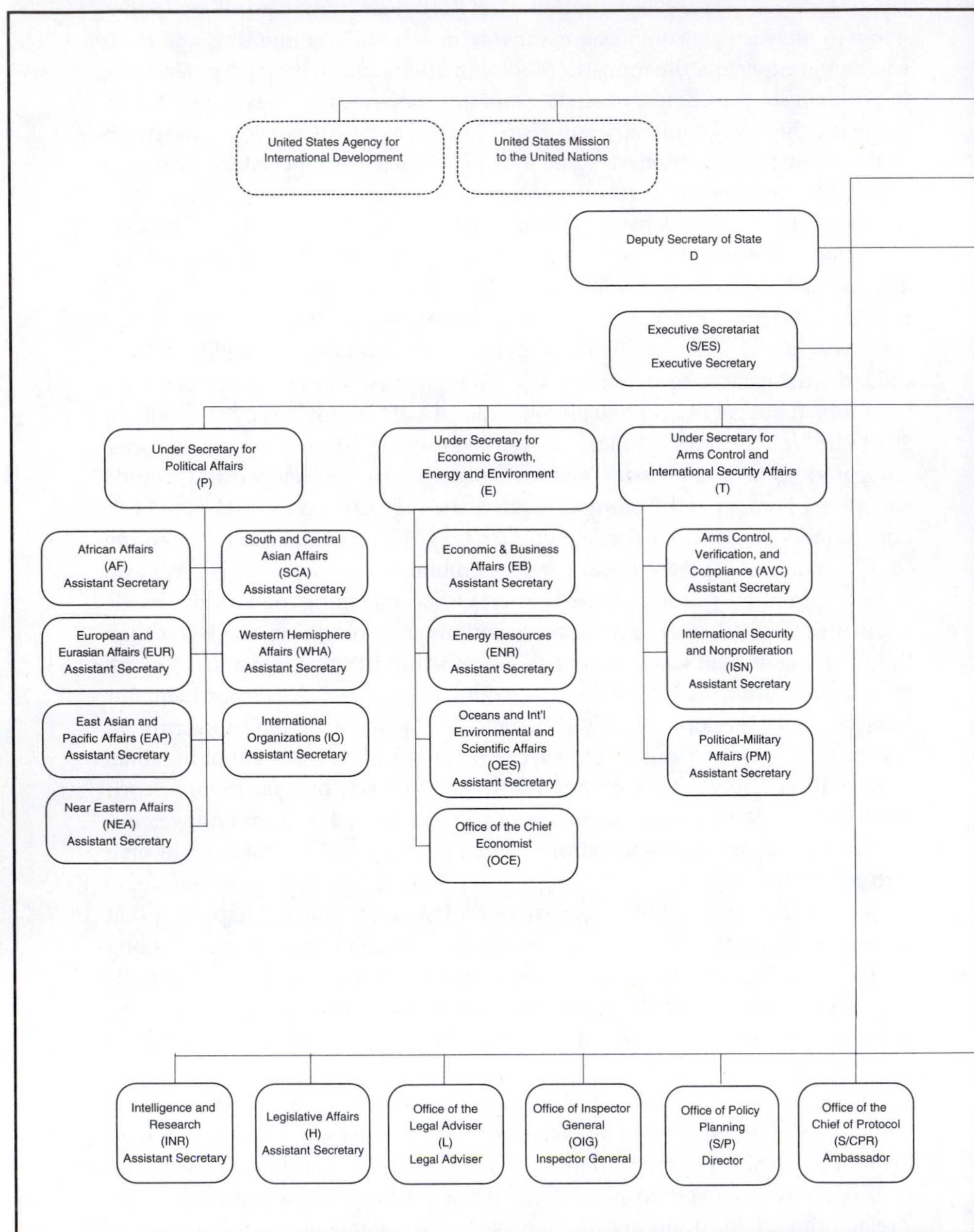

Source: U.S. Department of State, "Departmental Organization Chart: (image map) March 2014," http://www .state. gov/r/pa/ei/rls/dos/99494.htm.

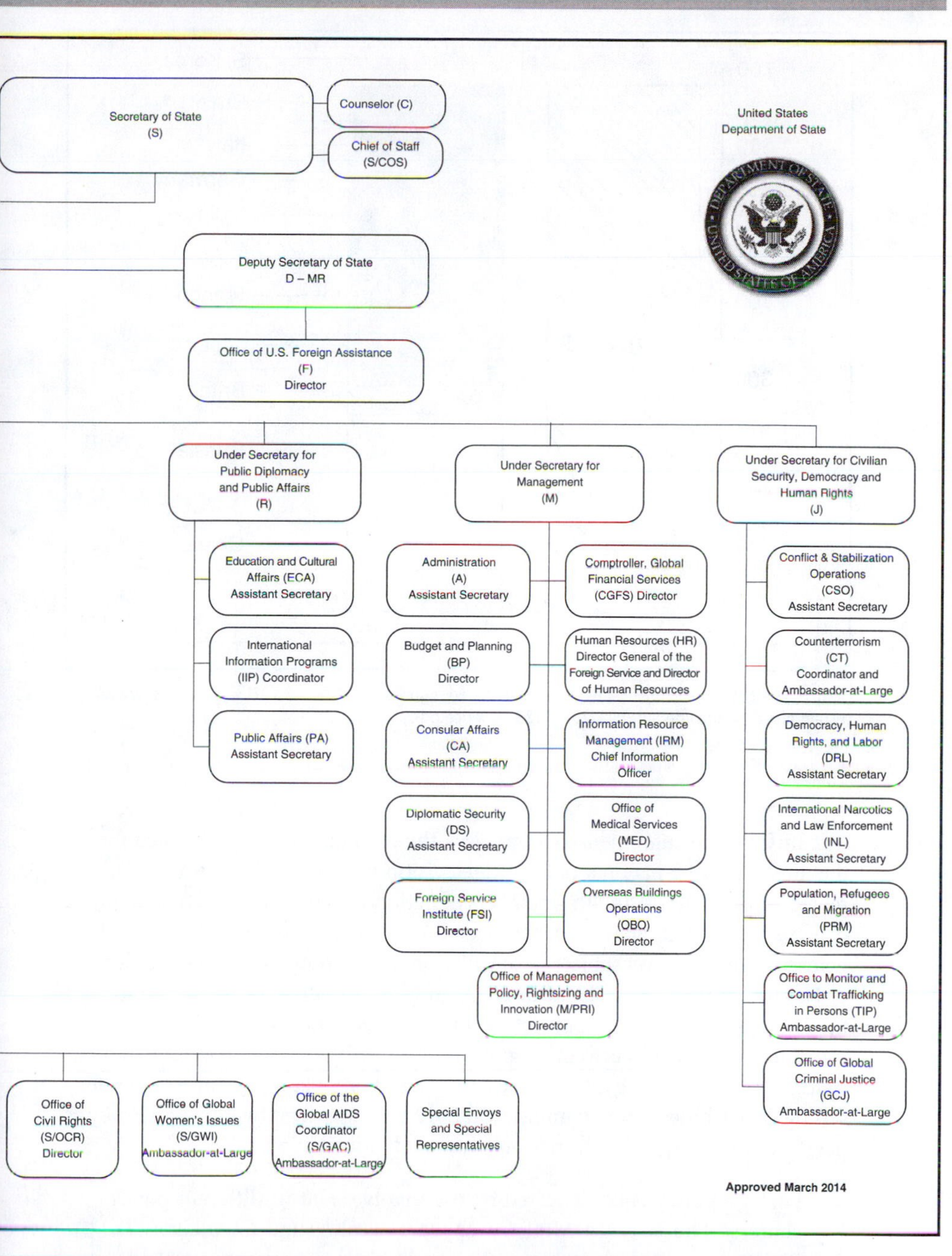
Secretary of State
(S)
Counselor (C)
Chief of Staff
(S/COS)
United States
Department of State
DEPARTMENT OF STATE
UNITED STATES OF AMERICA
Deputy Secretary of State
D – MR
Office of U.S. Foreign Assistance
(F)
Director
Under Secretary for
Public Diplomacy
and Public Affairs
(R)
Under Secretary for
Management
(M)
Under Secretary for Civilian
Security, Democracy and
Human Rights
(J)
Education and Cultural
Affairs (ECA)
Assistant Secretary
International
Information Programs
(IIP) Coordinator
Public Affairs (PA)
Assistant Secretary
Administration
(A)
Assistant Secretary
Comptroller, Global
Financial Services
(CGFS) Director
Budget and Planning
(BP)
Director
Human Resources (HR)
Director General of the
Foreign Service and Director
of Human Resources
Consular Affairs
(CA)
Assistant Secretary
Information Resource
Management (IRM)
Chief Information
Officer
Diplomatic Security
(DS)
Assistant Secretary
Office of
Medical Services
(MED)
Director
Foreign Service
Institute (FSI)
Director
Overseas Buildings
Operations
(OBO)
Director
Office of Management
Policy, Rightsizing and
Innovation (M/PRI)
Director
Conflict & Stabilization
Operations
(CSO)
Assistant Secretary
Counterterrorism
(CT)
Coordinator and
Ambassador-at-Large
Democracy, Human
Rights, and Labor
(DRL)
Assistant Secretary
International Narcotics
and Law Enforcement
(INL)
Assistant Secretary
Population, Refugees
and Migration
(PRM)
Assistant Secretary
Office to Monitor and
Combat Trafficking
in Persons (TIP)
Ambassador-at-Large
Office of Global
Criminal Justice
(GCJ)
Ambassador-at-Large
Office of
Civil Rights
(S/OCR)
Director
Office of Global
Women's Issues
(S/GWI)
Ambassador-at-Large
Office of the
Global AIDS
Coordinator
(S/GAC)
Ambassador-at-Large
Special Envoys
and Special
Representatives
Approved March 2014

Figure 3.3 **Military Spending 2012 ($ billion)**

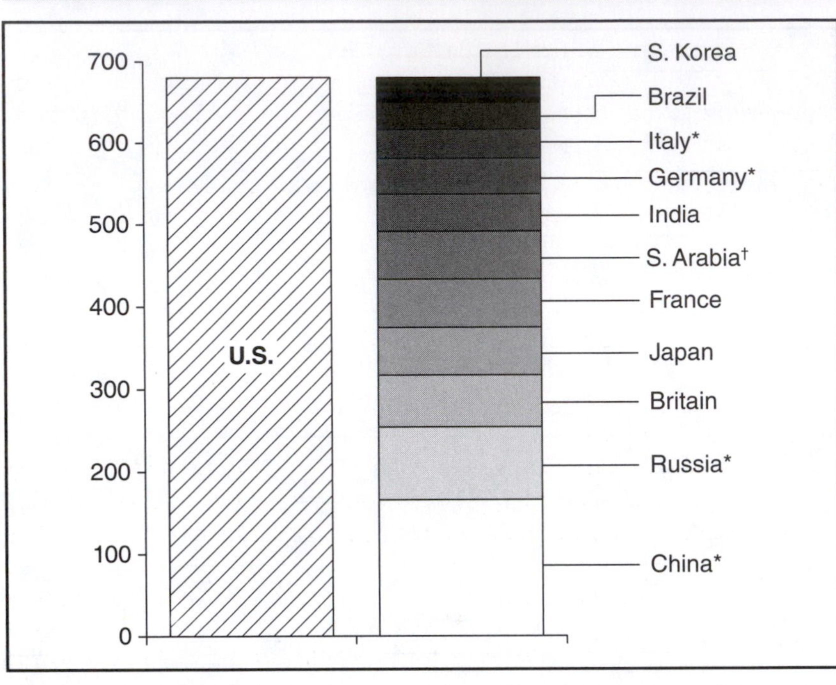

Source: *The Economist*, "Special Report: American Foreign Policy," Nov. 23, 2013, p. 7, http://www.economist.com/sites/default/files/20131123_america.pdf.

*Estimate

†Defense and security

In Iran, the supreme leader appoints the commanders of the armed forces, the director of the national radio and television network, the heads of the major religious foundations, and the members of national security councils dealing with defense and foreign affairs. Yet the elected head of government is the president, whose power is always subject to speculation. It was noticeable after the election of Hasan Rouhani as president in 2013, and his announcement that the foreign ministry would assume responsibility for the nuclear negotiations, that the website of the ministry underwent a significant refurbishment and updating. In other states, for example in Egypt and Pakistan, the military plays a major role in policy setting. The Chinese foreign ministry in 2012 was described by Jonathan Fenby as having only a marginal influence on Chinese diplomacy:

> Foreign policy is complicated by the involvement of different power centers. The Foreign Ministry appears weak. State Councilor Dai Bingguo, who derives his authority from the Communist Party's Leading Group on Foreign Affairs, outranks Foreign Minister Yang Jiechi. A constellation of interest groups affects policy, including the powerful Commerce Ministry; state-owned enterprises; the energy and metals lobbies; the security and ideological arms of the Party,

which want to keep "harmful" foreign influences at bay; and the People's Liberation Army.[9]

One function that the foreign minister or secretary of state normally retains in this changed climate is head of the administration that controls the resources of diplomatic or foreign service. Here, there is generally no ambiguity of influence. This gives the position a unique dual role distinct from most other heads of ministries in governmental systems. The foreign secretary in every developed country has at his or her command a vast global resource, with access to 24/7 information.

Few ministers of foreign affairs of major Western countries have been career diplomats. U.S. secretaries of state in recent years have been military (Colin Powell), academic (Condoleeza Rice), from law and politics (Hillary Clinton), and from Congress (John Kerry). Most British foreign secretaries have been career politicians, though some, like Douglas Hurd, did serve as diplomats before entering politics. Other diplomatic systems favor the professional career diplomat. An example of this is Sergei Lavrov, who has worked for over forty years, first for the Soviet Union and later for the Russian Federation, serving latterly as foreign minister. Another recent example is Miguel Ángel Moratinos, Foreign Minister of Spain.

Style in the job has varied greatly as well. John Foster Dulles traveled 56,000 miles in six years in office. Alexander Haig in 1982 traveled 34,000 miles in five days during the Falklands War. Hillary Clinton far exceeded all previous secretaries, telling *The Economist* in 2012 she had already traveled over 900,000 miles. This remains an advantage of the position of minister, as cabinet colleagues are required to limit their time out of the country. Personal familiarity with other foreign leaders can count for much.

But centralization of government has not left diplomacy unaffected. As William Hague has said, "Foreign policy runs through the veins of the whole government in a way that it has never done before."[10] The key decisions in many systems of diplomacy are increasingly taken at the center of government. The staff at Downing Street or in the White House report directly to the head of government and have direct input from intelligence agencies, many of which are autonomous from the ministry. Many heads of government second advisors from the foreign ministry to bring their expertise to the center. One institutional change that further undercut the role of the British foreign office was the creation by British Prime Minister David Cameron in 2010 of a new National Security Council, headed by former FCO officials. There are two deputy national security advisors—one for foreign policy and one for intelligence. This was modeled on the U.S. National Security Council, which was established in 1947.

ROLES OF EMBASSIES AND CONSULATES

What are the roles of embassies and other missions (consulates general and consulates) in this machinery? They remain the most visible and permanent institution of diplomacy. Tens of thousands of them exist, and many major capital cities host over one hundred permanent bilateral missions, as well as those of multilateral institutions like the EU, and UN agencies.

Every diplomatic mission has a head, and the formal aspect of the head of mission is, as we have seen, established in the VCDR and VCCR. The heads of missions are also responsible to the minister of foreign affairs or secretary of state, and many ambassadors, if career diplomats, will be members of the organization headed by the minister. Senior appointments of ambassadors in most systems are now approved by heads of government, and the competition for the jobs may involve nondiplomat candidates against professional diplomats. It is also important to remember that once appointed, the head of mission is a representative of the state, not the government of the sending state. This means that the credentials document of the head of mission is signed by the head of state, rather than the minister or secretary of state.

The characteristics of individual appointed ambassadors, as we have seen, are diverse and there are no formal qualifications required. The personalities, however, can eclipse an institution, and the task of fulfilling an effective representative role is more similar to a jazz musician than a conductor of an orchestral score. The institution of an embassy has enduring functions, but the nature of the tasks relating to those functions is impossible to predict. The head of mission must be strategic to maintain the enduring tasks but also responsive, creative, and willing to work with diverse partners to achieve results. Management and people skills are essential to motivate staff and bring organization to its vast output. In 2014, the U.S. embassy compound in Baghdad was the largest building area in the city after the airport and had accommodation for up to 35,000 people, including private contractors. The U.K. defense section in its Washington embassy alone employs over one hundred people.

The line between career diplomats and civil servants in embassies is increasingly blurred. Many missions are taking on private sector contractors or consultants in aid issues, media, and IT. As we will discuss in Chapter 9, state department reforms emphasize the need for diplomats to work with civil society, not just officials. And some well-funded embassies, so used to cultivating influence through charm, language skills, and entertainment, are now employing lobbyists to do some part of their jobs. In the context of this changing environment, what remains of those essential functions of the role of embassies identified by the VCDR?

First, embassies are the one-stop shop for relations between countries. No other entity can perform this role. However large they are, and the VCDR provides that they must be of a reasonable size agreed to with the receiving state, they must all be tracked in activities by the host country's ministry of foreign affairs. The VCDR provides that the embassy continues to be the only entity that can represent the sending state. But the modern reality is that the sending state's non-governmental organizations (NGOs), tourists, and businesses are also present in the receiving state.

Second, the embassy is the chief protector of foreign nationals of the sending country, whose staff must be prepared to offer continuous and imaginative assistance to nationals in difficulties or peril. The one attribute unaffected by any aspect of globalization is the attribution of nationality, so the responsibility of the embassy for such protection seems assured. The increase in world travel (which requires a constant updating by embassies of travel advice), families of dual or multiple nationality, and international education means that the problem-solving responsibility of missions will only grow in importance. There is discussion of sharing such protection responsibilities to save costs, and the Canadian and U.K. governments have announced they want to collaborate more. The British Foreign Office explained the objective: "It is about speed and flexibility, practicality, saving the taxpayer money in both countries, but also being able to operate effectively in a networked world . . . where we need to be present in more places than ever before."[11]

This kind of arrangement is nothing new and offers reciprocity. Canadians have worked out of the Australian mission in Cambodia, and the United Kingdom works out of Canada's office in Mali. Canada provides consular services to Australians in several countries, and the practice of interest sections, where one country represents the interests of another, is provided for under Article 46 of the VCDR. Examples of such sections are the Swiss acting for the United States in Cuba or the Swedes representing the United States in North Korea. Both are countries with which the United States does not have full diplomatic relations. The duties of the representing state include the protection of U.S. nationals.

This sort of pragmatic sharing of the functions of missions does not go down well with prickly concepts of national sovereignty. The Canadian politician Thomas Mulcair complained that the proposed United Kingdom-Canada arrangement would mean that Canada would "be represented by a desk at the British embassy instead of an independent Canadian diplomatic mission."[12]

The third core function of an embassy is its capacity to negotiate. Without an embassy, many of the elements of a negotiation would be impossible to achieve. For the sending state to negotiate effectively in the receiving state it needs an embassy. In many cases, embassies require backup expertise from their government at home to conduct these negotiations, but the continuous 24/7 existence of embassies is indispensable in supervising all the stages of a negotiation and implementing any agreements.

Fourth, the embassy is the only part of the mechanisms of diplomacy that can see the opportunities presented overseas for contacts, initiatives, and results. The ministry will give broad outlines on policy and objectives. But the officials in the capitals have neither the time nor knowledge to direct staff on the ground. The Foreign Office Department in London, which had responsibility for the U.K. policy toward Cuba, covered over thirty other countries. This would be typical of the staffing of many ministries. So if embassy staff members are always waiting to be told what to do by officials in a ministry, they are in the wrong job. Many diplomats seldom hear from capitals at all except when visits are planned. So the temptation is there to relax and stay quiet—not a good idea when promotion in a meritocratic service often goes to those who at least have looked busy and made sure the ministry has noticed. Real life examples of the life of a modern ambassador in a major post are shown in Box 3.1.

Box 3-1 Life of an Ambassador

To give a real life example of what an ambassador in a major post might be doing during a week, I went to the website of the German embassy in Washington. The ambassador helpfully reproduces some of the appointments he had. Here is a sampling from October 2013; of course, this excluded the reporting on policy, his U.S. contacts, and dealing with serious cases of protection of German nationals.

October 3. The ambassador attended a meeting of the EU heads of mission in Washington. The ambassador hosted a garden party to celebrate the Day of German Unity on the twenty-third anniversary of German unification.

October 4. The ambassador met with Jochen Köckler, member of the board of Deutshe Messe AG.

October 6. The ambassador attended the Shakespeare Theatre Company's annual gala in Washington, D.C.

October 7. The ambassador delivered the keynote address at the annual conference of International Economic Development Council in Philadelphia and spoke at a luncheon cohosted by the German American Chamber of Commerce and the Irish American Business Chamber in Philadelphia.

October 8. The ambassador met with the managing director of the Vodafone Foundation in Germany, Mark Speich. The ambassador met with Jim Barber, President of UPS International, and Frank Sportolari, President of UPS Germany. The ambassador met with former editor of Der Spiegel, Georg Mascolo. The ambassador hosted a dinner in honor of Andreas Dombret, member of the Executive Board of Deutsche Bundesbank.

October 9. The ambassador hosted a delegation of Atlantik-Brücke led by Freidrich Merz, chairman of the organization, at his residence. The ambassador attended a luncheon in honor of Atlantik-Brücke delegation with members of Congress at Capitol Hill.

Source: www.germany.info.

EMBASSIES LOSING THEIR GRIP?

What functions of embassies now raise problems and are causing a reassessment of the role of embassies and their unique usefulness?

The first is their visibility, the bricks and mortar nature of their status. The argument is that to fulfill their role, the institution cannot hide. It needs to fly the flag—literally and diplomatically—otherwise, how would the receiving state know it had diplomatic relations? Out of the U.S. State Department's annual budget of around $16 billion, over $2 billion is spent not on diplomacy but on securing buildings and equipment. Yet, in an era of open virtual discussion—spewing hatred or encouraging altruism—an embassy represents reality and tangibility in terms of a target. Every year brings new examples of embassies and consulates being used as a vent for anger or as a focus for ad hoc or organized protest. Diplomatic vehicl are also easy targets as they carry distinctive registration plates. A little research ca tell any would-be attacker what state they represent. In 2014, the Islamic State (IS) targeted Turkish diplomats in Mosul, Iraq, and held them hostage.

Second, embassies are increasingly competing with innumerable nonstate actors to obtain and disseminate information. Embassies still have a privileged entrée to official contacts and are used to transmit information, but that is no longer the whole story. Often they are seeking to control information about their own countries from competing sources. As the British Foreign Office noted in a policy document of 2006,

> States will remain the single most important international actors. But as the impact of new technology and globalization grows, a wider variety of participation will have international influence. This may be fuelled by further erosions of confidence in governments, international organizations and global business.[13]

Third, the reporting function of an embassy is no longer as unique as it was. The mission will still have access to senior officials and other diplomats who will talk in confidence about events that would not be accessible to the media. But the 24/7 capacity of the global media to report from anywhere in the world, coupled with the universal presence of cell phones for photos and talk, often means that embassies are responding to reports of others rather than getting their briefing to their ministers first. A minister of foreign affairs will have a TV set in his or her office, ready for breaking news and tuned to the likes of the BBC or CNN. Of course, a good embassy will not be far behind in its reporting speed but it is bound to be an unequal battle.

HOW ARE EMBASSIES STAFFED?

Embassies have an institutional conformity and similarity represented by the titles of their officers. This has obvious value for the sending and receiving countries and accords with a formal requirement in the VCDR. Thus, a head of mission can be an ambassador, a high commissioner (heads of mission in member countries of The Commonwealth) or a consul general. Consulates outnumber embassies in most countries, especially where the main centers of business and immigrant communities are outside the capital cities. Of the 270 missions in the U.S. foreign service system, 170 are embassies. Kosovo has currently fourteen overseas missions and had been recognized as a state by only a little more than half of the members of the United Nations by the end of 2013.

One feature of embassies that has contributed to their institutionalization is the common use of titles of other officials who serve under the head of mission. In no other profession, including the ranks of military, is the common branding so widely followed. In the corporate world, vice president or managing director may be common, nonexistent, or in practice signify very different levels of seniority. But the nature of the diplomatic relationship means that different interlocutors must seek out their equivalent level. A rank below ambassador that universally signifies a level of responsibility and seniority is the title of counselor, which is usually equivalent to a head of department in a ministry. In embassies, *counselor* is used to designate the senior specialist political officer, or those heading embassy responsibilities in commercial or inward investment promotion, consular issues, culture, and so forth. Military attachés are still common in embassies where there are defense issues of mutual interest to discuss. Below the ranks of counselors—a major embassy might have between five and ten of them—there will be larger numbers of first, second, and third secretaries. Again, many will carry designations according to their responsibilities—for example, First Secretary (Commercial). There are may be even larger numbers of second and third secretaries similarly identified. These ranks and titles are used as indispensable measures of equivalence in diplomacy. A junior diplomat in an embassy would not expect to be seen by a counselor in another mission, and this common heritage of diplomatic seniority facilitates the practicalities of diplomatic operations.

The role of local staff in an embassy is often neglected. These people give embassies real connection to local society, are a source of knowledge and experience, but also may constitute a risk to the sending state of infiltration and loss of confidentiality. Often over 80 percent of the staff of medium-sized missions will be from the receiving state or other countries. In the case of the embassy I headed in Cuba, we had over forty Cuban employees, some probably in the pay of our hosts as well as Her Majesty's government. But the running of the mission and dealing with agencies of the state, customs, transport, and administrative minutiae would have been difficult without them. Many had served for decades, and some were decorated by the British government (for which permission is required of the receiving state); also, the Cuban reaction to new British management initiatives not known in Cuba was very instructive. In discussion of some issues and on matters of confidence, it was not possible to include them, but they served with distinction. In Venezuela, the local staff of our embassy included non-Venezuelans—British, American, and Chilean citizens who had settled in Caracas.

Just as the ministry of foreign affairs is competing for influence at home, the provision of the VCDR requiring only one premises and one representational unit in the receiving country gives embassies continuing authority. Every modern embassy will have staff who come from a wide variety of disciplines and home departments. Officials from departments of commerce, treasury, environment, drugs enforcement, the branches of military, and homeland security or ministry of interior for visa and passport processing will serve alongside career diplomats. Intelligence officers in an embassy may be declared to the host government or may have a cover title to disguise their real functions. All these officers bring expertise and widely differing experience to a unit that must, according to diplomatic practice, remain under the charge of the head of post. This control is a great asset for the foreign minister and ministry. The administration of a large institution also brings in an additional set of experts with few or no diplomatic responsibilities. Missions have accountants, translators, directors of transport, and information technology experts. In some cases, such officers will be recruited from the local community. Despite their diversity of purpose, size, and quality, all missions share these fundamental characteristics. In tit-for-tat expulsions in a persona non grata dispute, titles and levels of responsibility matter.

NEW AND OLD TASKS

We have discussed how far trust and mutual benefit from relations is crucial to productive diplomacy. Yet, at the same time, the acceptance of permanent missions may stimulate distrust because of the opportunities they afford for espionage, including in the industrial and technology spheres, and disruptive activities. Some missions may be used for electronic surveillance of the very ministry to which they are accredited. Having privileged and immune officials of a government embedded in a country can readily form a base for activities against opponents of the government, liaison with sympathetic foreign groupings, and illicit activities such as drugs or arms running. With their increased mobility and the virtual contacts facilitated by digital technologies, diplomats are increasingly a burden on the security operations of the receiving country. Diplomatic missions, therefore, come with a downside. Most receiving countries will monitor the behavior of such missions to ensure that the disadvantages of their presence do not outweigh the benefits. As diplomacy values the insights into a government's activities acquired covertly, there is again a kind of mutual benefit from under the radar activities. As President Obama commented when the United States was accused of widespread eavesdropping, even on allies, "And I guarantee you that in European capitals, there are people who are interested in, if not what I had for breakfast, at least what my talking points might be should I end up meeting with their leaders. That's how intelligence services operate."[14] It's a game played by most, if not all, though given different proficiencies among states, it is usually not zero-sum.

If some of the traditional roles of embassies have declined in importance, others have developed and absorb more diplomatic time. Two activities that were hardly central to the intention of the drafters of the VCDR have developed apace. These are public diplomacy and active promotion of trade and investment opportunities.

In public diplomacy—engaging with overseas publics rather than officials—the embassy has to strike a sometimes fragile balance between promoting overt and possibly unwelcome propaganda and positive engagement with the civil society of the receiving state. This will be examined in more detail in Chapter 7.

The VCDR defines the third function of diplomats as protecting the interests of the sending state. These interests now include tasks such as proactive promotion of trade and investment of the sending state. These roles involve contact and negotiation with nationals of the receiving state. They also potentially involve the offer of incentives to companies of the receiving state to bring investment projects to the sending state. Many states, for example, are currently competing for new projects planned overseas by Indian companies. Their diplomatic agents call repeatedly on the same target companies in bidding wars. In export promotion, the sending country may be promoting the purchase in the receiving state of goods and services in direct competition with those produced by national companies in the receiving state. In my own career, I spent several years in the United States as consul for investment, promoting U.S. companies' investment in the United Kingdom. Based in New York City, I covered the six states of New England. I drove hundreds of miles every month selling different parts of the United Kingdom as a location for manufacturing, a service center, or to attract investment that would safeguard existing jobs. I was in competition with many other EU diplomats from France, Ireland, the Netherlands, and Germany, among others.

With tourism, global business, and education all accelerating, the diversity of demands on the diplomatic functions of the sending state has grown. And with global opportunities for trade and investment abounding, domestic taxpayers look to their governments for assistance to produce overseas commercial success. Power is no longer judged in solely military terms, and the emerging powers have shown that giving high priority to economic diplomacy will gain prestige. Economic leverage is now wielded directly by the state through companies it controls, not just through the medium of diplomatic agents. Sovereign wealth funds often speak louder diplomatically than squadrons of fighter jets. This will be discussed further in later chapters.

The hundreds of diplomatic missions that now exist in major countries mean that diplomatic institutions have been one of the growth industries of the last 150 years. The example of Germany shows how far the creation of diplomatic institutions has advanced. In 1874, Germany had only four embassies (in London, Paris, Saint Petersburg, and Vienna), with nonambassadorial representation at fourteen posts (in Athens, Bern, Brussels, The Hague, Constantinople, Copenhagen, Lisbon, Madrid, Rome, Stockholm, Peking, Rio de Janeiro, Washington, D.C., and the Holy See). In addition, Germany had seven consulates general with diplomatic status (in Alexandria, Belgrade, Bucharest, London, New York, Budapest, and Warsaw) and thirty-seven consulates and vice-consulates headed by consular officers. By 1914, Germany had around twenty major overseas missions. Today, Germany has embassies in 166 countries and some 350 honorary consuls. And in Washington, D.C., the total number of diplomatic missions is 176.

COMPETITION

The overseas missions of states have enormous opportunities in a globalized world. Through their efforts and initiatives they can bring jobs, deliver commercial orders, entice students to study and pay fees, and, through public diplomacy, perhaps improve their country's image and soft power. It is hardly surprising now that the pressure is on missions to outperform their competitors. Each government will receive reports from its citizens that competitor nations are doing better in markets, gaining access to who counts, and handling cases of distressed subjects. The activity of international relations, because of the growing public nature of the arena in which they operate, has taken on a new competitive edge. Increasingly, the domestic constituency holds its service providers to account. The media relish stories of incompetence or corruption of overpaid and underworked diplomatic staff.

In an exercise designed to produce better use of diplomatic resources, the U.K. Foreign Office in 2012 set up an expert panel of advisers. This panel of sixty politicians, journalists, and representatives from business and the NGO sector was "to assess the department's progress and to judge how it compares with diplomatic services around the world."[15] It would ask the British public what diplomats should be doing and what the role of diplomatic posts should be at home and overseas. Simon Fraser, head of the U.K. diplomatic service, told the Parliamentary Foreign Affairs Committee that the panel had judged France to have the most effective diplomatic service—although the United Kingdom came second!

> French diplomacy is very good at a single-minded pursuit of a perception of the national interest. This is something that perhaps British diplomacy could be a bit more focused in doing, whilst also pursuing the other things such as our values agenda, human rights and these other issues.[16]

Fraser said the United Kingdom's diplomacy aimed to be more "hard headed and focused on delivering the national interest" and more "bold and imaginative."[17]

The pressure on diplomatic institutions does not just come from competition with others. The protection of nationals, once perhaps an activity receiving little personal attention from ambassadors, has become a core activity, subject to enormous innovation. This will be discussed in more detail in the context of new technology in Chapter 11. Increasingly demanding and traveling publics mean there will continue to be pressure to raise charges to pay for consular services. It is not impossible to conceive of this function being devolved to the private sector, but the majority of taxpayers come into contact with embassies or consulates of their own country only when needing assistance. The idea of a commercially based helpline organization handling these cases with a credit card payment system seems far-fetched, but it might look good in a consultant's strategy review paper. However they are handled, crises seem bigger and more frequent in the modern era. The protection of national subjects is now increasingly not just an ad hoc response to individual problems or natural disasters. Most crises involve consular officials from many countries. They cooperate and compete, but having more states involved usually assists with collective problem solving. When diplomats are thrown into a crisis, their determination and versatility is severely tested, knowing that one result of applying intelligent diplomacy can be to save lives. One such example was the evacuation of citizens of various European countries from Libya in 2011.

In October 2012, the United Kingdom responded to its Libya experience by establishing a permanent crisis center to

> provide one of the most complete and advanced consular services in the world. . . . With increasing numbers of British nationals living, working and travelling abroad, and to a more and more diverse range of places, we need to ensure that we are innovative and make the most of emerging tools of communication, such as Twitter and Facebook, so that we can reach and help as many people as possible in a crisis.[18]

The U.K. statement noted that its crisis response capabilities had been tested thirteen times in the previous twelve months, including evacuating diplomats and their families from Tehran and helping those involved in the sinking of the Costa Concordia cruise ship off the Italian coast.

THE FUTURE OF DIPLOMATIC MISSIONS

In assessing the value of the permanent diplomatic mission, one enduring feature is the constant nature of diplomacy. Richelieu's rationale for diplomacy sees its best expression in the work of embassies and consulates. Despite regular changes in personnel—most diplomats do not serve longer than five years in a post—their activities, through regular contacts, meetings, and problem solving create a fund of knowledge and social capital that may be invaluable if relations become tense. Missions attempt to establish areas of common interest and to ensure that differences that do exist do not define the core relationship. The international agreements that exist bilaterally between sovereign states are testimony to the work of diplomatic missions. They separate the issues that matter and try to give substance and predictability to management of international relations. Few of the discussions hit the headlines—that is part of continuity in diplomacy—but the value in practical terms is immense in areas like double taxation, investment protection and promotion, and prisoner exchange negotiations. All are monuments to useful diplomatic activity. The smoothing of the edges between countries would be difficult, if not impossible, to achieve without diplomatic and consular missions.

Some of the activities of embassies are much less case specific. The collective lives of embassies are increasingly interwoven. There has long been camaraderie among the diplomats that serve in the missions. They share a wish for diplomacy to be valued and to function. Despite the appearance of separateness, they share contacts, compare the competencies of officials of the receiving state, and share experiences of local shops and schools. Many employ the same software and the same contractors, and they defend their collective privileges—for example, on taxes—and work together as a trade union for diplomacy. Diplomats enjoy each other's company, share their tales of past diplomatic triumphs and disasters, but will be wary of cooperating for the crown jewels. Diplomats will fight as hard as any brokerage dealer for insider information, commercial contracts, and access to media. The system breeds frenetic activity, skilled reporting, insights, and courageous assistance to protect nationals in crises. But in many respects, the work of missions also encourages overlapping and competitive activities.

A common role missions share is the hosting of visitors from their capitals. So frequent are such visits that many missions employ full-time visit officers, and they involve frequent contact with the host government's officials in the ministry of foreign affairs. Visits are one of the staples of the diplomatic diet. Their content follows predictable patterns: preparation of programs, the inputs from the mission to the briefing of visitors, the drafting of speeches, the calls on the local chamber of commerce with business representatives of both countries, and the likely inclusion of an item in the program involving civil society, reflecting global issues like education, the environment, or science and technology. The availability of key officials and how the visitors are entertained will inevitably reflect how the sending country is viewed relative to other missions. Status is a regular feature of diplomatic practice, in spite of the provisions of the VCDR insisting on equality of treatment.

One reason embassies continue to receive resources is because every sovereign state views them as measures of status and states feel comfortable with a system that treats all embassies as equals. One unique feature of diplomatic missions compared, say, to business organizations or non-governmental entities is that despite their vastly different degrees of sophistication and effectiveness, they receive equal status. Their officers will have different skills, including proficiency in languages, they will have different social skills, their work ethics vary enormously, and they will be regarded with different degrees of respect by their own home ministries. But all states agree that embassies add much to the identity and self-esteem of a state. But that also gives diplomacy some of its increasingly troublesome problems, as the appearance of states going through the diplomatic motions does not promote diplomatic innovation. The effects of underachieving diplomatic institutions will be examined more in the final two chapters.

Case Study

How Embassies Operate

One practical way to absorb the diversity of embassies is a survey of embassy and ministry websites. Of course, all modern institutions have recognized the requirement to be on the web. Their sites reflect both how they see themselves as institutions and how far they can be expected to be practitioners of effective diplomacy. The websites of ministries of foreign affairs

(Continued)

(Continued)

and embassies may not be viewed frequently by members of the public, but their diversity is striking. Some are impressive, funded with fulsome budgets and regularly updated to make them attractive to the surfer. Some are predictably boring, with bureaucratic prowess more evident than eye-catching presentation. Many are simply shoddily managed with little updating and with an amateurism that is comically inept. Government employees engaged in projecting incompetence for the world to see. There are no bankruptcies decided by market forces in diplomacy, yet all the institutions presenting themselves on the web are facets of the modern family of contemporary diplomacy.

The websites of major countries show a strong awareness of corporate branding. Each U.S. or French embassy will have a distinctive look common to all its posts. Some sites will stress the attractiveness of the country for tourism (the embassy of Kenya in the United States), some the excellence of their education system for overseas students (United States in India). Some will perhaps try to change the image they perceive the public has of their country. The German embassy in Washington has offered language prizes, items for children, impressive videos and message rooms. Embassy websites reflect the features of the relationship between the particular country and its host. Of the dozens of embassy sites maintained by major states, none will be the same, and within the same state some will be of a much higher standard than others. When I checked the site of an embassy of an EU member state in London in July 2013, it was elegant, well presented, and was appropriately updated with news. Yet the same country's embassy site in Islamabad on the same day had nothing more recent posted in news than a note from February 2013. Clicking on a link for visa information led to the site of a Pakistani dating agency. The English language website of the Ministry of Foreign Affairs of Iran was transformed in weeks after the election in 2013 of Hasan Rouhani and his appointment of the Western-educated Javad Zarif. No longer was the website out of date and uninformative, but its slickness compared favorably to the diplomatic market leaders. The ministry had acquired new importance within Iranian diplomacy.

One case study that illustrates the unsung value of having a permanent mission occurred during my own posting in Caracas in 1996. During one of the innumerable cocktail parties, I was doing my rounds of polite conversations, planning my exit to head to another tropical garden, when I saw a new face from the usual party crowd. We began talking and he said his name was Ronald Evans—an unusual Welsh name for a Venezuelan. He was a tax specialist from an accounting firm in New York who was seconded to the Venezuelan Ministry of Finance. I had just been dusting down some old files the embassy had on the draft United Kingdom-Venezuela Double Taxation Treaty. This had been stalled for years mainly due to bureaucratic inertia. Evans expressed what I assumed was a polite interest only, but invited me to call him. I duly did, and he said he could fix the problem quickly if the United Kingdom would send out a team of officials. We found a willing and able British team of tax experts and within a few weeks the United Kingdom and Venezuela had concluded a treaty. It is fair to say that without an embassy, this small step of diplomatic progress would not have happened.

Embassies of integrated diplomatic systems used by the sending state are part of the international projection of their image. Political leaders travel and like to be seen as intervening effectively in issues and expect their missions to play a role in implementing policy. With large public resources being devoted to overseas representation, accountability requires that those who authorize the resources—whether monetary or human, development or defense—are seen to be checking for themselves. No longer is the mission a self-governing, self-accounting unit. On-site inspections are required. Total government has meant that diplomatic institutions are now also part of a wider reality where there is little separation between domestic and international activity. Ministers in many governments come and go with frequency. From 1997 to 2011, the average length of stay of a junior minister at the British Foreign Office was eighteen months. Before leaving, all embarked on their rounds of visits overseas to countries within their purview and then moved on in their political careers. The embassies fulfilled their visit-organizing role. One former U.S. head of mission compared his role to a flight attendant. He made sure the visitors were comfortable, fed them, and then cleaned up the mess when they left.

In Afghanistan, the military and state-building operations that began in 2001 and continued for over a decade had enormous impact on the diplomacy of NATO and other states involved. Sherard Cowper-Coles, the United Kingdom's ambassador in Afghanistan from 2007 to 2009 and special representative for Afghanistan from 2009 to 2010, has described the task of his embassy in servicing, briefing, and feeding visitors from home:

> Each senior international visitor, civilian or military, had to be given a program of calls which accorded with his or her estimation of their own importance, each accommodated and transported securely. The handful of serious ambassadors in Kabul found themselves endlessly attending briefing suppers arranged by their colleagues for visitors from their respective capitals, with the same routine at each event.[19]

Cowper-Coles's experience in Afghanistan was in unusual times when NATO forces and advisors were administering large sections of the country. But his observations will ring true to many heads of missions. Diplomatic missions now are part of a morass of policy planning that applies pressure to and seeks to influence the behavior of other countries. As Cowper-Coles wrote,

> Back in London there was an alphabet soup of committees supposedly coordinating the British effort in Afghanistan: a Ministerial Committee, usually chaired by the Prime Minister; an informal trilateral meeting of the three Cabinet Ministers directly involved—the Foreign, Defence and Development Secretaries; an Afghan Strategy Group; an Afghan Senior Officials' Group; and others for specialized subjects such as media handling. All of these fed two illusions: first, that Britain could somehow have an independent strategy towards Afghanistan, and, second, that British Ministers could direct the military campaign in Afghanistan—in reality the military took their orders from the NATO command chain. But neither illusion stopped us spending many hours in often impassioned debate.[20]

(Continued)

(Continued)

Diplomacy for its own sake, being there, was the frequent default position. Diplomacy in modern systems needs to look busy, and embassies spend some of their time acting out their roles in this theater.

In the case of Afghanistan, Cowper-Coles knew that some embassies in Kabul—for example those of China, India, Pakistan, Russia, and Iran—were largely bent on noncooperation because they perceived their national interests as competing with NATO and the United States. But there was little attempt to use these missions in the widest intelligent use of diplomacy in Kabul to bring the regional stakeholders into an edge-smoothing discussion. The opportunity to demonstrate the value of the versatility of diplomatic missions was largely lost.

NEVERTHELESS ESSENTIAL

The institutions of bilateral diplomacy have served, and continue to serve, an important purpose in the practice of diplomacy. The question is not so much whether they should be maintained but rather whether the missions as diplomatic institutions have adapted to new problems and are configured to seize new opportunities. It may be that the institutions in their traditional form are engaged in a battle for survival like the one-pad cipher or French rules of precedence. The reality of serving in a major capital is one where the bilateral embassies are increasingly searching for new roles when individual countries and governments are not sure of what their influence or resources can achieve. They deploy smart, ambitious, and well-resourced officers, but the framework in which they operate breeds more competition than constructive collective diplomacy. The real issue with diplomatic missions is not a total redundancy of function but the redirection of effort. In recent decades, diplomatic reform has concentrated on creating permanent regional and international organizations where collective problems can be discussed continuously. That is the subject of the next chapter.

SUGGESTIONS FOR FURTHER READING

1. Cowper-Coles, Sherard. *Cables from Kabul: The Inside Story of the West's Afghanistan Campaign*. London: HarperCollins, 2011.

2. Leira, Halvard, and Iver B. Neumann. "Consular Diplomacy." In *Diplomacy in a Globalizing World: Theories and Practices*, ed. Pauline Kerr and Geoffrey Wiseman. New York: Oxford University Press, 2012.

3. Hocking, Brian. "The Ministry of Foreign Affairs and the National Diplomatic System." In *Diplomacy in a Globalizing World: Theories and Practices*, ed. Pauline Kerr and Geoffrey Wiseman. New York: Oxford University Press, 2012.

chapter 4

The Institutions of Multilateral Diplomacy

International and regional institutions are not new to diplomacy. The Congress of Vienna in 1815 and the Congress of Berlin in 1878 bookended a period when international conferences were used to try to maintain a balance of power in Europe and produce acceptable multilateral solutions. The Congress of Vienna also issued a ringing condemnation of a pressing global issue—slavery—which "has been considered, by just and enlightened men in all ages, as repugnant to the principles of humanity and universal morality . . . [so that] the public voice, in all civilized countries, calls aloud for its prompt suppression."[1] The Suez Canal was administered in the nineteenth century by a group of international shareholders. International conferences at The Hague in 1899 and 1907 are examples of attempts to build a collective approach on the rules of war. The periods post-World War I and II also produced other numerous examples of conferences and diplomatic agreements. A collective approach was the favored route to getting diplomacy back on track.

In technology, too, the world has established international norms and organizations where international collaboration was required for anything to function. The establishment of international telegraphic connections led to an International Telegraph Union in 1865, and postal use to the Treaty of Berne and the Universal Postal Union in 1874, first called the General Postal Union. Three global principles were established applying to postal use that themselves marked major advances and a dilution of national sovereignty to the benefit of the common good:

- A uniform flat rate to mail a letter anywhere in the world
- Equal treatment to foreign and domestic mail
- Each country to retain all money it collected for international postage

The increasing specialization of subjects had its impact on diplomacy. Two conferences before World War I showed that experts could combine their efforts with diplomats to produce practical progress. In 1909, the International

Automobile Conference settled the size and shape of international car license plates. The International Aerial Navigation Conference of 1910 originally attracted delegations of military and home-based civil servants. When the British Foreign Office heard that the French and German delegations included diplomats, they insisted that the British ambassador to Paris be appointed to head the British delegation. This shows an early example of diplomats being sensitive to losing turf battles on international issues.

World War I was one of the crises that shaped modern collective diplomacy. The responses to the carnage of the trenches and breakup of the old order, which included the Bolshevik Revolution in Russia, were to initiate fundamental reforms in diplomacy. War had exposed the flaws in the international diplomacy, and the struggle of nations for individual supremacy had produced collective damage. The concept of a peaceful community of nations had been proposed as far back as 1795, when Immanuel Kant's *Perpetual Peace: A Philosophical Sketch* outlined the idea of a league of nations to control conflict and promote peace between states. Kant argued for the establishment of a peaceful world community but not global governance. In his vision, each state would declare itself a free state that respected its citizens and welcomed relations with others.

There were further efforts in the nineteenth century at collaborative diplomacy and attempts to smooth the edges of power rivalry. The establishment of the International Red Cross in 1864, driven by an early example of collaboration between state and nonstate actors, led to agreements to regulate how wars were conducted. The forerunner of the League of Nations, the Inter-Parliamentary Union (IPU), was formed by peace activists William Randal Cremer and Frédéric Passy in 1889. The organization was international in scope, with a third of the members of parliaments (in the twenty-four countries that had parliaments) serving as members of the IPU by 1914. Its aims were to encourage governments to solve international disputes by peaceful means.

The origins of the idea of the League of Nations (LoN) are disputed. Whether it was Lord Robert Cecil (a British politician and lawyer, who also promoted the use in diplomacy of an international language—Esperanto) or Sir Edward Grey, the British Foreign Secretary from 1905 to 1916, it seems certain that one of the main objectives of launching it was the British aim to entice President Woodrow Wilson into the allied cause in World War I. Wilson adopted the idea as his own, though the irony of the U.S. Senate never ratifying the LoN treaty was a lasting bitterness. The United States ensured that this failure was corrected when the modified idea reemerged after 1945 as the United Nations. The LoN was an ultimately failed experiment in collective diplomacy and governance, but it showed that ideas and idealism matter for any changes to be made. The LoN established institutions such as its Council, with membership from the four principal allied powers plus four others; the Assembly; and the Permanent Court of International Justice (PCIJ), which became institutional models for the United Nations. Woodrow Wilson, Lloyd

George, and Jan Smuts were leaders of energy and vision who believed that diplomacy could avoid the horrors of war. The first secretary general of the LoN, Sir Eric Drummond, was British and his deputy, Jean Monnet, was French. Permanent diplomatic delegations were established in Geneva, despite Drummond's opposition, and by 1937—the twilight of the organization—there were forty-six missions representing the then largest concentration of permanent collective diplomacy in the history of the world.

The LoN also provided a forum for international discussion on major global issues such as disarmament. The First World War left many thinking that nothing short of widespread disarmament would prevent the inexorable decline of diplomacy. The LoN hosted the first world conference on disarmament in 1932, with sixty states attending in Geneva. It also tried to establish an institutionalized system of arbitration called the Geneva Peace Protocol with transgressing states facing the imposition of automatic sanctions applied against them. Despite its inadequacies and the disastrous record of diplomacy in the late 1930s, the LoN experience was a practical lesson in what might work and what was misguided. So the United Nations borrowed approaches from the LoN; its Council was reinvented as the United Nations Security Council (UNSC), and the ICJ was maintained. Indeed, the LoN was only formally wound up after World War II in 1946.

THE UNITED NATIONS

It might have been a more reasonable approach to multilateral diplomacy to try something new after 1945, but the deficiencies in the simple sovereign state model were perceived in similar ways as in the immediate aftermath of World War I. Nevertheless, the evils of National Socialism could have been seen as a temporary aberration in human progress due to catastrophic economic factors coupled with a new blend of mass populism. It was not inevitable that diplomacy's inadequacies would be seen as one of the causes of disaster.

In the United Nations (UN) Charter of 1945, the victors of World War II preserved the power structure that emerged in a new multilateral diplomatic institution. Most important, the powers worked in many guarantees to ensure such predominance would endure. That the major powers were practicing very different political and economic ideologies was of course evident, and so the Charter steered clear of entering into controversial areas such as the merits of communism against capitalism.

Just as in the case of the LoN, political leaders played a key role in setting up the United Nations. Churchill and Franklin Roosevelt had agreed on principles of self-determination and economic cooperation in the Atlantic Charter of 1941. And the origins of the war they were fighting were seen as having an important economic dimension. A redesigning of the international diplomatic system was required, and this had to involve a permanent conference to prevent and end the scourge of war.

Yet the task the United Nations set itself went beyond the creation of the institution. The objectives of Franklin and Eleanor Roosevelt, Churchill, and other postwar leaders included the stimulation of wider diplomatic efforts to correct the shocks that massive destruction had wrought on almost every continent. These leaders were applying intelligence to the needs of the time. Something different had to be tried. The permanent conference gave substance to continuous diplomacy not only to prevent threats to global peace and security but also to target financial reconstruction (the Marshall Plan), financial cooperation (the IMF and World Bank), and collaborative work on important global issues. The aspirations here exceeded the results as there are few indicators in the UN Charter that the United Nations itself was conceived as an instrument of consensus building on global issues. It provided fora for discussion but major issues such as self-determination, human rights, and fundamental freedoms, though mentioned in the Charter, are not defined.

The Dumbarton Oaks Conference between the major allied powers in 1944 was the first important step to implement Paragraph 4 of the Moscow Declaration of 1943 between Roosevelt, Churchill, and Stalin, which recognized the need for a postwar international organization to succeed the LoN. The drafting process of the UN Charter, which largely took place at San Francisco from April to June 1945, indicated that the world was moving into uncharted territory. And sovereign states recognized they might need permanent assistance from non-governmental groups. Indeed, some non-governmental groups like the Rotary Club and Lions International were also invited to participate in the drafting at San Francisco. A new layer of diplomatic activity reaching out beyond sovereign states was being added.

THE CHARTER OF THE UNITED NATIONS

Important central principles in the creation of the United Nations were that it would be permanent, that it would be open to all countries, and that it would not exclude regional organizations that would be seen as complementary to its diplomacy. The Charter made clear that all sovereign states would be equal in the United Nations, but the key feature of the world order at the time—the outcome of World War II—was also an important influence. The victorious powers knew that renouncing such power would render their diplomacy toothless.

Oscar Wilde wrote, "A map of the world that does not include Utopia is not worth even glancing at, for it leaves out the one country at which Humanity is always landing."[2] The United Nations never intended to create Utopia. It was an institution established at a time when the world was broken diplomatically and had to be reassembled. At its outset, it seemed bright, innovative, and hugely ambitious, and it benefited from the age of television. The ratings of proceedings of the UNSC were second in the United States only to The Bob

Hope Show in 1950! It drew on the experience of the LoN, which unexpectedly had attracted the adherence of almost all countries, despite its main architect state, the United States, failing to secure ratification of the treaty.

In one major feature, the UN Charter reaffirmed its faith in the traditional diplomacy—the system based on sovereign states. Those states would allow the United Nations to limit that sovereignty only in defined areas. Sovereign states would remain the most effective actors in the diplomatic system and the main units of international governance, commanding the loyalty and nationalism of their populations as in previous eras. This also implied that the influence of transnational religious and other movements would not undermine traditional loyalties. The problems of the post-1945 era, in the minds of the UN drafters, would in many respects be similar to those of pre-1939.

Like the LoN, the UN Charter did not envisage universal membership. Indeed, the prospects were not auspicious. It was hatched at the opening of a new era of ideological standoffs and conflict. The Berlin airlift (1948–1949) and conflict on Korean peninsula in the early 1950s were early convulsions at the start of a period in history that has produced massive changes in the way states interact. Since its foundation, the United Nations has operated continuously through the process of decolonization, the end of the Cold War, the war against terror, globalization, and the Internet. Its Charter has been amended rarely and only to adjust the number of members serving on its organs; for example, the Security Council was expanded from eleven to fifteen members in 1965, raising the number of nonpermanent members from six to ten.

Article 1 covers the purposes of the organization, which are defined as follows:

1. To maintain international peace and security, and to that end: to take effective collective measures for the prevention and removal of threats to the peace, and for the suppression of acts of aggression or other breaches of the peace, and to bring about by peaceful means, and in conformity with the principles of justice and international law, adjustment or settlement of international disputes or situations which might lead to a breach of the peace;

2. To develop friendly relations among nations based on respect for the principle of equal rights and self-determination of peoples, and to take other appropriate measures to strengthen universal peace;

3. To achieve international co-operation in solving international problems of an economic, social, cultural, or humanitarian character, and in promoting and encouraging respect for human rights and for fundamental freedoms for all without distinction as to race, sex, language, or religion; and

4. To be a centre for harmonizing the actions of nations in the attainment of these common ends.[3]

All UN members, by signing the Charter, assume obligations to settle all their disputes peacefully. They are obliged to use the organs of the United Nations and its mechanisms to supplement their own diplomatic efforts.

It is instructive to compare this ambitious agenda covering many more global issues than war and peace with the idealistic yet limited objectives of the LoN Covenant of 1919. Under this, the parties agreed

> to promote international co-operation and to achieve international peace and security by the acceptance of obligations not to resort to war, by the prescription of open, just and honorable relations between nations, by the firm establishment of the understandings of international law as the actual rule of conduct among Governments, and by the maintenance of justice and a scrupulous respect for all treaty obligations in the dealings of organized peoples with one another.[4]

The world had moved on in diplomatic ambitions but also in recognizing what factors needed to come together to make for successful diplomacy. This chapter will examine how the United Nations operates in practice as the world's major multinational diplomatic institution and how successful it has been.

THE ORGANS OF THE UN

The UN Charter establishes six major organs—the General Assembly, the Security Council, the Economic and Social Council, the International Court of Justice, the Trusteeship Council, and the UN Secretariat. It is perhaps helpful to see the General Assembly as the shareholders of the organization, the Security Council as the executive board, and the ICJ as the legal department. This is still the structure that determines its operation.

The General Assembly of the UN (UNGA) is the only organ in which all members of the United Nations are represented. It receives reports from the Security Council and votes, with one vote per state, to approve the budget. It is also the body that elects new members, but on most issues it is a recommending, not a deciding, body. It is not permitted to debate an issue that is currently under consideration by the Security Council. The UNGA functions through six issue committees: Disarmament and International Security Committee; Economic and Financial Committee; Social, Humanitarian and Cultural Committee; Special Political and Decolonization Committee; Administrative and Budgetary Committee; and Legal Committee. In addition, there are two procedural committees and two standing committees: one on the budget, one on contributions. It meets annually in plenary session beginning with the ministers' session and speeches on the third Tuesday in September. This is usually the only time of year that UNGA receives widespread attention.

Voting on all resolutions in the UNGA is one country, one vote. Some participants like the Holy See and the Palestinian Authority have observer status, as do international groupings like Association of Southeast Asian Nations (ASEAN), the African Union, and the European Union. Such observer status is granted by a UNGA resolution. It is based purely on practice, and there are no provisions for this in the UN Charter. Observers have the right to speak at assembly meetings and participate in procedural votes, but not to vote on resolutions and other substantive matters. Various other rights (e.g., to speak in debates, to submit proposals and amendments, to raise points of order, to circulate documents, etc.) are given to observers on an ad hoc basis. Of the regional organizations, so far the EU is the only international organization to hold these enhanced powers. Observer status also involves obligations. In 2013, the UN Committee on the Rights of the Child announced they would question the Vatican about child abuse scandals in the Catholic Church.

Full members of the United Nations have full voting rights. There is nothing in the UN Charter that prevents group voting according to established positions on issues agreed in regional or other blocs. The Non-Aligned Movement came into being after the 1964 UN Conference on Trade and Development and still meets in annual conferences, which include two-thirds of the UN members—some 130 states. Its bloc vote has been a regular feature of UNGA debates. It is not surprising that smaller countries value the collective clout that these groupings deliver and the access to expert advice on technical issues and drafting, which is all part of UNGA operations. The forum has, however, seldom been one for consensus building and UNGA, though the source of many important resolutions in diplomatic history, has made its name more by talk than action.

THE SECURITY COUNCIL

The UN Security Council (UNSC) is central to the structure and philosophy of the UN Charter. It also is vested with prime responsibility for the maintenance of international peace and security. The five permanent members—the United States, the Soviet Union, the United Kingdom, France, and China—were the victors of World War II and were given a guaranteed veto power over the development of the United Nations and what tasks it would assume. The Charter provides that the affirmative votes of all the five permanent members (the P5) of the UNSC are required for any amendment to the text. In this way, the permanent five ensured their national interests were not jeopardized by investing in this form of permanent multilateral diplomacy. The so-called realist theorists of diplomatic behavior would feel vindicated. Yet this was an unusual diplomatic arrangement—although the five shared victory and had common enemies in the war, they also had sharply different ideologies and regional ambitions. Even the three Western allies did not agree on important postwar issues like decolonization.

The five permanent members were originally supplemented by six nonpermanent members, elected from lists that in practice were compiled by regional groupings. A decision was made in 1963 and implemented in 1965 to accommodate the rapidly growing number of UN members by increasing the number of nonpermanent members to ten, making the UNSC fifteen in total. They were still elected to two-year terms by a vote of two-thirds of the UNGA as before, except that from 1966 forward, five were chosen each year. The ten nonpermanent seats are distributed on a regional basis as follows: five for African and Asian states; one for Eastern European states; two for the Latin American and Caribbean states; and two for Western European and other states. The role of smaller countries elected as members for two-year terms has also given a boost to diplomatic common practice. As all countries serve a term, their diplomatic capacity is improved and standards rub off. This has happened despite the existence of veto power.

The veto power of each of the five permanent members on any matter that is not purely procedural is established under Article 27 of the UN Charter. This article also provides that Security Council decisions on all substantive matters require the affirmative votes of nine members, raised from seven in 1965. Abstention is not regarded as a veto, despite the wording of the Charter, which refers to the requirement of "concurring votes of the permanent members."[5] In the history of the UNSC, up to 2013, China (formerly the Republic of China, then the People's Republic of China after 1971) has used its veto six times; France, eighteen times; Russia and the USSR, 123 times; the United Kingdom, thirty-two times; and the United States, eighty-nine times.

Despite the careful crafting of a multinational diplomatic institution that would suit the World War II victors, very early in its history, the UNSC proved itself dysfunctional. In 1950, the Soviet Union boycotted the council for almost a year, allowing the deployment of a UN force in Korea to pass without veto. Later in 1950, the UNGA, frustrated at the Soviet capacity to stymie all UNSC activity, passed Resolution 377A, the "Uniting for Peace" resolution as it has come to be known. This was initiated by the United States to avoid further Soviet vetoes during the course of the Korean War (1950–1953). It was adopted by fifty-two votes to five, with two abstentions. The preamble to and first paragraph of the resolution was as follows:

> *Reaffirming* the importance of the exercise by the Security Council of its primary responsibility for the maintenance of international peace and security, and the duty of the permanent members to seek unanimity and to exercise restraint in the use of the veto . . .
>
> *Conscious* that failure of the Security Council to discharge its responsibilities on behalf of all the Member States . . . does not relieve Member States of their obligations or the United Nations of its responsibility under the Charter to maintain international peace and security,

> *Recognizing* in particular that such failure does not deprive the General Assembly of its rights or relieve it of its responsibilities under the Charter in regard to the maintenance of international peace and security . . .
>
> *Resolves* that if the Security Council, because of lack of unanimity of the permanent members, fails to exercise its primary responsibility for the maintenance of international peace and security in any case where there appears to be a threat to the peace, breach of the peace, or act of aggression, the General Assembly shall consider the matter immediately with a view to making appropriate recommendations to Members for collective measures, including in the case of a breach of the peace or act of aggression the use of armed force when necessary, to maintain or restore international peace and security.[6]

Since 1950, the resolution has been used in several instances as a reminder that the UNGA does retain a function as a forum on global security when the UNSC avenue is blocked. In November 2011, again to avoid a Russian veto in the UNSC, the UNGA passed a resolution condemning the repression of the Syrian government and "gross human rights violations being carried out by Syrian Government forces"[7] by a vote of 131 to twelve with thirty-one abstentions.

UNSC reform has been on the agenda of the United Nations in earnest since the 1990s. The category of permanent members reflected the power patterns at the time of the drafting of the Charter in 1945 but now gives a grossly distorted picture of the world order of the twenty-first century. Indeed, the only objective measure of power in the current world order is reflected in the scale agreed for budgetary contributions to the central budget of the United Nations. This is based on the relative capacity of each country to pay, as measured by their gross national income, with adjustments for external debt and low per capita income. But the diplomatic mechanisms that exist have proved incapable of redesigning a new structure. The Charter itself sets a high bar for amendment. The relevant article is 108:

> Amendments to the present Charter shall come into force for all Members of the United Nations when they have been adopted by a vote of two thirds of the members of the General Assembly and ratified in accordance with their respective constitutional processes by two thirds of the Members of the United Nations, including all the permanent members of the Security Council.[8]

If the budget might offer a yardstick for reassessment, what might it show? The second and third largest contributors, Japan and Germany, are not permanent members. And the present criteria for permanent membership exclude African and Latin American countries and only China represents Asia. There

TABLE 4-1 **Contributors to UN Regular Budget 2012**

Member State	*Contribution (Percentage of UN Budget)*
United States	22.000
Japan	12.530
Germany	8.018
United Kingdom	6.604
France	6.123
Italy	4.999
Canada	3.207
China	3.189
Spain	3.177
Mexico	2.356
South Korea	2.260
Australia	1.933
Netherlands	1.855
Brazil	1.611
Russia	1.602

Source: United Nations, "Status of Contributions as at 31 December 2012," http://www.un.org/ga/search/view_doc.asp?symbol=ST/ADM/SER.B/828.

are also no Muslim majority countries as permanent members of the UNSC, though Muslims make up around 20 percent of the world's population

The failure to agree on reform of UNSC permanent membership is due to varied factors. But the formality of UN procedures and the deliberate elitism of the status of permanent members mean that any change made could not be easily reversed. Member states recognize that if a rival secures the prize, then the advantage secured could be irreversible. The United Nations has at its core a diplomatic trade-off between efficiency and inclusiveness. Diplomatic reengineering may be the answer. The juggling could be helped by creating a new status of membership, a voluntary renunciation of the use of veto, or longer terms (perhaps four years) for nonpermanent members. Sovereign states recognize that since the Cold War, the emerging economic power order reflects an infinitely more fluid world where influence shifts quickly. The age of permanence is fading, and the rivalries between India and Pakistan, Japan and South Korea, Brazil and Argentina, Nigeria, Egypt, and South Africa, and even Germany and Italy make for depressing reading to those interested in a rebooting of the functions of the UNSC.

If the struggle to ascend to permanent membership of the UNSC is a priority for foreign policy of several emerging powers, then some of the reasons can be found in the section of the Charter that gives the UNSC its uniqueness. The core powers of the UNSC are contained in Chapters VI and VII. The rationale of the UNSC is that a mixed panel of peer sovereign states can make decisions that will provide the basis for peaceful settlement of disputes in accordance with the responsibilities of all members of the United Nations. Under Chapter VII, Article 39,

> The Security Council shall determine the existence of any threat to the peace, breach of the peace, or act of aggression and shall make recommendations, or decide what measures shall be taken in accordance with Articles 41 and 42, to maintain or restore international peace and security.[9]

Article 41 gives the UNSC power to implement measures, such as economic sanctions, which stop short of the use of force. Article 42 contains some of the weightiest language of the whole Charter, and the powers it describes are expressly linked to the effect of action under Article 41.

> Should the Security Council consider that measures provided for in Article 41 would be inadequate or have proved to be inadequate, it may take such action by air, sea, or land forces as may be necessary to maintain or restore international peace and security. Such action may include demonstrations, blockade, and other operations by air, sea, or land forces of Members of the United Nations.[10]

If Article 42 measures are used, then diplomacy and the mechanisms of the United Nations have failed. Since the United Nations is the pinnacle of continuous multilateral diplomacy, it is not perhaps surprising that Article 42 has been used rarely. The only direct applications of this article that have taken place in the history are the "Uniting for Peace" Resolution in June 1950 and the UNSC resolution authorizing the use of force to expel Saddam Hussein from Kuwait in August 1990 (UN Security Council Resolution [UNSCR] 660). Indeed this most intrusive article of the Charter in reducing absolute sovereignty of states is tempered by Article 51—the right of self-defense of every sovereign state. "Nothing in the present Charter shall impair the inherent right of individual or collective self-defense if an armed attack occurs against a Member of the United Nations, until the Security Council has taken measures necessary to maintain international peace and security."[11]

ECOSOC

Article 61 provides that "The Economic and Social Council [ECOSOC] shall consist of fifty-four Members of the United Nations elected by the General Assembly."[12] Its functions are to provide a forum for discussion of the agenda of issues that are seen as supplementing direct UN action on security. ECOSOC's objectives are stated in Article 55:

> With a view to the creation of conditions of stability and well-being which are necessary for peaceful and friendly relations among nations based on respect for the principle of equal rights and self-determination of peoples, the United Nations shall promote:
>
> 1. higher standards of living, full employment, and conditions of economic and social progress and development;
> 2. solutions of international economic, social, health, and related problems; and international cultural and educational cooperation; and
> 3. universal respect for and observance of, human rights and fundamental freedoms for all without distinction as to race, sex, language, or religion.[13]

ECOSOC can "make or initiate studies and reports with respect to international economic, social, cultural, educational, health, and related matters and may make recommendations with respect to any such matters to the General Assembly to the Members of the United Nations, and to the specialized agencies concerned."[14] Given the UN's own genesis and the input of non-governmental representatives into its structure, the Charter acknowledges the role of ECOSOC in working with non-governmental organizations (NGOs). Under Article 71,

> The Economic and Social Council may make suitable arrangements for consultation with non-governmental organizations which are concerned with matters within its competence. Such arrangements may be made with international organizations and, where appropriate, with national organizations after consultation with the Member of the United Nations concerned.[15]

Though the Charter generally reflects the sovereign state model favored by realist theorists, which posits the unitary nature of the state acting on one set of objectives, its approach on economic and social issues shows a broader concept. The role of ECOSOC as set out in Chapter IX of the Charter is to reach out into the wider society of states for the promotion of far-reaching social and economic principles. By establishing ECOSOC, the United Nations recognized the value of multilateral diplomacy to build consensuses on issues, create habits of cooperation, and serve as a forum to set agendas. Yet the United Nations has never achieved the same central and unduplicated functions in the economic and social field as it did in security issues. Nevertheless, the establishments of multiple UN agencies that report to ECOSOC, discussed later, open many doors to cooperation with NGOs. Sensibly again, the United Nations built on a legacy that it saw as worth preserving. The International Labor Organization, which was set up Geneva in 1919, is still a functioning UN agency. But developments outside the United Nations have diluted its roles in some areas. While ECOSOC initiated such endeavors as the General Agreement on Tariffs and Trade (GATT), such activity is centered now in the World Trade Organization in Geneva.

INTERNATIONAL COURT OF JUSTICE

The other organ of the UN Charter that is an important part of the international diplomatic practice is the International Court of Justice (ICJ). The ICJ replaced the Permanent Court of International Justice, which had functioned since 1922. As Satow's guide says,

> Whilst few diplomats in the course of their careers are likely to appear before the Court as representatives of their governments the use of the Court to settle disputes and the impact of the Court's decisions are a significant feature of the conduct of international affairs.[16]

The ICJ is the top legal forum in the world for states wishing for multilateral consideration of contentious cases. The United Nations itself cannot bring a case against a state in its own judicial organ, but all members of the United Nations are parties to the Statute that governs the ICJ by virtue of their membership. The ICJ may hear cases only if both parties have agreed to accept its jurisdiction. It is possible that in a treaty between states they have made provision to refer disputes to the Court, so where this applies, one party would be entitled to bring the case. The Court may issue judgments and advisory opinions, which will form the basis of international law. It has fifteen judges elected from nominees by the UNGA and UNSC, and candidates must win a majority of both voting simultaneously. They serve for nine-year terms, which can be renewed. The importance of ICJ judgments is discussed further in Chapter 8.

THE UN SECRETARIAT

The UN Secretariat is the permanent administration or diplomatic machinery of the United Nations. It is headed by a Secretary General (UNSG) who serves a five-year term, which is renewable. That this position is important is undoubted. But the exact role the UNSG plays is not defined. Roosevelt said he hoped the UNSG would be a "world moderator," and the UN website has described the roles of the office as "diplomat and advocate, civil servant, and CEO."[17] Article 97 in Chapter XV of the UN Charter states that the Secretary General shall be the chief administrative officer of the organization, but does not describe specific obligations.[18] Different UNSGs have chosen different priorities and taken different attitudes to how far the diplomacy of the United Nations should be visible. The nationality of the UNSG has traditionally been from a state not readily identified with a major power in the world order. One exception is Ban Ki-Moon, who is a former foreign minister of South Korea, a strong U.S. ally.

DIPLOMATS AND THE UN

Within this inclusive model of all stakeholder states being represented in the United Nations, the role of permanent delegations has proved useful for many diplomatic systems. The expertise of the well-funded larger delegations and the experts in the permanent secretariat has performed an educational and developmental role for emerging countries and new members. Each member state has a mission, headed by a permanent representative, often called an ambassador, and serving in the mission will be officers such as counselors and first secretaries, mirroring those of a bilateral mission. The diplomats accredited to the United Nations have diplomatic immunities and privileges on a reciprocal bilateral basis depending on those granted by their governments to the UN's officials when they serve in or visit that state. Officials working for the United Nations and its agencies throughout the world generally have a more limited range of diplomatic immunities and privileges than granted through the Vienna Convention on Diplomatic Relations (VCDR). The General Convention on the Privileges and Immunities of the United Nations was adopted by the UNGA in February 1946. Only the most senior officials like the Secretary General have the fullest range of immunities. In general, officials accredited to the United Nations or officials working for the United Nations are not given total exemption from taxes or custom duties. The United Nations itself is generally exempt from income taxes and custom duties in countries where it operates.

THE UN'S DEVELOPMENT

In the first years of the United Nations, the passion and vision of its founders produced a series of groundbreaking approaches to issues as diverse as genocide, human rights, and the necessity for new international financial institutions and mechanisms to underpin global trade and economic activity. But at the outset, the global environment for building a new consensus could hardly have been more dismal. The United Nations, in many aspects of diplomacy, became an irrelevance. After meeting for over one hundred times a year in the 1940s, the UNSC was reduced to five meetings only by 1959. As we have seen in the years of the Korean War era, the Soviet Union boycotted the meetings.

Despite this, the United Nations survived, and its participants have increasingly seen its activities as a channel for them to participate in transnational issues. The constructionist theorists, which suggest that all countries do share some interests and that they work together on international norms and rules, can cite the UN's development as lending their theory some support.

Today the United Nations has over twenty accredited agencies. Many, like the UN Development Programme (UNDP), employ far more people than even the best-funded national diplomatic systems. These include The United Nations Children's Fund (UNICEF), The Food and Agriculture Organization (FAO), The International Atomic Energy Agency (IAEA), the UN Commission for Refugees, the UN Human Rights Council, The UN Environment Programme (UNEP), The World Food Program (WFP), The World Health Organization (WHO), and The United Nations Educational, Scientific and Cultural Organization (UNESCO). The official reporting status of all these agencies is through ECOSOC. It is indeed the cost of the agencies and the peacekeeping operations that now absorbs the greatest proportion of UN expenses.

The continuing interest of states in membership of the UN owes much to its inclusivity. As of January 1, 2014, there were 195 members, with some, like Kosovo, in line for consideration. And the election of members to bodies like the UNSC and ECOSOC from the regional groupings ensures that all countries are given their chance. The division of other UN jobs within the agencies is also open, with unspoken quotas and a balancing of representation being applied.

The United Nations is still central to multinational diplomatic activity, but its Charter envisaged greater effectiveness and coherence in problem solving. The United Nations is unmistakably a creation of a world order that no longer exists. It has adapted its functions, but its current capacity to undergo reform appears limited. Shortly after her appointment as U.S. permanent representative in 2013, Samantha Power, said though the United Nations had "done tremendous good in the world, there are times when the organization has lost its way, when politics and ideology get in the way of impact."[19] Before becoming the U.S. envoy, she was more forthright. Writing in *The New Republic*, she suggested the need for root and branch reform of the Security Council: "The U.N. Security Council is anachronistic, undemocratic, and consists of countries that lack the standing to be considered good faith arbiters of how to balance stability against democracy, peace against justice, and security against human rights."[20] It is instructive to look in turn at some of the key current activities of the United Nations, how it has lived up to its objectives, and what alternative diplomatic solutions may now be available.

Peace and Security

Since 1945, the United Nations has not guaranteed peace, nor has it lived up to its mission statement in the preamble to the Charter "to save succeeding generations from the scourge of war, which twice in our lifetime has brought untold sorrow to mankind."[21] Rarely, indeed, has it attempted to make peace; instead, its peacekeeping role is more developed.

Despite having the unprecedented powers under Chapter VII given to the UNSC to intervene to restore peace, they have, as we have seen, been used rarely. Conflicts like Vietnam and the Soviet invasions of Hungary and Czechoslovakia were never brought to the United Nations at all because of big power vetoes, potential or actual. The same applied in the U.S. interventions in Grenada and Panama. Circumstances were rare indeed when the UNSC could agree to use the intervention powers that the Charter had envisaged, and those powers did not cut across the interests of the P5. The case of Saddam Hussein's Iraq invading Kuwait in August 1990 met many of the classic criteria—armed aggression by a state against another that the UN Charter had envisaged. It happened a few months after the collapse of the Soviet Union and the end of the Cold War, and that helped craft a multilateral diplomatic and subsequently a military response.

The UNSC has increasingly used its powers in matters where different types of threats have been confronted, particularly in more recent years. An important use of the Chapter VII power occurred with the unanimous passing of UNSCR 1540 in April 2004. This resolution was prompted by the proliferation activities of the Pakistani nuclear scientist A. Q. Khan. By its terms, under Chapter VII of the Charter, all states must enforce appropriate legal and regulatory measures against the proliferation of chemical, biological, radiological, and nuclear weapons and their means of delivery to prevent the spread of weapons of mass destruction to nonstate actors. The resolution requires every state to criminalize various forms of nonstate actor involvement in such weapons and to enforce such legislation.

A second example of progress in use of the UNSC occurred in 2011. The problem of intrastate conflict has increasingly challenged the UN Charter and its operations as an institution. When a massacre of hundreds of thousands of Libyan rebels seemed likely by government forces in March 2011, UNSCR 1973 was passed by ten in favor (Bosnia and Herzegovina, Colombia, Gabon,

Lebanon, Nigeria, Portugal, South Africa, and permanent members France, the United Kingdom, and the United States) with five abstentions (Brazil, Germany, and India, and permanent members China and Russia). The UNSC demanded an immediate ceasefire and authorized the international community to establish a no-fly zone and to use all means necessary short of foreign occupation to protect civilians.[22]

The UNSC's underperformance in peace and security issues derives from three shortcomings. First, few security issues are ever viewed in isolation. Power relations are always set in a wider context—for example, the differing effects on neighboring countries—and the P5 rarely see security through the same prism. Second, the institutional composition and working rules of the UNSC militates against solving intractable problems. The threat of veto is still real, and the UN machinery often cannot deliver anything of legally binding effect at all. Third, the UNSC has not developed a coherent strategy on what forces it needs to apply and still has no standing peacekeeping force that is permanently available to the Secretary General. Each case is still dealt with ad hoc, the forces are assembled afresh, and specialist expertise, which could be harnessed in different peacekeeping scenarios, is generally not developed. In 2011, it took several weeks just to assemble a few hundred ceasefire monitors for Syria. By the time they were deployed, it was too late. In 2013, expressing general disapproval of the UNSC, its methods, and its failures, Saudi Arabia announced it would refuse an invitation to take its seat as a member. A senior UN official herself recognized this. Speaking to the Security Council in August 2014, the retiring UN Human Rights Commissioner, Navi Pillay, said that "short-term geopolitical considerations and national interest, narrowly defined, have repeatedly taken precedence over intolerable human suffering and grave breaches of— and long-term threats to—international peace and security."[23]

Peacekeeping

If peacemaking has not been as effective as hoped, what about peacekeeping? How successful has the UN peacekeeping been over the existence of the United Nations?

The peacekeeping operations of the United Nations number over 120 since 1945, dating from the early history of the United Nations acting as a mediator on the Palestine issue in 1948 to hybrid peacekeeping alongside African Union forces in Sudan and the Democratic Republic of Congo (DRC). An early successful use of peacekeepers was made after the Suez conflict in November 1956. In many instances, the peacekeepers have been a diplomatic bandage to a wound that continues to fester. Peacekeeping in Cyprus, Kashmir, and Lebanon have been holding, not solution building, operations. In accordance with the UN Charter, there has been cooperation with regional organizations, such as the EU in Kosovo and the African Union in Ivory Coast and Mali. Yet failures have often had catastrophic results. In 1994, the Canadian commander of a few hundred UN peacekeepers watched helplessly as hundreds of thousands of Tutsi were massacred in Rwanda, his pleas for reinforcements not heeded. In July 1995, the Srebrenica massacre of thousands of Bosnian Muslims happened in spite of the presence of a small Dutch peacekeeping force.

Peacekeeping is an irreplaceable role, increasingly required in situations of civil conflict, which now accounts for 95 percent of conflicts occurring. And it has expanded its objectives since first conceived. Developing roles of peacekeeping includes promotion of human rights, poverty reduction, protection of aid workers, and rebuilding civil police networks. The costs of such operations, which in June 2013 involved 114 UN members in providing personnel (with Pakistan, Bangladesh, and India prominent among the major suppliers), have risen 50 percent in a decade. In 2014, the budget stands at over $7 billion annually, compared to $5 billion for the central secretariat budget. Peacekeeping remains a unique task, and there are no obvious alternatives to the United Nations. Unsuccessful peacekeeping may give diplomacy a bad name, but its public failures mask wider problems of collective diplomacy.

An interesting hybrid of Chapter VII UNSC action and peacekeeping operations emerged in March 2013. Interpreted by some as the UN's first authorization of an offensive peacekeeping force, UNSCR 2098 of March 2013 called for the deployment of an intervention brigade to the DRC that could be used in offensive combat operations to neutralize and disarm Congolese rebel groups, in particular the M23 rebels responsible for taking over Goma in the east of the country. The differences in practice between this and peacekeeping may be small as the UN Stabilization Mission in the Congo (MONUSCO) was already authorized to conduct offensive operations under its Chapter VII mandate, and its rules of engagement authorized the use of force beyond self-defense. But the resolution showed a clear intent that the force deployed make more of an impact.

In its Agenda for Peace in 1992, the United Nations and its then Secretary General Boutros Boutros-Ghali differentiated preventive diplomacy from peacekeeping. It urged the United Nations to engage in "action to prevent disputes from arising between parties, to prevent existing disputes from escalating into conflicts and to limit the spread of the latter when they occur."[24] Boutros-Ghali was also the Secretary General who consolidated the UN peacekeeping operations in a new department (the DPKO) in 1992. Previously the operations had been managed by the Department of Political Affairs.

The Activities of the Agencies

The existence of UN agencies that operate throughout the world is a major achievement of the organization. No other period in human history can boast the global outreach that has been achieved. Yet the ambition and vision have produced bureaucratic negatives. The organizations take on their momentum and struggle with rivals for profile and funding. There are few examples of UN agencies ever having been wound up. Some groups have been consolidated into one, such as the recently named UN Women or UN Water. But the plethora of agencies in overlapping areas such as those working on food and nutrition (WFP, FAO, UNICEF) or the environment (some forty-four UN bodies have been estimated to be inputting into policy on environmental issues) suggest that the system may generate more heat than light in resolving key issues. With so many diplomatic cooks, the United Nations is in danger of serving multiple ingredients with an unappealing end product. Only in one area of activity, that of humanitarian response to disasters, is the UN official in charge called a coordinator.

An extract from the UN website describes with pride some of the many agencies that have some responsibility for activities in the area of health.

> It would be misleading to suggest that the entire work of the UN system in support of global health rests with the WHO [World Health Organization]. On the contrary, many members of the UN family are engaged in this critical task. Many health-related matters are addressed directly by the General Assembly and the Economic and Social Council, as well as through the efforts of the Joint United Nations Program on HIV/AIDS (UNAIDS); the work of the United Nations Population Fund (UNFPA) in support of reproductive, adolescent and maternal health; and the health-related activities of the United Nations Children's Fund (UNICEF).
>
> In addition, such members of the UN system as the International Labour Organization (ILO), the United Nations Relief and Works Agency for Palestine Refugees in the Near East (UNRWA), the Food and Agriculture Organization of the United Nations (FAO), the International Atomic Energy Agency (IAEA), the United Nations Environment Programme (UNEP), the United Nations Office on Drugs and Crime (UNODC), and the World Bank, among others, all play a key role in promoting global health.[25]

There is talk of turf wars, a loose framework of overlapping and competing mandates and behavior in some situations where the UN agencies foster a republic of NGOs. But there is now some recognition that coordinated UN management is needed. For example, the UNDP director in Vietnam is now responsible for coordinating twenty UN agencies. The Report of the UN Secretary General in 2006, *Mandating and Delivering*, appeared to put the blame for lack of delivery on member states:

> In the General Assembly, humanitarian agenda items are dispersed among the plenary and the Second and Third Committees. The plenary deals with coordination, staff security and natural disasters; the

Second Committee addresses humanitarian assistance to specific countries and regions, disasters, vulnerability and risk reduction; under the purview of the Third Committee fall assistance to internally displaced persons and refugees and the new international humanitarian order.[26]

And the report went further. "The result of such fragmentation is frequent overlap between the mandates issued. Member States could take practical action to address this problem."[27]

In terms of disaster relief, the report was starkly critical of the agencies involved: "Recent disasters have shown all too clearly, however, that there is no agreed institutional leader for early disaster recovery."[28] The case study at the end of Chapter 10 discusses the shortcomings of how the United Nations, the nonstate sector, and world diplomacy responded to Haitian earthquake in 2010.

The newness of challenges, how they interconnect, and the difficulty of integrating efforts into the existing format are now central to the future of these agencies. The Secretary General's report highlights the problems: "New programs and agencies have created a largely unmanageable complex of organizations. With such proliferation inevitably come duplications, contradictory goals for donors and recipients alike."[29]

The critical task for the UN agencies is to convince the governments that fund them and the NGOs that work with them that they have continuing usefulness in their current forms. Governments now have many options to implement their policies on global issues. They must decide whether their objectives in child policies, environmental protection, or health and nutrition are best served through using the UN agencies. And UN agencies receive the bulk of their funding through voluntary contributions from members. The budget of the UNDP alone at over $5 billion is larger than the UN central secretariat's. Another factor perhaps limiting the attractiveness of the agencies compared to NGOs is that the senior appointments are the result of national bargaining, with criteria for appointments not purely based on competence and the ability to lead politically and managerially in the modern world.

UNESCO, the scientific, cultural, and educational organ, has been periodically embroiled in political issues, lack of funding transparency, and politicization. The Cold War and North-South divides provoked heated disputes. In 1984, the United States withdrew funding on the grounds that UNESCO had "extraneously politicized virtually every subject it deals with, has exhibited hostility toward the basic institutions of a free society, especially a free market and a free press, and has demonstrated unrestrained budgetary expansion."[30] The United States had played a leading role in establishing UNESCO in 1945 as a major international educational agency, and distinguished Americans like William Fulbright and Archibald MacLeish were both strongly supportive. The United States did not formally rejoin (contributing 22 percent of the budget) until 2003, and shortly after, First Lady Laura Bush was named an honorary ambassador to the agency. But controversy returned. In 2011, UNESCO members voted to admit the Palestinian Authority (PA) as a full member despite the PA's not having such status in the United Nations. The UNESCO membership bid, which required approval by two-thirds of the agency's general conference, passed by a vote of 107 to fourteen, with fifty-two abstentions. The United States responded again by cutting its funding payment of $60 million.

UNICEF is an interesting model that may signal elements of a future way forward. The agency has to raise one-third of its annual budget of over $3 billion through private sources. Such initiatives as having their logo on Barcelona football shirts (paid for by the club), on Halloween collection boxes, and "Change for Good" collected from airline passengers shows what can be achieved in funding. And, like several UN agencies, UNICEF has used goodwill ambassadors to raise their profile. Dating back to 1954 with the appointment of the movie star Danny Kaye, sporting and other celebrities like David Beckham, Serena Williams, and Whoopi Goldberg have performed this role.

Human Rights

There are few references in the UN Charter to human rights. They are mentioned, as we have seen, in the "Purposes" part of the Charter but not defined. The issue was treated at length in a separate nonlegally binding document, the Universal Declaration in 1948 (see Chapter 8). Despite the obvious differences between member states in the treatment of such issues as the rights of women and freedom of speech, the United Nations has continued to try to smooth edges and include human rights in its agenda. As an inclusive body that does not expel its members, it continues to be the only world forum, which, despite its obvious imperfections, provides some diplomatic yardsticks. Human rights were an early UN priority. The UN Commission on Human Rights was established in December 1948 at the first meeting of ECOSOC and was one of the first two functional commissions set up in Geneva within the early UN structure. The UN Human Rights Council (UNHRC), formed in 2006, is the successor body to the UN Commission on Human Rights and is also based in Geneva. It is a forum for debate on human rights issues but no UNSC resolution has ever been passed that sanctioned a member state on human rights grounds alone. Nevertheless, the UNHRC has been used to raise the profile of the issue and has addressed the horrors of the Syrian civil war. In September 2012, the UNHRC voted to extend the mandate of the independent panel probing abuses in Syria and called on all parties to put an end to violence. This resolution was adopted by the forty-seven-member council, elected by the UNGA, by a vote of forty-one in favor to three against (China, Cuba, and Russia), with three abstentions. The regular work of the UNHRC includes a system of peer review of member countries on human rights records.

Disarmament

In the tradition of the founders of the League of Nations, the United Nations has supported the maintenance of a major global forum to discuss disarmament issues, following the first major conference on the issue in 1932. It broke down when Hitler withdrew the German delegation. The current Conference on Disarmament (CD) was established in 1979 and has been the negotiating forum used by its member states, currently numbering sixty-five, to negotiate, inter alia, the Chemical Weapons Convention and the Comprehensive Test Ban Treaty. While the conference is not formally a UN organization, it is linked to the United Nations through a personal representative of the United Nations Secretary General. Resolutions adopted by the UNGA request the conference to consider specific disarmament matters. In turn, the CD annually reports its activities to the assembly. In recent years, the CD has been less productive as a forum as deadlock has prevailed over the consensus requirement for agreement on a work program. Measures like the Fissile Material Cut-Off Treaty have been unable to make progress for years, and pressure is growing to remove the negotiation from this forum. The key international organization charged with regulating the peaceful uses of nuclear energy is also a UN-affiliated agency. The International Atomic Energy Agency (IAEA) was established as an autonomous organization in Vienna in July 1957. The IAEA reports to both the UNGA and the UNSC.

UN-hosted disarmament discussions have paved the way for many achievements in the field, including the Nuclear Non-Proliferation Treaty, the Group of Experts on Small Arms, the Chemical Weapons Convention of 1993, and the 2013 Arms Trade Treaty, which was passed by the UNGA because some of the P5 on the UNSC announced they would not be parties to it. In September 2013, the UNSC, for long deadlocked over the Syrian civil war, passed unanimously Resolution 2118 on the destruction of Syrian chemical weapons after UN-appointed inspectors had verified the use of such weapons.

Trade, Finance, and Economic Stability

The origins of the Second World War were seen as rooted in economic causes, not just political ambitions and aggression. The conference at Bretton Woods in July 1944 was named the United Nations Monetary and Financial Conference and predated the meetings at Dumbarton Oaks and San Francisco. The Atlantic Charter, which was so influential in framing the United Nations itself, was also a source document for the new trade and financial order. Trade flows were seen as a demonstration of a healthy international system. New financial institutions would be designed to encourage fixed exchange rates and predictability with the reconstitution of what had been lacking between the two world wars—a system of international payments that would promote trade stability and a forum for dispute settlement in trade issues, prohibiting discrimination.

The Marshall Plan on economic reconstruction for Europe was equally critical in addressing the aftermath of war and ensuring the peace. The generation of leaders of the postwar era was farsighted and aware of the symbolism of collective efforts that were necessary to achieve stability.

The Bretton Woods meetings created a legacy of institutions to take collective responsibility for structural imbalances, development, and trade. The creation of the institutions and machinery of the IMF and the World Bank were diplomatic triumphs alongside the United Nations and have endured during the same era. As a recognition of the new impact of developing countries, a trade and investment forum, the UN Conference on Trade and Development (UNCTAD) was established in 1964. Beyond these landmarks, during the UN's lifetime, the global economy has been transformed. Diplomacy has adapted to unprecedented globalization and many significant features of economic and commercial convergence. Some of the largest global companies in market value, such as Google and Facebook, did not even exist twenty years ago. The scope for massive global downturns has increased greatly. The global responses to the most significant downturn in 2008 and 2009 showed again the recognition that the world was capable of collective diplomatic, if not financial, policy convergence. However, the United Nations was not the center of the action, and in the rescue meetings, the United Nations was largely sidelined with the Group of Twenty (G20) and regional organizations like the EU taking the lead.

Crimes against Humanity

Another legacy of World War II was the aftermath of crimes committed not as acts of war by one military against another (which had been the main pattern throughout modern diplomatic history) but against civilians and those from certain ethnic groups. The holocaust and its perpetrators was a harbinger of the inexorable rise of conflicts or aggression against civilians by state and nonstate actors. This collective response to these global crimes was designed because the previous diplomatic model based solely on sovereign states had gaps to fill. Wider measures and global standards were necessary. The early outcome was again an achievement for the United Nations. This was the negotiation of the first global convention against genocide. The Convention for the Prevention and Punishment of the Crime of Genocide was adopted by the UNGA on December 9, 1948. So the legacy of Nazi extermination policies and camps was addressed in treaties, punishment, precedents, international law, and the setting of new norms—a strong diplomatic package. The crimes were punished at Nuremberg, not as victors' vengeance. The 1990s revived interest in global intrastate crimes against civilians and the United Nations responded again, albeit too late to prevent many of the crimes. The special tribunals for the former Yugoslavia and for Sierra Leone exacted punishments. And now the International Criminal Court is attempting to establish new global norms in criminal procedures and punishments (Chapter 8 discusses further aspects of international law).

Refugees

The UN Charter assumes that the world consists of responsible, capable sovereign states. Or at least it assumes that such states will develop once they assume obligations within the United Nations. Such states have their membership in the United Nations because they have demonstrated their right to be recognized as a state with authority over part of the planet's territory. But refugees—those expelled or abandoned by states or simply the victims of breakdown in civil society—are also covered by UN collective actions. Refugees have long been among the victims of failed diplomacy. World War II displaced millions of people in Europe. The UN Relief and Rehabilitation Administration— established in 1943 by the United States and its allies, which had by then taken the name of the United Nations—began to address the problem of those displaced in Europe by the war. It became a UN agency in 1945. In 1947, the International Refugee Organization (IRO) was founded by the United Nations. The IRO was the first international agency to deal comprehensively with all aspects of refugees' lives. The IRO did not last long and was replaced by the UN High Commissioner for Refugees (UNHCR) in 1950. It was not intended to last for long but has established a permanent role as the problem of refugees has also become a permanent global issue.

More progress in dealing with refugees came in 1951 with agreement on the United Nations Convention Relating to the Status of Refugees. Article 1 of the convention, as amended by the 1967 protocol, provides the one essential element of any diplomatic effort to address an issue—an international definition of a refugee:

> A person who owing to a well-founded fear of being persecuted for reasons of race, religion, nationality, membership of a particular social group or political opinion, is outside the country of his nationality and is unable or, owing to such fear, is unwilling to avail himself of the protection of that country; or who, not having a nationality and being outside the country of his former habitual residence as a result of such events, is unable or, owing to such fear, is unwilling to return to it.[31]

The convention obliges parties that have ratified the refugee convention to protect refugees who are in their territory. The UNHCR is funded almost entirely by voluntary contributions, with 93 percent coming from governments. A further 4 percent comes from intergovernmental organizations and pooled funding mechanisms, while the remaining 3 percent is from the private sector. In addition, the agency receives a limited subsidy from the UN regular budget for administrative costs, and accepts in-kind contributions, such as tents, medicines, trucks, and air transport.

The UNHCR was launched on a shoestring annual budget of $300,000 in 1950. The funding is increasingly chaotic, with major contributions coming from only a few donor states. Of the 2012 UNHCR budget, no country outside North America or Europe came in the top twenty donors. The United States gave seven times more than any other government at over $700 million. Some fifteen existing UN agencies gave a mere $60 million. Of the countries in regions like the Middle East and Africa, where conflict had produced numerous refugee crises, Saudi Arabia gave $2 million and Qatar $100,000. Voluntarism is not the way forward to fund increasingly frequent world emergencies, with the Syrian civil war alone producing over two million refugees. At the end of 2013, the UN humanitarian coordinator appealed for $6.5 billion in donations for the Syrian refugee crisis, its largest appeal in history. Over two-thirds of this was needed for refugees already outside the country, which the United Nations said had affected three-quarters of Syria's population of twenty-two million. One country with 0.3 percent of the world's population was stretching the global resources of the largest multilateral institution ever invented.

Most Palestinian refugees—those in the West Bank, Gaza Strip, Lebanon, Syria, and Jordan—do not come within the responsibility of the UNHCR, but instead are treated by the UN body established in 1949—the United Nations Relief and Works Agency for Palestine Refugees in the Near East (UNWAPR).

Responsibility to Protect

In the aftermath of the Rwandan and other massacres of the 1990s resulting from civil conflict, Kofi Annan, then UN Secretary General, proposed that the world address the quandary of sovereign states that did not demonstrate the capabilities and responsibilities that were associated with membership of the United Nations, and where noninterference in their sovereignty conflicted with human rights. He posed the issue: "If humanitarian intervention is, indeed, an unacceptable assault on sovereignty, how should we respond to a Rwanda, to a Srebrenica—to gross and systematic violations of human rights that affect every precept of our common humanity?"[32] A commission was set up under the leadership of former Australian Foreign Minister Gareth Evans. Titled the International Commission on Intervention and State Sovereignty, it produced a report in December 2001 called *Responsibility to Protect*. This concept argued that the rights of sovereign states were not absolute but needed an acceptance of responsibilities as well.

The responsibility to protect principle, or R2P, is an important variant of the sovereign state principle. As well as spurring interest in establishing an International Criminal Court, it also influenced the charter of the reborn African Union (AU) in 2005. This stated that "protection of human and people's rights" would be a principal objective of the AU and that the union had the right "to intervene in a Member State pursuant to a decision of the Assembly in respect of grave circumstances, namely war crimes, genocide and crimes against humanity."[33] The acceptance of a dilution of sovereignty was gaining ground.

The R2P principle was adopted at the 2005 World Summit, which took place as a follow-up to the acceptance of the Millennium Development Goals (discussed later in this chapter). In the concluding document of the summit, which otherwise was not as productive as hoped, the following paragraph was adopted as a summary of R2P.

> Paragraph 138. Each individual State has the responsibility to protect its populations from genocide, war crimes, ethnic cleansing and crimes against humanity. This responsibility entails the prevention of such crimes, including their incitement, through appropriate and necessary means. We accept that responsibility and will act in accordance with it. The international community should, as appropriate, encourage and help States to exercise this responsibility and support the United Nations in establishing an early warning capability.[34]

So far the principle has been applied when it has been practical to do so. As we have seen, UNSCR 1973 of April 2011 did authorize military operations to protect civilians in the conflict in Libya. And UN peacekeepers have on several occasions been deployed to intervene in internal conflicts, for example in the Ivory Coast in 2011. Nevertheless, successful long-term implementation of R2P seems far from certain.

Syria seemed to be another classic case requiring enforcement of the principle. But the different circumstances of lack of P5 consensus, the concerns of some that the Libya precedent would be used to make intervention in sovereign states commonplace, and the confusingly wide range of parties to the conflict came together to block any early UN-endorsed approach to the bloodiest civil war of the twenty-first century.

Beyond the failures in Syria, the R2P concept has made some states uneasy. Brazil abstained on UNSCR 1973 and has proposed a conditioning of the approach of R2P in the future. Dilma Roussef, the President of Brazil, in her UNGA address in 2011 proposed that the concept should be modified to be described as "Responsibility while Protecting."[35] Brazil's concern, which they circulated in the UNGA in a concept note, was that force would be used as a first resort rather than later and that the authority of the UNSC was being undermined by resolutions to protect civilians without specifying what legal force could be used. "The use of force must produce as little violence and instability as possible and under no circumstance can it generate more harm than it was authorized to prevent."[36]

R2P is work in progress, but it does at least show diplomacy and the United Nations grappling with the issue of how far sovereignty equates to impunity or whether it is something earned through good behavior. Diplomacy has to show new versatility and creativity.

The Law of the Sea, the Environment, Climate Change

The United Nations has been instrumental in major progress in consensus building and law making, affecting the exploitation of global resources of the planet, the oceans, the environment, climate, and the preservation of the planet. Like the issue of refugees, the United Nations convened the Law of the Sea Convention, resulting from negotiations that lasted from 1973 to 1982, settled and extended previous provisions from customary law and partial agreements defining ocean boundaries. The convention establishes general obligations for safeguarding the marine environment and protecting freedom of scientific research on the high seas. It also created an innovative legal regime for controlling mineral resource exploitation in deep seabed areas beyond national jurisdiction through an International Seabed Authority.

The pace of UN involvement in environmental diplomacy has increased over the last thirty years. Following UNGA Resolution 38/161 of December 1983, the then UN Secretary General, Javier Pérez de Cuéllar, asked the prime minister of Norway, Gro Harlem Brundtland, to create an organization independent of the United Nations to focus on environmental and developmental problems and solutions. This led to the Brundtland Commission. Its report, *Our Common Future*, was produced in 1987 and drew attention to the concept of sustainable development, defined as "development that meets the needs of the present without compromising the ability of future generations to meet their own need."[37]

The Rio Earth Summit of 1992 was another important milestone in international environmental discussions. Major outcomes of the conference include the Climate Change Convention—a climate change agreement that led to the Kyoto Protocol, Agenda 21, and a Convention on Biological Diversity. It also created new actors and an institutional framework—the Commission on Sustainable Development, tasked with the follow-up to the Rio Conference, and the United Nations Framework Convention on Climate Change (UNFCCC).

The process has been equally sustained. The UNFCCC led in 1997 to the legally binding addendum to the Climate Change Convention called the Kyoto Protocol. The objective of the treaty is to "stabilize greenhouse gas concentrations in the atmosphere at a level that would prevent dangerous anthropogenic interference with the climate system."[38] Since then, conferences of state parties to the UNFCCC have met annually since 1995, the latest being in Durban, South Africa, in 2011, Doha in 2012, and Warsaw in 2013. The Kyoto Protocol, which set broad limits on emissions targets for different categories of countries, expired in 2012. The Doha conference agreed to extend it until 2020, with a target date for a successor agreement set for 2015.

The United Nations has been crucial in setting the agenda and providing an international forum for discussion over the environment. It would have been impossible to conceive of progress in this area without its role.

Corruption and Lack of Accountability

Another measure of how far the United Nations has lived up to its objectives is to see how ready to respond to changed circumstances it has been and how far its activities have become accountable where crimes, fraud, or other damaging actions have been committed in the name of the United Nations.

For over fifty years, the governance of the United Nations did not receive attention on a systematic basis. It was only in 2008 that the United Nations established the Independent Audit Advisory Committee (IAAC) to assist the General Assembly in fulfilling its oversight responsibilities of UN activities. It provides expert advice on the scope, results, and effectiveness of audit and other oversight functions, and on other issues such as risk management, internal controls, accounting, and disclosure.

The fragmented structure of agencies and governance has also been recently addressed. The UN Management Committee was established in 2005 to ensure leadership and strategic direction on internal management and effective follow-up on the findings and recommendations of oversight bodies. In the same year, the Management Performance Board was created to strengthen accountability and monitor the performance of senior managers.

In 2006, the United Nations introduced Senior Managers' Compacts—annual agreements between the Secretary General and the senior-most officials—that set specific objectives and managerial targets in each year and outline clear roles and responsibilities for all managers. In 2010, the compact regime was broadened to include heads of peacekeeping and of special political missions.

A UN Ethics Office was established at the end of 2005 to address reports of misconduct and offenses by UN officials. Previously, when whistleblowers reported abuses, such as the trafficking of people involving UN officials during peacekeeping in Bosnia, they had gone unpunished. Now, the Ethics Office has a remit to protect "staff against retaliation for reporting misconduct and for cooperating with duly authorized audits or investigations."[39] Despite these steps, there has never been a prosecution of any senior UN official involved in corruption.

Indeed, it was an outside whistle-blower—Iraqi government documents recovered after the fall of Saddam Hussein in 2003—that revealed significant abuse and siphoning of funds by the senior UN officials involved in administering the Oil for Food program during the UN-administered sanctions on Iraq in the 1990s. Due to media pressure, an independent commission was set up headed by former chairman of the U.S. Federal Reserve Bank, Paul Volcker. The Volcker Commission documented how the UN chair of the program, Benon Sevan, a Cypriot official, used his position to take allocations of oil from Iraq during the years he oversaw the Oil for Food Program. The son of the UN Secretary General Kofi Annan, Kojo Annan, worked for a Swiss inspection firm on the program and did not tell his father he was lobbying for the company to get the contract. Annan had suspended Sevan, and the Volcker Commission recommended he be prosecuted for embezzlement. But Sevan managed to flee the United States before he could be arrested and take refuge in Cyprus. He remains free.

The peacekeeping budget is one part of the United Nations where enormous funds are spent. Again, there are instances of poor governance and accountability by the United Nations. The Nepalese government reported that $4 million had been diverted to private bank accounts of money intended for armored cars for a Nepalese contingent of peacekeepers to Darfur. A second scandal involving Nepalese peacekeepers was the cholera outbreak in Haiti in the aftermath of the January 2010 earthquake. Before the earthquake, there had been no cholera in Haiti. By October 2011, about 6 percent of the population was infected and more than 7,500 people had died—ironically, a higher toll than the political violence that brought the peacekeepers to Haiti. According to the WHO (itself of course a UN agency), the 340,000 cases in Haiti in 2011 were more than in the rest of the world put together. The United Nations has not accepted responsibility or agreed on compensation to Haiti for this tragedy. The United Nations continued to say the issue of whether its peacekeepers caused the outbreak remained unproven. Secretary General Ban Ki-Moon in a letter to petitioners on behalf of the victims said their claims were not receivable. At the time of writing, a U.S.-based advocacy group is lodging claims for the families of victims against the United Nations, which continues to claim immunity.

The United Nations has only the powers that its membership has given to it. It has on occasions sought to hold its own members accountable and investigate crimes that have gone unpunished. The assassination of the former Lebanese prime minister Rafic Hariri in February 2005 has been investigated by a special UN tribunal established under UNSCR 1595. The Lebanese authorities had requested this as the only way to guarantee a transparent legal process. Despite extensive reports produced by international prosecutors and a trial in absentia of some suspects at a special tribunal for Lebanon in The Hague, no individual or group has been punished for the crime.

The UN's decision making and administration generally remain opaque and poorly accountable compared to the sovereign states that operate oversight systems. Few know what senior officials are paid or on what basis they operate. There is little external oversight. For example, the International Labor Office in Geneva has a budget of over $700 million but has no requirement for external audit. The appointments and terms of senior officials are left vague with little scrutiny. One example is the position of Lakhdar Brahimi, the Algerian UN envoy and advisor on Syria appointed in August 2012. His mandate ended in May 2014. For most of this time, UN diplomacy had been going nowhere, yet member states knew little of the terms of his employment.

An Agenda Setter, a Creator of Standards, and Builder of Consensus

Though the United Nations is now increasingly in competition with NGOs and businesses for international attention, no organization can rival it for its clarion call capacity to raise the profile of an issue. The 2000 Millennium Development Goals (MDGs) are a good example. The MDGs are eight international development goals that were officially established following the Millennium Summit of the United Nations in 2000. All UN members have agreed to achieve the following goals by the year 2015:

1. Eradicate extreme poverty and hunger
2. Achieve universal primary education
3. Promote gender equality and empowering women
4. Reduce child mortality rates
5. Improve maternal health
6. Combat HIV/AIDS, malaria, and other diseases
7. Ensure environmental sustainability
8. Develop a global partnership for development.[40]

Some of the goals are impossibly ambitious, but the vision of rousing the world to fresh collective efforts is part of the role envisaged in the UN Charter. The results of global efforts on these goals will be discussed more in Chapter 9, and there is evidence that the United Nations is successfully partnering with individual sovereign states, foundations, and philanthropists. The results that have been achieved in the struggle against HIV and AIDS are one example of an ad hoc cooperation with nonstate actors with credit also due to, inter alia, President George W. Bush and the Bill and Melinda Gates Foundation. But the United Nations can justly claim some success as an agenda setter and implementer.

Equally, the United Nations has played a consensus-building role in its work on international statistics. The reports and research of UN agencies bear an international stamp. And it is difficult to conceive of any other body that could perform this function of universality in information. Such composites statistics as the Human Development Index (HDI) rank states on life expectancy, education, and income indices to give some measure of human development. Many other UN-originated statistics in areas such as health, labor, and nutrition are used as standards in diplomatic discussions and in setting criteria for overseas development assistance. Yet the statistics may not in practice tell the story they purport to tell. The UN officials compiling them seldom have full independent access to national statistics such as child mortality or educational measures. The scope for national manipulation is obvious. But the measures assembled by the United Nations have few equals, and this can again be rightly claimed as a considerable contribution to multilateral diplomacy.

Public Diplomacy

The founding era of the United Nations was, as we have seen, genuinely visionary. The drafters were indeed rebuilding international diplomacy. To what extent has the United Nations provided convincing evidence that in the post-World War II era it has revamped the way diplomacy is conducted?

First, we have seen many examples of big power rivalries being played out in UN institutions. The United Nations gives a stage that raises hopes for collective solutions but seems to encourage nationalist standoffs. The major powers seldom seem to agree on important issues and increasingly bypass the United Nations in favor of regional groupings, with the increased fragmentation of diplomacy laid at the UN's door.

The senior positions of any international organization are subject to complex diplomacy, but most major organizations would now undertake a global trawl with no predisposition to appoint the national of one country. This is still rare for core jobs in the United Nations. The head of peacekeeping since 2000 has always been a French diplomat—Jean-Marie Guehenno, Alain LeRoy, and Herve Ladsous. The executive head of UNICEF has been an American since its founding in 1946. The director general of the IMF has always been a European and the president of the World Bank an American. The G20 agreed that this should change, but no action has so far followed the words.

Second, in public perception, the United Nations often appears ineffective. Many decisions of the UNSC go unenforced, despite being legally binding. There were at least seventeen UNSC resolutions in force against Iraq after its invasion of Kuwait, and for over a decade they were not fully enforced and flouted by Iraq. UNSCR 1504 of April 2004 mandated action within six months of its date by all members to enact domestic legislation to prevent the proliferation of weapons of mass destruction. Two years later, sixty-two members of the United Nations had still not initiated measures to comply.

Third, the United Nations has succeeded in maintaining an inclusive system of diplomacy. The attraction of UN activities for small countries is obvious. The one country, one vote provision is the last outpost of the equality of sovereign states. This, as we saw, reached its apogee in the VCDR of 1961 and the Vienna Convention on Consular Relations of 1963. Seventy percent of the UN members have fewer than twenty million inhabitants, and diplomats from smaller countries have contributed significantly to the development of the United Nations. Dag Hammarskjöld of Sweden, Perez de Cuellar of Peru, and Kofi Annan of Ghana have all left their mark on UN diplomacy. And Gro Harlem Brundtland of Norway, Lester Pearson of Canada, and Tommy Koh of Singapore have all been instrumental in developing key policy areas. Arvid Pardo of Malta urged the creation of a negotiation of the Law of the Sea.

Fourth, the United Nations is seen by the world as a forum for negotiating 24/7 among representatives. As a one-stop shop negotiating venue, it has been used on innumerable occasions for behind the scenes exchanges—the lifeblood of diplomacy. Ethiopia agreed through UN contacts to participate in the first Gulf War coalition if the United States would get involved in the cease-fire negotiations with Eritrea. Permanent representatives at the United Nations develop a certain camaraderie and can work on issues where favors are offered and repaid. Sir Jeremy Greenstock, the former U.K. permanent representative, records that when he was at the United Nations, he agreed with his French colleague to be mutually supportive of U.K. and French respective interventions in Sierra Leone and Côte d'Ivoire. Without such continuous contact, the policies might have been seen in capitals as rivalry for influence.

Fifth, the United Nations has also demonstrated a key capability of a diplomatic institution by learning from past experience and failures. The disasters that befell peacekeeping in Somalia influenced Rwanda, and the state-building mechanisms used in Namibia and Cambodia were applied better to Kosovo and East Timor. Ignoring brutality or humanitarian emergencies in an age of mass 24/7 media, cell phone videos, and a well-funded NGO sector is increasingly not an option. Yet the fact remains that none of the major conflicts that have occurred after the founding of the United Nations, such as Vietnam, Serbia, Rwanda, and Syria, have been significantly influenced by Chapter VII actions.

Sixth, and in contrast to few authorizations of the use of force, the United Nations has shown an appetite for other coercive measures. Yet the many examples of UN trade and investment sanctions, and arms embargos have had mixed success. In the 1970s, the United Nations provided on many occasions little more than a forum to expose disagreements on key development issues but did eventually lead to a successful imposition of measures against apartheid in South Africa. In the 1990s, the UN inspections of Iraq were an unusually intrusive task. They did their job, but too slowly, and the big power divisions were brought to bear as post-Cold War features took shape. UN-mandated sanctions continue to be imposed and the monitoring of evasion and side-effects are all tasks that need to be perfected. But UN collective disapproval is one of the effective manifestations of its action. In 2013, a group from the Geneva Institute for the Study of International Governance and the Watson Institute at Brown University reported on twenty-two cases of UN-targeted sanctions covering al-Qaeda and the Taliban, Angola, Côte d'Ivoire, North Korea, Democratic Republic of Congo, former Republic of Yugoslavia, Haiti, Iran, Liberia, Libya, Sierra Leone, Somalia, Sudan, Eritrea-Ethiopia, Guinea-Bissau, Iraq, Kosovo, Lebanon, and Rwanda. They noted the different objectives contained in the sanctions. Some were to coerce or change behavior in countries, some to prohibit certain activities, some to stigmatize a state's conduct in the widest sense. The durability of these regimes, for example Iraq, suggests that sanctions are slow to take effect. But other successes, such as a change of behavior in Libya over weapons of mass destruction (WMD) possession, would suggest that UN-backed diplomacy has been successful. Whatever the truth, no other international organization can replace the United Nations in drawing attention to global issues. When Malala Yousafzai, on her sixteenth birthday in 2013, wanted to make maximum impact in affirming the rights of every child to education, she chose the United Nations as her podium.

What does the public think of the United Nations and does it matter? A World Public Opinion poll in 2008 found that most in the Muslim world thought the United States effectively ran the United Nations. This view was endorsed by 68 percent of Egyptians, 63 percent of Palestinians, 59 percent of Jordanians, and 53 percent of Turks. In 2009, majorities in nineteen of the twenty-five countries surveyed by Pew Research gave a favorable view of the United Nations, including 61 percent in the United States. Nevertheless, the poll also showed that one thing that the Israeli and Palestinian publics shared was that a majority in each country had an unfavorable view of the institution.

As former U.S. ambassador to the United Nations Richard Holbrooke observed, to blame the United Nations for failures of diplomacy is like blaming Madison Square Garden for the losses of the New York Knicks basketball team. One point that is perhaps in the UN's favor is that since the end of the Cold War, no country has worked out how to make the United Nations work for its national interests consistently. That is no bad thing, but the image of ineffectual and feckless diplomacy contributes to the search for alternative fora, alternative agencies, and alternative diplomacy. Insiders to the organization, who have experienced its working methods, may have a different perspective. The jobs may be dangerous and disruptive to family life, but they are well paid and many salaries are tax free, including generous cost-of-living adjustments. United Nations personnel include officers who mirror the functions of major global corporations, including equities analysts for pension schemes. Yet, despite the attention it pays to its staff, it does not seem to all that it meets standards of efficiency and integrity. Former UN Deputy Secretary General, and later Minister in the British Foreign Office, Mark Malloch Brown told the *New York Times* in 2011 that "there's a huge redundancy and lack of efficiency" in the UN system, and the budget is "utterly opaque, untransparent and completely in shadow."[41]

So in public diplomacy terms, the United Nations arouses positives and negatives—perhaps not unexpected because it reflects a world that is also often chaotic and dysfunctional.

The Future of the UN

What are the challenges to the future of the United Nations? Which of its core functions are still unique to multilateral diplomacy, and which might be replaced or more regularly supplemented by other procedures through other bodies?

The United Nations is increasingly being challenged as an agenda setter and implementer by other groups, both state and nonstate, and by other multilateral bodies frustrated at logjams and sovereignty impasses when it comes to problem solving. Our next chapter will examine what value some of these global and regional diplomatic groups bring to diplomacy. Yet the United Nations remains central to dispute-solving and as a source of inclusiveness. No state sees itself as having a complete identity without UN membership.

The United Nations remains a first point of call for relief from disasters. And of course it is true that bureaucratic failures and turf wars are not confined to the United Nations. But speed of response, expertise, and efficient administration has developed in newer, more focused organizations, which in turn reflect the decline of the sovereign state. In disaster relief, transnational organizations like Médecins Sans Frontières and Partners in Health are used as implementers. National governments adopt an à la carte solution to which agency they choose as project managers. The United Nations bureaucracy may be seen as an unattractive partner when customized solutions are needed.

In terms of bureaucracy, the United Nations is among the world's largest. There are currently five main centers of staff—New York, Geneva, Rome, Vienna, and Nairobi—plus many smaller ones. The *New York Times* reported that in Geneva alone, the United Nations held 10,000 meetings in 2009, ran 632 training workshops, and translated 220,000 pages of documents for various reports. In this guise, the United Nations has become a massive think tank with guaranteed funding but serving only vaguely defined ends. The UN Economic Commission for Europe (UNECE) worked on a project for Bolivia to draw up a list of standards for the trade in llama and alpaca meat. The UNECE duly published its report in 2008 offering global norms for the fat thickness and trimming of llama cuts, the means of avoiding ragged edges and ensuring that cross-sectional surfaces form approximate right angles with the skin surface. The same UNECE report also offered a color gauge for in-shell walnuts and walnut kernels and a seventy-five-page brochure on red and green peppers.

DIFFERENT WORLDS: DIFFERENT UN

What differences does the contemporary world show from the world the UN's authors envisaged? Back in 1945, the UN drafters were not naïve; they did not assume that conflicts would cease, but the primary source of them was still seen as sovereign states. And the equally critical diplomatic issue of economic development was still framed in largely sovereign state terms. Governance, self-determination, and freedoms had of course been central to the causes of

World War II, but the converging interests of all in poverty (freedom from want), climate change, and such nonstate driven activities as terrorism and cyber hacking could not have been predicted.

Failures in area of security, often with the Security Council locked with no password, and diplomatic deadlocks are to be set alongside progress in health and information indices. The work of the WHO in eliminating some endemic diseases and in promoting vaccination policies has shown collective efforts as impressively productive. The IAEA is the only internationally recognized agency whose objective is to prevent the proliferation of nuclear weapons. The United Nations has established itself as a brand with appeal in the most multipolar world diplomacy has known. But the implementation of decisions and the funding of activities still depend on sovereign states. There have been no universal levies imposed and the United Nations must ultimately satisfy the sovereign states who see it as an institution beneficial for their survival. States still behave as separate entities and have not progressed far into the creation of a continuous consensus-building mechanism where a united nations of collective interests is regularly seen to exist.

International legitimacy derives from the universal acceptance of legal obligations of the UN Charter. There is no higher authority than the United Nations in terms of legally binding resolutions. But equally, to give the United Nations a report card is difficult when there has never been an equivalent. Compared to the 1940s, governments control less of the economy as most have privatized major sectors previously in state hands. Wars are not only a failure for diplomacy, but they also are expensive and limit what governments can deliver in other areas. So the capacity of governments to wage wars has declined but the capacity of nonstate actors to cause and conduct conflicts has increased. Now governments engage in less direct economic activity and employ far fewer people. But they are still expected to provide services and security. Meanwhile, the expanded private sectors cause crises through poor decisions, breach of rules, or the absence of rules. They are acting within a framework that pays little heed to the existence of sovereign states. The United Nations, as a collection of sovereign states, is bound to seem less and less central to solutions, and diplomacy is compromised.

In terms of future challenges like climate change and governance of the Internet, will the UN model be followed or will its past failures and sovereignty issues be gradually eclipsed by a more hybrid system of multilateral diplomacy? Will the United Nations be seen by history as an organization that was increasingly concerned with its own survival or does it contain the seeds of regeneration that makes the objectives set in the 1940s still valid? Just as states need to adapt domestically to the information and technology revolution, so does the United Nations.

Irrespective of what the United Nations does in the future, the search for collective security and organizations capable of responding to shared interests with shared actions will continue. Diplomacy has not yet worked out enduring solutions. On global issues such as conflict, disarmament, development, human rights, and poverty, the universality of the United Nations produces a multiplicity of opinions, some constructive but others blocking initiative. That these discussions and forums still happen and that states still wish to belong and pay for it is an achievement in itself. But we now see emerging models that recognize the shortcomings of the United Nations, and alternative avenues are available to diplomacy. The regional organizations that we discuss in the next chapter are part of the response. We will examine how far they are more effective diplomatic institutions than the United Nations and the motivations that led to their development.

Case Study

The UN Charter and the UNSCR— The Iraq Crises of 1990 to 1991 and 2003

How did the United Nations and multilateral diplomacy perform in both Iraq crises?

The United Nations was central to both crises. The United States, though widely seen as engaging in diplomacy that paid little attention to the United Nations and multilateral institutions, did in reality try to engage the United Nations in performing the functions for which it was designed.

At the time of the first crisis, the United Nations had weathered the end of the Cold War and in 1990 was looking forward to a new era of operations. It was widely believed that if it were not "the end of history," there would be a new convergence between the powers and the world would take the opportunity to build a new diplomatic architecture.

Of course not all the world changed overnight, and one country rooted in the past was Iraq, governed since 1968 by Saddam Hussein, a leader who had already invaded his neighbor, Iran, in one of the bloodiest conflicts that occurred during the Cold War. Between 500,000 and 1.5 million people died in that war. He had also used chemical weapons against his own population, killing thousands, mostly Kurds, in Halabja.

On August 2, 1990, Saddam Hussein invaded Kuwait, taking advantage of a world looking elsewhere for trouble and seizing an opportunity for settling old territorial disputes and claims to oil deposits with Kuwait, particularly in the Rumaila peninsula. Some have argued that U.S. diplomatic signals from the then ambassador April Glaspie had given Saddam reason to think that the United States would treat Iraqi disputes with Kuwait as none of its business. The United States believed that Saddam was only interested in pressurizing Kuwait to forgive debts Iraq owed from Kuwaiti loans during the Iraq-Iran war and that he wanted to persuade Kuwait to reduce oil production to raise prices.

The United States viewed this assault on sovereignty as an event that would start the post-Cold War era on the wrong footing and believed that an international response must be orchestrated. The U.S. President George H. W. Bush was a former U.S. ambassador to the United Nations under President Nixon and vice president under President Reagan. Diplomacy had an experienced and effective leader. The United Nations was used as a physical location to negotiate the participation and organization of the coalition he put together. Within hours of the invasion, the Kuwait and U.S. delegations requested a meeting of the UNSC, which passed UNSCR 660, condemning the invasion and demanding a withdrawal of Iraqi troops. On August 3rd, the Arab League passed its own resolution, which called for a solution to the conflict from its own members and warned against outside intervention. Iraq and Libya were the only two Arab League states, along with the PLO, that opposed UNSCR 660. UNSCR 661, passed by the UNSC by thirteen to zero on August 6th, put in place a trade and financial embargo on Iraq. By August 25, 1990, the UNSCR 665 had instituted a naval blockade to be enforced against Iraq and twenty-three countries had agreed to provide vessels to participate in the action.

Meanwhile, Saddam had begun his own diplomatic efforts to improve his chances of securing some international support. He linked his invasion with other popular Arab causes like the Israeli occupation of Arab land after the 1967 war. On August 12th, Saddam called for Israel to withdraw from occupied territories in Palestine, Syria, and Lebanon, and for Syria to withdraw from Lebanon, which would be accompanied by mutual withdrawals by Iraq. From the beginning of the crisis, President Bush was strongly opposed to any linkage between Iraq's occupation of Kuwait and the Palestinian issue.

On November 29, 1990, the United Nations voted in UNSCR 678 to authorize the United States and its allies to expel Iraq from Kuwait if it had not left by January 15, 1991. The resolution was adopted by twelve votes to two against (Cuba and Yemen) and one abstention by China. China, which had usually vetoed such resolutions authorizing intervention against a sovereign state, abstained in an attempt to ease sanctions placed on it after the Tiananmen Square protests of 1989. Various members of the council were rewarded for "yes" votes—for example, with aid packages and trade concessions—and those who initially opposed the resolution were discouraged from voting "no" with threats of economic penalties. The United States played hardball in the United Nations. Yemen, which voted against, incurred the wrath of Saudi Arabia, which expelled its migrant workers, and the United States stopped its aid programs.

Saddam continued to try to divide the states ranged against him. In December 1990, Iraq offered to withdraw from Kuwait provided that foreign troops left the region, an agreement was reached regarding the Palestinian problem and Israel dismantled its weapons of mass destruction. The United States rejected the proposal. The United States stuck to its position that there would be no negotiations until Iraq withdrew from Kuwait and that they should not grant Iraq concessions. The Iraqi government remained obdurate and seemed to believe there would be a UN climb-down. U.S. Secretary of State James Baker met with Iraqi Foreign Minister Tariq Aziz in Geneva in early 1991, but Aziz reportedly made no concrete proposals and there were no further direct diplomatic contacts. On January 14, 1991, France proposed to the UNSC a compromise to fold in a wider conference on Arab-Israel questions alongside withdrawal from Kuwait. The United States, the United Kingdom, and Russia rejected it, and France dropped the proposal when Iraq greeted it with no interest.

After the ultimatum in UNSCR 678 went unheeded, air strikes by the United States began on January 15, 1991, and a ground invasion on February 24th. Over thirty countries contributed personnel or equipment to the invading forces commanded by U.S. General Schwarzkopf,

(Continued)

(Continued)

and several other countries like Japan and Germany gave significant funding. In a few days, Saddam Hussein had been ejected from Kuwait. Diplomatically and militarily, the expulsion of Saddam Hussein from Kuwait was a textbook case of the United Nations acting as it been intended to by the drafters of the Charter forty-five years before, resulting in a diplomatic and military triumph.

Following Diplomatic and Military Success: New Tasks

The international community then set itself the task of deciding what do about an offending sovereign state, when the government still remained the recognized authority of the state and a member of the United Nations. The United Nations was entering uncharted territory.

UNSCR 687 of April 3, 1991, was one of the most ambitious in UN history. It reaffirmed the previous resolutions 660, 661, 662, 664, 665, 666, 667, 669, 670, 674, 677, 678 (all 1990) and 686 (1991), and was carried by twelve votes to one.

The resolution was divided into nine sections. It urged Iraq and Kuwait to respect the boundary between the two countries and requested the Secretary General to submit a plan for the deployment of the UN Iraq–Kuwait Observation Mission along a demilitarized zone, which was established to be 10km into Iraq and 5km into Kuwait.

UNSCR 687 threw the book at Saddam Hussein on Iraq's international treaty obligations, some on arms control dating from many decades before. Extensive disarmament obligations were imposed on Iraq. The main legal authority for demanding the destruction of Iraq's chemical and biological weapons was the Protocol for the Prohibition of the Use in War of Asphyxiating, Poisonous, or other Gases, and of Bacteriological Methods of Warfare, usually called the Geneva Protocol of 1925. Resolution 687 also stated that Iraq had breached its obligations as a non-nuclear weapon state under the Nuclear Non-Proliferation Treaty of 1968 by attempting to develop a nuclear weapon. The limits imposed by the resolution on maintaining ballistic missiles with a range greater than 150km had no global instrument to support them other than the recognition by members of the Missile Technology Control Regime that such longer range missiles were destabilizing. The UNSC ordered Iraq to submit, within fifteen days, a report declaring all locations of all these prohibited items and to agree to urgent, on-site inspections. It then established the United Nations Special Commission (UNSCOM) to undertake some of the most intrusive weapons inspections in history.

Resolution 687 also discussed reparations and compensation, holding Iraq liable for loss, damage, and injury inflicted upon Kuwait and demanded that Iraq hand over any remaining property seized from Kuwait. It also declared null and void any statements by Iraq regarding its refusal to repay its foreign debt and set up a fund to handle these compensation claims (UNSCR 692). Resolution 687 stated that international sanctions against Iraq did not apply to foodstuffs or medical aid to the civilian populations of Iraq. However, sales of weapons and other related material to Iraq would continue to be prohibited. Resolution 687 also required Iraq to facilitate the repatriation of prisoners of war and cooperation with the International Committee of the Red Cross and to inform the UNSC that it did not commit or support terrorism and would not allow such acts to take place in its territory.

Never before had a UN member been subjected to such demanding and wide-ranging on-site weapons inspections. The United Nations was in effect ordering Iraq to behave within its territory only according to international rules. If Iraq failed to comply, it would not regain its full sovereignty under the UN model. By April 18, 1991, after Iraq had formally accepted the provisions of Resolution 687, the Secretary General submitted to the Security Council his report regarding the establishment of UNSCOM. He appointed Swedish Ambassador Rolf Ekéus as the executive chairman and on May 1, 1991, twenty other UN members of the commission were appointed. The bulk of the costs of UNSCOM were derived from Iraq's own funds, supplemented in kind by its members. The UNSCOM inspectors reported regularly to the United Nations and, at first, seemed to carry out their tasks productively.

UNSCOM and UNMOVIC Success

The issue for the inspectors was not whether Iraq had WMD (though tabloid history has often assumed so), but whether it had destroyed them under the UN-mandated inspections. Immediately following the termination of hostilities in 1991, Iraq did show good cooperation. Iraq turned over militarily significant holdings of weapons of mass destruction, and the destruction of them and facilities that were associated with them was carried out mainly by Iraq itself under the supervision of UNSCOM and the IAEA.

By the mid-1990s, significant quantities of Iraq's nuclear, chemical, and biological weapons programs had been destroyed or rendered harmless under UN supervision. In 1996, the IAEA reported to the Security Council that no nuclear weapons had been manufactured in Iraq, that nuclear material had been removed from the country, and that no clandestine nuclear weapons program remained. At the same time, UNSCOM was also able to account to the Security Council for 817 of the 819 short-range Scud missiles known to have been held by Iraq. Indeed, UNSCOM itself had destroyed forty-eight Scud missiles and fifty warheads and was able to confirm that Iraq had destroyed the rest.

By the early 1990s, Iraq had turned over more than 40,000 chemical weapons, mainly shells, half of which were drained and subsequently destroyed by Iraq, again under UNSCOM guidance. UNSCOM also supervised the destruction by Iraq of an additional 700 tons of bulk chemical weapons agents, 3,600 tons of precursor chemicals, and more than one hundred pieces of equipment used to produce chemical weapons. Yet it increasingly became clear that Iraq was engaging in a deliberate and increasingly ambitious plan to delay and deceive the inspection teams. The inspectors' record in locating and understanding Iraq's biological weapons were particularly weak. Indeed, biological weapons inspections became a priority only after the 1995 defection of Saddam's son-in-law, Hussein Kamal. The defection compounded suspicions of covert Iraqi programs and scientists with much to hide.

The Iraqi authorities were also now actively suggesting to foreign oil and other companies that there would be massive new opportunities in Iraq once the UN sanctions were lifted. The government showed adeptness in dividing the major inspecting countries. In 1997, a new head

(Continued)

(Continued)

of UNSCOM was appointed, an Australian diplomat, Richard Butler, and the level of cooperation dropped abruptly. He made numerous visits to Iraq, received new assurances of cooperation and unrestricted access, but eventually he concluded that the inspections could not be carried out effectively. Saddam Hussein increasingly sought to link full cooperation with a lifting of UN sanctions. In 1998, the inspectors pulled out altogether. In December 1998, U.S. and U.K. planes bombed Iraq as a punishment for noncooperation in inspections and for breaches of the UN-mandated no-fly zone.

A lot happened to U.S. diplomacy between 1998 and 2002, when the inspectors returned. The world had hoped to reap a peace dividend from the Cold War, but the removal of economic and ideological divisions increased unpredictability and loosened adherence to international norms. The use of chemical weapons by Iraq was a leading motivation for a major new treaty—the Chemical Weapons Convention of 1993, negotiated under UN auspices in Geneva. And the Additional Protocol produced by the IAEA in 1993 was designed to provide inspectors with greater capability of detecting cheating by those who were non-nuclear weapons states parties to the Non-Proliferation Treaty. Russia now needed enormous economic and security assistance from the United States to prevent its own holdings of WMD from falling into the wrong hands. African genocides and the breakup of the former Yugoslavia generated new kinds of instability. The UN's diplomacy sat on the sidelines as NATO and the United States tried to restore order in the Balkans. Yet the message many countries took from this period was that the world was now unipolar and that the United States would act whenever it could unilaterally outside any diplomatic constraints.

In the midst of this new world order, the events of 9/11 exploded. But in Iraq, nearly three years on from the inspectors exit from the country in 1998, there was still no international verification of what was happening with its weapons programs. Even before 9/11, UNSCR 1267, adopted unanimously on October 15, 1999, had already established a sanctions regime to cover individuals and entities associated with al-Qaeda, Osama bin Laden, and the Afghan Taliban. After 9/11, U.S. diplomacy returned to the UNSC. UNSCR 1368, adopted unanimously on September 12, 2001, condemned the September 11th attacks against the United States, expressed the council's determination to combat threats to international peace and security caused by acts of terrorism, and recognized the rights of individual and collective self-defense under the Charter. The resolution called on all countries to cooperate to bring the perpetrators, organizers, and sponsors of the attacks to justice and said that those responsible for supporting or harboring the perpetrators, organizers, and sponsors would be held accountable.

After the successful ousting of the Taliban from power in Afghanistan, the United States set about establishing a government that would not harbor terrorists (see "Case Study of The New Agenda: Nation Building in Afghanistan" in Chapter 9).

U.S. diplomacy again shifted back to the United Nations. In September 2002, President George W. Bush outlined his new National Security Strategy. In this, he said the U.S. government's duty to protect the American people gave it a responsibility to "anticipate and counter threats, using all elements of national power, before threats can do grave damage."[42] And that to prevent hostile acts by adversaries of the United States, the country would

> if necessary, act preemptively in exercising our inherent right of self-defense. The United States will not resort to force in all cases to preempt emerging threats. Our preference is nonmilitary acts. And no country should ever use preemption as a pretext for aggression.[43]

This seemed to suggest to many a revival of U.S. interest in Iraq and the unfinished compliance issues dating from UNSCR 687. The caveats to the Bush doctrine, even at the height of U.S. anger and confidence in its abilities in September, are worth remembering. The United States was couching its strategy still in diplomatic terms.

U.S. diplomacy was now put in top gear to secure another UN resolution to add to the formidable dossier that lay unimplemented by Iraq. The United States was in many ways trying to restore both its own and the UN's credibility. The result was one of the most contentious resolutions in the history of the United Nations. In UNSCR 1441, passed unanimously on November 8, 2002, Iraq was instructed to allow UN inspections to resume within forty-five days and gave Iraq thirty days to provide a complete declaration of all aspects of its programs to develop chemical, biological, and nuclear programs. UNSCR 1441 said Iraq would be given a final opportunity to comply. It warned Iraq there would be serious consequences from its continued violations.

Weapons inspectors of the newly constituted United Nations Monitoring, Verification and Inspection Commission (UNMOVIC) returned to Iraq for the first time since being withdrawn by the United Nations in 1998. Two officials shared the responsibility. Hans Blix, a former Swedish foreign minister who had been director general of the IAEA was the head of UNMOVIC, and Mohamed ElBaradei, the director general of the IAEA. In early December 2002, Iraq filed a 12,000-page weapons declaration with the United Nations. After reviewing the document, the United States, France, and the United Kingdom found it an inadequate declaration. On December 19, the United States claimed Iraq was in material breach of UNSCR 1441.

Rumors persisted that Iraq was still not coming clean. Even the slightest unexpected discovery fueled speculation of deception. In January 2003, inspectors discovered eleven empty 122mm chemical warheads. These components had not been previously declared by Iraq. Iraq dismissed the warheads as old weapons that had been packed away and forgotten. On January 27, 2003, UN inspectors reported that Iraq had cooperated on a practical level with monitors, but had not demonstrated a genuine acceptance of the need to disarm unilaterally. They noted that some Iraqi scientists had refused cooperation.

The United States returned to the United Nations in February. On February 5, 2003, U.S. Secretary of State Colin Powell appeared before the United Nations to prove that Iraq still remained a threat. Powell showed photos of what he said were mobile biological

(Continued)

(Continued)

weapons plants, chemical weapons bunkers that had not been destroyed, and claimed that Iraqi commanders were being tipped off about new UNMOVIC inspections. Differences of opinion now surfaced between the United States and the head of UNMOVIC. On February 14, 2003, Blix presented a report to the Security Council, stating that the Iraqis were now more proactive in their cooperation. Blix questioned the interpretations of the satellite photos shown by Powell and believed that alternate interpretations were possible. ElBaradei of the IAEA also said that he did not believe the Iraqis had a nuclear weapons program.

The United States was now drafting a second resolution with the objective of finding Iraq in material breach and that the serious consequences of Resolution 1441 should be implemented. The United States, with input from the United Kingdom and Spain, claimed that further action against it should be authorized. It built a case based partly on Blix's expressed skepticism over Iraq's claims to have destroyed its stockpiles of anthrax and VX nerve agent in *Time* magazine. Blix had said he found it "a bit odd" that Iraq, with "one of the best-organized regimes in the Arab world,"[44] claimed to have no records of the destruction of these illegal substances.

On March 10, 2003, French President Chirac announced that France would veto any resolution that would lead automatically to war. His Prime Minister Dominic de Villepin declared that "such intervention could have incalculable consequences for the stability of a scarred and fragile region."[45] The avenue of the UNSC was effectively blocked off for enforcing final Iraqi compliance.

On March 12, 2003, Blix made what turned out to be his final report on the status of UNMOVIC's efforts to verify Iraq's disarmament. On March 16th, the United States, United Kingdom, and Spain announced a deadline of March 17th for military action and that no further resolution was required beyond 1441. The attacks and subsequent invasion of Iraq began on March 18th and 19th.

Conclusion

The first Iraq crisis showed the United Nations machinery working smoothly with major national interests aligned with enforcement of UN authority and of Iraq's treaty obligations. The second Iraq crisis showed the United Nations and new post-9/11 era diplomacy struggling to produce consensus-building efforts. There is no question that Saddam Hussein had defied the United Nations over many years and seemed convinced in the inability of the international community ever to act. The UN inspection teams seemed to have satisfied most members of the United Nations. Further attempts to reaffirm Iraq's compliance with its obligations were fruitless amid a mixture of indifference and promises of large commercial contracts. But the United States saw its own national interests as being obstructed by UN dithering. Others, unlike in 1990, feared that a new unipolar order was taking shape and fell back on UN checks to block American ambition.

The means of implementation of international treaties (which, as we shall discuss in Chapter 8, have to be registered with the United Nations) have rarely been defined, and so each issue of noncompliance raises new issues. In many respects, the United States invasion, however ill-conceived in terms of political expediency and in the price that was paid in loss of life and resources by the United States, its allies, and Iraqi civilians over many years, was an effort to reinforce the power of UN resolutions. For many states, these had proved easier to ignore than take seriously. Iraq had cheated on treaties and deceived the inspectors. As we have seen, reforms in the enforcement of international norms resulted from the lessons of the Iraq crises. The IAEA Additional Protocol on nuclear safeguards was one. The Chemical Weapons Convention was concluded in 1993 and took effect in 1997. Later, suggestions that the Pakistani nuclear scientist A. Q. Khan had been helping Iraq's nuclear weapons program led to UNSCR 1540 in 2004, which puts additional obligations on member states.

Who was right? Had the Iraqis disarmed during the years of inspections so that there were no WMD left? It appeared that way for several years. Then, in 2009, when the new Iraqi government joined the Chemical Weapons Convention, Rogelio Pfirter, the director general of the new Organization to Prohibit Chemical Weapons (OPCW) announced, "Iraq submitted its initial declaration on 12 March 2009, and has declared two bunkers with filled and unfilled chemical weapons munitions, some precursors, as well as five former chemical weapons production facilities."[46] Yes, there were still some chemical weapons in Iraq. No one had found them despite the most intrusive inspection regime in human history.

A second question, whether the removal of Saddam would herald a more inclusive government in Iraq and a state capable of assuming new international responsibilities within the United Nations, also received a disturbing answer in 2014. The creation of an Islamic State (IS) out of large swathes of northern and western Iraq in 2014 showed the perils of collective action to disrupt an existing sovereign authority, however brutal. In September 2014, over 30 countries, including all the P5, came to a conference in Paris to discuss united action against a new collective threat to sovereign states. Russia, itself then subject to American and EU sanctions over Ukraine, attended, showing the grave issues IS had raised for all. The United Nations was only marginally involved.

The United Nations and the Iraq crises show diplomacy struggling to bring order to a world with important new features. From 1990 to 1991, it performed well, because the cause of the problem was clear, U.S. power was at its height, and sovereign states happened to align to produce an ad hoc solution. In 2003, the United Nations failed to be the forum where the world could agree on an issue of international compliance orchestrated through the United Nations. National rivalries ensured diplomacy took a back seat. Since then, though multipolarity has firmly taken hold in the world, the United Nations has not devised any new mechanisms to meet the needs of a changed world order. Iraq in 2014 seems more troublesome than ever.

SUGGESTIONS FOR FURTHER READING

1. The Charter of the United Nations, 1945, http://www.un.org/en/documents/charter/index.shtml.

2. Wiseman, Geoffrey, and Soumita Basu. "The United Nations." In *Diplomacy in a Globalizing World: Theories and Practices*, ed. Pauline Kerr and Geoffrey Wiseman. New York: Oxford University Press, 2012.

3. Mingst, Karen A., and Margaret P. Karns. *The United Nations in the 21st Century*, 3rd ed. Boulder, CO: Westview Press, 2007.

4. Knight, W. Andy, ed. *Adapting the United Nations to a Postmodern Era: Lessons Learned*, 2nd ed. New York: Palgrave Macmillan, 2005.

chapter 5

Regional Diplomacy, Summits, and the Gs

The Rise of Summitry

The UN Charter envisaged the use of regional arrangements and made clear that the Charter did not preclude such arrangements influencing diplomacy on issues like peace and security. Innovations in regional diplomacy have indeed taken shape throughout the world. Many are long-standing experiments in diplomacy that have developed into influential and effective organizations. Some have bloomed and faded, only to be reinvented in different configurations. Most reflect some recognition that the modern UN cannot address some problems as effectively as smaller groups of states with more common interests and with perhaps more urgency to act diplomatically.

THE NONALIGNED MOVEMENT

One trend that the UN also foresaw was the movement of self-determination and the creation of newly independent states in continents where there had been few. This created a certain common identity outside the two military blocs. The nonaligned movement (NAM), founded in 1961, showed at least a common interest of countries from all continents in trying to assert a new collective identity. The Group of 77 (G77) was formed among developing and newly independent states in the UN in 1964 and has since expanded to over 130 countries.

Both the NAM and G77 have persisted as loose groupings with membership growing to over 70 percent of the states in the world. But as countries became more active in the global economy and sought to attract foreign investment from many sources, states could align themselves less easily simply on the grounds of being nonaligned. Fidel Castro, with the ambition and capacity to seize a leadership role for Cuba, aligned himself more for economic than ideological reasons with the Soviet Union. But he also became a focal figure in the NAM with Cuba assuming the chair in 1979.The Soviet invasion of Afghanistan in 1979 saw him having to choose between supporting the Soviets and opposing an intervention that alarmed many in the NAM. He chose to stick with the Soviets.

The unwieldy bloc of seventy-seven gradually outlived its diplomatic usefulness, and regional groupings mostly based primarily on common interests in economic and commercial issues have taken its place. That the G77 still meets in global summits suggests that one of the faults of diplomacy is that clubs survive beyond their relevance. Nevertheless, the NAM does occasionally attract attention. The 2012 summit in Iran provided a forum for Egypt to support the Syrian opposition that led to a walk-out of the Syrian delegation.

The evolution of some other regional groups will be examined to assess how far each has added value to their members' diplomacy and how far they are a model for how collective diplomacy may develop.

THE EUROPEAN UNION

The European Union's (EU) origins go back over five decades, during which it has developed into the world's most advanced and complex institution of collective diplomacy. Like the UN, the early European experiments in regional diplomatic groups depended on the leadership of politicians. They sensed that diplomacy would not function effectively without new institutional arrangements and a focused vision of evolution. And the continuous nature of diplomacy was to be encapsulated in a system of meetings and permanent administration that would ensure that a culture of negotiation would become permanent.

Europe had a common cause after World War II. The continent needed to be reconstructed and such a reconstruction involved every aspect of diplomacy. Many were attracted to the example of the main liberator of war-torn Europe—the United States. Indeed, the term *United States of Europe* was first used by Winston Churchill, whose mother was American, in a speech he made on September 9, 1946, at the University of Zürich: "We must build a kind of United States of Europe. In this way only will hundreds of millions of toilers be able to regain the simple joys and hopes which make life worth living."[1]

The response of Europe was to confront the conflict and destruction of the continent after World War II through cooperation on economic and trade policy. The U.S. Marshall Plan and the NATO Charter were equally crucial diplomatic foundations for the future reconstruction of the continent. Fragmentation had led to continent-wide conflict twice in less than thirty years. And, perhaps most important for the prospects of a new diplomatic grouping, the United States was fully supportive of Europe becoming more capable and more united.

Just as the evolution of the UN in key areas has benefited from the ideas and leadership of smaller countries, several of the founding fathers of the European Union were from smaller countries. Robert Schuman was originally from Luxembourg, the crossroads of many European power exchanges, and Paul Henri Spaak was from Belgium. Schuman took up Churchill's cause and proposed a European assembly.

> Our century, that has witnessed the catastrophes resulting in the unending clash of nationalities and nationalisms, must attempt and succeed in reconciling nations in a supranational association. This would safeguard the diversities and aspirations of each nation while coordinating them in the same manner as the regions are coordinated within the unity of the nation.[2]

After conferences in The Hague in 1948, the Council of Europe gave effect to the idea of a supranational European assembly. The Council of Europe was created by the Treaty of London in 1949.

The original idea of the European Coal and Steel Community (ECSC) was also first proposed by Schuman, who was then the French Foreign Minister, in May 1950. He declared his aim was to "make war not only unthinkable but materially impossible."[3] Europe's first supranational economic arrangement was formally established in 1951 by the Treaty of Paris, signed not only by France and West Germany but also by Italy, Belgium, the Netherlands, and Luxembourg. Between these states, the ECSC would create a common market for coal and steel. The ECSC was governed by a new supranational authority headed by Jean Monnet, a French diplomat and former deputy secretary general of the League of Nations. Monnet had far bigger visions than the ECSC and in 1943 had written,

> There will be no peace in Europe, if the states are reconstituted on the basis of national sovereignty . . . The countries of Europe are too small to guarantee their peoples the necessary prosperity and social development. The European states must constitute themselves into a federation.[4]

The ECSC was merged with two other similar institutions in 1957 under the Treaty of Rome—the European Economic Community (EEC) and the European Atomic Energy Community (EURATOM)—with which it shared its membership and some institutions. In 1967, all institutions of the ECSC were merged with that of the EEC, but it still retained its own independent identity. However, in 2002, the original Treaty of Paris expired, and all the ECSC activities and resources were absorbed by the European Union. During its existence, the ECSC had succeeded in creating a common market but could not prevent the decline of the coal and steel industries.

So a diplomatic initiative produced unexpected results. What was conceived as a strategic way of sharing coal and steel took political wings. The institutions of the EEC saw the abolition of trade barriers, the creation of a single market, and the convergence of policies between member states as central to the group's growth. Dynamism would also be provided by extending the inclusiveness of the EU. For the first time in history, sovereign states would be encouraged to renounce sovereignty in important areas of policy in return for a common commitment to promote convergence, provide infrastructure help, and create common approaches to diplomacy. Today, the EU, through a cumulative series of treaties, has grown from the original six members to twenty-eight with the accession of Croatia in 2013. The treaties that have been the legally binding building blocks have pushed the EU forward in areas such as migration policy, a common currency (eighteen countries use the euro), and foreign and defense policy (the creation in 2010 of a new European External Action Service).

Diplomatically, the EU has evolved as an edifice with extensions, new floors, and new wiring and plumbing. A short survey of the treaties that have been agreed upon will describe the phases of the project: 1951, Treaty of Paris (ECSC); 1957, Treaty of Rome (EEC and EURATOM); 1972, Accession of the United Kingdom, Denmark, and Ireland; 1981, Accession of Greece; 1985, Accession of Spain and Portugal; 1985, Schengen Treaty; 1986, Single European Act Treaty; 1992, Treaty of Maastricht (establishing the European Union and the euro currency); 1995, Accession of Austria, Finland, and Sweden; 1997, Treaty of Amsterdam; 2001, Treaty of Nice; 2004, Accession of Czech Republic, Estonia, Cyprus, Latvia, Lithuania, Hungary, Malta, Poland, Slovenia, and Slovakia; 2007, Accession of Bulgaria and Romania; 2009 (signed in 2007), Treaty of Lisbon; and 2011, Accession of Croatia (realized in 2013).

The EU mirrored other diplomatic initiatives aimed at boosting collective security. The United States had also come to similar conclusions about Europe, and the Marshall Plan and the NATO alliance were initiatives designed to recast the diplomatic architecture alongside the EU. The NATO Charter, signed in 1949, formalized the wartime North Atlantic alliance into a commitment for collective defense. Article 5 of the charter states that an attack on one is an attack on all.

Despite many differences on policy issues with individual EU members, the United States has always been a strong supporter of the integration process in the EU. In 2013, just after British Prime Minister David Cameron announced his commitment to a referendum and a renegotiation of the United Kingdom's terms of membership, the senior U.S. State Department EU expert said the United States would regard with alarm any fragmentation of the EU: "We have a growing relationship with the EU as an institution, which has an increasing voice in the world, and we want to see a strong British voice in that EU. That is in America's interests. We welcome an outward-looking EU with Britain in it."[5]

The EU, as its own model acknowledges, has important features of supranational institutions that combine their activities with existing diplomatic institutions and mechanisms that provide for continuous diplomacy between member states. The main supranational bodies are the European Commission, the European Parliament (whose most significant power is over the budget), the European Council, the European Court, and the European Central Bank.

The EU has set the bar high for other regional groupings in collective governance. The single market achievement has been a unifying feature to promote other actions. But, as we shall see, the activities and joint development of EU competences in many other areas shows the EU in its most pioneering light as an exercise in diplomatic innovation. An important principle that has been developed is the division of competences between the supranational authorities and member states. This issue is at the core of diplomatic tensions that exist between the supranational institutions of the EU and the member states. The Treaty of Lisbon in 2009 clarified the division of competences between the EU and member states. It introduced a precise classification for the first time since the founding treaties, distinguishing between three main types of competence: exclusive competences, shared competences, and supporting competences. The Lisbon treaty also created a new legal entity, the European Union, which has legislative authority to exercise the competences conferred upon it to the full extent. Fundamental to the working of the organization as a diplomatic entity is the principle that the EU is only competent to act within the scope of the powers allocated to it. Any measures adopted by the EU institutions must be based on powers conferred in treaties. A summary of how these competences have evolved follows.

EU Competences

The EU's Exclusive Competences cover

- customs union,
- establishment of competition rules necessary for the functioning of the internal market,
- monetary policy for member states that use the euro,
- conservation of the biological resources of the sea as part of the common fisheries policy,
- common trading policy, and
- the conclusion of an international agreement when this is within the framework of EU legislation, when it is necessary to help the EU exercise an internal competence, or if there is a possibility of the common rules being affected or of their range being changed.

Joint Competence of EU and Member States

The EU and the member states are jointly responsible for

- the internal market;
- social policy with regard to specific aspects defined in the treaty;
- economic, social, and territorial cohesion;
- agriculture and fisheries, except for the conservation of the biological resources of the sea;
- the environment;
- consumer protection;
- transport;

(Continued)

(Continued)

- trans-European networks;
- energy;
- areas of freedom, security, and justice;
- joint security issues with regard to aspects of public health;
- research, technological development, and space; and
- development cooperation and humanitarian aid.

Member States' Exclusive Competence

The member states have exclusive competence in

- protection and improvement of human healthcare;
- industry;
- culture;
- tourism;
- education, professional training, youth, and sport;
- civil protection; and
- administrative cooperation.

Special Competences

The EU has special competences reserved to it in some areas.

- The coordination of economic and employment policies. It is required to define the broad direction to be followed by member states.
- The Common Foreign and Security Policy (CFSP). The EU has competence in all fields connected with the CFSP. It defines and implements this policy through the President of the European Council and the High Representative of the Union for Foreign Affairs and Security Policy, whose roles have been defined by the Treaty of Lisbon.
- The Flexibility Clause (Article 352 of the Rome Treaty). This clause enables the EU to act beyond the power of action conferred upon it by the treaties if the objective pursued so requires.[6]

THE EU AND DOMESTIC POLICIES

The EU is much more than a diplomatic organization. It frames and debates policies in many areas that have historically been the preserve of sovereign states. The EU's economic, social, regulatory, and financial policies are beneficial collectively to the member states. The policies that are implemented regularly through jointly funded budgets have made the EU the most integrated multinational bloc in the history of the world. Diplomacy over many decades has created a new diplomatic structure.

The EU now refers to these collective programs as solidarity policies (in regional, agricultural, and social affairs) and innovation policies, which provide joint projects in areas such as environmental protection, research and development, and energy. The EU funds these programs through an annual budget of more than €150 billion, which is derived from import duties of goods that are imported into the EU, a proportion of the value-added tax levied by member states, and from a budget contribution from each member state that is set at a maximum of 1.24 percent of the combined gross national income of all member states. The EU Commission has said that the average EU citizen paid only sixty-seven cents per day to finance the annual budget in 2010. The proposed resource spending is drawn up by the European Commission and requires unanimous approval from the member states and negotiation and agreement with the European Parliament. How is this money spent?

Solidarity Policies

The main purpose of the solidarity policies is to support the completion of the single market and to correct any imbalances in regions or industrial sectors. Through its regional aid, the EU continues to promote convergence between member states, helping the least developed countries and regions catch up more quickly with the EU average by improving conditions for growth and employment. It also aims to encourage regional competitiveness and cooperation between regions within the EU.

The EU applies resources to promote these policies with two structural funds—the European Regional Development Fund (ERDF) and the European Social Fund (ESF), which provides funding for vocational training and job creation initiatives. In addition to the structural funds, the EU operates a Cohesion Fund, which finances transport infrastructure and environmental projects in EU countries whose GDP per capita is lower than 90 percent of the EU average.

The Common Agricultural Policy (CAP)

Among the most ambitious objectives and most significant achievements of the EU has been to adapt the principles of the founders, based on security of coal and steel production, to the vital area of food production. The Europe that emerged from World War II was short of food, and large parts of the continent's productive capacity had been devastated by fighting. The aims of the CAP were set out in Article 39 of Treaty of Rome in 1957; the farming community's standard of living has been protected, markets have been stabilized, supplies reach consumers at reasonable prices, and farming infrastructure has been modernized. Consumers enjoy security of supply, and the prices of agricultural products are kept stable, protected from fluctuations on the world market. Indeed, the subsidies provided under CAP have been too successful. Production in many areas has grown far faster than consumption, placing a heavy burden on the EU budget. Agriculture has long been the dominant expenditure of the EU. In 2006, support for the sector represented over 46 percent of the EU budget, with this percentage set to decline to 32 percent in 2013.

Article 38 of the Treaty of Rome also establishes a common fisheries policy created to manage fish stock for the EU as a whole. The EU aims to reduce the overcapacity in fishing fleets, preserve fish stocks, and provide financial assistance to allow fishing communities to develop other economic activities.

The Social Dimension

EU legislation guarantees important social rights throughout the member states. Some of these rights are enshrined in the treaties—for example, the right of women and men to equal pay for equal work. Others are set out in directives concerning the protection of workers and essential safety standards.

In 1991, the EU adopted the Community Charter of Basic Social Rights, defining the rights that workers in the EU should enjoy. These include free movement, fair pay, the right to form associations and to undertake collective bargaining, the right to vocational training, and equal treatment of women and men. At Amsterdam in June 1997, this charter was integrated into EU treaties. The Charter of Fundamental Rights of the European Union, which was the product of a special European convention, was solemnly proclaimed at the time of the Treaty of Nice in 2001 but did not have any binding legal effect. Only in 2009, with the entry into force of the Treaty of Lisbon, did the charter become legally binding on EU institutions and national governments.

The Environment and Sustainable Development

The EU has also assumed responsibility in driving forward environmental policies with an action program called "Environment 2010: Our Future, Our Choice." The EU aims to mitigate and slow down climate change and global warming. The EU shares negotiating mandates with member states for international obligations in discussions on climate change and carbon emissions targets.

Technological Innovation

The founders of the EU rightly saw that Europe's future prosperity would depend on its ability to remain a world leader in technology. They saw the advantages to be gained from joint European research. In 1958, alongside the EEC, they established EURATOM. Its aim was for EU countries together to exploit nuclear energy for peaceful purposes. As part of this, the Joint Research Centre (JRC) was created, consisting of nine institutes to combine efforts across the EU. The EU's current research budget of over €50 billion is applied in areas such as health, food and agriculture, information and communications technology, nanoscience, energy, the environment, transport, and space.

Energy and Climate Change

Fossil fuels—oil, natural gas, and coal—account for 80 percent of energy consumption in the EU. The EU in 2014 imported 50 percent of its gas and oil, with a projected growth to 70 percent by 2025. Energy highlights the complexity of issues facing a multinational organization in negotiating a common position on issues like climate change. The European Commission has made ambitious commitments in energy policy, notwithstanding the economic turbulence it suffered in the global financial crisis. By 2020, the EU has committed to cutting its emissions to 20 percent below 1990 levels. The EU has offered to increase its emissions reduction to 30 percent by 2020 if other major emitting countries in the developed and developing worlds make further commitments.

THE EU INSTITUTIONS: A MODERN CRISIS OF SUPRANATIONAL DIPLOMACY?

Robert Schuman viewed supranational unions as a new stage in human development. They contrasted with nationalist-driven policies of the nineteenth and twentieth centuries and the destructive wars that resulted. In his speech to the United Nations General Assembly in 1948, Schuman saw the rolling back of nationalism as essential.

> Europe must unite to survive. A European public opinion is already being created. Already concrete efforts are taking shape that are marking the first steps on a new road. . . . We are, of course, only at the start of what is a great work. . . . Let us hope, God willing, that those who are presently hesitating will not take too long to be convinced about it. An economic union implies political cooperation. The ideas of a federation and a confederation are being discussed.[7]

In terms of supranational institutions, the EU's founders believed the organization was heralding a new era. The European Commission is the first modern governance group not administered by officials responsible to sovereign states. The Commission is the permanent secretariat of the EU with each area of responsibility headed by a Commissioner who is appointed by the member states. With the accession of Croatia in 2013, there are twenty-eight commissioners who form a multinational cabinet in promoting the EU's common agenda. The President of the Commission attends major multinational summits alongside the new EU President of the Council of Ministers—the important supranational appointment created under the Lisbon Treaty.

One of the earliest common EU institutions is the Court of Justice of the European Communities, created by the Treaty of Paris, which also established the ECSC in 1952. It has now been renamed the European Court of Justice (ECJ). It consists of one judge nominated by each member state and nine advocates general. The ECJ is the highest court of the EU in matters of EU law but not national law. It is not possible to appeal the decisions of national courts to the ECJ, but rather national courts refer questions of EU law to the ECJ, and their interpretations are applied in national cases. The court is an essential arbitrating instrument in the EU and has powers to sanction members for not applying rules. In practice, these powers have been seldom used. The court acts more as a part of the negotiating culture of the EU, part of its diplomacy of continuous negotiation. Ultimately, member states recognize they have to make their institutions work, and they need to show commitment to the wider cause. So the ECJ has an unusual type of authority in which the national courts often accept the supremacy of the ECJ and apply its rulings even against their own national governments.

The European Central Bank (ECB) is the sixth of the seven institutions of the EU as listed in the 1992 Maastricht Treaty. It is the central bank for the euro and administers the monetary policy of the eighteen EU member states (most recently, Latvia joined in 2014) that constitute the Eurozone, one of the largest common currency areas in the world. It is thus one of the world's most important central banks. The capital of the bank is owned by the central banks of all twenty-eight EU member states. The ECB was established by the Treaty of Amsterdam in 1998 and is headquartered in Frankfurt, Germany. It was cast in an unexpectedly crucial role during the Eurozone crisis, which has been one of the most enduring fundamental crises that the EU has faced.

The crossroads that the EU faces goes well beyond the powers of the ECB. The commitment of eighteen countries to a common currency has, of course, been recognized as an important pooling of sovereignty. But equally, the political decisions to enable such a common currency to fulfill all its functions have not been taken. Thus, each member of the Eurozone maintains its own fiscal policies, pension arrangements, and has widely diverging debt to GDP ratios. The global financial crisis exposed the vulnerabilities produced by the diversity and contradictions within a single market without a common currency. The result was a shock to the EU project. After over half a century of evolution, the EU, consisting of four of the world's ten largest economies, was forced collectively to seek the assistance of the International Monetary Fund in providing bailouts for its members.

The crisis highlighted the economic fragility not of the collective EU economy but of certain member states. The EU responded by taking collective measures to defend the sovereignty and viability of some of its member states. In addition to the loan bailout of Greece, the European Financial Stability Facility (EFSF), financed by contributions from members of the Eurozone to address the crisis, was established by the EU's twenty-seven member states in May 2010. The EFSF is authorized to borrow up to €440 billion. A separate entity, the European Financial Stabilization Mechanism (EFSM), a program reliant upon funds raised on the financial markets and guaranteed by the European Commission as collateral, has the authority to raise up to €60 billion.

As of mid-2013, the EFSM had been activated for Ireland and Portugal for a total amount up to €48.5 billion.

IS ACCOUNTABILITY A PART OF THE EU?

The Council of Ministers is the first branch of the bicameral EU legislative system; the other is Parliament. The Council consists of ministers from members states in different configurations. The membership depends on the issues discussed (e.g., agriculture and energy). The presidency of the Council rotates every six months, continuity being provided by the preceding and succeeding member state—the trios. The Council operates by qualified majority voting and shares legislative and budgetary powers with the Parliament. Thus, the Council inserts the elected officials of member states into the supranational process of the EU. The EU Commission proposes new legislation that is discussed by both the Council of Ministers and Parliament. The European Council comprises the heads of state or heads of government of the EU member states and was formerly recognized under the Lisbon Treaty. While the European Council has no formal legislative power, the Lisbon Treaty gives it responsibility for the general political direction and priorities of the EU.

The only directly elected institution of the EU is the European Parliament. The EU, therefore, has another feature of what would be seen as a normal range of institutions in a sovereign state. Together with the Council and the European Commission, it exercises the legislative functions of the EU, and it is unique among legislatures in the world. The European Parliament is currently composed of 751 members, who represent the second-largest democratic electorate in the world and the largest transnational electorate with some 400 million eligible voters.

Since 1979, the Parliament has been directly elected every five years by universal suffrage. However, turnout at European Parliament elections has fallen steadily and has been under 50 percent since 1999. In 2014, it was 42.54 percent of all European voters and was under 50 percent in eighteen out of twenty-seven member states. In 2014, the elections showed strong support for anti-EU parties in several major members, such as France and the United Kingdom. The U.K. prime minister seemed to accept the end of new ambition for the EU: "We need an approach that recognizes that Brussels has got too big, too bossy, too interfering. We need more for nation states. It should be nation states wherever possible and Europe only where necessary."[8] The French president said the EU had become "remote and incomprehensible."[9]

The European Parliament has legislative power over approximately two-thirds of the EU's policy agenda. On some questions (e.g., taxation or industrial and agricultural policy), the European Parliament gives only an advisory opinion, known as the consultation procedure. And the Parliament does not formally possess legislative initiative such as exists in most national parliaments of EU member states. The Parliament is known as the first institution of the EU since it is mentioned first in the treaties and has diplomatic precedence within the EU. It likewise has equal control over most of the EU budget with the Council, with the exception of agriculture. Finally, the European Commission, the executive body of the EU, is accountable to Parliament. The Lisbon Treaty gives the European Council the power to nominate a candidate for President of the Commission, "taking account of elections to the European Parliament."[10] Parliament has the right to approve new members of the Commission, and can force the entire Commission to resign through a vote of no confidence. This requires two-thirds of those voting and a majority of the total membership of the Parliament. Parliament threatened to use the power against the Commission headed by Jacques Santer in 1999 over allegations of corruption.

THE EU'S SUCCESS IN DIPLOMACY

The EU's success in diplomatic terms cannot purely be judged in terms of internal achievements. In the decades of evolution, it created an interdependent group of sovereign states in a defined contiguous territory. Collectively, the EU consists of over 500 million people and represents over 25 percent of the world's GDP. It has struck a chord that has resonated throughout many countries of different ethnic, economic, and political backgrounds and has shown that collective diplomacy can be more coherent than national. There are no precedents to predict how the EU might develop. As Vivien Schmidt has noted,

> It is the first region-state, meaning a regional union of nation-states which have over the years pooled together more and more areas of sovereignty, eliminated most of their internal borders as they massively extended their external ones through new memberships, and merged their markets.[11]

It is indeed the first of its kind.

First, it produced a successful regional economic model that broke down internal barriers, allowed workers to move across borders, and provided assistance to less affluent regions. It did not promote single political ideologies and has continued its collective experiment despite having many forceful leaders of national governments. It was a model of establishing a negotiation culture, taking account of national differences, and its formative years were during the Cold War when different power blocs dominated diplomacy.

Second, the EU has also provided an attractive political model over different periods of history. During its early years, it did not define what its membership criteria were. In 1963, the powers of veto were used by President de Gaulle to exclude the United Kingdom. Yet the British joined in 1973 alongside Ireland and Denmark. Spain and Portugal, though founding members of

NATO, were not admitted until they established democratic institutions. The criteria for membership needed to be defined more precisely after the end of the Cold War as many new applicants appeared. The membership terms, known as the Copenhagen Criteria, were defined at the Copenhagen Council of Ministers in June 1993. The membership criteria have three components:

- Stable institutions guaranteeing democracy, the rule of law, human rights, and respect for and protection of minorities
- A functioning market economy and the capacity to cope with competition and market forces in the EU
- The ability to take on and implement effectively the obligations of membership, including adherence to the aims of political, economic, and monetary union[12]

The EU's recent crises in governance and economic management provide a case study in halfway houses. Diplomatically, the arguments for maintaining the EU as a collective entity remain strong. The drive for convergence and collective economic policy has highlighted the paradoxes of semisovereignty. When conditions are tough, the lowest performer has the capacity to drag down the highest. Indeed, the indicators that determine EU policy—economic and social statistics—are still collected nationally because many functioning parts of EU economic policy, such as social security benefits, depend on national states. In mid-2013, unemployment rates were 12.5 percent in the Eurozone collectively, yet Germany had 5.2 percent while in Greece and Spain rates were over 27 percent.

The common euro currency has encouraged markets to judge the EU as a whole. An adjustment of the value of one Eurozone member's currency is, of course, not available where there are seventeen other states using the same unit. The very diversity of disagreements visible in the EU between the ECB, national banks, the EU commissioners, and national political leaders mean public and business perceptions of crises are exacerbated. The reluctance of political entities to relinquish control of such issues as fiscal policy, pensions, and wage rates is something that diplomacy can do little about. As Vivien Schmidt has commented, the EU model has set the objective of further integration but "for real economic governance, the EU would need to create an ongoing process of macroeconomic policy formation, tied to the budgetary cycle, as national governments normally do."[13]

On foreign policy, the EU has used its collective diplomatic clout judiciously in areas such as the Middle East peace process, Iran's nuclear program, protection against pirates off Somalia, and in Kosovo peacekeeping. But member states differ significantly on core issues, including new membership admissions. Turkey submitted its bid to join the EU in 2005 but has made slow progress. The United Kingdom and Italy are strong supporters, but Germany and France (under Sarkhozy) remained opposed. Spain and Greece, among others, do not support the majority EU position that Kosovo should be recognized as an independent state. The record of the EU in agreeing on responses to major crises is also not impressive. Only the United Kingdom, Spain, and Poland joined the United States in actively supporting the invasion of Iraq in March 2003. In 2011, Germany abstained in the United Nations Security Council (UNSC) when France and the United Kingdom sought approval of NATO implementation of UNSC Resolution (UNSCR) 1973 to protect civilians in the Libyan conflict.

The world that created the EU has also changed. Through the 1970s and 1980s, the attractions of a country acquiring an EU identity were considerable: the blue flag with gold stars, access to the single market of over 300 million consumers, functioning regulatory institutions, and the institution's internal 24/7 diplomacy-enhancing national efforts. There appeared to be a tangible diplomatic objective—solidifying Europe for democracy and free enterprise, in contrast to the Soviet bloc to the east. After the collapse of the Soviet Union and the disappearance of barriers, countries emerged looking for new identities. The EU set some minimum standards and the sovereignty of those joining was willingly diluted. The EU also provided a useful consensus-building piece of diplomacy for newly constituted democracies such as Poland, the Czech Republic, Slovakia, Romania, and Bulgaria. The EU accession process itself helped unify sparring political factions. But time has moved on, and perceptions of the EU's objectives vary greatly. The utility of the EU for Malta or Cyprus is vastly different from how it is perceived in Germany or France. And the United Kingdom, which is not part of the Eurozone but is a major global economy, sees the organization through yet another prism.

Equally, the threat of war within Europe has declined, and the EU project has realized already the most obvious benefits of pooling sovereignty. Meanwhile, the growth of the Brazil, Russia, India, China, and South Africa (BRICS) and other non-EU economies keen to do business in Europe has proved alluring to EU members. In 2012, German exports to non-EU countries rose by over 10 percent while those to EU fell by 5 percent. Nevertheless, the shift can be overstated. The United Kingdom's exports to Ireland alone in 2011 were equal to its exports to China, India, and Russia combined. The EU project has to make some new consensus decisions. Are there to be new chapters in integration or federalism? Will the EU regain momentum, or has it plateaued so that it will have to fight to maintain its existing achievements? The final question is whether the Eurozone crisis can be seen as a force for deeper integration, with the extension of shared liability via rescue mechanisms and new economic governance rules, or for deeper division such as between Northern and Southern Europe or between Eastern Europe and the rest.

THE EU AS A DIPLOMATIC SERVICE

It is against this background that the Lisbon Treaty in 2009 inaugurated a new integrated External Action Service (EAS) for the EU, which is in effect a collective diplomatic service without the name. The Lisbon Treaty also established a President of the European Council with a renewable two-and-a-half-year term and a High Representative for foreign affairs and security policy with a five-year term.

The EAS will eventually infuse the diplomatic community with another six thousand diplomats. The treaty was debated at a high point of EU confidence in 2007 when nothing seemed beyond the organization. For the first time in history, diplomats from individual sovereign states will serve in the same capitals and be accredited to the same states alongside diplomats representing a regional diplomatic grouping to which those same states belong. This was perhaps a natural development. The EU appears to have many of the attributes of a diplomatic actor. It tries to promote a common foreign policy, has a large overseas aid budget, and has collective responsibility and competence over issues like trade policy.

Catherine Ashton, an existing member of the EU Commission and of the unelected British House of Lords, was appointed in November 2009 as the High Representative. She described her functions as "to make EU foreign policy more consistent and coherent."[14] The EAS will not automatically harmonize the views of all EU members. But progress has been made. Past successes have included peacekeeping in the Balkans and organizing joint patrols to protect shipping from pirates off the Horn of Africa. The EU is a member of the Quartet—alongside the United Nations, the United States, and Russia—which is working for peace in the Middle East. And Baroness Ashton has chaired the UNSC permanent members plus Germany group negotiating with Iran on its nuclear program. The EU and its member states are the world's largest aid donor, so there ought to be much more that a collective diplomatic presence can do.

Yet EU common diplomacy does not function quite as well in practice as the organograms and press briefings might suggest. In 2013, the government of Mali appealed to France to prevent its collapse in the face of Islamic insurgency. The African Union's delay in organizing a military force appeared to be handing a victory to the insurgents. Despite repeated calls from France to members of the EU, only a handful of members offered airlift support and none offered troops on the ground. The EU now envisages two full time battle groups that would be deployed in such crises at short notice, but due to lack of contributions this has been dropped to one. Nevertheless, the EU is taking on some military training missions in Africa.

The EAS will generally have higher pay levels than national diplomatic services, and up to one-third of its staff will be recruited from former diplomats of member states. Another third is to come from the Commission and one-third from the old secretariat of the Council of Ministers. The first career head of the EAS, the executive secretary general, was the former ambassador of France to Washington, Pierre Vimont.

Box 5-1 **Top EU Delegations**

The EU's top 10 diplomatic delegations in terms of staff numbers in 2013 were as follows:

Ankara (137)

Beijing/Hong Kong (116)

Moscow (102)

Belgrade (100)

Ramallah/Tel Aviv (97)

Kiev (93)

Sarajevo (92)

New Delhi (87)

Washington (86)

Nairobi (85)

Source: EU Observer, "Turkey and China Host Biggest EU Outposts," http://euobserver.com/enlargement/116052.

The EU has already established a large number of missions, many of which had been posts of the EU Commission reporting to its former external affairs commissioner, who is now replaced by Baroness Ashton. They are still called delegations, not embassies. This begs the question what changes to staff the member states are making in these same capitals. Many national diplomatic services have been cutting staff and now will pay a collective €500 million for funding the EAS. Major member states are not likely to reduce their presence in capitals just because the EU has come to town. In 2013, the United Kingdom had 270 diplomatic staff in Washington, 245 in Beijing, and 230 in Moscow. The numbers for France were 421 in Washington, 305 in Beijing, and 224 in Moscow.

These numbers do not tell the whole story. Member states' embassies, like those of the United Kingdom and France, include diplomats and consular staff. The EU does not do consular or visa work because it is not a state. And the EAS has not resolved turf battles with the Commission, whose officials retain responsibilities for EU enlargement and development aid. Beyond this, there are some odd features of staffing priorities. The EU has forty-three people in Barbados, thirty-three in Fiji, and seventy-seven in Nicaragua, which prompted members of the European Parliament to ask if they were there to enjoy the sunshine.

Like a national diplomatic service, the EAS is expanding as new opportunities present themselves. The EU is pushing for greater access to all of the UN's diplomatic mechanisms through its enhanced observer status, including the right to vote alongside full members. In 2013, it signed an establishment agreement—a template for diplomatic relations—for a new embassy in Myanmar. Iran is a future possibility if tensions relax. Member states have shown interest in colocating some of their embassies with the EAS in single compounds, called Europe houses, to save money. Several EU countries already operate out of the same building in Tanzania, and there are plans for a pan-EU compound in Afghanistan.

Case Study

EU Case Studies

Although the EU has become a region state, the nation-state is never far away. Member states themselves lobby fiercely for positions in the EU administration and EAS. The United Kingdom has a published target aiming to secure 10 percent of senior positions in the service. My own EU experience spanned two decades. From 1979 to 1980, I was private secretary to the British EU ambassador. The period was dominated by Prime Minister Thatcher's aim to secure the United Kingdom a better deal on the EU budget. U.K. diplomats used their skills and twisted diplomatic arms to deliver on a domestic issue that went to the heart of the EU, but did not suggest that in the early years of its membership the United Kingdom was truly *communautaire*. Hard-edged negotiations, changing the rules of the club, and lobbying officials to gain advanced warning of decisions were the core activities. Domestic issues predominated, and our staffing reflected this. Our own post included a generous mixture of officers from the Bank of England, the Treasury, and the Departments of Trade and Energy, reinforced on a daily basis from London. A sovereign state behaving as a sovereign state.

From 1997 to 2000, I participated in numerous EU working groups on issues such as the India-Pakistan nuclear explosions and the Nuclear Nonproliferation Treaty review conference. The EU usefully coordinated positions (called Common Positions or Joint Actions), issued statements, and agreed to vote as a bloc in the United Nations. In 1998, the United Kingdom assumed the six-month rotating presidency of the EU, a long-standing role of nation-states in the EU that has driven short-term agendas for the group. As head of the United Kingdom's nonproliferation department, I chaired a group of experts on arms export licensing that produced the EU code of conduct on arms exports. It was a U.K. government priority and designed to produce a step forward in ethical foreign policy. The EU provided a ready-made forum for diplomacy. We produced an agreement that was a forerunner of the UN Arms Trade Treaty of 2013—a good example of an EU practice leading to global action.

If the EU has undoubtedly made a difference to diplomacy, it has also, like the UN, created a new bureaucracy with perks to be defended. On many visits to Brussels, I marveled at the conditions of those working in the permanent bureaucracy. The various cafeterias, heavily subsidized, surpassed the quality of the food of the investment bank's staff canteen in London where I had worked two years earlier. No meeting ever took place without beautifully served coffee or tea through the catering services. Dining rooms for special meetings were luxuriously elegant, and shops and duty-free arrangements for EU staff were also highly prized. It was a club for affluent diplomats. In addition, the six weeks of summer shut down gave leave entitlements to EU staff well in excess of the normal in the United Kingdom.

Another of my posts, Cuba, involved regular coordination with other EU missions in Havana. Part of the EU culture is that missions of EU member states meet regularly to coordinate work in third-country capitals. They contribute to the drafting

(Continued)

(Continued)

and implementation of formally agreed diplomatic strategy binding on the EU, and position papers that set the guidelines for diplomatic activity. And such diplomacy has consequences. Our diplomatic work in Cuba was greatly influenced by The Common Position the EU adopted on Cuba in 1996. It committed all EU members diplomatically to a policy of critical and constructive engagement with Cuba, with full cooperation conditional on greater openness in political and economic rights in Cuba.

THE EU BALANCE SHEET

As a diplomatic actor, the EU is an odd model. It has little in the way of democratic accountability, and its record suggests an à la carte method of conducting diplomacy. It is also hard to see the activities of the EU as backed by popular legitimacy. The Council of Ministers and Parliament are involved in major decisions involving diplomacy. The Council takes decisions by weighted or qualified majority voting according to a system devised and modified by several EU treaties including the latest, the Lisbon Treaty of 2009. Anything less than majority in the EU means, of course, some individual sovereign states disagree. The President of the Council and the High Representative for foreign affairs are elected by no one. Neither are the members of the EU Commission.

How far have the leaders of the EU responded to the vision for Europe of Schuman and Monnet, and how far do they generate positive public diplomacy? A Pew Research Global Attitudes Project survey from May 2012 gave a grim picture. Conducted in the middle of a Eurozone crisis, it may overstate the mood. But the malaise with the EU had spread well beyond the immediate member states in the eye of the storm. Pew found that

> across the eight European Union member countries surveyed, a median of only 34% think that European economic integration has strengthened their country's economy. Indeed, majorities or near majorities in most nations now believe that the economic integration of Europe has actually weakened their economies. This is the opinion in Greece (70%), France (63%), Britain (61%), Italy (61%), the Czech Republic (59%) and Spain (50%). Only in Germany (59%) do most people say that their country has been well served by European integration.[15]

The EU model, while having left an indelible mark on the history of continuous diplomacy, faces an uncertain future. There are few who now see the EU as likely to reach higher levels of integration. But it does offer another option for diplomacy of member states, adding some versatility that is often convenient. As the British foreign secretary said during a visit to Germany in 2013, "Finding the right balance between integration in Europe for those who need it, and flexibility where it is best for our economies and our democracies, is the great challenge of German and British diplomacy over the next few years."[16] What happens in the EU will be closely watched by other evolving regional groups.

THE AFRICAN UNION

The African Union (AU) replicates several features of the EU. When launched in 2002, it was a conscious remodeling of a former organization—the Organization of African Unity (OAU)—that had been founded in 1963. Postcolonial leaders like Kwame Nkrumah of Ghana and Julius Nyerere of Tanzania had long called for Africa to unite and create a United States of Africa. But the OAU was widely seen by its members as having failed the continent during some of the worst atrocities committed in modern history. The objectives of the AU were ambitious. The AU's first president, Thabo Mbeki of South Africa, promised that the Union would liberate the African people from their misery, abject poverty, and perennial underdevelopment. Kofi Annan, Secretary General of the UN and from Ghana himself, struck a note of realism and urged the member states "not to mistake hope for achievement."[17] Perhaps inauspiciously, in view of future events, many of the key decisions to wind up the OAU and establish the AU were taken in 1999 at a summit in Sirte, Libya, the hometown of Muammar Gaddafi and where he was killed in October 2011. Gaddafi had built up wide support among African leaders, in particular from Nelson Mandela.

Africa has a long history of attempts at integration. The Southern African Customs Union (SACU), which was established in 1910, remains the oldest functioning regional organization involving Botswana, Lesotho, Namibia, South Africa and Swaziland. But the vast area of Africa, its enormous diversity in resources, and cultural and ethnic history has made significant integration a formidable challenge. Currently, there are fifty-five sovereign states in the territory of Africa, which is bigger than the area of the United States, China, India, Japan, and all of Europe combined. Unsurprisingly, the sovereign states have found more in common economically with their immediate regional neighbors than with the whole of the continent. So several smaller group organizations supplement the activities of the AU. The oldest, the fifteen-member Economic Community of West African States (ECOWAS), was established in 1975. The Economic Community of Central African States (ECCAS) that links eleven countries was set up in 1983, and a Common Market for Eastern and Southern Africa (COMESA) that covers nineteen African countries was founded in 1993. The Southern Africa Development Community (SADC) has thirteen member countries and was established in 1993.

The Constitutive Act of the AU, agreed at a summit in Togo in July 2002, governs the AU's behavior. All countries on the continent are full members with the exception of Morocco, which has observer status because of its dispute over the territory of Western Sahara. Its core principles include sovereign equality and interdependence among member states, popular participation in the AU's activities, the establishment of a common African defense policy, the prohibition of the use of force or threat to use force among its members, and noninterference in the internal affairs of another. The AU is also intended to accelerate the political and economic integration of the continent, promote and defend African common positions on issues of interest to Africa, achieve peace and security in Africa, and promote democratic institutions, good governance, and human rights.

The African Union is made up of both political and administrative bodies. The highest decision-making organ is the Assembly of the African Union, and consists of all the heads of state or government of member states of the AU. The AU also has a representative body, the Pan-African Parliament, which consists of 265 members elected by the national parliaments of the AU member states. The AU's secretariat, the African Union Commission, is based in Addis Ababa, Ethiopia, where the permanent representatives of member states deal with day to day business.

The institutions of the AU certainly have clear similarities with the EU. And the AU has developed a flexible format where decisions are made. In both the assembly and in the executive council, decisions can be either based on consensus or a two-thirds or simple majority. And Africa is coming together diplomatically when it is also attracting more attention for its economic potential. But it is still not on track to integrate economically. There is little economic interdependence between African countries, and the trade relations are still dominated by flows to other continents. An AU study in 2011 called "Action Plan for Boosting Intra African Trade" lamented the lack of intra-African trade. It recognized that other regions did much better, and this assisted the process of integration. "Intra⊠African trade stands at around 10 percent compared to 60 percent, 40 percent, 30 percent intra⊠regional trade that has been achieved by Europe, North America and ASEAN respectively."[18]

If the AU is not likely to emulate the EU in economic matters, how far has it lived up its Constitutive Act in terms of preservation of peace and security in Africa and promotion of human rights? In 2003, the AU deployed its first peacekeeping troops to Burundi, but it was a hesitant and ineffective move. The AU initially dispatched a sixty-member AU Mission as observers in Sudan (AMIS) in the spring of 2004, which two months later the AU Assembly revised upward to eighty. In 2006, the AU deployed up to 7,000 military personnel in Western Sudan, most of whom were from Nigeria and Rwanda. The AU/UN hybrid peacekeeping operation in Darfur, referred to by its acronym UNAMID, was established in July 2007. Its mandate has been extended regularly. The AU was also active in pressing for a peaceful solution to the Libyan conflict in 2011, though the prominent role of Gaddafi in the founding of the AU diminished their status with the rebels. On human rights abuses, the report is mixed. The AU has moved from being a supporter of the utility of the International Criminal Court (ICC) to a more skeptical position, disconcerted with the apparent concentration of ICC attention on crimes committed in Africa. Nevertheless, with 800 million cell phones in the continent now, the AU is well placed to tap into a pan-Africanism, which was the dream of its founders over half a century ago.

In contrast to the EU, the AU has included all countries in the continent as members. Yet it did not start with a nucleus of consensus as was the case in Western Europe. It now has to try to find ways of building common positions and coordinated diplomacy in a continent with a record of civil conflicts, border disputes, and rivalries between the main economies such as Nigeria and South Africa. Rich in resources of every mineral and a major producer of fossil fuels, the AU's operations are now being encouraged by emerging powers from other continents. China has led the surge of investors, with generous deals necessitated by the voracious demands of the Chinese economy. Chinese diplomacy has been underpinned with a fat checkbook—the new African Union headquarters in Addis Ababa was constructed with $200 million of Chinese money.

Africa has progressed as a diplomatic force since the largely ceremonial, status-conscious organization of the OAU in the 1960s. The AU offers an alternative diplomatic avenue to bilateral diplomacy with coordination in Addis Ababa or through the UN. It has been remarkably decisive in expressing disapproval when elections have been rigged or elected governments removed from power. In its brief history, it has suspended member states for perceived anti-democratic practices, including Niger, Madagascar, Mali, and the Ivory Coast. It has also contributed to nation rebuilding in Somalia with peacekeeping forces operating alongside those of Kenya. Since its foundation, peaceful changes of power through elections have been achieved and the AU has played its part. It offers a similar incentive to good domestic behavior as the EU has provided for its members. For the future, the AU has talked of a customs union, a common central bank, and a common currency within ten years. For the moment, the AU is still work in progress, but its ambition to show that African countries can work collectively themselves on Africa's problems is well on the way to being realized.

ASEAN

If the AU has evolved quickly into political diplomacy, then its main Asian counterpart, The Association of Southeast Asian Nations (ASEAN), has been more active in economic and commercial integration. ASEAN is an organization of ten countries located in Southeast Asia that was formed in August 1967 and had as its original members Indonesia, Malaysia, the Philippines, Singapore, and Thailand. It is headquartered in Jakarta.

ASEAN was formed at the peak of China's cultural revolution and its support for several communist movements in Southeast Asia. There was also widespread fear that the United States would withdraw as a strategic guarantor to countries in the region after its experience in Vietnam. So the noncommunist countries came together with the objective stated by Thailand's foreign minister, Thanat Khoman, "to be master of their own house and to enjoy the inherent right to decide their own destiny."[19] Apart from Indonesia, the organization's founding states were dependent on either Britain or the United States for their defense. Additional members have since joined. Brunei was admitted in 1984, Vietnam in 1995, Laos and Myanmar in 1997, and Cambodia in 1999.

The member states of ASEAN had few common features in their governments. Many were led by the military, while others were pursuing a path to democracy with governments focused on economic development. The region has generally seen steady economic growth with little ethnic conflict in a postcolonial setting. The main feature of ASEAN that has influenced its operations is the absence from the original organization of the big Asian powers. China, Japan, South Korea, India, and Pakistan have never been members, suggesting there has not been a common recognition of the advantages of regional integration. The region still reflects competing ambitions of several large, but so far not overwhelming, states that have preferred to form alliances to bolster their power rather than committing their sovereignty to a full cooperative project.

ASEAN did not move beyond a purely diplomatic organization for many years. It was only in 1992 that harmonizing tariff policies and moving towards a free trade area was agreed in the ASEAN Free Trade Agreement (AFTA). And, unlike in the EU, AFTA does not apply a common external tariff to imported goods to the member states. ASEAN members have revised their agenda for economic cooperation, realizing that their capacity to reach out to giants of the region could bring mutual benefits. The regional financial crisis in 1997 and 1998 was for ASEAN what the demise of the OAU was to the African Union. It gave an impetus for renewed attention to the benefits of integration and demonstrated dramatically the region's shared interests and vulnerabilities. In particular, ASEAN saw the advantage in greater financial cooperation with the bigger regional powers like Japan, South Korea, and China. This led to the establishment of the ASEAN Plus 3 finance ministers' group and related structures, such as the Chiang Mai Initiative and the Asian Bond Markets Initiative. The ASEAN Plus 3 initiative began in 1996, incorporating China, Japan, and South Korea, and the first leaders' meetings were held in 1996 and 1997, signaling that the United States' diplomatic influence or focus on the region was declining.

ASEAN now also sponsors an East Asia Summit, a pan-Asian forum attended annually by leaders of sixteen countries in East Asia and the region. The members of the summit are all ten members of ASEAN plus China, Japan, South Korea, India, Australia, and New Zealand, and it met formally for the first time in Malaysia in 2005. This group represents nearly half of the world's population, and has so far discussed such issues as trade, energy, and security.

In October 2010, Russia and the United States were formally invited to participate as full members, and the presidents of both countries now attend East Asia summits.

The tone of the ASEAN Charter, though professing to move closer to an EU-style community, is grounded on the principle of noninterference in internal affairs. There has been no attempt to take joint foreign policy initiatives, and the ASEAN group has rarely acted together. Does ASEAN show consensus building or diplomacy, or a group that sweeps problems under the rug? It has been seen as both. Unlike other regional diplomatic groupings, ASEAN is obligation light. As Joshua Kurlantzik of the Council on Foreign Relations observed in 2012,

> The ASEAN Secretariat in Jakarta runs with a skeleton staff one-tenth of the size of the European Commission's and also smaller than the African Union's. Unlike the African Union, ASEAN possesses no peacekeeping force; unlike the Organization of American States (OAS), it has no strong mechanism for enforcing human rights; unlike the Arab League, ASEAN's top leaders attract little attention from the international media; and unlike the European Union, ASEAN has continually failed to adhere to commitments for deeper economic integration and broader free trade.[20]

Yet ASEAN meets regularly, another feature of the ASEAN way of diplomacy. According to the ASEAN Charter, which entered into force in December 2008, ASEAN holds at least two summits a year, each hosted by the member state holding the ASEAN chairmanship. In practice, the first of the year's summits is devoted to ASEAN affairs and the second to ASEAN's relations with its neighbors and the wider world. Some ASEAN leaders have proposed that voting should be introduced to increase the speed and efficiency of decision making, and that more issues should be aired where in the past noninterference had prevented discussion. The United States has taken note of ASEAN's role in a region where the United States now wishes to show itself a Pacific power. In November 2012, President Obama attended both the ASEAN–U.S. summit and the East Asia Summit.

The treatment of Myanmar illustrates the ASEAN way. During years of military rule, the country was never sanctioned or suspended by ASEAN. As Burma, Myanmar had been a prominent diplomatic force in the region and in the world. U Thant, then the Union of Burma's permanent representative to the UN and former secretary to the prime minister, was elected Secretary General of the UN in 1961, a position he held for ten years. Among the Burmese to work at the UN when he was secretary general was a young official, Aung San Suu Kyi, who went on to become the winner of the 1991 Nobel Peace Prize. Myanmar was admitted to ASEAN in 1997, despite the military rulers' refusal to recognize free elections held in 1990. Since then, political reforms have begun. In 2011, ASEAN issued a statement that it hoped Myanmar would continue on the path to democracy, and it nominated Myanmar for the chair of ASEAN in 2014. Meanwhile, the United States and the EU had used tougher diplomatic means to encourage change—they had long imposed sanctions to apply pressure on the military leaders. ASEAN left most of the diplomacy to others but the desired result was achieved.

In another challenge to how the modern ASEAN will evolve, the member states have become embroiled in territorial disputes. The Philippines, Vietnam, and Cambodia all dispute sovereignty over several small islands, with offshore oil discoveries a factor in the claims. China is also involved in several disputes, and the United States is now asserting its presence in the region. Even India has expressed its concern about ensuring freedom of navigation in the waters of the region. ASEAN now has a chance to prove it can be a productive diplomatic forum for solving disputes that divide but also potentially damage all their members. The former ASEAN Secretary General Surin Pitsuwan warned that "the South China Sea could evolve into another Palestine"[21] if countries did not try harder to defuse, rather than inflame, tensions.

These political disputes have developed at a time when ASEAN has an ambitious economic agenda, targeting the creation of an ASEAN Economic Community by 2015. ASEAN has also concluded free trade agreements with China, Korea, Japan, Australia, New Zealand, and India. In 2012, intraregional trade and trade with China accounted for more than 37 percent of ASEAN's total trade, up from 26 percent in 2000. ASEAN now has observer status and is a "partner of dialogue" with the UN and has announced it will promote a joint bid to host the 2025 Soccer World Cup.

ASEAN has a strong platform on which to build. The larger powers of Asia still prefer to do their diplomacy bilaterally but increasingly share common interests in preserving economic stability. Two major neighbors—India and Pakistan—barely interact commercially with each other; bilateral trade is only 5 percent of their total. In comparison, ASEAN has developed impressively and performs its central functions well, giving the smaller diplomatic actors a collective identity. That said, ASEAN is an organization yet to prove its diplomatic worth in testing times.

LATIN AMERICA

If the dynamic of regional cooperation in Southeast Asia has been to provide economic and political solidarity against powerful neighbors, in Latin America, the common denominator in many of the regional initiatives since World War II has been the relationship of the region with the United States. Simon Bolivar, in the early nineteenth century, had originated the idea of a grouping of newly independent Latin American states, and in the late nineteenth and early twentieth centuries, the United States also supported the concept of a Pan-American Union. One of the oldest regional groupings of the twentieth century, which owed much to U.S. diplomatic efforts to defend the continent against communism, was the Organization of American States (OAS). It was founded in Bogota in 1948 and has its headquarters in Washington. In the words of Article 1 of the charter, the goal of the OAS members was "to achieve an order of peace and justice, to promote their solidarity, to strengthen their collaboration, and to defend their sovereignty, their territorial integrity, and their independence."[22]

The OAS, like the UN Charter, had a strong security agenda that was a priority for the United States post-World War II. And the turbulent history of the continent since 1948 showed that the United States' main interest was to maintain stability and to counter what were seen as potentially hostile interests to the United States—a modern exposition of the Monroe doctrine. U.S. ambitions to promote free trade in the region did not produce a lasting monument until the NAFTA agreement of the 1990s. But since then, Latin American regional ambitions have gained momentum.

One lasting problem the region has experienced is the political and economic rivalry between the largest countries—Brazil, Mexico, Argentina, and Colombia. In 2012, intraregional trade made up only 27 percent of total trade in South and Central America, compared to 63 percent in Europe and 52 percent in Asia. The dissimilar economic and political characteristics of the states have also been obstacles to Bolivar's dream. The oil wealth of a few countries, such as Venezuela and Brazil, and the difficulty of establishing representative democracy in face of military interventions have stood in the way of cooperation. *Competitive authoritarianism* is a term that describes many of the features common to Latin American governance. Yet one issue where Latin America can claim to have been a diplomatic pioneer was over the issue of nuclear proliferation. The shock of the Cuban missile crisis in 1962 and the decisions of Brazil and Argentina to renounce nuclear weapons provided the basis for the 1967 Treaty of Tlatelolco, creating the first nuclear weapons free zone in the world.

Yet this lumpy progress and the global ambitions of states like Brazil and Mexico have not prevented diplomatic efforts at regional integration. The yearning for a regional diplomatic impact has persisted, spurred no doubt by the successes of other continents. Latin America could not reasonably be the only part of the world without a collective voice. Progress in creating a regional grouping now has its most credible face in the Union of South American Nations (UNASUR/UNASUL) headquartered in Quito.

Founded formally in 2008, UNASUR is currently a junior partner in the world with its first objective being to integrate previous subregional organizations called Mercosur (a free trade organization of Brazil, Argentina, Uruguay, and Paraguay) and the Andean Community (Bolivia, Colombia, Ecuador, and Peru). In December 2010, Uruguay became the ninth state to ratify the UNASUR treaty, meaning it entered into force in March 2011. The organization has plans to locate a South American parliament in Cochabamba, Bolivia, while the headquarters of its bank, the Bank of the South, will be in Caracas, Venezuela. It has a wish list of cooperation projects in areas such as defense and security, but it is too early to judge whether past differences will be overcome.

While the continent can claim a strong historical pedigree in promoting early models of regional organizations, Latin America continues to show more appetite for forming new groupings than in making them do anything effective. Even as the foundation stones of UNASUR are being put in place, parallel organizations are taking shape. CELAC (the Community of Latin American and Caribbean States) was founded in 2010 under the leadership of the former Venezuelan President Hugo Chavez. He conceived it as an alternative grouping to the OAS and excluding the United States and Canada. Unlike the OAS, which has suspended Cuba from membership in 1962, CELAC includes Cuba as a full member, and indeed nominated Cuba to be an early chair of the body. Meanwhile, the Pacific Alliance is a newly formed group of free-trading countries—Colombia, Mexico, Peru, and Chile. The EU has been pressing for free trade negotiations with the wider groupings, but so far the Latin American side has remained divided. And, despite years of anti-U.S. rhetoric by some leading politicians, the Latinobarómetro poll in 2013 found that 69 percent of respondents had a favorable opinion of the United States with only 49 percent thinking that Latin America needed an institution that excluded the United States.

OTHER REGIONS

The Arab League is an example of an organization, largely moribund and backslapping for many years, that came to recognize that real diplomacy was necessary if its members were not to lose their collective grip on how their region developed. The League was founded in Cairo in 1945 by seven countries: Egypt, Iraq, Lebanon, Saudi Arabia, Syria, Transjordan (Jordan from 1946), and Yemen. Since then, it has increased to twenty-one states. Despite containing few supranational features, the League has played a prominent role in some diplomatic initiatives. The issue of Palestine has been central to the League's agenda since its foundation, and a delegate from Palestine has played a full part in its activities throughout its history. The founding pact of March 1945 stated,

> The States signatory to the Pact of the Arab League consider that in view of Palestine's special circumstances, the Council of the League should designate an Arab delegate from Palestine to participate in its work until this country enjoys actual independence.[23]

If Palestine has been a binding issue, so have the preconditions of any future peace with Israel. The League has been split over several peace initiatives, and Egypt and Jordan have established diplomatic relations with Israel. Yet eighteen of the twenty-two members of the Arab League either do not recognize Israel or do not have diplomatic relations. Another collective challenge to the League came in the Arab Spring of 2011, where many of the uprisings were directed at removing long-standing rulers. The League had long been focused on promoting Arab unity in causes where the members were already largely united. Now the choice was to allow events to run their course and sit on the sidelines or risk the region devolving responsibility to others to restore stability. Both the League and the AU tried to broker a deal that concerned one of their prominent members—Muammar Gaddafi—but with no success. The League tried a different approach in an evolving Syrian civil war, suspending the Syria of Bashar al Assad from membership and eventually proposing monitors to administer a nonexistent cease-fire. Yet in a development that may well be repeated, a transnational media organization founded by one of the League's member—Qatar's influential and well-funded Al Jazeera—has become a powerful medium that reduces the impact of state controls on information. The League is entering the digital age with pan-Arabism again potentially a powerful impetus to united action. The common interests that many share include the threat of transnational insurgency, Islamic fundamentalism, sectarian divides—all of which are causes that may shake the foundations of the existing sovereign states. The Islamic State (IS) in 2014 represented the most direct challenge to current states since the League's foundation. The Arab League may yet have to assume much greater diplomatic importance.

OTHER GROUPS

Other regional groups do not base themselves solely on geography but on other perceived common interests. The Shanghai Cooperation Council includes Russia, China, and the central Asian republics; APEC (Asia Pacific Economic Cooperation) includes some twenty-one Pacific Rim countries; and the BRICS now meet as a group not just as a creation of an investment bank analyst. Indeed, in July 2014, the BRICS leaders announced the creation of their own development bank based in Shanghai. The Gulf Cooperation Council (GCC) includes six Arabian Gulf states that are also members of the Arab League. The GCC in particular shows that a smaller grouping of interlinked economies—Bahrain, Kuwait, Oman, Qatar, Saudi Arabia, and United Arab Emirates—can be effective by concentrating on a small numbers of issues. The threat from Iran has been a unifying force for Arab countries before, and the readiness of Saudi Arabia to bolster the Sunni Arab government of Bahrain in 2011 showed that regional security structures and economic integration in the Gulf are proving a significant diplomatic reality. The majority of the states are small, share family connections in ruling families, and see the rise of regional powers that are potentially hostile.

The success of another regional grouping—the Arctic Council (AC)—is another illustration of a common defined interest. Established in 1996 by the Ottawa Declaration, it consists of eight states that have territory within the Arctic Circle—the United States, Canada, Denmark (representing Greenland and the Faroes), Finland, Iceland, Norway, Russia, and Sweden. The region's strategic importance is growing fast. The UN Law of the Sea has given the group a legal basis to prepare agreements on unprospected oil, gas, and minerals under national jurisdiction. Global melting now permits ships to sail from the Far East to Europe, cutting costs by taking the Arctic route. So interest in the AC is burgeoning beyond the existing membership. Applicants to join the group are also growing with China, the EU, Greenpeace, and the International Association of Oil and Gas producers among those in line.

One phenomenon that besets some organizations, perhaps in similar vein to UN agencies, is the "time to call it quits" decision. Few organizations are ever wound up. Some survive for reasons more akin to a social club than a meaningful diplomatic organization. *The Economist* described the Commonwealth, a group of fifty-four countries drawn originally from former British colonies that continued to use the English language, in the following terms:

> The Commonwealth runs a decent sports championship but is otherwise cash-strapped, unsure of its purpose and increasingly obscure. In a recent poll, half of Britons and Canadians could not name any Commonwealth activity. A quarter of Jamaicans thought Barack Obama was its head.[24]

The Commonwealth serves as a reminder of common heritage, and in Europe, too, tradition also still secures budgets to sustain groupings. One of the oldest of all is the Council of Europe, which was part of Jean Monnet's original European vision. It rarely interests diplomatic commentators but still exists, absorbing resources of over €240 million a year. Its budget document runs to some 247 pages for those citizens of forty-seven European member countries who might be interested.

The panoply of regional organizations is rich and varied. Many more will be invented. Most date since the foundation of the UN, which may be one of the reasons why they appear to have attracted so many members. No state wants to be left out in diplomacy, especially where a group of a few dozen offers more chance of influence than a global diplomatic forum. And each region's efforts have spurred others to imitate. Yet it would be wrong to put much faith in their contributing to consensus on global issues. Many are not configured to produce consensus at all because large sovereign states are the lead actors. The strongest among them, of course, exert most influence within each group. And the formula of regional meetings, free trade arrangements, and some discussion of regional problems is probably all that can be hoped for. The organizations generally lack infrastructure to follow up on implementation. With the exception of the EU they have no permanent mechanisms to promote consensus. Across the regions, there is no domestic pressure for action, no coordinated non-governmental organization lobby, and currently no blogosphere looking for collective progress. Leaders comfortably fend off accusations of failure and plan for the next meeting. There is seldom a downside to lack of achievement. Nevertheless, the regional groups can claim to have extended the options available for diplomacy. They have added another layer to diplomatic activities with some permanent delegations who may conduct day-to-day business and regional summits between leaders that come round with surprising rapidity. They have created opportunities for leaders of states to meet direct frequently and in doing so have undercut part of the traditional rationale for the roles of embassies and ambassadors.

SUMMITS AND THE Gs

Summits share some of the characteristics of regional groupings. But a successful summit is ad hoc and issue focused. Other summits—dubbed serial summits by G. R. Berridge—are often less successful because they form part of a regular calendar and contribute to diplomacy's rituals. But all share a feature that is important for diplomacy—the key decision makers are present, as the name suggests. In the words of David Dunn, they are meetings between those who "by virtue of their position . . . are not able to be contradicted by any other individual."[25]

Summits have a long-standing role in diplomacy. The power of the monarch or ruler predated professional diplomacy, and the rarity and grandeur of such meetings was seen as fitting for the important issues of state. Some had a specific objective—for example, to negotiate peace after conflict. This was the purpose of the complex process of meetings that culminated in the Peace of Westphalia in 1648. Delegations were sent by sixteen European states and sixty-six imperial states with a vote in the Diet of the Holy Roman Empire.

In 1652, Ferdinand III, the Habsburg monarch, held a summit in Regensburg with a delegation of 3,000 people to meet the Diet and the empire's princes, bishops, and other dignitaries. When Ferdinand left again for Vienna, he was accompanied by 164 ships floating down the Danube. This was grand imperial pomp, but such displays of power and flamboyance have survived as an important element of summit diplomacy.

With all the promise of high-level contacts but none of the inconvenience of permanent institutional structures or treaty documents, the summit is often the solution of choice when sovereign states are called to take urgent action. The term *summit* seems to have been used first by one of their most enthusiastic practitioners, Winston Churchill. Yet the modern practice, facilitated by ease of travel, can be traced to events like the Versailles Peace Conference of 1919. Woodrow Wilson, David Lloyd George, and Georges Clemenceau, all of whom spent several months at the meeting, treated Versailles as an extended summit. But the idea of Wilson to have a conference open to the public was not realized and the proceedings at Versailles took place behind closed doors.

The World War II summits between Roosevelt, Stalin, and Churchill were also the key events in the reframing of the world order. The EU holds regular summits of member states, and the other regional organizations we discussed have put strong emphasis on such meetings to maintain any momentum in their programs. Do summits indicate a failure of conventional diplomacy, or are they useful supplements to previous efforts? The answer is usually both. Summits, to prove themselves as necessary, rather than mere photo opportunities, should add value, but the status of the leaders is something that diplomats may find introduces an unhelpful ingredient. Diplomats represent a state but leaders, well known often for many years to international media, may in practice come to represent themselves.

Diplomacy in the contemporary world tends to look more to leaders to bridge gaps and produce results. The reasons for this are the complexity of issues, the unwieldy bureaucracies involved in policy decisions, and the capacity of world leaders to respond to public pressure. Being seen to be busy with diplomacy is now a 24/7 concern for many of the major world leaders. Many publics see the international credentials of politicians as important qualifications for the job. So the serial summit meetings have proliferated as faith in the diplomatic capacity of permanent organizations has declined. The multiple actors present in UN and the cumbersome process of securing agreements from 190-plus members all make a smaller decision-oriented body more attractive. If institutional and committee-based diplomacy cannot solve issues, then a process that brings individuals together where failure may be seen as a personal disaster for the politicians attending has obvious attractions.

The fact that many leaders now meet frequently in different fora means that the quality of diplomacy—familiarity and confidence in interlocutors—may also be improved. A U.S. president typically attends every year summits of Group of Eight (G8), Group of Twenty (G20), NATO, APEC, ASEAN Plus 3, the Summit of the Americas, and others. This does not mean that diplomatic agents are absent in the planning of such meetings, but the leaders invest in their own capacity to give diplomacy an extra ingredient. Not all summits produce results in terms of lasting outcomes, but the symbolism is important and needs careful attention. Bilateral summits between British Prime Minister Edward Heath and French President Pompidou had a diplomatic effect in changing the climate for the United Kingdom's entry into the EEC that no official gathering could have replicated. And the meeting between Mao Tse-tung and U.S. President Nixon in 1972 is not remembered for its content but for the images of the two unlikely political leaders sharing a well-publicized encounter.

The longest surviving nonregional summit organization is the G8, a forum created for the governments of eight of the world's largest economies. (It excludes, however, two of the current eight largest economies by nominal GDP: China, second, and Brazil, sixth.) The G8 originated in a 1975 summit hosted by France that invited leaders of Germany, Italy, Japan, the United Kingdom, and the United States, thus leading to the name Group of Six or G6. The summit became known as the G7 the following year with the addition of Canada. In 1997, Russia was added to make it the G8, and suspended over Ukraine in 2014. The EU is represented within the G8 but cannot normally host or chair summits.

We have seen the impact of crises on significant diplomatic innovations. Another example of such a major crisis happened in 2008, when the world's financial system was convulsed by a contagious collapse of confidence. There was no escaping its impact, but it did not appear to threaten the physical security of states. Neither political leaders nor diplomats understood the private sector financial instruments central to the crisis, which were of such complexity that few had even heard of them. President George W. Bush convened a new summit of the major economies. The G20 group had previously existed only as meetings of finance ministers. Now, the U.S. president decided he would not risk diplomatic wrangling by agonizing over what group to convene. He invited those who could make a difference to the issue at hand. Needless to say, this upset some countries because they sensed that a new club was being created. Spain and the Netherlands were among those who lobbied intensively to attend.

The G20 has been reluctant to define its operations or create a bureaucracy that might be a reliable signal of intention to be permanent. Its chairmanship rotates annually among the members with similar respect for regional balance as shown by the selection of candidates for the UN Security Council. The G20 has so far also been reluctant, perhaps to the disappointment of critics of the UN, to engage in discussion of issues that still remain the domain of the UNSC. The G20 seemed to herald innovation at the time, but it has reverted to cautious discussions with long communiqués that seem to be drafted to emphasize diplomatic opacity. Already there are many criticizing what it represents in exclusivity. Some have argued over the basis for the calculations of the GDP figures that form the group's basis. As President Obama has said, "Everybody wants the smallest possible group that includes them. So, if they're the 21st largest nation in the world, they want the G-21, and think it's highly unfair if they have been cut out."[26] Meanwhile, Norway's foreign minister has called the G20 one of diplomacy's "greatest setbacks since the Second World War."[27]

INNOVATION FROM GROUPS

There is no evidence so far that a commitment to become a member of these regional organizations indicates any interest in diplomatic innovation. Even the EU, with its half-century of history, has a budget of only 1 percent of the collective GDP of its members. It votes in the UN mostly as a bloc, but EU coordination has not eradicated sovereign state diplomacy that promotes commercial and consular services. The regional state is a long way off and the commitment to participate in regional groupings remains an à la carte option. Summits involve less commitment of time and money than permanent organizations. To new leaders, many of whom will remain in office only a few years, the idea that a grouping of individuals can add value to diplomacy even without institutions or written rules is appealing. Leaders, of course, also regularly use social media like Skype and Twitter. They are conscious that through information technology, nonstate actors and global social media can be reached 24/7, and summits are one more opportunity for hashtags. These issues are explored further in Chapters 10 and 11.

ISSUE GROUPS

Aside from regional or summit groups, some international issues have been discussed in customized collective diplomatic fora made up of interested parties. Examples are the Quartet on the Middle East Peace Process, composed of the UN, the United States, the EU, and Russia. Established in Madrid in 2002, former British Prime Minister Tony Blair is the Quartet's current special envoy. Another example is the group that has negotiated with Iran on its nuclear program composed of the five permanent members of the UNSC plus Germany. Another group of six countries meets on issues on the Korean peninsula. This includes North and South Korea, Japan, China, the United States, and Russia.

The participation of traditional diplomatic agents in these processes reinforces what is a prime quality of diplomats—their versatility. A diplomat will use the confidential discussions in these ad hoc groups to add to other processes. And part of their value is their visibility. Diplomacy is seen to be happening. The issue may not lend itself to institutional solutions, nor are there often precedents or treaties that can be easily applied. Indeed, many of the processes we have examined have achieved little. A settlement between Palestine and Israel has remained beyond reach, and the behavior of the Democratic People's Republic of Korea in missile and nuclear proliferation has so far proved largely unresponsive to an ever changing mixture of diplomatic carrots and sticks. Diplomatic failure is nothing new, and the lack of obvious solutions goes to the heart of why negotiations happen that involve sovereign states. Sovereign states are sometimes immune to negotiations and other activities of diplomacy, and they survive despite diplomatically egregious behavior. This may be because the processes of diplomacy and the negotiation techniques used are defective. How do the participants, the range of issues, and the order they are dealt with affect the outcomes? It is a good time to begin discussion of diplomatic negotiations and what makes them a worthy topic for discussion.

SUGGESTIONS FOR FURTHER READING

1. Bátora, Jozef and Alan Hardacre. "Regional Institutional Diplomacies: Europe, Asia, Africa, Latin America/The Caribbean and Other Regions." In *Diplomacy in a Globalizing World: Theories and Practices*, ed. Pauline Kerr and Geoffrey Wiseman. New York: Oxford University Press, 2012.

2. European Union External Action Service. http://eeas.europa.eu.

3. Berridge, G. R. "Summitry." In *Diplomacy: Theory and Practice*, 4th ed. New York: Palgrave MacMillan, 2010.

4. Dunn, David H., ed. *Diplomacy at the Highest Level: The Evolution of International Summitry*. New York: Palgrave Macmillan, 1996.

chapter 6

Negotiations

In August 2012, Lakhdar Brahimi was appointed UN and Arab League envoy to try to negotiate a cease-fire and an end to the Syrian civil war. By February 2013, after numerous meetings with all sides in the conflict and stakeholders in the international community, and despite having all the resources of the UN behind him, he had come to a point of desperation. "All that is left is the wider international world," he said. Only the UN Security Council (UNSC) could find a solution. "You are the last appeal." As for the UNSC members, "Please do your job. . . . We need a clear decision from the Security Council to set the agenda for a peaceful solution of the problem."[1]

The content of the negotiations that Brahimi orchestrated was not known and took place in multiple locations. The salaries of the officials, as well as the hotel and travel bills involved, were paid for by international taxpayers but produced little perceivable results. Brahimi had admirable credentials as a former Foreign Minister of Algeria and a senior official of the UN. But his negotiations made little progress: "Frankly now as we speak, I am much more conscious of the difficulties and of the country being broken, day after day than I am of a solution around the corner."[2] Brahimi spoke to both sides of the conflict, brought in the major powers and neighbors. He appeared to have produced an opening. Mouaz al-Khatib, a Syrian opposition leader, expressed willingness to engage in talks with President Bashar al-Assad's government but wanted the release of 160,000 detainees as an expression of good faith. There was willingness to talk but the diplomatic key did not fit the door.

As one diplomatic negotiation foundered, another took shape. In August 2012, the government of Colombia announced that they had negotiated an understanding with the rebel group FARC that, after over fifty years of conflict, they would begin talks on a permanent peace. Though not between two sovereign states, the process contained many elements of a state-to-state negotiation. And the cooperation of other states with differing interests was also integral to the process. The framework agenda had been agreed at talks in Cuba, and the first phase of the negotiations proper were held in Oslo. Norway, Venezuela, Chile, and Cuba had agreed to act as guarantors of the process.

Countless smaller and less visible negotiations happen in diplomacy every day. How successful are the structures that diplomats can apply to these problems, and what special factors apply in diplomatic negotiations that seldom impact other types of negotiation such as those in commercial life?

FRAMING AN ISSUE

The Charter of the UN requires all members to negotiate and "settle their disputes by peaceful means in such a manner that international peace and security and justice are not endangered."[3] So a commitment to negotiation is one of the requirements to be recognized as a sovereign state. For a diplomatic negotiation to be formalized in this way means that the alternative solutions have been exhausted. These might involve military action, economic sanctions, or some offers for development assistance or commercial advantage. So, as Berridge notes in his summary of the prerequisites for a successful negotiation, the existence of a stalemate is a good starting point.[4] There is usually no other way to move the issue forward. In other words, every alternative to negotiations has already been tried or has been seen to have failed. Or the factors that applied during the last attempt at negotiation have changed. In diplomacy, the problem is often how long such a fragile convergence of interests that may have led to negotiations will hold. A stalemate has existed on several occasions in the negotiations between Palestine and Israel, only to be broken as a result of new violence—perhaps deliberately staged to stymie the process—or changes in domestic political circumstances or pressure from external stakeholders.

But many new to diplomacy will argue a stalemate or a special situational alignment is necessary in all forms of negotiations, and diplomacy is not a unique case. A deal will not be made until every alternative has been tried. The concept of Best Alternative to a Negotiated Agreement (BATNA) will be discussed further under Strategy and Progress later in this chapter. All negotiations involve give and take, relative bargaining strengths, and the discussion of terms on which mutual benefit may be possible. What if my Internet server offers me a reduced-term contract when a rival is offering a $100 discount to commit myself for two years? My neighbor says he will remove an easement that affects my property if I agree to maintain the drive up to my home? Will I buy my coffee at Starbucks if they contribute to fair trade causes or simply use the coffee machine at home?

THE RAW MATERIAL OF DIPLOMATIC NEGOTIATIONS

Let us examine how far what states negotiate merits special attention. What are the important characteristics of diplomatic negotiations?

First, the subject matter of diplomatic negotiations usually will have lasting significance. For diplomats to roll into action, there is usually something that matters in the long-term. Short-term fixes apply in diplomacy, particularly in crises, but diplomats try to produce predictability and a framework for relations. That is why the subject matter of a diplomatic negotiation is often designed to impact the legal basis of the relations between the two countries. It may deal with territory, boundaries of rivers, or mutually beneficial arrangements like agreements on extradition or investment protection. Or they may enhance mutual security—for example, through arms control negotiations supported by on-site inspections.

Second, the parties to diplomatic negotiations are representative of governments, international organizations, or entities with legal capacity to decide questions that have international repercussions. The parties are not—and should not—be negotiating for personal gain or advancement. But they will usually be experienced in other similar negotiations, so they may come to talks with preconceived expectations of how they will be conducted. Just as in corporate negotiations, on some occasions leaders will conduct the negotiations themselves. This is often viewed with alarm by diplomats. But the practice of leaders inserting themselves in negotiations or attempting to probe positions is becoming more common due the ease of communicating and the frequent meetings between world leaders at the proliferation of summits.

Third, there is seldom an alternative interlocutor in diplomatic negotiations, either as a state or individual leaders, to those that conduct them. There have been many instances in modern history of leaders who disliked each other—U.S. President Lyndon Johnson and British Prime Minister Harold Wilson, Fidel Castro and Mao Tse-tung, or U.S. President Nixon and Indian Prime Minister Indira Gandhi. Diplomats use cables to report on the personalities of the leaders they deal with. Leaks and unguarded remarks can cause damage to perceptions and turn what should be impersonal diplomatic issues into insults and slights that obstruct progress. Whatever the degree of congeniality, one key factor about diplomacy is that there is no alternative to the leaders on offer. States do not trade CEOs. Unlike in a commercial organization where some senior officers may have worked for rivals and are moving on for career advancement, leaders often stay around for years. Term limits apply, but many sovereign states seldom change their leaders. In 2013, over a dozen African states had had the same leaders for fifteen years or longer.

Fourth, there must be a conceivable outcome to the negotiation that is at least possible for a sovereign state to accept. No state is going to enter into negotiations where a possible result might threaten its existence. So the likelihood of a successful negotiation under duress is small.

Fifth, diplomatic negotiations do not normally deal with monetary payments. This is not impossible, for example in reparation payments for wars or in development assistance, but payments between one government and another simply to achieve a settlement of a contentious issue are rare. Adjusting financial terms is a straightforward and common device in commercial negotiations but in many cases is not available in diplomacy. It was noticeable that despite the billions of dollars of military and other assistance the United States has provided to Egypt, the diplomatic influence and leverage this gave to the U.S. in the aftermath of the removal of President Mubarak was minimal.

Sixth, states have no competition in identity. There is only one for each area of the world. Unlike commercial organizations, there is no competition within a country. Countries endure and maintain a history of alliances, achievements, failures, and cultural makeup. They contain natural resources and have more or less strategic importance in the space they occupy on the planet. So this gives inherent features to each state as a negotiating partner. Companies rise and fall, they merge and disappear. Several of the largest companies in the world in the 2020s will not have existed in the twentieth century.

Seventh, cultural differences between the parties are a central issue to most diplomatic negotiations. This is a fascinating study in itself, and it marks another distinctive feature that is never absent in diplomacy and, of course, may influence negotiations in other contexts.

CULTURE

To define culture is an important starting point. The concept has been developed by anthropologists to encompass what makes a particular society distinct in terms of customs, manners, and the rules commonly observed of the society's members. As Raymond Cohen explains in *Negotiating across Cultures*, it is not to be confused with national character, personality, or indeed language.[5] It affects how states are organized, their economic success, and thought processes. Culture is a determinant of traditional behavior, how diplomats may react to systems of rewards and punishment, the role of gifts and bribes, and the use of facial and body movements.

Culture impacts a society rather than individuals. It is what remains when formal common elements between individuals, such as being educated at the same institution, are stripped away. The culture may extend to the role of diplomacy itself and the foreign ministry, and how much influence the process has. In business negotiations, it would be wrong to say that cultural differences never play a role. If a European company is negotiating with a Chinese state-owned entity, then their cultural differences will impact the negotiation. But the common perception of the commercial issues, the common language of profit and markets, will produce common ground sometimes unavailable in diplomacy.

Diplomats try to frame issues in terms that smooth edges, despite acknowledging the differences of culture. The issues of arms control or double taxation are examples of universal issues that are regarded as important in different cultures. But those who maintain that context matters would point to differences between how countries would treat their discussion of the same issue. Cohen argues convincingly that some cultures like the United States are low context, whereas Chinese, Japanese, Indian, and Mexican cultures are high context. For this latter group, this means that the significance of a diplomatic negotiation goes well beyond the issues themselves.

What specific examples of cultural differences can be cited? A sample of those discussed by Cohen will suffice to make the point. Japanese culture favors caution in revealing positions in any clear statement. Chinese culture favors stating Chinese positions and requirements before the negotiations begin. Indian culture pays strong attention to status, and Korean to the issue of "face." And what of others? U.S. culture loves sporting metaphors, perhaps suggesting they aim for clear outcomes. And in Arabic there is no word for compromise.

In my own experience, I discussed nuclear weapons proliferation with a range of interlocutors from 1997 to 2001. The noticeable culture differences are not easily anticipated, especially in discussions with countries where there is a little tradition in these exchanges. At a meeting in Tehran, the British female delegate was excluded from greetings by the Iranians, which we expected. What was less expected was a two-hour opening presentation by the head of the Iranian delegation on their history of being attacked, their regional struggles, and advances since the Revolution. In China, the atmosphere was professional, the hospitality lavish, and the exchanges fluent. But the Chinese did not ask us at any stage what we thought. In India, the discussions were highly scientific, the atmosphere dignified, and there was much Indian emphasis on respect among states but little attention to the global issue of nonproliferation. In Israel, the interlocutors were expertly informed, drew heavily on intelligence sources, and seemed to attribute a very low value to any diplomatic efforts to deal with nonproliferation.

As we have seen in discussing protocol and the common treatment of immunities and privileges, diplomatic practice has long anticipated the barriers to international dialogue that national differences erect. The use of a common language—Latin or French—was one convention seen as a necessary but not a sufficient condition for progress in diplomacy. The fact that such languages were often used by the transnational aristocracy and royal families of the age created an additional bonding. As we have seen, certain terms in Latin or French survive to the modern era. Today, language barriers are overcome through translators and interpreters. All international agreements have authenticated texts in several languages. During a fast moving conversation or tough questions from one side, the use of an interpreter can buy valuable time for the participants to think of an appropriate reply. Fidel Castro, though known to speak and understand English well, always used an interpreter in meetings.

Differences in cultures also impact the implementation of agreements achieved through negotiation. As Cohen says, "For high-context societies, an agreement is seen as a provisional step on a never-ending journey, yet another move in an open-ended relationship."[6] The United States' can-do, results-oriented, technology-driven diplomacy, interested in combining a military and civil approach to solving a host of global issues, is a world away from a Pakistani diplomat whose background may be entirely in the military and who sees only one big issue in everything on an agenda—the balancing of relations with India. Culturally, an Israeli may have attended an American or French college, may like American movies or Spanish soccer teams, but will still have as an overriding objective Israel's national survival. The scene may be set for a meeting of minds in diplomacy, but cultural differences still predispose the diplomat to a role of separateness.

No state adopts the same approach to every type of negotiation. And the same state will shape its approach according to the interlocutor. This would, of course, also be true for a major corporation with a small supplier of components. Yet the context of a diplomatic negotiation is seldom solely concerned with the merits of the issue. It encompasses the many linked issues that all countries deal with in the totality of their relations. Aside from the constants of differences in culture, India will negotiate with Sri Lanka differently than with the United States and will treat China differently than it will Myanmar. The act of negotiating itself has many facets. The level of expertise and authority brought to a diplomatic negotiation also differs greatly. I have been in meetings with diplomats where they have read word for word a technical manual of export control regulations for over ten minutes, with a minister of the interior who played music in the background for fear of being bugged by his own security apparatus, and with officials who were fearful of saying anything other than what I had said had been noted.

Despite all these pitfalls, some diplomatic negotiations succeed. From centuries of history, it is possible to identify certain features that will give a negotiation a reasonable chance of success and will help identify likely stumbling blocks. What then are the key ingredients of a diplomatic negotiation that have to be settled to give the negotiation a reasonable chance of success?

ELEMENTS REQUIRED FOR SUCCESS: PRENEGOTIATIONS

Even before negotiations proper get underway, there will be a period of prenegotiations where the sides meet for talks about talks. Such initial contacts can be explored often by resident diplomats, either direct with the foreign ministry in the capital to which they are accredited or by diplomats of the countries involved in another location. Or they could be explored by mediators who may have no formal diplomatic status. The example of the negotiations between Colombia and the FARC discussed at the start of this chapter included a period of six months of such prenegotiations in a neutral capital city, Oslo, away from the glare of media publicity.

Before the negotiations can begin, the venue for the talks must be decided. The venue could be in a third country as when Gorbachev and Reagan chose the Icelandic capital Reykjavik for arms control discussions. The United States and Vietnam chose Paris for their peace talks. Another option might be the UN delegations in Geneva or New York, or a home-and-away alternating series. The Israelis have been keen to hold peace talks with Arab and Palestine negotiators in the Middle East to emphasize their presence in the region. The Afghan Taliban and the United States have been discussing the possibilities of peace in the privacy of Qatar, which wishes to promote itself as a diplomatic actor. Whatever the geographical location of the venue, good communication facilities and diplomatic missions (for internal consultations) will usually be essential.

Second, all successful negotiations must settle the issues to be discussed, and such issues must be defined in the agenda. An important assumption of negotiations is that the states involved will be rational and competent actors aware of the pros and cons of different courses of action. If this is indeed the case, no sovereign state is going to enter negotiations with every aspect of its existence on the table or if it sees no acceptable outcome compared to the alternatives. Military force or commercial or economic pressure may have been considered but rejected in favor of negotiations. The common way of limiting outcomes is to stick to an agenda. The agenda will be specific to an issue or issues, territorial or substantive, long standing or short-term. Only when the agenda has mutual support will the first essential element of trust have been established.

Once a venue is decided and the agenda agreed upon, the details of the format of the negotiations must be settled. There may be contention over who will be invited as a party to the talks. In January 2014, the inclusion of Iran in the second Geneva Syria peace conference was supported by the Syrian government, Russia, and the UN but not by the United States or the Syrian opposition groups. Once the parties are settled, then there must be agreement on the level and size of the delegations, the frequency of sessions, the format for the talks, the size and shape of the table, or if there will be no table at all. A planned session of talks between North and South Korea in 2013 was scrapped when North Korea professed itself surprised at the lowly rank of the South Korean who awaited them. Other aspects include press handling. Will there be an opening joint announcement? Will there be regular press arrangements? Will there be a time limit? Will there be alternating venues between the participants? What role, if any, will third countries have?

If the negotiations progress to this point, there will have been many occasions where the goodwill and trust of both sides will have been tested. Contacts will have been made, relationships developed, and some genuine social capital built up. Often officials involved in a joint negotiation will bond. That can be important. It happened between Soviet and U.S. military officials during the Cold War and subsequently. Egyptian President Sadat seemed genuinely to like his Israeli counterparts. The young President Kennedy liked the much older, patrician Harold MacMillan and was keen to deliver a nuclear weapons cooperation deal with the United Kingdom. Officials of member states in the EU know each other very well. In some cases, they will have negotiated on the same issues for years.

The context of many diplomatic negotiations is contentious, however. Though the stalemate exists, this does not mean that the path is clear for a negotiation that is issue specific. The likelihood in postconflict situations is that trust will be in short supply. And even when relations are extensive and significant—as in the case of Japan and China, the latter today accounting for over 20 percent of Japanese trade—this has not prevented tensions over such fractious issues as contested territorial sovereignty. Claims to small islands often are still beyond the capacity of the smartest diplomats to resolve.

MEDIATION

National diplomatic systems, however sophisticated and well resourced, may be unable to even start negotiations without outside help. In this case, the role of a mediator may be crucial. Indeed, the appointment of a mediator itself requires some agreement that may be difficult to achieve as few candidates of experience will be seen to be wholly impartial. Some countries volunteer for the job, as was the case with Turkey and Brazil in 2010 and their efforts to broker a deal over the Iranian nuclear program. Turkey and Brazil were both then nonpermanent members of the UNSC and promoted a swap deal that would have given Iran access to nuclear fuel. This appeared to be based on previous ideas floated by the permanent members of the UNSC but had then been rejected by Iran. In accepting the role of the Brazilian and Turkish mediators, Iran seemed, at least for a while, to see this as a step forward.

When Kofi Annan was appointed as the UN envoy (mediator) in the Syrian civil conflict, he appeared to be acceptable to both sides and was able to start discussions sufficiently to draw up a plan for a cease-fire. Yet the very hostility of the two sides and the volatility of the conflict where neither side was clearly in the ascendancy produced an unworkable document. It had few deadlines, had few enthusiastic supporters, and the balance in the conflict was swinging in favor of the rebels, however fragmented they were as a political entity. The cease-fire proposal never gained any traction. There was no stalemate. A different set of circumstances produced a better outcome. In the protracted sectarian violence in Northern Ireland, the employment of George Mitchell, a former U.S. Senator, and John de Chastelain, a Canadian general, proved invaluable facilitators outside the region to smooth the peace process. Another U.S. mediator, Richard Haass, helped progress sensitive discussions in 2013 and 2014 on the practice of parades and use of flags in Northern Ireland. During President Obama's visit to the Middle East in March 2013, he used his time not only to talk directly to Israeli, Palestinian, and Jordanian leaders but also to mediate between Turkey and Israel, who had feuded since the Israeli attack on a Turkish flotilla heading to Gaza. Obama persuaded Israel's Prime Minister Netanyahu to apologize to Turkish Prime Minister Erdogan and reopen diplomatic communications.

The mediator in diplomatic negotiations has a variety of roles. Zartman suggests that the role of mediators can be divided into three categories according to the types of obstacles to be overcome: they can play the role of communicators for when the parties cannot talk to one another; they can be formulators when they cannot come up with ways to resolve ideas; and they can be useful as manipulators when the parties do not see large enough benefits to outweigh the costs in what is being negotiated. A successful mediator will combine elements of all three.[7]

STRATEGY AND PROGRESS

If the talks get underway, further progress may need new inputs. In most diplomatic negotiations, there are not the same incentives to do a deal as in commercial negotiations—movements in markets, competition from rivals, personal rewards, and media pressure. The stance of diplomacy is often to wait. States last forever and you never know what may turn up. Unlike in commercial deals, where rival bids may come in or companies are taken over, there are seldom any absolute deadlines that threaten the existence of a state. Saddam Hussein probably never believed the world would be roused from its summer slumbers in August 1990 when many diplomats would be on vacation. He tried to adopt a negotiating strategy of hints, bluster, and efforts to divide the formation of a coalition. Similarly, after he was expelled from Kuwait in 1991, he played his negotiating hand skillfully through the 1990s to drive wedges between the UN members that were charged with inspecting his destruction of weapons and missiles.

Within the content and course of a diplomatic negotiation, there are strategies that differentiate them from negotiations in other fora. Bankers, lawyers, parents, and children are all regular negotiators. They work out their tactics and strategies to achieve results. A diplomat is representing a complex set of stakeholders in a state. He is negotiating on behalf of an entity that must continue to function in the international community. The diplomat may be under deadlines, which could bear no relation to the issues at hand and must be concealed from the other side. He may represent a state with severe financial problems, secret alliance commitments, and threatened with internal political instability. He may be under personal pressure for family or health reasons. Throughout everything, a successful diplomatic negotiator must be a smoother of edges, an enlister of experts, a networker of resources, and a person of versatility and patience. A skillful diplomatic negotiator should ensure there are strategies employed that will produce movement toward the objectives set. Such strategies might involve linkages with wider issues, making concessions perhaps long planned and perhaps intending to convince the other side that the concessions were more important than in reality they were—the so-called Homans rule from the sociologist who framed it. And diplomats must of course be aware of the real alternatives that exist for the other state or states involved the principle of BATNA. Preparation and intelligence will take into account what other avenues exist should the negotiations collapse. A diplomat will be on the look-out for "costly signals," a concept that shows the strength of a state's commitment to negotiate. Does what has been offered involve a cost for the state? If it does, it may signal sincerity and suggest ultimate success. This has been discussed by Todd Hall and Keren Yarhi-Milo as one of several key personal issues that can impact diplomatic negotiations.[8]

Diplomats must also use media briefings and be aware of public opinion in all countries involved in the negotiations and in the wider world. And any negotiation that is no longer a secret will involve the media probing for stories of deadlock, impasse, and train wrecks. By contrast, the diplomat will want to maintain the atmospherics of trust, dialogue, progress, and the inevitability of agreement. Yet trust may be built up only to conceal a real intent to deceive or delay action. In the April 2014 negotiations in Geneva over the status of rebel strongholds in Eastern Ukraine, there was an unstated interest of Russia to buy time for the separatists under the cover of diplomatic activity.

Few states, having committed to a negotiation, will readily accept that the process has proved unproductive. Therefore, metaphors of movement may be used to talk up progress and perhaps pressurize the other side—*green lights*, *tracks*, *hurdles*, and *road maps* are widely used in the description of negotiations. If a negotiation fails, pencils are sharpened and text messages sent to explain why the other side or external influences were to blame.

Case Study

The INF Negotiation 1980 to 1987

The Intermediate Nuclear Forces (INF) negotiations between the Soviet Union and the United States are a good illustration of the various stages that a complex negotiation must sometimes undergo to produce success. The world order at the beginning of the 1980s appeared predictable. There had been over thirty years of standoff with rival forces stationed in Europe and high-stakes disputes, including over the status of Berlin.

Arms control agreements between the United States and the Soviet Union had recognized the mutual interests of both blocs in reducing offensive weapons and in a treaty on missile defense. The Strategic Arms Limitation Talks (SALT I 1969–1972) and the Anti-Ballistic Missile Treaty (ABMT 1972) were monuments to a new coexistence and diplomatic understanding. Under the presidency of Jimmy Carter, there were follow-up negotiations to reduce existing stockpiles and impose limits on the developments of new missiles—SALT II. But the Soviet invasion of Afghanistan in 1979 scuppered the ratification process in the U.S. Senate.

The painstaking progress that had been made between the United States and the Soviet Union stuttered in the late 1970s. The nuclear strategy of the Soviet Union appeared to be changing at the same time as the West was condemning its actions in Afghanistan. Arms control had so far concentrated on strategic nuclear weapons (those with a range exceeding 5,500 kilometers). The new Soviet SS-20 missile, an intermediate range missile not covered by the SALT talks, began to be deployed in Soviet territory in Eastern Europe in 1977. Western strategists were unsure what this represented in Soviet motivations and whether there were divisions in Soviet leadership. The implications appeared to be that the Soviet Union was trying to challenge NATO to respond to Soviet missile deployments in the hope this would undermine NATO unity. In any case, the move shook the trust between the negotiating parties that had been established. The Soviet leaders knew the anxiety SS-20 deployments would cause among the populations of Western European countries. They saw the common interest in arms control had been shaken and that an opportunity had arisen to explore how far their negotiating leverage could go. They gambled on the influence of a nonstate actor—the antinuclear movement in Europe.

NATO responded with an agreed alliance strategy in two parts. The first was to pursue arms control negotiations with the Soviet Union to reduce INF arsenals. The second was to deploy in Europe from 1983 ground-launched cruise missiles (GLCMs) and Pershing II ballistic missiles. The chosen locations for these missiles were the United Kingdom, the Federal Republic of Germany, and Italy. Preparations were also made for deployments in Belgium.

In a classic period of prenegotiation, the Western powers recognized that there was no stalemate because the Soviet Union was still hoping that European publics would prevent the deployments. The Soviet Union argued that NATO had superiority in other weapons systems like sea-launched missiles and they already had deployed other short-ranged nuclear weapons in Europe. In their view, NATO was not justified in the spirit of Cold War world order diplomacy to respond to the SS-20s with counterdeployments. The danger in the mid-1980s was that arms control achievements would be reversed and would inaugurate another arms race in Europe.

Now NATO decided to match another part of Soviet strategy. They, too, would work on public opinion. NATO officials met with think tanks and editorial boards. Marshaled by the U.S. ambassador to NATO, David Abshire, they argued that a counterdeployment would bring the Soviets back to their previous stance on nuclear weapons and that the deterrence of mutually assured destruction would restore equilibrium.

As Nicholas Cull has shown, Abshire's and NATO's approach did not seek to convince the Soviet negotiators to change their positions. Instead they worked on key opinion formers in Europe to support the rationale for deployments.

> Abshire was the founder of the Center for Strategic and International Studies (CSIS) in Washington DC and already had a special relationship with the European think tank circuit and defense journalists. He also knew senior people in the European peace movement.[9]

Gradually, key non-governmental contacts in Europe began to swing around to the view that that the rise in tension was not due to NATO's proposed counterdeployments but to the Soviet aggressive intent with SS-20s.

In 1984, despite widespread public protest, the United States began to deploy missile systems in West Germany, Italy, and the United Kingdom. Meanwhile, a change of political leadership in the Soviet Union led to a change in outlook. Mikhail Gorbachev became the Soviet Leader in 1985. President Reagan and Prime Minister Thatcher decided that Mr. Gorbachev was a man they could do business with—shorthand for someone who could be a negotiating partner. The scene was set for a new stalemate to emerge. In March 1986, negotiations between the United States and the Soviet Union resumed, covering not only the INF issue but also separate discussions on strategic weapons (START I) and space issues. And the Soviet Union accepted a key condition that had long prevented progress on wider nuclear issues. There would be no other parties to the nuclear agreements. There would be no constraints imposed on British and French nuclear forces.

A series of prenegotiation meetings in August and September 1986 led to the Reykjavik Summit between Reagan and Gorbachev in October 1986. The ground had been prepared well. For the first time in history, two countries had agreed to eliminate a

(Continued)

(Continued)

whole class of existing missiles, those within a crucial intermediate range and they agreed to the terms of the INF treaty. Under its terms, nuclear and conventional ground-launched ballistic missiles and cruise missiles were eliminated with ranges between 500 and 5,500 kilometers. The INF treaty was signed on December 8, 1987, by President Reagan and President Gorbachev and entered into force on June 1, 1988. Despite excluding the United Kingdom and French systems, the United Kingdom and other NATO allies were involved directly in the negotiations as the terms of the verification of the dismantlement and destruction of the missiles involved access arrangements into the territory of the states where the deployments were made. As a junior officer in the Arms Control Department in the U.K. Foreign Office, I was part of the diplomatic team that negotiated the regime for the INF treaty inspections. U.K. sovereignty dictated that it must agree to the conditions on which the Soviets could inspect our bases.

A negotiation succeeded due to a carefully constructed stalemate between two negotiating entities, the United States/NATO and the Soviet Union, which, though they did not trust each on many issues, had long established a basis for mutual interests in arms control. It involved a massive diplomatic effort on detail, significant new defense expenditure, public diplomacy, management of an alliance, and a renewed personal trust between leaders. But the result was that the United States/NATO balance of power with the Soviet Union was back on track. The INF treaty was a successful negotiation for the 1980s, the final decade of the Cold War. But in diplomacy, nothing is final. Now the treaty's value is disputed by some as inappropriate for the security environment of the twenty-first century. Sometimes diplomacy's negotiating successes depend on a combination of factors that are hard to repeat.

CONTINUOUS NEGOTIATION

Diplomatic negotiations seldom have as far-reaching consequences as the INF treaty. To interact with other countries and fulfill their functions, diplomats must be negotiating. As we have seen, the VCDR designates negotiating as one of the functions of a diplomatic mission in the receiving state. There are innumerable daily examples of diplomatic negotiations. Every embassy is concerned with daily administrative arrangements, visits, visa and passport issues, and changes of staff at the mission. Within the framework of international institutions, contacts, discussions, proposals, and linkages are constantly in play to produce diplomatically agreed solutions.

Within regional groupings like the EU, and in international regulatory organizations like the World Trade Organization (WTO), diplomats are the actors for dispute solving, working for their national interests but also with their distinct preference for smoothing edges and with an incentive to produce agreements that will have wider significance than pure national interests. Both the EU and WTO are permanent negotiating fora that serve to promote and hone negotiating skills and have established an internal negotiating culture. Beyond its own internal negotiating culture, the EU negotiates as a bloc on trade issues and is the partner for any issues where the WTO has competence.

There have been proposals for discussion between the EU and the United States on a new free trade agreement, the largest in history. Before the EU adopts its formal negotiating stance for these talks, it must be preceded by protracted internal negotiations between the member states.

The framework of international organizations also reflects the negotiating ethos of the times. In the tradition of the United Nations, inclusiveness of all countries and the provision of one country one vote is the basis of negotiation. Yet there are few consensus-building mechanisms that are expressly designed to produce negotiated agreements. No authority can insist on a negotiation if states fail to agree. Diplomacy seldom forces the issue of negotiation, but likewise, without it, little would happen.

Summits are often useful staging posts for negotiations and provide an incentive for momentum. The summit is an occasion where evidence of diplomatic progress is often required and leaders will ask for deliverables—the results of prolonged negotiations—to make the event worthwhile. One example was at the Asia Pacific Economic Cooperation summit in Russia in September 2012, where the United States and Russia signed new agreements on Antarctica, the Bering Straits, and visa arrangements, and progressed talks on trade preferences. These were not headline-grabbing agreements perhaps but show a meeting that was prepared and scheduled in a way that was diplomatically useful.

Embassies can also be a means of checking the ripeness of positions for negotiations. As well as preparing the ground to move to a negotiation, the embassy is also best placed to initiate and manage it. Embassies are more focused on bilateral issues than a ministry of foreign affairs, which will have its own priorities, perhaps far-removed from the context of a local embassy. Indeed, a successful embassy within a national system may well be seen as one that is proposing an active negotiating agenda that they themselves will undertake. After all, modern diplomatic services are competitive organizations where those who show flair and drive will be earmarked for promotion. To negotiate a deal might offer a good chance to be noticed.

Case Study

Negotiation in Cuba

In the British embassy in Cuba, we decided to stage a major public diplomacy festival in 2002 to celebrate one hundred years of unbroken diplomatic relations between the United Kingdom and Cuba. Another motive was to show engagement in areas where the United Kingdom and Cuba could claim to have common interests. We had a sensitive relationship with Cuba. One of our diplomatic objectives, agreed within the EU, was to promote a more open and tolerant society with greater respect for freedom of expression. In proposing the festival, we were not abandoning this, and we were also showing Cuba that we regarded them as an important partner for the United Kingdom.

(Continued)

(Continued)

Nevertheless, the negotiations were not straightforward. It seemed simple enough to stage a centenary in 2002 as Cuba achieved independence from Spain in 1902. And we were not asking for any money from London—always a good selling point—as all the funding for the events was to come from British business. But the problem went deeper. Fidel Castro had never accepted that Cuba achieved real independence in 1902. The United States had still retained significant influence over Cuban foreign and defense policy with the Platt Amendment and maintained its military base at Guantanamo Bay. Over several months, we were in touch with a senior Cuban official who, like us, wanted to stage this festival (of over forty events spread over two months). But he, too, had a sensitive negotiating job to do to achieve a consensus. In the end, we compromised on the key issue of the one hundred years and chose instead another diplomatic peg, which was the brief British occupation of Havana in 1762. This enabled our collage of events to be staged. They included the participation of a distinguished British historian, who had written the authoritative history of modern Cuba in which he had made some critical remarks about Fidel Castro. He also was invited to lecture on Cuba and the United Kingdom as long as he stuck to 1762. The festival was a success and showed the United Kingdom's and Cuba's common interest in subjects as varied as The Beatles, mahogany furniture, Winston Churchill, sport, and nanotechnology.

CONCLUSION

This chapter has argued that diplomatic negotiations do exhibit special characteristics, and if they fail, the consequences are often much more serious than in the world of commerce or personal relations. Diplomatic negotiations, of course, take place at points or periods of time when specific alignments of interests and circumstances are favorable. Though the requirement and skills of the negotiator are timeless, some of the challenges of the modern world are new. Among these are the pressure from 24/7 media, instantaneous communications, and the necessity of involvement of many state and nonstate stakeholders. We now turn to an influence on diplomacy that has long been present but its importance has forced itself much more into diplomatic calculations—the issue of public diplomacy.

SUGGESTIONS FOR FURTHER READING

1. Zartman, I. William. "Diplomacy as Negotiation and Mediation." In *Diplomacy in a Globalizing World: Theories and Practices*, ed. Pauline Kerr and Geoffrey Wiseman. New York: Oxford University Press, 2012.
2. Cohen, Raymond. *Negotiating across Cultures: International Communication in an Interdependent World*, rev. ed. Washington, DC: United States Institute of Peace, 1997.
3. Hall, Todd, and Keren Yarhi-Milo, "The Personal Touch, Leaders' Impressions, Costly Signaling, and Assessment of Sincerity in International Affairs." *International Studies Quarterly* 56 (September 2012): 560–73.

chapter 7

Public Diplomacy

This book has so far concentrated on what diplomatic machinery exists for contacts between sovereign states, how their representatives behave, and how they negotiate. We now consider diplomacy that aims to engage with nonstate entities and individuals. For this reason, it is called public diplomacy.

Two different definitions, written at an interval of forty years, show common elements in how public diplomacy is seen but also how the activity has evolved.

> Public diplomacy . . . deals with the influence of public attitudes on the formation and execution of foreign policies. It encompasses dimensions of international relations beyond traditional diplomacy; the cultivation by governments of public opinion in other countries; the interaction of private groups and interests in one country with another; the reporting of foreign affairs and its impact on policy; communication between those whose job is communication, as diplomats and foreign correspondents; and the process of intercultural communications.[1]

> Traditional diplomacy is an international actor's attempt to manage the international environment through engagement with another international actor; public diplomacy is an international actor's attempt to manage the international environment through engagement with a foreign public.[2]

How do the institutions, professionals, and methods of diplomacy operate with the wider publics overseas? If diplomacy is about intelligence and tact in relations between sovereign states, why does it matter at all what ordinary people think? And how far is trying to engage with ordinary people simply an activity that is all about propaganda, which by its nature in sometimes distorting the facts will undermine the trust and respect that needs to exist among diplomats?

PUBLIC DIPLOMACY IN THE PAST

Anwar al-Awlaki was born in New Mexico in the United States in 1971 to parents from Yemen. His father, Nasser al-Awlaki, was a Fulbright scholar doing graduate work at universities in the United States. He later was appointed minister of agriculture in Yemen and president of Sana'a university. Anwar al-Awlaki became an Imam and used his religious platform on the Internet through many YouTube videos to promote jihad and attacks on the United States. He died in a U.S. drone attack in Yemen on September 30, 2011. Two weeks later, al-Awlaki's sixteen-year-old son, Abdulrahman al-Awlaki, a U.S. citizen who was born in Denver, was killed by a drone strike in Yemen. Nasser al-Awlaki released an audio recording condemning the killings of his son and grandson as senseless murders.

The following story appeared in the *New York Times* in February 2012.

> Twenty-seven years ago, a young man named Xi Jinping, on an agricultural research trip from his home in China, came to rural eastern Iowa and slept in Eleanor and Thomas Dvorchak's sons' room. The boys had just gone off to college—their room still stuffed with the things of childhood—and Ms. Dvorchak said she felt bad. She had grown up reading Pearl S. Buck novels about the travails in rural China, and now here was a visitor, perhaps from that same hard place, and they had put him in there with the Star Trek action figures.[3]

Both of these examples show U.S. public diplomacy in action. The two individuals, al-Awlaki and Xi Jinping, have impacted U.S. official diplomacy in significant ways. Both had been beneficiaries of U.S. public diplomacy—al-Awlaki's father had received a Fulbright scholarship, one of most prestigious awards for overseas students and a building block of U.S. public diplomacy for decades. In 1991, al-Awlaki himself returned to the U.S. state of Colorado to attend college. He earned a bachelor's degree in civil engineering from Colorado State University. Obviously, the United States' engagement with this family did not produce diplomatic benefits but nevertheless shows skilled American diplomacy in engaging with a prominent Yemeni family. The second example shows U.S. diplomatic efforts to use United States and Chinese shared interests in agriculture to build bridges with Chinese society, sow seeds of contact and perhaps goodwill. By 2013, Xi Jinping had become the president of China. Chalk one up to public diplomacy success. No one could have known that among the thousands of other Chinese junior officials and experts he would be the one to advance. Like many such public diplomacy exercises, the effect is uncertain, and the Iowa Star Trek bedroom may turn out to have had no diplomatic effect at all. But some spark of affection seems to have been ignited because Xi Jinping wanted to return to Iowa when he visited the United States as vice president in 2012.

Both of these examples show public diplomacy in ordinary times. In times of war, public opinion has long been a prime target of diplomacy because wars are not fought just by officials. William Joyce, with his nickname

Lord Haw Haw, was thought to be an asset to Nazi Germany during World War II. His creepy voice mocked the British and their version of how the war events were going. Set in a different context and with different objectives, the United Kingdom organized a public diplomacy campaign against U.S. neutrality in World War II. Again, the target was not U.S. officials. In the United Kingdom's case, the BBC played a part in influencing U.S. opinion. Americans used it to listen to Churchill's speeches and Britain's war was brought into America's homes by broadcasts and an American voice, CBS's Ed Murrow on the BBC.

A dedicated agency, the U.S. Information Agency (USIA), played a major role in psychological warfare in the U.S. intervention in the Dominican Republic of 1965 and the Vietnam War and was prominent in a counterdisinformation role in the Cold War. Similarly, the BBC's external services during World War II were fed material by the arm of the British Foreign Office and Secret Intelligence Service.

Diplomacy has of course long engaged with representatives of the media, who are normally (though not in all countries) distinct from representatives of the receiving government. Press conferences by ministers of foreign affairs are nothing new, and embassies have had press and information attachés for well over fifty years. An amusing example of ambassadors interacting with radio happened in 1948 when a question was asked of resident ambassadors by a Washington, D.C., radio station. Perhaps it was merely a time-filling exercise, and the question "What would you like for Christmas?" seemed easy enough for diplomats to handle. The French ambassador uttered some sugary platitude about world peace; the Soviet ambassador scored a cheap political point about "freedom from imperialist enslavement." The reply by the British ambassador, Oliver Franks, was simple and honest: "It's very kind of you to ask," he said. "I'd quite like a small box of crystallized fruit."[4]

PROPAGANDA?

Some see these efforts to engage by diplomats as really nothing more than propaganda. Berridge claims that public diplomacy is only a euphemism for propaganda because in contemporary diplomacy it is simply unacceptable to describe propaganda for what it is.[5] I think there are signs of an evolution in approach to the activity that will be discussed below, but it is true that propaganda and diplomacy were full partners for many years.

I experienced the traditional propaganda approach during my posting to the British embassy in Portugal. The Falklands War of 1982 was the only prolonged multitheater conflict that engaged the United Kingdom alone against another state in the lifetime of my generation of British diplomats. It was—and is—a classic international dispute over territorial arrangements that were the subject of much inconclusive diplomatic activity, UN meetings, and bloc alignments of support. When the war broke out, both Spain and Portugal were ripe to take sides and enter the public diplomacy debate. Spain of course had affiliations with Argentina and was involved in territorial issues with the United Kingdom over Gibraltar. The issue of the proximity of island territories to the nearest landmass did pose some contextual issues for the Spanish case—the Canary Islands are geographically closer to Morocco, and the Spanish-administered Ceuta and Melilla are in North Africa. But the colonial British were fair game, and Argentine television and press coverage of the war and the Argentine case for the seizure of the islands dominated Spanish television. As the press attaché in our embassy, I knew that the issues raised would be of interest to the Portuguese government but also the wider public. Portugal had some territory a long way from the mainland—the Azores—and Portugal was a party to one of the oldest bilateral treaties in the world with the United Kingdom, the Treaty of Windsor of 1386.

So, like many other U.K. posts, the embassy in Lisbon was given material to use to work on with political leaders and the media. We received a toolkit of material, statistics, and videos detailing the British origins of the Falklands population; descriptions of the military operations and capabilities of each side; and the important principles at stake of a military-led regime invading a peaceful democratic society that had its own representative government and where the population all spoke English. This was not just a public communications exercise. We needed Portuguese cooperation for logistical support for naval ships going down to the South Atlantic. So we naturally made our case with Portuguese foreign ministry officials and ministers as well. But it was primarily with the media that we used this material. Television and radio were important forces, but in those days they had specific domestic audiences and did not cross international boundaries.

In 1982, we had little possibility of engaging with the Portuguese wider public. There were no websites, Twitter feeds, or YouTube videos to advance your case. We had some successes with what we did, but the effort put into this small but significant conflict shows that there has always been a battle for hearts and minds. The growth of multinational diplomacy has meant that most countries like to convince foreign media and publics of the justice of their cases. One inevitable by-product of fighting a diplomatic public relations battle in a third country capital was the tension that it imposed on the embassy staff of the protagonists. We had good friends at the Argentine embassy in Lisbon. Obviously, that friendship was a victim of professional representative duties. Our consular duties of protecting British nationals in Portugal also had an odd public dimension. At the start of the conflict, the world roller hockey championships were taking place in Lisbon. As luck would have it, the United Kingdom was drawn against Argentina, one of the world powers in the sport. I was asked by the team if the game should go ahead. It was a Saturday afternoon and I advised that there seemed no point in causing further acrimony, so the game was played, resulted in a crushing Argentine victory dubbed by the British tabloid press as a war on roller skates.

The British mainstay of public information material for use overseas was over many decades the output of the Central Office of Information. Every

British post was fed a diet of annual "Handbooks on Britain," a solid if uninspiring narrative of all that was good in British institutions, education, science, and culture. This was supplemented by regular articles written by in-house and external journalists who again aimed to show the world what Britain was doing. Little of this material was tailored to each individual country, nor was there any invitation to discuss or debate the issues.

So while what we used in traditional public diplomacy was not spreading falsehoods, it was essentially self-promotion without any systematic attempt to obtain feedback. We were giving a narrative to another country that what United Kingdom was doing was right and that the British were talented and effective. Beyond that, there was perhaps a message that all the United Kingdom represented was basically worth emulating by others. We were using our diplomatic presence to represent our state, like a lawyer representing a client. It is obvious that the likely effect of every one of 190 or so states in the world engaging in propaganda is unlikely to be productive. The meeting of minds and mutual advantage, which is the bedrock of diplomacy, is unlikely to happen. And with the increasing access of all overseas audiences to new information and to a huge array of commentaries on every aspect of international relations, states can no longer expect the target audience of public diplomacy to be so malleable.

PUBLIC DIPLOMACY FOR TODAY'S WORLD

Let us try to answer three questions. How does the modern approach to public diplomacy differ from propaganda? Why is public diplomacy now a targeted activity for every sovereign state and indeed many multinational organizations? And how is it best carried out?

Some argue that traditional propaganda and cultural diplomacy have long been part of diplomatic activity to influence public opinion and set the scene for the modern era. Nothing fundamental has changed, though most would admit that old methods limited what was possible. The evidence in my view is different. I believe there are fundamental changes in the diplomatic environment that affect how public diplomacy is practiced. Nicholas Cull has identified several differences from the old and new roles of public diplomacy.[6] He notes the impact of the technology in the digital age, the pressures on states to undertake public diplomacy, the growing influence on diplomacy of nonstate actors, and the objectives that states hope to achieve compared to previous eras.

Beyond these differences with the past, the central motive in the modern world for promoting public diplomacy is the dilution of the influence of states in determining outcomes in diplomacy. States recognize they have neither the time nor resources to fashion the complete range of diplomatic behavior. They know that their economies are highly interdependent, jobs and investment flow across borders, and information flashes around the world before traditional diplomacy either knows or can intervene. Publics—in the widest sense of the term—are now a diplomatic factor that states ignore at their peril. And it is for reasons of national interest that states now see the need to engage with overseas publics. In the context of these significant changes, what are the factors that influence how modern public diplomacy is conducted?

First, domestic and overseas policies and decision-making processes are increasingly blurred. The impact a country makes on investors, tourists, and those searching for educational opportunities will be affected by a country's image and capacity to act in a way that appeals to others. A country is competing for influence, prosperity, and resources with many actors, some of which are not sovereign states and many of which have no allegiance to or identification with one sovereign state. Much of the public diplomacy agenda is therefore directed towards differentiating your country from others.

Second, access to information through global seamless communications is open to actors of all genres. Such communications have greatly enhanced the risks and opportunities for those who seek to manage international affairs. This has meant that governments face unpredictable threats that inflame tensions at the click of a search engine. Equally, states also have opportunities for outreach that no government even twenty years ago could have dreamed of. Two examples will show how global interconnection challenges and helps diplomacy. The attackers on the Mumbai hotels in November 2008 scouted their locations on Google Maps. They did not need to risk doing conventional reconnaissance in person. In the same country, the website of the U.S. embassy in New Delhi provides information, SAT test venues, and links for innumerable U.S. education institutions to attract Indian students—outreach over the Internet.

Third, though governments feel the need to engage with publics, the results and methods they use are outside the conventions of traditional diplomatic activity. There is no specific mention at all of public diplomacy in the Vienna Conventions. There are neither prescribed methods nor negotiated limits. The line between engaging with overseas publics and seeking to influence internal events challenges diplomatic norms and the separateness that remains a central feature of diplomatic functions.

Fourth, Thomas Jefferson observed that "as men become better informed, their rulers must respect them the more."[7] This is more than ever a tenet of promoting the new approach to public diplomacy rather than relying on pure propaganda. Publics are more informed, better wired, and more discriminating. Many have almost costless access to any piece of information they want. This poses another challenge for exponents of public diplomacy.

Fifth, the task of diplomacy has always been to project a clear message and make as substantive and convincing case as possible to promote common understanding of an international issue. Now the core task of making an argument and making it heard in the midst of innumerable distractions is demanding for even the most sophisticated and well-funded team of diplomats. A diplomatic system of any country is now swamped with data from a myriad of sources. Publics and their own information output demand attention as well as the torrents of material from other sovereign states. Publics themselves can now fulfill some of the traditional functions of diplomacy. They report on a foreign country. They can assist in protecting other citizens, for example, by using cell phones to alert authorities and identify dangerous locations in real time. And they can damage a state's reputation just as much any official actions. A football hooligan rioting in a foreign city may be just as much identified with the United Kingdom as the royal family. Indeed, the public's appetite and capacity to communicate means public diplomacy is often a reactive task. The information publics put out is unfiltered, unverified, and uncensored in many fora. But it provides part of the raw material for diplomacy within and between sovereign states. Jihadist websites are just as accessible as those for the U.S. embassy. And a figure like the Reverend Terry Jones and his Florida church of fifty members can have a hugely disproportionate influence. Edward Snowden, a former U.S. government employee and contractor, achieved his desired effect of raising awareness of U.S. surveillance not by communicating it discreetly to other governments but by leaking documents to mass media. Diplomats themselves would have been aware that spying is part of modern diplomacy. But the effect on the general public was what Snowden wanted to achieve, and U.S. official public diplomacy has had to respond.

EFFECTIVE PUBLIC DIPLOMACY

Recognizing all these challenges, what are the best methods that diplomats can use to implement their public diplomacy?

A country that is concerned about how other publics see it gives an impression that it values foreign relations. It is concerned with what others think of it. Some U.S. presidents, including both Wilson and Obama, have called the United States a "beacon" that by its example will inspire others. It is true that some countries do borrow and copy elements of governance that have worked elsewhere. But to call your own country a beacon is not a good start in developing relations with other countries whose publics may regard your light not so much as a beacon but as a dangerous fire.

In undertaking practical public diplomacy, most countries will have a more hardheaded interest. There is little to be said diplomatically by simply projecting an attractive image of your country. Diplomacy is not a popularity contest. But favorable opinions held by overseas publics can bring real benefits. A global public does not spend all its time agitating on blogs or communicating on social media. Such publics also spend money across borders and can now access products at the click of a switch. A country's international products and services reflect brands carefully crafted through corporate advertising. And the country of origin often incorporates elements of that brand. A German car is associated with German engineering prowess, thoroughness, and reliability established over decades. Italian flair and design is not something created by Italian diplomacy, but it can be used to its benefit. It is not only commercial products that carry a country image. So does a country itself as a destination for tourism, education, and foreign investment. A global customer for these services is certain to access material to help with making such a decision. So public diplomacy in these areas is not an option, it is a necessity. States have no choice but to compete in the attraction business. Joseph Nye's concept of *soft power*[8]—or the power to influence through attraction—is an ingredient of successful diplomacy. This will be examined in more detail when the results of public diplomacy are considered.

Effective public diplomacy is one of the most fascinating issues of modern diplomatic practice. As in other areas of diplomacy, good practice is imitated and competition is recognized between sovereign states. But when we analyze the components of good public diplomacy, there are few elements that can be read from a guidebook. The specifics of how to implement public diplomacy test the versatility of diplomats and resources of their states. And countries are not only engaging with different overseas publics but competing with each other. Unlike the titles of diplomats, their immunities and privileges, there is no uniformity, no one size that fits all.

The question every sovereign state faces in public diplomacy is to translate what it sees as its assets and uniqueness into a format that will engage overseas publics and perhaps convince them that it can be a useful and attractive partner. The objectives of public diplomacy may be similar to the old approach of propaganda, but that exercise is no longer seen as intelligent for the reasons we have identified. Amid all the opportunities and the competition for attention of overseas publics, states need to focus on productive elements that suit the circumstances of modern diplomacy. What guidance can our analysis provide?

First the activity of engagement in public diplomacy implies a relationship. A country needs to show commitment and interest in another to prepare for engagement. There is little room in modern public diplomacy for a situation where one side speaks and the other listens. The relationship needs to be a two-way street. Each side must be attentive to what the other is saying about it. Listening to what is being said, reading what is written, and composing a response need acute diplomatic antennae. The skillful and versatile mission will recognize that simply being in the country is no guarantee for fruitful interaction. Years of quiet formal diplomacy, carefully crafted strategy papers, immaculate dress and manners, and exchanging pleasantries with officials will not make any impact in public diplomacy.

Second, public diplomacy needs to take account of its locale. If a diplomat has been a successful performer in the formal, choreographed atmosphere of a capital like Rome, where status and bonhomie are the currency of diplomacy, it does not mean that success is guaranteed in a capital like Caracas. Versatility and intelligence will recognize that, just as marketing a product takes account of the consumer audience, so the style of public diplomacy must adapt. The same country cannot just deploy the same messages and content to its public diplomacy throughout the world. Russia's public diplomacy efforts towards the Georgian public will differ greatly from what it uses in the United States.

British public diplomacy in Argentina will bear little resemblance to what it deploys in Japan.

Though every partner country in public diplomacy wants to feel special, the reality is that states do also adopt a regional approach to messages. It would indeed seem odd if the United States were deploying different public diplomacy messages in Morocco and Algeria, or between Kenya and Tanzania. So countries may find common themes. Indeed, the United States has established regional hubs to coordinate such approaches. Yet engaging with countries generally requires customized messages, even where the target publics do share some common culture. Any regional specialist will know that the demographics, geography, history, and ethnic composition of Libya, Egypt, and Syria are very different. Smart public diplomacy must recognize this.

Third, a country may appear a more attractive diplomatic partner because it appears to emphasize global issues rather than its own agenda. Overseas publics may be more inclined to share a view with another country on an issue such as climate change or renewable energy sources rather than on issues where nationalist rivalry is more evident. Using diplomacy to discuss exchanges in science, sport, and culture may also be productive. Such messages can often be deployed globally, and the country engaging in the debate may improve its own reputation as a trustworthy and active diplomatic partner.

Fourth, public diplomacy is also only one element of diplomacy, one input to foreign policy. So it is pointless to choose themes for public diplomacy if they are at odds with your policy. Though public diplomacy likes to be responsive and agile, foreign policy has a history that is not easy to reshape in a period of a policy cycle. India and Pakistan cannot simply wipe their slates clean because public diplomacy campaigns argue they should. And if public opinion is generally already favorably disposed towards your country, then public diplomacy, as an absorber of scarce diplomatic resources, may not be a priority. Every state has to prioritize. Equally, starting afresh with a public diplomacy campaign in a hostile environment may take years to produce any result. Former colonial powers in Africa and Asia still have a negative hangover on certain issues. Yet, even here, it is important to listen to what the particular audience is saying. Perhaps surprisingly, an opinion poll published by the Jamaican newspaper *The Gleaner* in 2011 recorded that 60 percent of those surveyed preferred Jamaica when it was a British colony.

Fifth, the best voices and means of communicating may not always be those of the state itself. If you can work towards a position where the audience itself starts to articulate your messages and arguments, then this will appear more credible and effective. An article about the compassionate treatment of immigrants in a country will have more weight if written by a UN official or by a director of Oxfam International than by an official of the foreign ministry.

Sixth, public diplomacy must be responsive and take into account new developments. And public diplomacy mechanisms have diverse uses. It is not all about upside from the engagement. It may have damage control as its major objective. The United Kingdom was launching a major trade offensive in Brazil in 2012. Large delegations accompanied a visit by the British Prime Minister, and new staff had been posted to Brazil to promote trade and investment. This all should have been very positive for British public diplomacy. But at the same time, the media were full of news that Brazilian students were being sent home from the United Kingdom for not having proper student visas. It was terrible public diplomacy timing as many of the students were already in courses in UK universities. As a result, student applications to the United Kingdom from Brazil fell by one-fifth. A short-term blip perhaps, but UK public diplomacy needed to work hard just to restore the previous position.

A conflict involving a state or an attack on its citizens may signify failure of state-to-state diplomacy. But it may also indicate a problem for public diplomacy. Since the attacks of September 11, 2001, the United States has invested vast resources in public diplomacy efforts in the Middle East. A sustained and well-resourced public diplomacy campaign has been used as part of a wide range of diplomatic measures in part to address a security issue. Some would argue that the task is beyond the capacity of U.S. public diplomacy, simply because of its links with and support for Israel.

PUBLIC DIPLOMACY IN PRACTICE

Theory is one thing, but in terms of diplomatic practice, what specific activities might produce successful public diplomacy? We will not focus on any one country but rather on the strategies that seem to offer most returns to diplomacy as a whole. We will then look at examples of what states have done in practice and the results they have achieved.

Objectives

To be effective, a public diplomacy campaign must have objectives. The United Kingdom, like many countries, has reviewed repeatedly its objectives in public diplomacy. The Carter Review of 2005 gave a short definition of what they viewed as Public Diplomacy: "Work which aims at influencing in a positive way the perceptions of individuals and organizations overseas about the UK, and their engagement with the UK."[9] In 2012, the UK Foreign Office defined the activity as follows:

> Public Diplomacy is a process of achieving the UK's international strategic priorities through engaging and forming partnerships with like-minded organizations and individuals in the public arena. So beyond traditional government-to-government channels, we talk to [non-governmental organizations], think tanks, opinion formers, young people, businesses and individual citizens (FCO 2012).[10]
>
> It's not just about delivering messages but holding a two-way dialogue, listening to and learning from audiences around the world, in

order to get a better understanding of the changing perceptions of the UK and its policies.[11]

It is clear that some of the recommendations that flow from modern analysis have been accepted by the management of British diplomacy. And that British public diplomacy is part of the wider efforts of British foreign policy to achieve the United Kingdom's international strategic priorities.[12] In 2012, the United Kingdom's strategic priorities were defined in simple terms as follows:

- Safeguard Britain's national security.
- Build Britain's prosperity.
- Support British nationals around the world through modern and efficient consular services.[13]

So in areas where diplomacy might previously have been seen to be an activity between sovereign states and their representatives—such as security, counter-terrorism, and protection of nations—the United Kingdom believes that public diplomacy must also play a role in all it major responsibilities.

The history of the U.S. Information Agency (USIA) is illustrative of how the setting of objectives for public diplomacy has changed. Founded in 1953, USIA was the coordinating agency for U.S. information diplomacy. Its stated aims reflected the rationale for U.S. propaganda efforts in the Cold War. It is noticeable, in contrast to the modern approach of engagement, that the flow of information to other countries' publics is described only in terms of emanating from the United States:

- To explain and advocate U.S. policies in terms that are credible and meaningful in foreign cultures
- To provide information about the official policies of the United States, and about the people, values and institutions which influence those policies
- To bring the benefits of international engagement to American citizens and institutions by helping them build strong long-term relationships with their counterparts overseas
- To advise the President and U.S. government policy-makers on the ways in which foreign attitudes will have a direct bearing on the effectiveness of U.S. policies[14]

Nevertheless, the USIA founded and administered some programs that have been seen as enduring successes in public diplomacy. The Voice of America broadcasts in the Cold War and the Fulbright educational exchanges had their origins in USIA work. In October 1999, the USIA was integrated into the State Department. At the time of its dissolution, the USIA had a budget of over $1 billion and a staff of over 6,000, more people than the whole of the UK Foreign Office. The Office of the Undersecretary for Public Diplomacy and

Public Affairs was created in 1999 to oversee the public diplomacy programs that USIA had administered.

The 9/11 attacks resulted in a major reassessment of U.S. public diplomacy. New objectives became a priority. The attacks were the largest ever on the U.S. homeland and, as the perpetrators were nonstate actors, part of the analysis concentrated on the failures of U.S. public diplomacy. The attackers were not armed or paid by a sovereign state but were attracted by a violent doctrine of revenge, promoted by a transnational activist, Osama bin Laden. As Joseph Nye has noted, bin Laden essentially used soft power to stimulate the attack. "Why do they hate us?" became a debating point in U.S. media. And the report of the U.S. 9/11 Commission in July 2004 put the activity of public diplomacy as central to the strategy of fighting the War on Terror: "Long-term success demands the use of all the elements of national power: diplomacy, intelligence, covert action, law enforcement, economic policy, foreign aid, public diplomacy, and homeland defense."[15]

We will look at how successful this role of public diplomacy when we discuss what in practice makes for good public diplomacy. But a look at a post-9/11 U.S. assessment of public diplomacy objectives can be seen in a statement by Judith McHale, Undersecretary at the Department of State for Public Diplomacy in 2011.

> In a world where power and influence truly belongs to the many, we must engage with more people in more places. That is the essential truth of public diplomacy in the Internet age. But it is not just a diffusion of power that necessitates greater engagement. The landscape of actors looking to influence that power has broadened as well. In years past, we were content to wait for the world to come to us. We expected that they would. And when we were the most attractive option, perhaps they did. Not anymore. Today, we must contend with an increasingly savvy and motivated set of influencers on a global stage, each armed with a vast array of affordable, adaptable tools to spread their message. Powers such as China, Brazil and Iran are flexing their economic and political muscle and establishing their own networks of cultural centers and language instruction around the world.[16]

Her successor as undersecretary, Tara Sonenshine, defined public diplomacy in this way: "The challenge of public diplomacy is to explain America. What are its policies, its practices, its values, its ideals and its ideas? And how do we bring that narrative into a rapidly expanding and deepening global conversation?"[17]

Engagement, conversation, and narrative are common terms used to describe the objectives of public diplomacy, even for the world's most powerful country. The United States' example is mirrored by the rest of the states that practice diplomacy in the twenty-first century.

Messages

Once a public diplomacy campaign has its objectives, the policy managers must decide what will form the content of the engagement. The attention given to engaging with particular publics shows that they are considered worth the effort, but beyond this, what messages in the conversation and narrative should be central to a public diplomacy campaign?

It is a wise approach when engaging with any audience not to assume you know everything about them and their opinions. Therefore, the messages crafted for public diplomacy need to be preceded by listening. What do they think about us and why? How does this influence their behavior? What messages would address any "image deficit" that our state might be perceived as having?

The first principle of a public diplomacy message is that it is not a diplomatic document. It is not something to be constructed and interpreted by committees of officials. And it is not a message reproducing a bureaucratic recitation of the strategic priorities. It needs to be simple, bear repetition, and give the audience reason to explore further. And a message can be given through different means. Actions that attract public attention may often speak louder to a foreign audience than words. Visual themes and events that have a popular content will open eyes and ears. And a message that could be effective in public diplomacy may suggest a sharing of interests, a two-way street, and a willingness to have a conversation. In 2002, we chose a date for our public diplomacy festival in Cuba that had importance to both countries, and we called the series of events "Islas y Ideas." The United Kingdom and Cuba might not appear to share much in common from their histories and economic systems, but no one could deny that they are both islands.

Targets

The sophistication of modern public diplomacy goes beyond just targeting overseas publics. This is too vast an audience for practical purposes. Many members of the audience will not pay attention. Some will be have no interest at all in international issues. Modern technology may suggest that the size of the world is the only limit. But there is little point in a scattergun approach to public diplomacy. Who might be the most productive targets? In most cases, the young will be seen as part of any public diplomacy target. One day they will travel, one day perhaps they will seek education overseas, one day they will run businesses. Equally, it is a sad reality that few public diplomacy campaigns target the over-80 age group. Women may be another target, particularly in societies where they have unequal opportunities. And in some countries, literacy may present a major problem to what messages can be deployed—in Pakistan over 50 percent of women can't read and write.

Cuban public diplomacy in the United Kingdom had specific targets. They worked closely with the local "Cuba Solidarity" organizations so their priority targets were left-leaning groups, often trade unions and anti-U.S. groups. Their hospitality was famously lavish. They devoted attention as well to the British public, holding open town hall meetings and they were good at what they did. Other targets for public diplomacy can include the state's own public. By hosting the Beijing Olympics in 2008 and the Shanghai World Expo in 2010, China was not only targeting world public opinion but also its own domestic constituency to generate pride in China's achievements.

Methods

There is little in diplomatic guidelines about the best methods of doing public diplomacy. The formal statement at a press conference by a foreign minister, a YouTube video by a startled-looking ambassador in a flowery tie, a visit by a children's choir, and a scholarship program for graduate students may all be regarded as worthwhile exercises. Anwar al-Awlaki, the Muslim cleric who was mentioned at the start of the chapter, used Facebook, YouTube, and many blogs to advance his cause. The Saudi news agency Al Arabiya described him as the "bin Laden of the Internet."[18]

The good news for public diplomacy practitioners is that there are many actors who may be capable and interested in playing a part in a public diplomacy. There are resources as well to be tapped because a country's attractiveness matters to many entities in the private sector. In Cuba, the British government paid nothing toward our public diplomacy festival. We raised $50,000 split between the dozen or so British commercial companies with a presence in Cuba. They were interested, partly at least because they might need the British government to lobby for their interests in the future but also because in a largely state-run economy, the government of Cuba could bestow many benefits to a company that was seen as a good partner and also make life difficult for those who were not. No participant in our festival was paid a fee but received expenses only. The U.S. parties hosted by diplomatic missions overseas to celebrate July 4th are paid for by businesses like Starbucks and Coca Cola. The U.S. Congress insists that such public diplomacy outreach never comes from the taxpayer's pocket.

Assuming the resources can be found, how should smart public diplomacy be managed? The versatile and intelligent diplomat will need to look at the market of public opinion. Who are the opinion formers? What would be an eye-catching message? What do we share with the country in popular culture? Tailored messages require tailored methods. The impression of an engaged embassy reaching out to varied elements of society also brings added benefits to diplomacy. Valuable contacts are expanded and assist greatly with the reporting on developments function described in the Vienna Convention on Diplomatic Relations.

A country may also choose methods that reach out to the global public by demonstrating its international credentials, expertise, or diversity. The staging of sporting events that attract global attention is a high level of engagement with the public. They are among the most prized platforms for showing off a country (old propaganda) but also now have been crafted to project other messages, including engagement. During the 2012 Olympics in London, the United Kingdom staged numerous events to impress foreign investors, promoting the UK music, film, and fashion industry, and British business expertise in sustainable energy, renewables, and modern transport. The Olympic movement and other global sporting events were conceived as contributions to internationalism and the promotion of world peace. Indeed, the instigator of the modern Olympics, the Frenchman Pierre de Coubertin, described his objective in terms that would be familiar to modern practitioners of public diplomacy:

> Let us export our oarsmen, our runners, our fencers into other lands. That is the true free trade of the future; and the day it is introduced into Europe the cause of Peace will have received a new and strong ally.[19]

Yet sovereign states appear to have diverted this intent to a new adjunct of nationalism. And the flag waving, medals tables, and fanatical support in sport has showed that major sporting occasions have a divisive as well as a uniting element.

States now face many rivals for international attention of publics. The methods used by NGOs and interest groups stimulate imitation. Religious organizations are some of the largest NGOs in the world and influence the opinions and motivations of large percentages of the world's public. When Pope Francis was inaugurated as head of the Catholic Church on the balcony of the Vatican before thousands of faithful in 2013, there were Argentine flags being waved—pride in a native son of the country and a plus for Argentine public diplomacy. One of the world's leading transnational religious organizations with followers of over one billion people had selected a candidate for its top job according to national considerations. Soon after his election, Pope Francis was asked by the president of Argentina to arbitrate in that ever simmering territorial dispute with the United Kingdom—the Falkland Islands. In 2014, the Islamic State (IS) produced slick videos encouraging recruits from all over the world to come to join their movement; they offered adventure, money and a new state that would ultimately change the world. Conventional diplomacy played little part in their brutal methods. But public diplomacy certainly did.

Technology has opened up many new possibilities for public diplomacy, and these will be discussed in greater detail in Chapter 11. Old methods, such as the printed page, are no longer staple fare. But some may still be seen as useful. At least the Japanese foreign ministry's calendar of flower arrangements called Ikebana, produced in thousands for distribution through diplomatic missions worldwide, had a year's usage and the pages suggested beauty, order, and peace, transmitting an effective public diplomacy message.

We saw in Chapter 3 how embassy websites are a method of public diplomacy used by many countries. A properly managed website will project different messages and use different methods in different contexts—Cairo, Pristina, or Moscow. Embassy and ministry websites have many other functions but most countries seek to use them at least in part to make a public diplomacy impact. Many ambassadors have tried blogging on their sites to appear in touch with the overseas public. Evidence suggests that few read, and even fewer bother to comment on, ambassadors' opinions—a message to note for the discerning public diplomatist.

It may be difficult to determine the objectives of public diplomacy campaigns. But their methods are and should be visible. Any strategist needs to take full account of the activities of others and the risks of imitating or overloading an approach to the same public. The missions of most countries will hold national days, celebrations of their culture, food tasting, and informative events. Some of these are for reassuring the resident nations of the mission that their country is flying the flag. But such events become part of the diplomatic ritual, and a natural result would be for them to cancel each other out. So it is not surprising that the contest for attention has spread into new areas.

Whatever the methods, public diplomacy has become an obligatory feature of modern diplomatic systems. It is not just a facet of the Western, liberal tradition. China now runs its Confucius Institutes. Founded only in 2004, they operate under the management of Hanban, which is formally described as non-governmental but receives extensive government funding for its cultural and language centers that now operate in over one hundred countries. Since 2006, the Indian Ministry of Foreign Affairs has a website devoted purely to Indian public diplomacy. A year after its foundation, Indian public diplomacy had more than 26,000 Twitter followers and 45,000 on Facebook. Iran runs a sophisticated media organization called Press TV, broadcasting in English, Spanish, and other languages.

The British Council, founded in 1934, has long played a role in promoting UK arts and science, as well as language education. The reputation of Britain in public diplomacy is closely associated with this rather oddly named but globally recognized organization. Today it raises considerable funding from its commercial activities as consultants and teaching language classes. Less than a third of its resources now comes from the British government. In 2009, the Director of Arts of the British Council told *Monocle* magazine enthusiastically,

> The arts are the most powerful tool you have to build a dialogue discussion across boundaries. It was only very recently that I heard a member of the Foreign Office say for the first time that arts are now as important as sanctions in the toolkit.[20]

The range of choice for public diplomacy methods is perhaps intimidatingly vast. The decision maker best placed to judge which methods are used is the resident diplomat. The task is so specific to the local audience and conditions that public diplomacy is now an increasingly important function of the diplomatic mission. Partnering with NGOs, opinion formers and cultural and sporting organizations may also produce dividends. A celebrity visit, a Twitter feed, a partnership in education, or a sustained thematic campaign over months are all now realistic options. But an understanding of a sophisticated and better-informed public is central to its effectiveness. The very versatility of a diplomatic mission may be the key message and method. And if the methods fail to work then obviously diplomacy needs to be agile enough to listen, think again, and make changes.

Organization

In the complexity of overseas relations, the public diplomacy effort needs to be properly coordinated. The U.S. State Department budget for public diplomacy in 2013 was over $370 million. The money needs to be allocated, balancing large and minor projects and combined where possible with other sources from the private sector. Beyond that, every actor in government needs to take account of the content of the campaign. As we saw when discussing ministries of foreign affairs, they now fight battles within their systems simply to retain control of diplomacy. Many who work in government think they know what needs doing to influence public opinion. The organization needs to be rigorous, sustained even through setbacks (such as the Brazilian visa issues), and flexible enough to show flair rather than resort to bureaucratic compromise. It will need to be proactive in damage limitation. A scandal at a military base involving your country's nationals may damage your hard work in creating a public diplomacy campaign designed to highlight your state's education opportunities.

Results

The application of strategy to public diplomacy shows that it is not an exercise easy to commit to paper. Bureaucrats like to see what an organization is delivering, but the exasperating part of public diplomacy is that it is difficult to measure results and even more difficult to explain what is happening to change the public perception of your state.

No aspect of diplomacy should be assessed without an appraisal of performance. The continuity of diplomacy militates against freezing time to take measurements, and a public diplomacy success can turn sour quickly. In any case, public diplomacy is only one part of the overall activity. And even after a sustained public diplomacy campaign, which members of an overseas public should be asked their opinion? Is diplomacy aiming at newspaper editors, heads of NGOs, youth leaders, or simply Joe or Jane six-pack?

The success of the U.S. public diplomacy instruments during the Cold War is widely cited as the result of sustained efforts that could not have been achieved through conventional diplomacy. The broadcasts of Voice of America, academic exchanges, and the projection of Western values weakened Soviet totalitarianism and communist ideology. In particular, President Reagan saw U.S. diplomacy's overall mission was to contribute to winning the Cold War. He also ended what he saw as a decade of détente-oriented policies toward the Soviet bloc and embarked on a major military buildup. Reagan provided America's public diplomacy organizations with significant new resources, and changed their mandate to reengage in the ideological struggle with the Soviet Union to prove the superiority of the Free World. This had not always been the case. The broadcasts of Radio Free Europe in the 1950s seemed to encourage armed uprisings against communism. But in the Hungarian uprising of 1956, the United States appeared unwilling or unable to intervene, so public diplomacy messages delivered in Hungarian were widely seen as discrediting U.S. policy.

One unexpected result that came to light after the collapse of the Soviet Union was the Russian public's view of the Watergate scandal. Public diplomacy might suggest that the scandal of a U.S. president bugging an opponent and covering up what had been done would be viewed negatively overseas. On the contrary, the evidence suggested that the Soviet public were favorably impressed with the accountability of its political leaders that the U.S. system had shown. It was the type of thing that would never have happened under communism.

Acceptance of results of public diplomacy may come as an unpleasant surprise. There must be an honesty to admit failure, but public diplomacy engages with the real world that politicians may prefer to ignore. During the Vietnam War, President Johnson dealt with the decline in the international standing of the United States by canceling the polls. Richard Nixon ended the practice of receiving a digest of editorials from around the world and rarely read what was written about the United States overseas.

Even if the feedback from overseas publics is favorable, results may be difficult to attribute to a specific policy or may merely show a persisting image problem with an overseas public that would have been much worse without the efforts. One obvious way of assessing results is if the public diplomacy efforts with sections of the media have resulted in more favorable coverage or a change in the balance of arguments on an issue. In our Falklands campaign, we monitored what our journalist interlocutors wrote about the British case compared to what they were writing before our contact and delivery of material.

One frustrating feature of public diplomacy is that there may be no correlation to the effort or resources devoted to it and the results. The United States Educational Foundation in Pakistan (USEFP) is a commission dedicated to improve Pakistan-U.S. relations through educational exchange opportunities. Since 1951, the USEFP has sponsored more than 2,000 Pakistani students to study in the United States and brought 800 Americans to Pakistan. The USEFP is also one of fifty-one Fulbright Commissions worldwide and runs the largest Fulbright program in the world. On the face of it, a sustained program over many years targeting young educated Pakistanis and an estimated $43 billion of U.S. aid to Pakistan since 1947 (according to former Pakistan ambassador to the

United States, Husain Haqqani) should have produced some positive results. But as the Pew Research Center figures have shown, the U.S. favorability standing in Pakistan is abysmally low—only 12 percent of Pakistanis have a favorable view of the United States.[21]

Results may also show changes in public perceptions on issues through effects that have little to do with direct public diplomacy efforts. The case of Vietnam might have seemed a particularly difficult public diplomacy challenge for the United States. Yet U.S. products such as Coca Cola and McDonald's are now leading brands in Vietnam, and some U.S. companies such as Nike have built factories there. The number of Vietnamese living in the United States is over 1.5 million, and affluent Vietnamese parents now see the United States as a prime location for their children to study. U.S. prosperity and openness has obviously contributed to this, and it may be that the Vietnamese government's decision to promote foreign investment and a new wealthy middle class had more to do with the boost in U.S. image than any systematic public diplomacy campaign.

Many countries devote resources now to probing the views of overseas publics to identify what public diplomacy produces the best results. The British Council has run "Through Others Eyes" surveys. The Pew Research Survey of favorability ratings of various countries has a particular relevance to public diplomacy as it has been conducted over an extended period. For the United States there were major "image deficits" identified by Pew from 2002 to 2008 even in the publics of NATO allies like Germany, France, and the United Kingdom. Pew's results showed a marked upswing in the later years of the decade following the announcement of the U.S. withdrawal from Iraq and more emphasis on public diplomacy in the Muslim world.

Yet the results in Muslim countries where the United States devoted major resources, such as Egypt and Pakistan, were at best mixed and overall very discouraging. Most show a considerable decline since the first year of the Obama administration. The favorability indices in Egypt and Jordan have slipped back and were never better than 27 percent overall of those Egyptians asked. With $1.5 billion a year in U.S. military and civil aid to Egypt in this period, it is clear money can't buy affection. In Pakistan, the favorability figures were even worse. Significantly, Pew Research found that U.S. public diplomacy campaigns were perhaps ill conceived in the case of Pakistan. Some 94 percent of Pakistanis considered themselves first Muslim and second Pakistani. And Pakistani dislike of America predates the modern era. Even before the wars in Afghanistan and Iraq, Pew found 70 percent of Pakistanis did not view the United States favorably. Equally, years of being a U.S. ally in NATO have not altered the unfavorable views of a majority of Turks or Greeks. By contrast, Kenya, a country not covered regularly by Pew, shows consistently that over 90 percent of its population has a favorable view of the United States. And this was the case before the election of the President Obama, who had a Kenyan father. Deciphering public diplomacy results often defies common sense and may lead to disenchantment with the activity. Yet, as we have seen, total abandonment is also not seen as an option.

Figure 7.1 **U.S. Favorability Ratings, Obama versus Bush**

	Percentage Favorable toward U.S.			Percentage Point Change	
	Bush era	Obama era			
	2008 %	2009 %	2012 %	2008–2012	2009–2012
Italy	*53**	--	74	*+21*	--
France	*42*	75	69	*+27*	*–6*
Poland	*68*	67	69	*+1*	*+2*
Britain	*53*	69	60	*+7*	*–9*
Spain	*33*	58	58	*+25*	*0*
Czech Rep.	*45**	--	54	*+9*	--
Germany	*31*	64	52	*+21*	*–12*
Greece	--	--	35	--	--
Russia	*46*	44	52	*+6*	*+8*
Lebanon	*51*	55	48	*–3*	*–7*
Tunisia	--	--	45	--	--
Egypt	*22*	27	19	*–3*	*–8*
Turkey	*12*	14	15	*+3*	*+1*
Jordan	*19*	25	12	*–7*	*–13*
Pakistan	*19*	16	12	*–7*	*–4*
Japan	*50*	59	72	*+22*	*+13*
China	*41*	47	43	*+2*	*–4*
India	--	--	41	--	--
Brazil	--	--	61	--	--
Mexico	*47*	69	56	*+9*	*–13*

Source: Pew Research Global Attitudes Project, "Global Opinion of Obama Slips, International Policies Faulted," June 13, 2012, http://www.pewglobal.org/2012/06/13/global-opinion-of-obama-slips-international-policies-faulted.

*Figure from 2007

PEW RESEARCH CENTER Q8a.

Soft Power

The most sought-after result from public diplomacy is what has been termed *soft power*. What is soft power and why does it matter in diplomacy? And how does soft power differ from public diplomacy?

Joseph Nye formalized the concept of soft power that in previous iterations might have been termed public affection, a special relationship, or a predisposition in overseas relations to be attracted to another country. As Nye has explained, hard power is a form of power where countries can achieve their objectives through force of arms or through economic might. Soft power involves neither tanks nor money but is the power of a country to attract others. Diplomats and states are not the only strivers for soft power. The concept is akin to *social capital*, which enhances the stature or influence of an individual or group through social networking.

Many organizations and individuals seek soft power, either for commercial sponsorships or to raise money from their activities. These include agencies of the UN and regional groupings like the European Union. Public diplomacy is part of the process of creating such soft power. As with most diplomacy, the results are difficult to measure and even more difficult to attribute. We have seen that some of the positive results of attraction are now foreign investment, overseas students paying fees, and tourism. Yet diplomacy tends to operate on specific issues and seldom applies itself to the full range of international relations. So inevitably, public diplomacy is an inexact science and soft power an amorphous concept. However well Japanese culture, cars, and businesses are regarded in China, they did not stop the Japanese ambassador's car from being attacked and its flag stolen in Beijing at the height of tensions over disputed islands in August 2011. Soft power is never the only objective of a relationship with another country. It is part of complex system of international outreach, other parts of which involves dialogue, coercion, trade-offs, and some elements of hard power.

And yes, the modern passion for measuring and league tables has even reached soft power. Since 2010, *Monocle* magazine has published an annual Soft Power Survey, ranking countries according to their ability to promote themselves in the world via culture, diplomacy, and trade. In 2012, the United Kingdom was declared the winner.

CONCLUSIONS AND CASE STUDIES

Public diplomacy is done for a wide variety of reasons, but the core reasons are more defensive than offensive. The explanatory statements of ministries recognize the declining influence of states, the power of the many, and the dangerous openness of media and instantaneous communication. These features suggest that public diplomacy is being engaged in with greater regularity because the world is becoming more chaotic and less predictable. Countries see others doing it, the frightening ease with which false rumors can be spread, and recognize how the extremists have grasped so enthusiastically and sometimes expertly the opportunities of modern communications and social media. Diplomacy's objective to smooth the edges of tension has been threatened. We will examine the full implications of the communications revolution in Chapter 11.

Case Study

The Shanghai World Expo 2010

In my own career, I saw some notable examples of where engaging in public diplomacy did serve national interests, producing results that could not have been obtained by other more conventional diplomacy. From the early planning stages, I was project director for the UK presence at the Shanghai World Expo of 2010. The United Kingdom's Public Diplomacy Board, which included many non-governmental experts in marketing and business, had to agonize over funding for the event, but their conclusion at an early planning meeting was simple. The Board gave us a simple message: "Do it well. Do it big." And, after it was all over, a careful cost-benefit analysis was made for the investment that the United Kingdom made. For six months, from May until October 2010, 73 million people visited the Shanghai Expo. It was the largest of its kind in the history of expos (which dated back to the Great Exhibition in London in 1851) and the first in an emerging—by 2010 already emerged!—economy. The site spread over 5.3 square kilometers with 192 nations and fifty international organizations exhibiting on the theme "Better City, Better Life." Each major pavilion occupied a site in downtown Shanghai the size of a football field. Internationally known architects and designers vied with each other and other states to wow the visitors. In 2010, Shanghai was the biggest show on earth—an extravaganza of public diplomacy.

Real Life Benefits

Here is how the British embassy in Beijing summarized the real benefits to a UK university, the University of Nottingham, and its business community from committing to a presence at the Expo.

> A University in the United Kingdom has helped to cement good relations with China after committing to a six-month presence at the World Expo in Shanghai.
>
> It was the only U.K. academy that exhibited for so long at China's Expo 2010 in Shanghai and because of that effort, the University of Nottingham's venture is now paying dividends.
>
> New business and research partnerships are emerging from the 17 expert-led conferences and workshops attended by more than 1,000 key stakeholders as well as the many meetings that took place during the exposition. Hundreds of thousands of visitors explored through words, pictures and video Nottingham University's research in sustainability . . . based on the theme, "Zero Carbon, Zero Waste."[22]

> The embassy described the benefits of the Expo to the wider region of Nottingham.
>
> In [2011] Chinese car manufacturer Chang'an Automobile will establish its U.K. research and development facility at the Nottingham Science Park, creating up to 200 jobs. During the course of the Shanghai exhibition, the university received more than 400 serious business inquiries. . . . July's drug discovery conference led to several prominent pharmaceutical companies beginning to develop an R&D center in Shanghai. . . .
>
> The global food security event strengthened relationships with multinational food producers, enabling visits to their R&D bases in Shanghai; plans are under way to establish a waste-reducing, post-harvest technology center of excellence with existing partners.
>
> One green manufacturing workshop launched the Sino-U.K. low-carbon manufacturing consortium, a unique multi-disciplinary research and educational partnership between international academics, industry and government bodies in China and the United Kingdom.[23]

For the UK as a whole, the results of the expo are of course harder to define. The UK pavilion won the gold medal for design in the category for the largest pavilions, the expo's top award. And the tourism growth to the United Kingdom from China since the expo has been impressive. A record 149,000 Chinese visitors came to the United Kingdom in 2011. According to the organization Visit Britain, China showed the largest absolute growth in all countries in terms of amounts spent between 2009 and 2013.[24]

Box 7-1 **Registering Disapproval**

Not all public diplomacy is about what might be seen as positive activities like education, culture, and tourism. Engagement with overseas publics can register disapproval of internal government policies and underpin the importance of human rights.

During my posting in Cuba, the government arrested seventy-five members of the peaceful opposition in March 2003. They were imprisoned for long periods after sham trials. It was our stated diplomatic policy to promote more openness and tolerance in Cuba. The United Kingdom and other countries of the EU, having made their displeasure felt directly to the Cuba government, decided to engage in some more public diplomacy. Parties held to celebrate national days are useful occasions for embassies to invite officials, members of civil society, the media, and others—a public diplomacy exercise. They normally take place in the head of mission's house. It is an embassy's right to decide who will be invited. In 2003, we decided to invite some of the spouses of the imprisoned opposition as guests to our parties alongside the representatives of the government. The government representatives stayed for a while but decided to walk out, and subsequently announced they were freezing contracts with the EU.

(Continued)

(Continued)

Public diplomacy became more conventional diplomatic practice when, in June 2003, EU ministers agreed to include this policy of invitations in the list of diplomatic sanctions against Cuba for the imprisonments. Did this unusual measure have an effect? The answer is not immediately. The Cuban government was not allowed to forget about the imprisonments as the EU had some fifteen missions in Havana, so similar parties with opposition guests invited happened at regular intervals. Perhaps not surprisingly, EU diplomats were not invited to government parties. *The Economist* newspaper dubbed it "the cocktail party wars."[25] There was, however, a serious purpose. The spouses themselves felt safe in the gardens of an inviolable mission and formed a peaceful group to walk in Havana called the "Ladies in White." This group attracted widespread international attention. In 2010, the Cuban Catholic Church took up the cause of the prisoners, and the Cuban government released all the seventy-five detainees. Perhaps again a small result of public diplomacy.

UNLIMITED IDEAS

In diplomatic practice, the opportunities for creativity abound in public diplomacy. The range of ideas that have been applied is immense. Some are recent, made feasible by new technologies. Some are long standing. Here is a short list of some noteworthy public diplomacy initiatives by states and private entities.

1. The German embassy in Washington sent a brightly painted bus around the United States. It invited Americans to take smartphone photos and email them in. Objective: to make Germany seem outgoing and fun.

2. In 2012, U.S. Secretary of State Hillary Clinton invited U.S. chefs to form an American Chef Corps to promote U.S. cuisine overseas. Objective: to show that not all U.S. food is fast.

3. In 2013, President Obama made a YouTube video sending the Iranian people best wishes as they celebrated Nowruz. Objective: to send a direct message of engagement. Risk: Few will watch and the government will distort or block.

4. Businessman Mo Ibrahim's annual Prize for Achievement in African Leadership is awarded to African political leaders who deliver security, health, education, and economic development to their people, and then transfer power democratically to their successor. Objective: to promote good governance and show non-governmental commitment to transparency and accountability. African publics see rewards for performance rather than from simply retaining power. The prize of $5 million is one of the largest international awards offered. And Ibrahim has sent his own message to the public by announcing in four out of the last five

years it would not be awarded because there was no worthy winner. Ibrahim explained his decision. "It's up to people to draw their own conclusions—you're grown up."[26]

5. Angelina Jolie used her Hollywood fame and her role as Special Envoy for the UN High Commissioner for Refugees to attend events highlighting violence against women. Objective: to raise the public profile of a major transnational issue and to partner with the British government to show commitment of states.
6. Juanes' Peace Concert was held in Havana in 2009. The Colombian musician promoted the event and performed for over one million people in Havana Revolution Square. Objective: to bring together Cuban, Cuban-American, and Latin American musicians in the cause of peace by drawing a massive audience and reaching out above politicians.
7. In the weeks after 9/11, the United Kingdom promoted a public diplomacy event in New York City. They changed the name from "UK in New York" to "UK and New York." Objective: to show solidarity through public diplomacy, promoting the message that New York City was back in business.
8. The U.S. Peace Corps was founded in 1961 by President Kennedy as a challenge to Americans to offer their service for the good of others. Perhaps the most sustained government-funded worldwide public diplomacy project. Objective: to demonstrate U.S. volunteer commitment to global causes. Over 8,000 serve annually, and the average age is 27 years old. Since its foundation, some 210,000 Americans have served in 139 countries. The Peace Corps is known throughout the world and has been around so long it seldom makes the headlines today, perhaps reducing its current public diplomacy impact.
9. Nobel prizes began as a bequest to the world from the fortune of Alfred Nobel, which was made from the manufacture of armaments and explosives. Objective: to recognize those who confer the greatest benefit on mankind in various fields, including peace. The prize draws public attention to those who assist diplomacy in achieving peaceful resolution of conflicts.
10. Royal and state visits have long been a part of diplomacy. Objective: draws public attention to a country and its leaders, bringing glamour and interest. These visits are useful for outreach and are sustained opportunities over several days for public diplomacy. Leaders can engage with overseas' publics. While the visits show the highest level of formal diplomatic attention, they are now becoming rarer and perhaps have less impact.
11. Google Ideas is a foundation created by one of the world's largest companies. Objective: to show a massively successful company is still innovative and trying to address major world issues.

These examples show states, individuals, and companies have reached out to the public. They have made a mark for a short or long time. No one can be called more successful than the others. No other country has a Peace Corps funded and managed in the same way as the United States. The British Royal Family has created a uniquely appealing image, but it has also suffered less successful periods. Collectively, the world witnesses actions that open eyes and suggest a higher meaning to diplomacy than mere state-to-state interaction. Following Satow's definition of diplomacy, each illustration shows an intelligent application of public diplomacy, maximizing its originators' chances of impacting the issues of the time.[27]

SUGGESTIONS FOR FURTHER READING

1. Cull, Nicholas. *Public Diplomacy: Lessons from the Past*. Los Angeles: University of Southern California Figueroa Press, 2009.

2. Cull, Nicholas. "The Long Road to Public Diplomacy 2.0: The Internet in U.S. Public Diplomacy." *International Studies Review* 15, no. 1 (March 2013): 123–39.

3. Leonard, Mark, Andrew Small, and Martin Rose. *British Public Diplomacy in the "Age of Schisms"* London: Foreign Policy Centre, 2005.

4. Melissen, Jan, Donna Lee, and Paul Sharp, ed, *The New Public Diplomacy: Soft Power in International Relations (Studies in Diplomacy and International Relations)*. New York: Palgrave Macmillan, 2007.

chapter 8

Public Goods

Treaties and International Law

Public diplomacy is a new must-do activity of diplomacy. It is a diplomatic activity for which the modern world seems to offer both enormous opportunities and pitfalls. It is unusual in that the choreography is largely unwritten, its results uncertain, and its predictability nonexistent. Fortunately, there are other areas of diplomacy that offer much more predictability. In their contribution to the search for international norms and legally enforceable international agreements, diplomats perform one of their most valuable functions.

Diplomacy has created multilateral institutions, as we have seen, and it has established norms and common forms of behavior in legally binding agreements like the Vienna Convention on Diplomatic Relations (VCDR). In its widest sense, the objective of diplomacy is to produce predictability and to create a framework where international agreements can be relied on, used as points of reference, and treated as public goods. In this way, common reference points can be established for the behavior of diplomats. And the fabric of international law we apply in many aspects of our lives owes much to the efforts of diplomats.

TREATIES

The treaty is the ultimate instrument for diplomats seeking to create a legally binding international agreement. It may deal with a universal issue to sovereign states like the issue of immunities and privileges. It may be a bilateral agreement. It may be called something other than a treaty—a convention, a pact, a protocol, an accord, or a charter—but in whatever form, a treaty is one of the recognized sources of international law. It is also one of the most definitive because the subject matter is clear. Other sources of international law, which will be discussed later in this chapter, are sometimes vaguer, sometimes based on opinion, and rarely tested. The treaty is a deliberate effort made by the parties to give predictability and legal force to their agreements. Treaties help frame diplomacy for years to come.

A treaty, like the diplomatic negotiations that led to it, may seem remarkably similar to an agreement in business and follow the law of contract. But there are distinctive features of a treaty that make it an instrument with a different pedigree. The definition of a treaty, internationally agreed in the Vienna Convention on the Law of Treaties of 1969 (VCLT) is that it is "an international agreement concluded between States in written form and governed by international law, whether embodied in a single instrument or in two or more related instruments and whatever its particular designation."[1]

Beyond this, a treaty embodies some important features. First, the parties to a treaty are states, not governments (temporary representatives of states), business corporations, or individuals. In 1986, the VCLT added the category of international organizations as having "legal personality under international law."[2] It was, however, stipulated that international organizations cannot be used in counting the minimum number of parties required for entry into force of a treaty.

Second, in agreeing a treaty, the parties are making an agreement about a significant issue between the states or international organizations—such as territory, arms control, or trade regulations. Third, to be seen as valid, a treaty must confer legally binding rights and duties. It must define specific actions or undertakings. So an international agreement that falls short of conferring legally binding rights and obligations will not normally be a treaty. Fourth, a treaty can only confer rights and duties on the actual parties to the document. No state can have obligations imposed on it by others. Fifth, a treaty must be ratified to enter into force. Ratification is a process determined by national legislative traditions or constitutional arrangements. And sixth, to be enforceable under international law, an international treaty must be registered with the United Nations.

Treaties have existed for centuries. Many ancient examples, like the Treaty of Windsor between the United Kingdom and Portugal in 1386, remain in force. The Peace of Westphalia of 1648 was actually a series of treaties, and the parties included sixteen European states and sixty-six imperial entities.

Treaties generally follow a similar format. Commonly they have a preamble that gives a background and some statements about what the agreement is intended to achieve. Then the numbered articles follow, giving the details of the legally binding provisions. A treaty will also include provisions on when and under what conditions it enters into force. This will usually follow ratification through the national processes of the two parties, if bilateral, or ratification by a sufficiently large number of parties in the case of a multilateral treaty. The text of the treaty will be stated as authentic in a designated number of languages. Other common provisions are the duration of a treaty, which may be indefinite but may also be subject to a review date. And though a treaty is supposed to have lasting effect, there may be a clause permitting withdrawal of the parties, perhaps in defined circumstances such as in cases of overwhelming national interest. A treaty may also provide for the terms under which an amendment may be made.

By agreeing to obligations with other sovereign states, treaties can be seen as a dilution of sovereignty. In some agreements that require specific actions to be performed, there are provisions to benchmark progress or to agree verification of implementation, such as destruction of stocks of chemical weapons under the Chemical Weapons Convention. There may be detailed arrangements for onsite inspections or use of remote telemetry for use in inspections, which may authorize unusual access to the territory of another sovereign state. Arbitration is also commonly used, for instance, in investment protection treaties when a decision on the valuation of corporate assets may have to be made and an outside expert will rule to satisfy both parties.

Treaties are not the only sources of international law and practice. They sit alongside other laws drawn from such sources as customary rules, civilized practice, and judicial decisions. Customary law and civilized practice indeed were the basis of diplomatic immunities and privileges respected for many centuries. Their status was accepted as akin to the sanctity of churches and the concept of a safe haven. The modern international governance of the Internet also has grown up in a contemporary version of customary practice, what has worked well, and what experts saw as making technological sense. Internet governance has produced some legally binding agreements but also a regulatory authority based on informality with strong involvement from multiple stakeholders and a practice that has become almost universally accepted. This will be discussed further in Chapter 11.

The purposes of treaties reflect the treatment of issues of the time. They also reflect the extent to which sovereign states have seen themselves and have been seen as strong enough actors to make and implement treaties. International conventions have often dealt with new developments in technology that had international implications and that societies had not regulated. Major powers seldom make treaties with weaker states, but the growth of multinational arrangements has highlighted the growing interdependence of sovereign states. The world has called for agreements and diplomats have delivered them in areas such as the rules of international civil aviation, international telephone dialing codes, the practice of international insurance, international recognition of intellectual property rights, the treatment of maritime practice, and banking swift codes. All are forms of treaties that most in the world take for granted but without which their lives would be greatly inconvenienced.

So diplomacy has a large number of successes in its legal portfolio. It has addressed some of the greatest collective challenges that affect our planet and sought to remedy the effects of disasters and wars that have caused millions of deaths. Despite the littering of history with failed treaties—the Kellogg-Brand pact, the League of Nations, the Anti-Ballistic Missile Treaty of 1972—sovereign states return to the formula. Though powerful countries reject certain treaties—for example, the United States, China, and Russia are not parties to the Rome Treaty establishing the International Criminal Court—no state has ever suggested it will never participate in any legally enforceable international agreement. Even the modern example of a renegade state in the international community, North Korea, withdrew from the Nuclear Nonproliferation Treaty (NPT) using the formal provisions of the treaty. It gave three months' notice in January 2003 under Article X of the NPT on the grounds that "extraordinary events, related to the subject matter of this [t]reaty, have jeopardized the supreme interests of its country."[3]

LAWS, RULES, AND DIPLOMACY

In this section, we will investigate how far diplomacy has been able to set new rules that govern international behavior in peacetime, how far it has failed, the reasons for this, and the current climate for new experiments in consensus building.

We saw in Chapter 2 that diplomacy evolved from theories, practice, and creation of rules going back to ancient civilizations of Greece and Rome. The growth of canon and Roman law spread common approaches, and as international trading developed within the Hanseatic League and among the city-states of Italy, commonly accepted rules developed.

In the modern era, the United Nations has proved a key coordinator of legal progress. Its Charter provides for the General Assembly to initiate studies and make recommendations on codifying international law. The United Nations also has a central role in registering treaties and in producing UN Security Council Resolutions (UNSCRs)—now over 2,000 since its foundation—that are legally binding. In addition, the International Law Commission (ILC) was established by the United Nations General Assembly (UNGA) in 1947 for the "promotion of the progressive development of international law and its codification."[4] The ILC, consisting of thirty-four legal experts, has proved instrumental in moving diplomacy forward in key areas of international law—the VCDR, the International Criminal Court (ICC), and, though it has not been universally ratified, the VCLT. The ILC is a lobbying and facilitating group behind diplomatic efforts to promote the development of international law.

Describing the results of collective diplomatic endeavors over many decades is best achieved by taking some examples of issues where there has been progress. We will then draw some conclusions about the circumstances in which diplomacy is most productive in producing enduring public goods after examining the following topics: War and Its Rules, The United Nations, Genocide, Terrorism, Human Rights, Nuclear Proliferation, Climate Change, and World Trade/World Finance.

WAR AND ITS RULES

War and its rules sit at the very core of diplomacy because the outbreak of war shows diplomatic failure. The destruction of war has threatened the fabric of all major sovereign states, and there has long been a collective interest in trying to control war and limit its scope. Diplomacy saw that, even when at war, states still functioned and might have common interests. So, contradictory as it may seem, the purveyors of peace were called into to make war more diplomatic—less violent, more limited in scope, and consensus based in its conduct.

Yet the major impetus to treating the effects of war and its humanitarian impact did not come from sovereign states but from an issue activist and non-state actor—Henry Dunant and the organization that became the International Committee of the Red Cross (ICRC), founded in 1863. In June 1859, Dunant, a Swiss businessman, traveled to Italy to meet French emperor Napoléon III to discuss difficulties in conducting his business in Algeria, then controlled by France. On his journey, he witnessed the Battle of Solferino, where in a single day thousands were killed or wounded. Dunant was shocked at the lack of medical attention given to the wounded and committed himself to raise awareness of the savagery of war, particularly its effects on civilians and the wounded. As a diplomatic facilitator, he wrote books, convened meetings, energized governments, and created a purposeful organization that has become a unique combination of volunteers and national organizations. The ICRC, based in Geneva, has produced a franchise consisting of scores of national organizations. It has been the catalyst for a wide-ranging series of conventions, known collectively as the Geneva Conventions on Humanitarian Law. There are four main conventions that were most recently comprehensively updated in 1949: the first Geneva Convention protects wounded and sick soldiers on land during war; the second protects wounded, sick, and shipwrecked military personnel at sea during war; the third applies to prisoners of war; and the fourth affords protection to civilians, including in occupied territory.

An important breakthrough in extending the scope of the conventions came with the incorporation in 1949 of a new Article 3 to all four conventions extending their coverage to situations of noninternational conflict and civil wars. The ICRC now will extend its services to parties to noninternational conflicts. In the decades that followed the adoption of this new article, the number of noninternational conflicts and wars of national liberation grew enormously. In response, two protocols in addition to the four 1949 Geneva Conventions were adopted in 1977. They strengthen the protection of victims of international (Protocol I) and noninternational conflicts (Protocol II), and place limits on the way wars are fought. An obvious problem that such legal measures face in such noninternational conflicts is the status of the parties to conflict. How can disparate groups in civil conflict be held responsible? So recent publications of the ICRC have recognized the difficulty of defining the key actors once sovereign states lose control. For international humanitarian law to apply, the ICRC acknowledges the problems: "The many different causes of non-international armed conflicts, and the diversity of the participants, also means that those hoping to assist the parties involved in respecting the law must bring to their task patience, wisdom and knowledge."[5] We will discuss later the implementation issues that arise when crimes against humanity are committed and the efforts diplomacy has made to ensure they are not ignored, particularly with the creation of the ICC.

Despite the problems of implementation, the Geneva Conventions represent a major success of diplomacy. The four main conventions have been ratified by 195 states, including all UN member states as well as the Holy See and the Cook Islands.

Sovereign states, having come together in humanitarian law because of pressure from an outside facilitator, pursued other legal instruments in diplomatic efforts both to avoid war and, in cases where war did break out, to limit its scope and results. Tsar Nicholas II of Russia saw the interests of Russia in preserving peace—he was an early nominee for the Nobel Peace Prize. He not only conducted conventional sovereign state diplomacy in consolidating Russia's alliance with France but he also convened the first Hague Conference of 1898 to discuss the rules of war. This resulted in the first Hague Convention that covered, inter alia, the Pacific Settlement of Disputes, created a permanent court of arbitration, consolidated the laws and customs of wars on land, amended the maritime warfare sections of the first Geneva Protocol (of 1864), and banned what were seen as particularly destructive weapons. These included the launching of projectiles and explosives from balloons and the use of projectiles for the diffusion of toxic gases. It also banned the use of bullets that expanded after entering the body.

The second Hague conference was called at the suggestion of American President Theodore Roosevelt (who did receive the Nobel Peace Prize in 1906) in 1904 but was postponed because of the war between Russia and Japan. It was held from June to October 1907 and added to the first Hague Convention, modifying some parts and adding others, with an increased focus on naval warfare.

The conventions that resulted were indeed a credit to diplomacy because they show an early example of an attempt at preventative diplomacy—a premonition of the devastation and carnage of World War I. And they have provided a base on which further progress has been built. One of the horrors of the First World War was a result of global industrial advances and the macabre recognition of the weapon potential of new gases. The Geneva Protocol of 1925 (a protocol for the prohibition of the use in war of asphyxiating, poisonous, or other gases, and of bacteriological methods of warfare, added to the existing Hague Convention), invited states to ban the use of chemical and biological weapons. It had no verification provisions in its terms and relied on diplomatic peer pressure to bring about a taboo on using such weapons of mass destruction. The Geneva Protocol took time to become universal. Most of the European powers ratified within a few years, but Syria did not until 1968, and the United States did not formally renounce the use of chemical weapons until 1975. Nevertheless, despite the later closing of the gaps in treatment of chemical weapons by the Chemical Weapons Convention of 1993 (which Syria had not at that time ratified), the international reaction to chemical weapons use by Bashar al-Assad in the civil war from 2012 to 2013 showed the lingering value of a 1920s treaty.

After World War II, further diplomatic efforts were made to address the impact of new weaponry following the development and use of atomic bombs in 1945 and the implications of the space race between the United States and the Soviet Union. The Outer Space Treaty of 1967 was a landmark agreement of extraterrestrial importance and prohibited the deployment of nuclear weapons in space or on any celestial body. Space exploration has been an unusual human endeavor where exploration for its own sake reached a peak before most of the impact of a globalized economy and the information and communications technologies revolution. There is now more computing power in the average smartphone than in the Apollo space landing craft of 1969. It seems likely that the Outer Space Treaty, which does not limit the use or deployment of conventional weapons, will sooner or later return to diplomats' desks as unfinished business.

The Nuclear Nonproliferation Treaty of 1968 is widely called the cornerstone of post war collective security diplomacy (see the Nonproliferation of Nuclear Weapons section later in this chapter). By limiting the possession of nuclear weapons to those treaty members that had tested before 1967, it attempted to limit the impact of the most dangerous genie that had escaped in human history. Its success was marked after the end of the Cold War by renunciation of nuclear weapons by countries such as Ukraine and South Africa. In response to the Ukrainian renunciation, the Budapest Memorandum was an ancillary agreement signed by the United States, United Kingdom, and Russia, guaranteeing the sovereign integrity of Ukraine. That part of the deal was less successful—Russia made no reference to it when annexing Crimea in 2014. The Biological and Toxic Weapons Convention of 1972 was also a landmark agreement that has become near universal in banning the development, manufacture, and deployment of biological weapons. So far, however, there has been no comprehensive agreement on verification measures. But the Organization for Prohibition and Prevention of Chemical Weapons in The Hague that was established in 1997 has become the paradigm for global efforts to eliminate a class of weaponry.

The tradition of diplomatic efforts to limit the effects of conflict continues to produce results. As in the case of Dunant and the ICRC, nonstate actors have more recently combined with states to produce the Arms Trade Treaty, treaties to ban the deployment of antipersonnel landmines and cluster bombs, and an informal organization to take direct action against the proliferation of weapons of mass destruction—the Proliferation Security Initiative. Diplomatic efforts to limit the development of armaments and the destructiveness of conflict have further monuments in the contemporary world.

THE UNITED NATIONS

The UN Charter is itself a monumental treaty. Despite the experience of the League of Nations, it has become nearly universal with new countries being eager to be admitted (which the Charter was unsure about) and increasingly regional groupings pressing their case to attend. Under Article 102, the United Nations has the central role in relation to other treaties. This article provides that "no party to any such treaty or international agreement which has not been registered in accordance with the provisions of paragraph 1 of this Article may invoke that treaty or agreement before any organ of the United Nations."[6] The UN treaty, as we have seen, has enduring value. But its strict legal framework, designed in a very different world order, is a limit on any flexibility it has to change or adapt to modern circumstances. The amendment provisions of the Charter ensure that it is unlikely to change in fundamentals. And if the United Nations itself does not serve as an adequate forum for consensus building, then the organization must be seen as an obstacle to further progress in some areas of international law and diplomatic predictability.

GENOCIDE

If weapons produced treaties in the history of diplomacy, so did atrocities. The diplomatic failures of World War II not only devastated states and their populations but showed another consequence of such failures—the Holocaust and the issue of genocide. The war showed that sovereign states could exercise their power not just to fight other states or to repress their own civilizations, but to attack and destroy an ethnic or religious group irrespective of nationality. The issue, therefore, transcended sovereign states and the rules of war or weapons. Indeed, the issue of genocide was named not by a government but by a Polish-Jewish legal scholar, Raphael Lemkin, during the 1930s. Lemkin had previously written about the slaughter of Armenians by the Ottoman Empire in the First World War.

The challenge for the diplomatic system was enormous. In the aftermath of war, and with no functioning international institutions, diplomacy had to decide what global issues were priorities for the postwar world. How important was it to deal with crimes so horrific that few could contemplate them being repeated in the future? How could the perpetrators of the crimes be prosecuted? How could the crimes be defined and what courts could try them? And how could such crimes be outlawed forever in a system based on sovereign states?

The answers came in two stages. In June 1945, the Allies declared they had assumed "supreme authority with respect to Germany, including all the powers possessed by the German Government."[7] Following these steps, the way was open for a new judicial authority and new crimes to be tried. The London Charter of August 1945 established the laws and procedures by which the Nuremberg trials were to be conducted. It defined three classes of crime: war crimes, crimes against peace, and crimes against humanity. These were based on existing laws and included an important new agreement that would enter into international law. The key principle established by Article 8 of the London Charter was that no official could argue in defense that he was merely obeying an order. The victors' justice was also accomplished in a careful judicial procedure rather than in a spirit of vengeance. It was a conscious attempt to add to the precedents of the rule of law and to set new norms. Judge Robert Jackson, one of the Nuremberg prosecutors, said that "if it is to serve any useful purpose, it must condemn aggression by any other nations, including those that sit here now in judgment."[8] Of twenty-four former Nazi officials indicted, twelve were sentenced to death, three acquitted, and the rest received prison terms.

The Nuremburg trials did not prosecute the crime of genocide, but the second diplomatic response was to address the definition of what had occurred so that law could be framed for the future. Again, diplomatic progress was assisted by a non-governmental actor. Lemkin successfully campaigned for the universal acceptance of international laws defining and forbidding genocide. In 1946, the first session of the UNGA adopted a resolution that affirmed that genocide was a crime under international law, but it did not provide a legal definition of the crime. In 1948, the UNGA adopted the Convention on the Prevention and Punishment of the Crime of Genocide (CPPCG) that legally defined the crime of genocide for the first time. The CPPCG entered into force in January 1951. The definition of genocide agreed in the Convention was

> any of the following acts committed with intent to destroy, in whole or in part, a national, ethnical, racial or religious group . . . (a) Killing members of the group; (b) Causing serious bodily or mental harm to members of the group; (c) Deliberately inflicting on the group conditions of life calculated to bring about its physical destruction in whole or in part; (d) Imposing measures intended to prevent births within the group; (e) Forcibly transferring children of the group to another group.[9]

One important omission from the agreed definition of a group whose destruction was at the core of the crime was the absence of "political" as one of the groups within the scope of the crime. Destruction and murder of political groups would of course qualify as other crimes, and despite this omission, the Genocide Convention represents a significant milestone. The convention does not, however, establish any international jurisdiction over the crime of genocide or incitement to genocide. Article 6 states,

> Persons charged with genocide or any of the other acts enumerated in Article 3 shall be tried by a competent tribunal of the State in the territory of which the act was committed, or by such international penal tribunal as may have jurisdiction with respect to those Contracting Parties which shall have accepted its jurisdiction.[10]

The wait for that international tribunal was long—until 2002—when the ICC was established. This will be discussed later.

TERRORISM

A global issue that has been a problem for diplomacy long before the post-9/11 campaign produced the phrase "War on Terror" is terrorism. The word itself has its origins in the *terrorisme*, used to describe the actions of the Jacobins during the Reign of Terror in the French Revolution. It has made many subsequent appearances on the international stage. The use of terror for domestic or international purposes often signals again that diplomacy has failed or is unavailable.

Violence is never helpful to diplomacy but sometimes, in a prenegotiation scenario, is part of the preliminary process that produces the necessary stalemate to begin a dialogue. Following the example of genocide, international action to establish norms against terrorism required a definition of the activity. Yet, though few if any deny that terrorism exists, the global community has not so far been able to agree on a universally applicable definition. Many countries have domestic legislation designed to counter terrorism and the core components of the activity are widely recognized—the use of indiscriminate and unpredictable violence against civilians and noncivilians for political or ideological ends. But, beyond that, there is a history of disagreement among sovereign states over which organization or informal groups are terrorists as opposed to freedom fighters, insurgents, or activists. Many modern groups that have resorted to bombings to destabilize and terrorize have had political units, and some have eventually renounced violence and participated in peaceful political processes. The Irish Republican Army (IRA) and the Basque Separatist Group (ETA) are recent examples.

Diplomacy wants order and predictability. Terrorism wants to disrupt order, make society unworkable and peaceful resolution of issues impossible. Yet terrorism may be sponsored by states as part of their foreign policy, and the arming of proxy militias to foster conflict was common throughout the Cold War. The power of a small unit of disrupters is ever greater in an interconnected international society with many points of vulnerability. The sponsor or organizer of terrorists may even be able to persuade the actors to move from planting the car bomb to planting himself or herself as a human suicide bomber. That is the ultimate weapon against society—most conventional defensive strategies assume that the attacker wants to survive. Neither diplomats nor military, however skilled, are of much use in these circumstances.

Diplomacy also sees terrorism as a serious threat to sovereignty. There are few examples of successful diplomacy being implemented by a state that is unable to provide security for its population. Diplomacy has few responses when terrorism takes hold as preferable to state-to-state negotiations. And, as we observed in Chapter 3, diplomats and diplomatic institutions are in many cases the first targets of terrorism because they symbolize to the terrorist the norms of a system they want to dislodge. Much of diplomacy depends on a common objective of guaranteeing the security of the peacemakers and the lives of the messengers.

Most countries that participate in the diplomatic system recognize that their own sovereignty would be undermined if terror became a standard method of conducting international relations. It undermines the fabric of any settled government and favors anarchy or a fragmented society. The Islamic State (IS) is a recent exception where terror appears integral to its establishment.

Nevertheless, diplomacy, to its credit, has not abandoned efforts to encourage diplomatic action against terrorism. Instead of laboring toward a global convention that would of course require a global definition, it has concentrated on producing agreements that deal with the effects of or results of terrorism.

The United Nations set up a working group to look at collective actions against terrorism in 1996. And an array of UN legally binding conventions now exist to enjoin states to take measures against terrorist groups. The 1999 UN International Convention for the Suppression of the Financing of Terrorism defined the crime of financing terrorism. The UN Security Council (UNSC) has passed legally binding resolutions requiring all members not to assist terrorist groups or allow them sanctuary on their territories (for example, UNSCR 1373 after the September 11, 2001, attacks). The United Nations also has promoted in 2005 a treaty on measures to protect countries from nuclear terrorism—the International Convention for the Suppression of Acts of Nuclear Terrorism.

So while the definition of the crime of terrorism may lack universal definition, the actions of governments against it do have an international legal basis. Intelligence, surveillance, and interception of terrorism funds and cargos have some legal framework. But as U.S. Attorney General Eric Holder said in 2012, "The terrorists only have to be successful once" in evading the best that states' diplomacy, military, and intelligence can devise.[11] States will therefore try to exploit the global interconnection of communication to stop an impending attack. Diplomacy is responding to evolving new threats from nonstate actors, who usually need to communicate to plot their activities. It is an intelligent response, but the trust and separateness of diplomats is being compromised. Another challenge in defining norms of international behavior awaits diplomacy.

HUMAN RIGHTS

Human rights are a challenge for diplomacy because if there were a universal recognition and application of what human rights are, then there would be much less need for diplomacy itself. A common appreciation of human rights would clear the way for consensus building on such issues as economic systems, rights of workers, equal pay, property ownership, and the role of women in society. Universal acceptance of political rights would recognize free elections, freedom of expression, an independent judiciary, freedom of trade unions, and access to a free media.

All diplomats see that the real world differs greatly in all these areas. The role of an individual in sovereign state societies is not defined by similarities of the human species but by historical, geographical, and anthropological differences. Governments may wish to engage internationally, but history has treated states very differently. The world of human rights is seen differently if a country has been invaded, occupied, or colonized. And some states would dispute that there might be any universality of such rights at all. The traditions of marriage, relationships, and other cultural practice are elevated above universal human rights. Indeed, some experts argue that words like *justice* and *freedom* have different meanings according to cultural backgrounds.

It was again the seismic shock of world war that prompted the most sustained attempt in modern times to give all citizens of the world a "Bill of Rights." The yearning that produced it was in fact already incorporated in the UN Charter, which in its preamble implores "universal respect for, and observance of, human rights and fundamental freedoms for all without distinction as to race, sex, language, or religion."[12]

The UN Universal Declaration of Human Rights is certainly universal and massively comprehensive. It was adopted by forty-eight votes in favor and zero against on December 10, 1948. Eight countries abstained: the Soviet Union, Ukraine and Byelorussia (both part of the Soviet Union), Yugoslavia, Poland, South Africa, Czechoslovakia, and Saudi Arabia.

The declaration is a document that reflects an imperfect world. It sets aspirational standards rather than codifies international norms. In the preamble, the signatories are urged to keep the declaration constantly in mind, and to "strive by teaching and education to promote respect for these rights and freedoms and by progressive measures, national and international, to secure their universal and effective recognition and observance."[13] The fact that it is a declaration and not a treaty means it is not legally binding. The countries involved in the drafting were diverse and included Australia, Belgium, Chile, China, Egypt, France, India, Iran, Lebanon, Panama, Philippines, United Kingdom, United States, the Soviet Union, Uruguay, and Yugoslavia. The chairperson of the drafting commission was Eleanor Roosevelt, former first lady of the United States. Her husband, President Franklin Roosevelt, in his State of the Union Address in 1941 had indeed defined four freedoms: freedom of religion, freedom of expression, freedom from want, and freedom from fear. For him, these were realistic diplomatic objectives.

> That is no vision of a distant millennium. It is a definite basis for a kind of world attainable in our own time and generation. That kind of world is the very antithesis of the so-called new order of tyranny which the dictators seek to create with the crash of a bomb.[14]

The young United Nations also had a role. The actual drafting was led by John Peters Humphrey, a Canadian official who had just been appointed as first Director of the UN Division of Human Rights. The document he oversaw has now been translated into 403 languages. And the aspiration to agree to legally binding provisions was eventually realized by splitting the declaration into two binding instruments. The first document became the International Covenant on Economic, Social, and Cultural Rights (ICESCR) and the second became the International Covenant on Civil and Political Rights (ICCPR). Both were adopted in 1966. The ICESCR entered into force in January 1976 and at the time of writing it has 160 parties. A further seven states, including the United States, have signed but not yet ratified the covenant. The ICCPR entered into force in March 1976 and has 167 parties.

Diplomacy has taken on an issue where there is compelling evidence that the world is not converging toward a universal paradigm on human rights. Amnesty International estimates that over 150 countries still practice some form of torture, an infringement of Article 5 of the UN Universal Declaration of Human Rights. But the top of the universal mountain is still visible, though it would be an exceptionally optimistic diplomat who would suggest that substantial further progress is likely. In 2000, the Islamic countries that are members of the Organization of the Islamic Conference (OIC) adopted the Cairo Declaration on Human Rights in Islam—an alternative document that states that "all the rights and freedoms stipulated in this declaration are subject to the Islamic Shari'ah"[15] but that there should be no discrimination on grounds of "race, colour, language, sex, religious belief, political affiliation, social status or other considerations."[16]

The United Nations is supported in efforts to enforce human rights accepted in the legally binding conventions by the review activities of the UN Human Rights Council and some regional treaties such as The European Convention on Human Rights (ECHR). All Council of Europe member states are parties to the ECHR. The European Court of Human Rights enforces the provisions of the ECHR and gives individuals living in those states that are parties to it recourse to the court on the grounds that their rights under the ECHR have been violated by national courts.

NONPROLIFERATION OF NUCLEAR WEAPONS

Prima facie, nuclear weapons might appear to raise analogous issues for diplomacy to The Hague Conventions and the Geneva Protocol that dealt with weapons and the rules of war. In 1945, the atomic bomb—the most destructive weapon of all time—was used by a major power. It had shown its immediate and lasting impact, and the term fallout entered the language. But the destructive power of nuclear weapons was not just like a new form of bullet or airborne weapon that worried the drafters of The Hague Conventions. The same power, the genie out of the bottle, had enormous potential for energy, medicine, and other peaceful uses. The classic dual-use problem of nuclear and other weapons of mass destruction was born. Simple outlawing of nuclear weapons or a reduction in numbers would not solve the issue. Technology trumped a tidy diplomatic solution.

The diplomatic problem that nuclear weapons posed was the new capacity of sovereign states with nuclear weapons not only to inflict mass devastation on each other by using a small number of weapons but also potentially to destroy the whole of human civilization. Indeed, the first diplomatic solution proposed by the U.S. administration, a few months after it dropped the bombs on Hiroshima and Nagasaki, was to press for total elimination of such weapons. In November 1945, President Harry Truman (who gave the order to drop the bombs), British Prime Minister Clement Attlee, and Canadian Prime Minister Mackenzie King jointly proposed that "a commission should be set up under the United Nations" to prepare recommendations on "entirely eliminating the use of atomic energy for destructive purposes" and promoting peaceful uses. Their reasoning was that states could not be trusted with halfway measures. "No system of safeguards that can be devised will of itself provide an effective guarantee against the production of atomic weapons by a nation bent on aggression." They also called for the new UN commission to devise "effective safeguards by way of inspection and other means to protect complying states against the hazards of violations and evasions."[17]

The issue became the most pressing for the new United Nations. In January 1946, the UNGA adopted a text on nuclear disarmament as its first official resolution. Shortly after, the U.S. Secretary of State Byrnes commissioned a report by Dean Acheson and David Lilienthal that endorsed the proposed approach for dealing with the weapons, arguing "there is no . . . security against atomic warfare in a system of international agreements to outlaw such weapons controlled *only* by a system that relies on inspection and similar police-like methods."[18] But the report went further. It called for international control covering the operation of all dangerous nuclear activities, including virtually the entire nuclear fuel cycle and the operation of uranium and thorium mines. The new Atomic Development Authority would also conduct research including into weapons.[19] The Baruch plan, taking its name from the U.S.-appointed negotiator, argued that only such international oversight would prevent the use of the veto by the permanent members of the UNSC. The Soviet Union, which in August 1949 had conducted its first test of a nuclear device, negotiated for some years but by 1950 had withdrawn from UN discussions. Cold War tensions intensified, and the renunciation of the veto became impossible to agree.

There then followed a nuclear arms race between the Soviet Union and the United States and its NATO allies. But the U.S. approach continued to favor international regulation. President Dwight Eisenhower gave a speech to the UNGA in December 1953 titled "Atoms for Peace." In it, he talked of the universality of the threat of nuclear weapons. "If a danger exists in the world it is danger for us all. If hope exists in the mind of one nation, it should be shared by all."[20] Eisenhower saw that the technology of nuclear weapons could not be disinvented and the atom had enormous potential for peaceful uses, but also that the world had to live in a new era of deterrence. One of the objectives of the speech was to persuade the United States' European allies to accept the NATO strategy of nuclear weapons stationed in Europe as a basis for deterrence.

Eisenhower was lofty in his vision: "My country's purpose is to help us move out of the dark chamber of horrors into the light." He was effusive in his praise for the United Nations. "Those same great concepts of universal peace and human dignity which are so clearly etched in"[21] the UN Charter. The U.S. president of the modern era who had seen personally more of the direct effects of war than any other proposed a peaceful solution that designated a pivotal role for a new international energy agency. This agency would receive contributions of fissile materials from the states producing them and would allocate those materials to all countries for peaceful uses of nuclear energy.

By the mid-1960s, the United States and the Soviet Union were reaching a stage where a mutually beneficial approach to preventing nuclear proliferation made diplomatic sense. They recognized that whatever other differences they had over ideology and economic and political systems, they could come together on this issue. The Nuclear Nonproliferation Treaty of 1968 was born. The five nuclear powers that had tested nuclear weapons before January 1, 1967, were defined in a class of state parties that could not be enlarged. The NPT served the interests of the nuclear powers in preventing transfer of technology and proliferation of weapons. The fact that the nuclear powers were the dominant members of the Cold War blocs of adversaries made the deal all the more feasible. The nonnuclear economic powers of the 1960s like Germany, Canada, and Japan were conceded a commitment in Article 6 of the NPT "to pursue negotiations in good faith on effective measures relating to cessation of the nuclear arms race at an early date and to nuclear disarmament, and on a treaty on general and complete disarmament under strict and effective international control."[22] Some skeptics have argued that the diplomatic skill of smoothing edges produced wording on disarmament with no cutting blade at all. Nevertheless, in return for accepting these obligations of nonproliferation, all nonnuclear weapons states received the inalienable right to the benefits of peaceful uses nuclear energy. Their obligations not to misuse this right would be verified through safeguards agreements and inspection under the International Atomic Energy Agency (IAEA) based in Vienna (see Chapter 4).

The approach of the NPT remains controversial. Though today it has been signed by nearly all states, the NPT took time to gain acceptance. It was only in the 1990s that China and France joined as nuclear weapon states. The treaty has never secured the signatures of India, Pakistan, and Israel, and all three have acquired nuclear weapons. India and Pakistan have also overtly tested them. Iraq was discovered to have been cheating by UN weapons inspectors and the verification powers of the IAEA were strengthened. North Korea has withdrawn from the treaty and has tested nuclear devices. Iran has shown ambitions to develop an advanced nuclear program and perhaps renounce its status as a nonnuclear weapon state. Though Iran has been sanctioned repeatedly under UNSC resolutions, it is in fact exploiting a loophole in the treaty that has not prohibited enrichment of uranium by nonnuclear weapons states. This has been recognized as the Achilles heel of the nonproliferation regime by a former director general of the IAEA, Mohamed ElBaradei. On the disarmament commitments, the treaty provides no timetable, and the article is so hedged in verbiage and general conditions that it is fertile ground for diplomatic hairsplitting. The NPT therefore has several fundamental flaws. Yet its success has also been considerable. Clandestine nuclear programs like those in South Africa and Libya have been terminated and dismantled, and there have been no new detonations of nuclear weapons in conflict.

Yet the risk of proliferation now stems more from threatened or actual use by a nonstate actor than from a sovereign state. In Pakistan, the nightmare seems to have most real life elements. Militants exist of many varieties with ambitions to target the United States and Western interests, and government control of territory and installations is feeble. The former head of Pakistan's nuclear program, A. Q. Khan, was for years the world's leading proliferator. He acted as a private entrepreneur but clearly had powerful supporters in the Pakistan government. Nevertheless, the world today has fewer "loose nukes" due to shared initiatives by the United States and Russia since the end of the Cold War. But the disproportionate power of weapons produced from a few kilograms of fissile material is still the most dangerous shared threat confronting diplomacy in the world.

Diplomacy has ensured the NPT has done its job for almost half a century. The approach adopted depended on the particular circumstances of the haves and have-nots at the time when it was agreed. The five permanent members of the UNSC (the P5) ultimately have shown far more joint commitment on nuclear weapons proliferation than on most other issues. The message they have given to Iran shows they recognize the extreme dangers that a nuclear breakout by an NPT nonnuclear weapon state could cause to the Middle East and the world. So a diplomatic negotiation, legally based, has established global norms against the possession and use of nuclear weapons. The model of the NPT, however, would seem to offer few precedents for dealing with proliferation of a new generation of weaponry—space based, laser, cyber, and new biological pathogens. Questions abound as to whether contemporary diplomacy has the capability to unite around such issues again where the drive for competitive advantage in a multipolar, multiactor world makes such fundamental commitments much more difficult to achieve.

CLIMATE CHANGE

Climate change is an issue that has arrived more recently on the diplomatic scene. It results from a study of scientific data that empirically suggest scenarios so unexpected and disturbing that the very future existence of the planet in the way we have known it is threatened. An increase in carbon emissions and global warming could mean major changes to the physical characteristics of many sovereign states and produce a variety of destructive forces that would undermine their security more seriously than anything in history.

The global diplomatic response to date has been perhaps the most comprehensive in history. States have scratched their heads and pooled information. Innumerable non-governmental organizations have connected virtually in the same cause and produced graphic videos. Yet the diplomacy of climate change has so far produced no consensus. In the case of climate change, the haves (industrialized states) and the have-nots (emerging or developing states) live on the same planet but have not found a negotiating basis for agreement. Unlike the destructive power of an atomic bomb, climate change does not seem to be the immediate priority for diplomatic activity. And diplomacy is seldom comfortable addressing a possible future calamity. Beyond that, states will not commit to a diplomatic agreement until the scientific data that is predicting changes and effects are interpreted in the same way. Once there is consensus on this, states' willingness to negotiate will be conditioned by the time horizon of not just whether but when action is required. Most of the solutions require major shifting in resources and a recasting of energy, environmental, and other policies. It is not hard to see why diplomacy is struggling to craft durable arrangements to respond to climate change.

The task for diplomacy of information building in the absence of current tangible effects is a new one. In the case of wars, new technology such as telephony, or the obvious lack of clarity over important provisions of the law of the sea, the facts, or the consequences of the facts, were clear. Nevertheless, the progress diplomacy has made from the first organized global discussions—the Rio Earth Summit of 1992—has been considerable. The first success of diplomacy is to have placed climate change on the agenda of world discussions. Other challenges remain. The shared actions that must be taken by all countries on the planet are recognized, but those countries are at different stages of development and there is as yet no agreement on the policies that would be most effective. And the impact of policies, such as carbon taxes, is also not universally agreed.

There are analogies to the case of nonproliferation. The Second World War revealed a new power structure and a growing recognition that nuclear weapons had shifted power. The five powers saw the essential value of the new nuclear currency but also recognized that the currency would be devalued and the world destabilized if the weapons became universally available. Two classes of parties were therefore created in the NPT. The diplomacy of climate change must reengineer a global issue into one where there are balanced gains and losses for all countries. The United States and China share a major stake in the issue. Currently, they are the top two emitters of greenhouse gases, China accounting for nearly 30 percent of world totals and the United States 16 percent. In terms of emissions per head, the United States is the leader. China consumes 40 percent of global production of coal, copper, steel, and aluminum, and its dramatic industrial growth has created numerous other problems like polluted air and water supplies. Both countries have set ambitious targets for use of renewable energy sources. If climate change is a reality for the planet, then much of its destiny depends on what happens in China over the next half-century.

Diplomacy has begun to outline a range of possible measures to respond to this global issue. Approaches involving capping emissions, trading carbon credits, transfers of development aid, and varied treatment in a common cause may offer a productive negotiation. But a fundamental problem that does not arise with the issue of weapons is measurement and verification. Even if the international agencies lack inspection access to determine fully whether Iran is complying with its obligations under the NPT, there would ultimately be irrefutable physical evidence of the veracity or otherwise of Iran's claims that it is not developing nuclear weapons. Diplomacy has a benchmark. But in the case of climate change, if legally binding obligations are assumed, the actions, payments, and further agreements will depend on measurements that so far can only be determined fully by national statistics on energy consumption. The scope for cheating and massaging of statistics would be great. Will sovereignty ultimately be further diluted and worldwide governance measures be accepted? Or could a World Trade Organization type of dispute settlement governance be instituted? If so, what would be the ultimate sanctions that would be imposed, who would levy an international carbon tax, and what would be the sanctions for noncompliance?

The diplomacy of climate change at the time of writing is at a halfway house. It has not ignored the issue and there is a huge international nongovernmental lobby looking for state action. It is often relegated to a lesser priority for governments with four- or five-year election cycles. Yet the process is now over twenty years old, and annual conferences of state parties (COPs) to the UN-framed Intergovernmental Panel on Climate Change (IPCC) ensure the issue receives continuing attention. Indeed, the United Nations, as we have seen, can rightly claim to have used its forum well. Unwittingly, the diplomatic efforts have produced many new business opportunities and new attention to extreme weather patterns. It has also produced innovative public diplomacy. The President of the Maldives, Mohamed Nasheed, in 2009 held a meeting of ministers under the ocean, drawing effective attention to the plight of low-lying islands under climate change.

WORLD TRADE/WORLD FINANCE

In contrast to climate change, trade is a traditional, bread-and-butter issue of diplomacy. It is the stuff of recognizable gains and losses, not elusively measured invisible gas emissions. Adam Smith set out in the *Wealth of the Nations* in 1776 the core arguments of why trade produces shared interests or comparative advantage to states.

> If a foreign country can supply us with a commodity cheaper than we ourselves can make it, better buy it of them with some part of the produce of our own industry, employed in a way in which we have some advantage.[23]

As we have seen, trade was one of the driving influences in modern diplomatic evolution. Trade has enhanced trust, expanded markets, and increased the interdependence of states. Peaceful, mutually beneficial trade exchanges have been at the heart of much of the perceived benefit of international relations.

In diplomatic terms, trade has passed from being a bilateral matter to being regional and global. A globalized world has come to see that countries could all benefit from the predictability of free trade without attempting to safeguard their sovereignty by putting up barriers to protect their industries and service sectors. Protectionism was a recipe for global recession as consumers turned away from overseas purchases and investments. And recession led to social and political instability that threatened the security of states. It sowed the seeds of conflict as common interests receded and rivalries and aggression seemed to offer a better chance of survival.

After World War II, when the memories of world recession and the effects of economic collapse were vivid, the diplomatic reconstruction of the world included a strong commitment to reviving world trade. The postwar leaders saw that economic development was as much an essential ingredient to stability as security. The General Agreement on Tariffs and Trade (GATT) was a diplomatic response to the prewar recessions and protectionism, just as the United Nations itself was an institutional correction to diplomatic failure and the World Bank and International Monetary Fund (IMF) offered international remedies to financial crises, imbalances, and inequality.

The origins of GATT were in prewar diplomacy and academic thinking that sought to redefine the world order through trade. As President Roosevelt's Secretary of State Cordell Hull said, "Unhampered trade dovetail[s] with peace; high tariffs, trade barriers and unfair economic competition, with war."[24] And he believed that "enduring peace and the welfare of nations are indissolubly connected with friendliness, fairness, equality and the maximum practicable degree of freedom in international trade."[25]

The initiative not only had the support of prominent diplomats, it was grounded in new economic thinking. James Meade, later a Nobel Prize winner for economics, and John Maynard Keynes had proposed an International Commercial Union, a trade counterpart of Keynes's idea for an International Clearing Union for postwar finance. The British government endorsed Meade's plan, and British and American officials began informal discussions about the shape of the postwar trading system, giving another example of diplomats and non-governmental experts combining their talents. These informal meetings eventually led to the 1947 GATT conference, attended by twenty-three countries. The U.S. administration insisted that the most-favored nation (MFN) clause—ensuring nondiscrimination in trade—be fundamental to the GATT agreement because it wanted to prevent the spread of the existing British imperial preferences that discriminated against its exports. The United Kingdom sought large American tariff cuts in exchange for a reduction in preferences. It also wanted the freedom to impose quantitative restrictions on imports in case of balance of payments difficulties, something that became Article XII of the GATT. Overall the GATT, though producing a lasting agreement, was a partial diplomatic failure as the intention had been to create a full international trade organization. Nevertheless, its role did gain widespread support. By the time of the 1986 Uruguay round of GATT discussions, over 120 countries were attending the negotiations.

The creation of a permanent trade organization had to await the creation of the World Trade Organization (WTO). It succeeded GATT in 1995 and is headquartered in Geneva. Its establishment coincided with a new turbulence in trade issues with a wave of post-Cold War economic reforms affecting countries in different ways. The WTO now provides a forum for trade dispute settlement between 159 member countries (in 2013) with the details left to the parties, but the principles that are to guide their discussions and negotiations are set down in the WTO rulebook. This runs to some 30,000 pages consisting of about thirty agreements and separate commitments—called schedules—made by individual members in specific areas such as customs duty rates and market-opening provisions for services. The WTO has shown a capacity to integrate new members—the Russian Federation was admitted as recently as August 2012—and has become sufficiently global that its massive set of regulations has effectively championed key principles like nondiscrimination and reciprocity. The bedrock rule is the original GATT MFN status. Provisions against antidumping of underpriced goods have also been central to many discussions.

In terms of diplomatic practice, the WTO dispute settlement arrangements are ground breaking. A procedure for settling disputes existed under GATT, but it had no fixed timetables, rulings were easier to block, and many cases dragged on inconclusively for a long time. Members of the WTO have agreed that they will use multilateral methods of settling disputes within the framework of consultations. Nevertheless, in a recognition of similar diplomatic reciprocity to transgressions under the VCDR, the WTO does recognize the right of retaliation. The WTO guidebook permits states harmed by violations to retaliate against the offending state by suspending equivalent "concessions and other obligations under the covered agreements."[26] A state may ask the Disputes Settlement Body (consisting of all members) of the WTO to set up a panel of experts to adjudicate. Once the case has gone through all designated procedures and appeals, sanctions can be imposed and retaliation permitted. And, unusual in modern diplomacy, small countries do sometimes win judgments. In a dispute starting in 2003, a WTO panel ruled that Antigua and Barbuda could retaliate against the United States to the equivalent of $21 million in trade per year because of U.S. actions penalizing online gambling based in Antigua.

So the diplomacy of the WTO is continuous, pragmatic, generally case by case, and without major recrimination. There are so many discussions and disputes underway, a WTO issue seldom takes on extraordinary significance, and the diplomatic way forward can always play out. Trade is indeed a constant in diplomacy, and few issues have crisis written into them. Diplomacy has adjusted to the times, provided a flexible forum, acknowledged that there will always be problems but established a norm that appears to be standing the tests of time.

In the field of financial diplomacy, the IMF has long occupied center stage. It has near-universal membership with 188 states, and like the WTO, it has devised some innovative diplomacy. Unlike the UNGA, where each country has one vote, decision making at the IMF reflects the position of each member country in the global economy. Each IMF member country is assigned a quota that is used to calculate its financial commitment to the organization as well as its voting strength. IMF voting is the most complex and carefully calculated of any international institution. In 2013, the 188 members split no more or less than 2,515,719 votes with the largest shareholder, the United States, having precisely 421,961.

The IMF, which employs over 2,400 people, has multiple roles and covers, inter alia, surveillance of and technical assistance to the international financial system and lending to its members. Many of these roles are complementary to the WTO's. Its objectives are to achieve international monetary cooperation and exchange rate stability, facilitate the balanced growth of international trade, and provide resources to help members in balance of payments difficulties or to assist with poverty reduction. It also readily admits that its areas of responsibility are meeting new challenges, recognizing in 2011 the flaws in the system:

> The current international monetary system . . . has a number of well-known weaknesses, including the lack of an automatic and orderly mechanism for resolving the buildup of real and financial imbalances; volatile capital flows and exchange rates that can have deleterious economic effects.[27]

So the IMF is the lender of the last resort to sovereign states—and has collaborated with the EU in its euro crisis—but it does not control every aspect of the world's financial health. Globalization has hugely increased the volatility of capital movements, and bailouts have become much more significant as Figure 8.1 shows. Interdependence and highly sophisticated computerized trading have exacerbated vulnerabilities that the global economy must confront. The IMF has therefore implicitly encouraged sovereign state interference such as through policies like quantitative easing, which are designed to reduce such violent swings. Exchange rate manipulation comes in many

Figure 8.1 **Number and Size of IMF Bailouts**

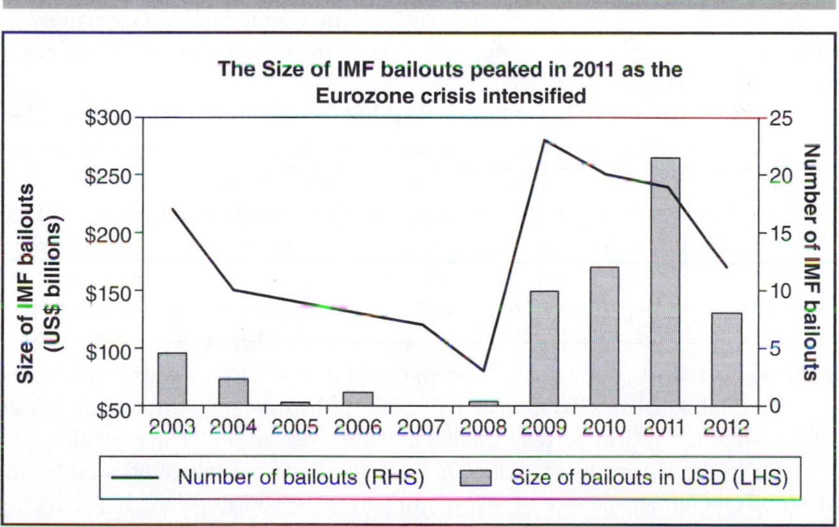

Source: IMF Annual Report Appendices, 2011 & 2012, St. Petersburg International Economic Forum Foundation, http://www.flickr.com/photos/spief_spb/8958056134/in/photostream/.

forms in the modern world, and it is all part of new global diplomacy. States accept it like the use of intelligence services, except when behavior is seen to be overly aggressive. In those cases, cries of cheating and threats of retaliation seem to have a public diplomacy effect, particularly by unsettling investors.

DIPLOMACY AND LAW: THE PROBLEM OF ENFORCEMENT AND IMPLEMENTATION

These examples illustrate that the quest for predictability, rules, and laws for diplomatic interchange has been productive. Few sovereign states have ever argued for a lawless system because they recognize that sovereignty requires mutual respect and recognition. Development of conventions and rules show a common interest. Diplomats recognize, however, the incompleteness of the coverage of rules and norms. Terrorism and human rights are existing examples, and important new challenges like cyber security and Internet governance have largely been untouched. One issue that has restricted the impact of rules and norms is the lack of enforcement mechanisms and penalties that diplomacy can impose on transgressing sovereign states. Meanwhile, UNSC resolutions go unimplemented and mandatory sanctions imposed as obligations on all UN members are breached.

The establishment of international courts has long been a diplomatic preoccupation. The League of Nations established the Permanent Court of International Justice, and from its foundation in 1922, it considered over twenty cases involving disputes throughout the world. Though an American judge was one of the early appointments, the United States only accepted the court's jurisdiction in December 1935 and it never ratified the League of Nations treaty itself. The court was based in The Hague but the German invasion of the Netherlands in 1940 made operations impossible and the court personnel moved to Switzerland.

The International Court of Justice (ICJ) has developed a steady and respected presence as an organ of the United Nations. It is the most widely used supranational authority in the world and has jurisdiction over all members of the United Nations. The disputes it considers must be submitted by interested parties, and the ICJ can only hear a case if the states involved have agreed to accept jurisdiction. One exception is if there is a treaty between the states that provides for submission of disputes by one party only. States differ in their approaches to use of the ICJ. Japan has not pressed for the ICJ to get involved in its dispute with China's claim to Senkaku/Diaoyu, but it did request an opinion in its dispute with South Korea over the Dokdo Islands. In another territorial and sovereignty dispute, the status of Kosovo, the UNGA referred the 2008 unilateral declaration of independence of Kosovo to the ICJ for its opinion. This was the first case regarding a unilateral declaration of independence to be brought before the court, and the ICJ delivered its advisory opinion on Kosovo in July 2010. By a vote of ten to four, it declared that "the declaration of independence of the 17 February 2008 did not violate general international law because international law contains no prohibition on declarations of independence."[28] This has proved a useful, though not conclusive, stimulus to Kosovo's continuing campaign for diplomatic recognition.

The ICJ has the authority of the UN Charter to enforce a decision. Under Article 94, states are required to comply with the decision of the court in any case to which they are parties. However, not all decisions have been straightforward to enforce. In the case of the Mexico and Other Nationals v. United States of America (2004), known as the Avena case, the ICJ determined that the United States should review the convictions of some Mexicans as a result of U.S. violation of their obligations to allow consular access by Mexico to prisoners under the Vienna Convention on Consular Relations. The U.S. administration tried to enforce the decision, but the U.S. Supreme Court ruled that ICJ decisions were not directly enforceable in U.S. courts. A second case illustrating the limits of enforcement occurred in 1984 with The Republic of Nicaragua v. The United States of America. The United States refused to pay reparations for their actions against Nicaragua—for example, mining the entrance to ports—and comply with other parts of an ICJ judgment. The case was taken to the UNSC by Nicaragua in October 1986. The United States twice vetoed draft UNSC resolutions calling for compliance with the judgment.

As we have seen, the ICJ is not the only transnational court dealing with disputes. The European Court of Human Rights has added another dimension to international law. And transnational courts have been incorporated into other regional organizations like the African Union.

Diplomats have long promoted the practice of arbitration in disputes and the WTO forum sees regular use of arbitrators. International treaties and bilateral legally binding agreements also commonly make such provisions for settlement of disputes. So bilateral and multilateral mechanisms to enforce agreements exist beyond formal court procedures. Some international crimes have been tried by special tribunals established to address particularly egregious acts in internal conflicts where criminal courts of the state are incapable or unwilling to try them. One example is the UN International Criminal Tribunal for the former Yugoslavia, established in 1993 by the UNSCR 808 under Chapter VII powers. This has prosecuted serious crimes committed during the civil conflicts in the former Yugoslavia and was followed by the creation of other special tribunals. One was established to investigate the atrocities committed in Rwanda. The authority for these tribunals is derived from the UNSC's capacity to prosecute breaches by states of international law:

> all parties are bound to comply with the obligations under international humanitarian law and in particular the Geneva Conventions of 12 August 1949, and that persons who commit or order the commission of grave breaches of the Conventions are individually responsible in respect of such breaches.[29]

Diplomacy, therefore, did find a legal basis for trying those who had committed crimes in internal conflicts, despite the sovereign state model.

The major development of the twenty-first century in implementation of international law and enforcement of international diplomacy is the establishment of the ICC. The UNGA first recognized the need for a permanent international court to deal with atrocities of the kind committed during World War II in 1948, following the war crimes tribunals in Nuremberg and Tokyo. It invited the ILC "to study the desirability and possibility of establishing an international judicial organ for the trials of persons charged with genocide."[30] The commission drafted two statutes by the early 1950s, but these were shelved as the Cold War removed any chance of an international consensus.

The ICC's modern genesis owes something to the initiative of a small state, thus exemplifying the contributions made in other diplomatic endeavors of leaders who think creatively to advance the public good of diplomacy. It also shows the United Nations in its role as an international convener and facilitator of the creation of an international institution that was not intended to be an agency of the United Nations. In 1989, A. N. R. Robinson, then Prime Minister of Trinidad and Tobago, proposed the creation of a permanent international court to deal with the illegal drug trade. His request led the UNGA to request that the ILC resume its work on drafting a statute. In 1994, the ILC presented its work to the UNGA, which created the Ad Hoc Committee on the Establishment of an International Criminal Court. The nonstate sector also contributed to the diplomacy. Non-governmental organizations (NGOs) and media active in conflict zones and the evidence of testimonies of the special tribunals on the former Yugoslavia and Rwanda ensured that pressure on diplomacy was irresistible. The NGO Coalition for an ICC (CICC) grew to over 2,500 civil organizations and included on its steering committee such groups as Amnesty International and Human Rights Watch.

The UNGA convened a conference in Rome in June 1998 with the aim of finalizing a treaty. On July 17, 1998, the Rome Statute of the ICC was adopted in the UNGA by a vote of 120 to seven, with twenty-one countries abstaining. The blocking votes of the P5 in the UNSC, the majority of which have not becomes parties to the statute, were thereby avoided.

Following a decade that had shown the increasing impotence of diplomacy to deal with criminal acts committed by or in the name of governments against their own people or in civil conflict, the ICC was a major step forward. Many had predicted that the 1990s would see an inexorable movement toward democracy and representative government that would combine with globalization and new technologies to pull millions out of poverty. Yet realignments after the Cold War appeared to herald an unraveling of the sovereign state model with diplomacy largely wringing its hands in face of mass killings, beyond the worst nightmares of the UN founders.

The ICC statute is, however, carefully circumscribed in its intrusions on sovereignty. The ICC's areas of competence are strictly defined. The ICC can only try a criminal case committed after July 2002, the date of the Rome Treaty.

It can try three categories of crimes so far agreed—war crimes, crimes against humanity, and genocide—while discussions continue on adding others, such as the crime of aggression.

The ICC cannot try a crime unless it has jurisdiction over the person concerned. It may only try the person accused of the crimes defined in the statute if one or more of the following states are parties to the Treaty of Rome:

a. The state on whose territory the crime was committed

b. The state of which the suspect is a national

The ICC does, however, have power to try cases referred to it by the UNSC under Chapter VII of the UN Charter. For example, Sudan was not a party to the ICC when in 2005 the UNSC referred to the court the crimes committed by nationals of Sudan, including the then president of Sudan, Omar Bashir, for events that occurred in the conflict in Darfur.

Even if the case meets all of the above criteria, the case would not be admissible to the ICC if the national authorities of those involved in the crimes or the national territories of the states where they were committed are investigating or prosecuting them, or if they have already done so. Article 17 of the Rome Statute allows the ICC to determine that the national authorities have shown themselves unable or unwilling genuinely to try the case. The ICC sees itself as complementary with national courts and a forum that should only be used a last resort. And as at present constituted, the ICC does not have the resources to try hundreds of cases.

One example of the complexities of the ICC's jurisdiction is shown by the case against those accused of inciting violence and murders in the Kenyan election campaign of 2007. The ICC was called in by the government of Kenya (a party to the statute), which approved the involvement through a vote in parliament because it considered its own courts as incapable of trying the cases. One of those accused, Uhuru Kenyatta, was elected president of Kenya in 2013. Shortly before the 2013 election, the ICC's Chief Prosecutor, Fatou Bensouda, announced that the cases against four of the accused were being dropped not because the charges were baseless but because some key witnesses had died and others had expressed themselves too frightened to give evidence. How this case evolves will create several important precedents for the operations of the court.

Nevertheless, the ICC has shown progress. At the time of writing, there are 122 state parties to the statute and it has indicted thirty individuals, all for crimes in Africa. One of those indicted, Muammar Gaddafi, died. By 2013, it had convicted just one—Thomas Lubanga—for crimes in the Democratic Republic of Congo. Yet despite its success or increased international profile, the threats to national sovereignty have proved a stumbling block in achieving participation from many of the world's major powers. The United States, Russia, India, and China have not signed or ratified the treaty. All these countries have been engaged in conflicts since 2002. They believe that accepting the jurisdiction of ICC would jeopardize their ability to project power and engage in military operations, fearing that those involved might be indicted under the broadly drawn terms of the Rome Statute.

The ICC showed commendable energy in addressing crimes committed in recent intrastate conflicts in Ivory Coast and Libya. Though there is no explicit reference in the definition of war crimes to chemical or biological weapons, the ICC also expressed its interest in investigating such use in the Syrian conflict. Its threat of supranational jurisdiction has introduced a new element to the diplomatic toolkit, but its de facto concentration on cases arising in Africa has caused growing suspicion in that continent. The appointment of a Gambian lawyer, Fatou Bensouda, as chief prosecutor was designed to correct the appearance of victimization. Even if the results of prosecutions have so far been patchy, the ICC should serve as a new deterrent to the flouting of internationally agreed standards of behavior—genocide, crimes against humanity—and leave doubt in the minds of the perpetrators that they will escape unnoticed and unpunished. Perhaps it is no accident that the high profile ICC case of the Kenyan politicians encouraged an election largely free of violence in 2013.

While examples of flouting of international laws abound, it is of course true that enforcement of laws in a domestic legal system is also incomplete—many speeding offenses or burglaries go unpunished. And several of the sanctions available to domestic law enforcement such as fines, probation, and jail do not exist for diplomacy. States, however, can be subjected to sanctions, backed by regional and UN-mandated authority. But states also have avenues available to them to evade punishments that individuals do not. Many sanctions regimes have existed for years without changes in behavior or a remedying of activities that the international community condemned.

The lack of implementation of many UNSCRs has regularly undermined the legal authority of the international community. UNSCR 242 is one of the most commonly cited as having been ignored. Adopted unanimously in November 1967 under Chapter VI of the UN Charter, it sought to reverse the result of an Arab-Israel conflict in specific ways. This affirmed the "inadmissibility of the acquisition of territory by war and the need to work for a just and lasting peace in the Middle East in which every State in the area can live in security."[31] And it prescribed the following to meet the fulfillment of Charter principles:

> (i) Withdrawal of Israel armed forces from territories occupied in the recent conflict;
>
> (ii) Termination of all claims or states of belligerency and respect for and acknowledgment of the sovereignty, territorial integrity and political independence of every State in the area and their right to live in peace within secure and recognized boundaries free from threats or acts of force.[32]

Over four decades later, this resolution has not been implemented and lies at the heart of one of the world's most protracted disputes, which diplomacy has failed to solve. Political arguments for why it has not been implemented are not hard to find, but the list of unimplemented UNSCRs has mounted over the years. UNSCR 1737 of 2006, also adopted unanimously, requires termination of Iran's nuclear activities. The resolution requires Iran to suspend certain "proliferation sensitive nuclear activities."[33] The resolution also imposed a freeze on those assets supporting or associated with Iran's nuclear activities and established a committee (known as the 1737 Committee) to oversee their implementation.

It is not surprising that the sovereign state model is reluctant to concede the UN authority when fundamental issues are at stake. Territorial disputes and, in Iran's case, the interpretation of a treaty—the NPT—go to the root of a state's existence. But the terms of implementation of other UNSC resolutions, such as UNSCR 1540 discussed in Chapter 4, involve a reaffirmation of sovereignty and the imposition of national controls against weapons of mass destruction proliferation within each state and over its citizens. Yet, some nine years after its mandatory orders, only 166 states had even filed a report of their measures that are required under the resolution.

Another example of a diplomatic inability to enforce implementation involves the murderers of Rafic Hariri, the former prime minister of Lebanon killed in 2005. They are still at large despite the United Nations having established a special tribunal to investigate the crime, which was never tried in Lebanon. And President Omar Bashir is increasingly traveling in Africa and the Middle East with impunity despite his ICC indictment. Like all diplomacy, implementation is a mixture of failure and success. In April 2013, a Qatari lawyer employed by the United Nations presented a check for $28 million to the new president of Tunisia from funds embezzled by the wife of the deposed Tunisian President Ben-Ali. Sometimes enforcement scores a modest victory.

Do lack of implementation and the lack of a UN military capacity to enforce render all such attempts at collective action pointless? Is international diplomacy a waste of time if the resolutions never get beyond the paper on which they were drafted? The analogy of domestic legal enforcement again gives part of the answers. The act of setting standards, common approaches, and norms gives focus to diplomacy. There are few instances of a total rejection by member states of the terms of treaty to which they are party (for example the UN Charter) or the authority of the UNSC. And diplomatic solutions may be possible sometimes outside the confines of the United Nations. In some cases, legally enforceable measures may be desirable but not necessary to achieve the same effect. Many issues are never put to the UNSC because lack of support or a threat to veto are known in advance.

CONCLUSION

Our survey has shown that diplomacy makes uneven progress in both formation of new norms and implementation. A successful display of unanimity, for example over intervention in Libya in 2011, can produce a collective closing of ranks by sovereign states against a precedent that might herald serial intervention in internal conflicts under the guise, in the view of some countries, of regime change. Indeed, diplomatic successes seldom come simply in the form of law enforcement. To produce the combination of diplomatic carrots and sticks that contributed to political reforms in Myanmar took years.

Not all states use their diplomacy to support progress toward collective rule books and harmony. Some may see their roles more as spoilers of other states' diplomatic agendas and are suspicious of the term public good applying in the international arena. The search for norms is not universal, and some may see an advocacy of a global agenda as a front for wider intervention and an attack on sovereignty. Others will see it as a vital function of modern diplomacy to define issues in global terms, and extend the rule of law and creation of norms. They recognize that in a thoroughly multipolar world, new norms are necessary because no country can achieve results on its own. What is not in dispute is that the range of treaties, agreed definitions, and implementation measures provide the fabric that gives the states of the world much of their basic tools for coexistence. It is a major drawback that their enforcement still depends to an uncomfortably large extent on the UNSC, but any more efficient mechanism in a fragmented world with weaker states seems a forlorn hope. Diplomacy must do its best with the world of reality.

International law shows best the painstaking and cumulative efforts of diplomacy. Despite its gaps, vague texts, and incomplete achievement of universal norms, all states at some time accuse others of a breach of international law. What has been put in place in the form of lasting public goods matters. And our next chapter—the agenda of diplomatic reform—will concentrate on other new quests for predictability and more effective diplomacy in a world that seems less law abiding than ever.

SUGGESTIONS FOR FURTHER READING

1. von Glahn, Gerhard, and James Larry Taulbee. *Law among Nations: An Introduction to Public International Law*. 10th ed. New York: Pearson, 2013.
2. Dunoff, Jeffrey L., and Mark A. Pollack, ed. *Interdisciplinary Perspectives on International Law and International Relations: The State of the Art*. Cambridge: Cambridge University Press, 2013.

chapter 9

The New Diplomatic Agenda

The Challenges for Diplomatic Reform

We have now completed the survey of current bilateral and multilateral diplomatic practice. We have looked at what diplomatic mechanisms exist today to respond to the issues on the world's agenda. The system that has evolved has been versatile and produced some impressive monuments to diplomatic progress. In any analysis of diplomatic practice, it is appropriate to ask how far the achievements of diplomacy in the past will be adequate for what diplomacy needs in the future. Equally, we will examine how much of what exists in current diplomatic practice is perhaps diverting resources into less productive areas. The issue of reform is one that diplomacy has regularly faced. Its adequacy and underperformance are now center stage and provide an invigorating series of what-ifs to a new generation of diplomats.

WHY REFORM?

Diplomatic reform is widely discussed because diplomatic leaders sense that something does not work sufficiently well in the contemporary world. This chapter examines how far diplomatic reform will be adequate for the new diplomatic agenda and what mechanisms are available to diplomacy to fulfill the tasks that it faces.

The machinery of diplomacy is unquestionably smoother and better funded than at any time in history. Bilaterally, many embassies are better equipped than they have ever been. Their technology is sophisticated, they have access to consultants on every conceivable issue, they have professional human resources experts and finance directors, and they are equal opportunity employers. They even employ lobbyists in key capitals like Washington. They are well primed to play a facilitator role and reach out to non-governmental organizations (NGOs). They meet targets and deliver outcomes.

But what is the outcome agenda to which these slick machines are applying themselves? Is it an agenda that is significantly different from the issues facing previous generations? And how far are diplomatic systems equipped to problem solve internationally rather than impress at an audit review? We have already seen how some issues have stalled in the diplomatic efforts to produce the shared actions that their shared interests suggest. The Syrian civil war, in one of the most dangerous parts of the world, showed a collective failure of diplomacy. The global governance of the Internet, the threat of cyberweapons, and the arguments over the scientific basis for climate change are all significant avenues for future diplomacy that have remain largely untraveled at the time of writing. There are many things wrong with the world, and one important complication is that states disagree over what *is* wrong. Nevertheless, a question that interests them all is how far it is fair to blame diplomacy—rather than the world being a mighty complicated place—for such disagreements.

One obvious feature of the contemporary diplomatic system is the declining power and influence of states. Strong powers help diplomats secure agreements because power, threats, and leverage usually focus minds. If a country is dependent in its position in the world order on another, either militarily or economically, then diplomacy has a predictable outcome. In a world where power is diffused or where leading powers have a reduced resource capacity to use that power, then discussion and process matter more. Diplomacy has to ensure it is as productive as it can be and that the pressing issues are given maximum attention. This capacity to self-evaluate and jettison the superfluous, ritualistic elements of diplomacy; reengineer the core functions and machinery; and adjust to changes is a fair test of how healthy, responsive, and versatile the system is. How far can diplomacy reform itself to work better?

Some experts think there is an overarching problem and that the contemporary world is just too complicated for our present system to function adequately. Hamilton and Langhorne, in their book *The Practice of Diplomacy* suggest, "Global problems may demand global solutions, but in a world of more than 190 sovereign states, and a multitude of non-governmental and transnational bodies, diplomacy has yet to design mechanisms capable of achieving global consensus."[1] Paul Sharp, in his work *The Diplomatic Theory of International Relations*, agrees that traditional diplomacy may no longer have all the answers. "Some of the codes, particularly those of the modern state system, may no longer be as useful as they once were, at least for now, but the problems they were developed to address remain broadly the same."[2]

We have seen that the classic architecture of diplomacy—its immunities and privileges, its major global institutions, and its traditional functions—is still active and relevant to today's issues. This chapter will examine how traditional diplomatic systems of different states are confronting reform and whether there are any identifiable trends between states. Is there still a preference for the traditional state-to-state solutions, where interstate rivalries are played out through diplomacy? Or are the institutions and their capabilities moving in the direction of preventive diplomacy and creating new fora for discussion and solution of problems? Is the system on a trajectory of reform that may produce radical solutions on the lines of the post-World War II generation? Or is the world now so configured that only ad hoc solutions are feasible, crafting diplomatic responses as each problem arises?

The traditional diplomatic system that evolved since World War II provided a framework for treatment of issues because of the order brought to the world by its division into ideological, economic, and political blocs. Now that order is fragmenting, few issues are settled by the same small group of powers. Interests of states converge on some issues but diverge on others. The new diplomatic agenda needs to adjust to a crowded field of international activity and myriad international entities competing for funds, influence, and outcomes. The diplomat and the system of diplomacy must again show intelligence to recognize the particular circumstances of the era to adapt their methods to deliver successful outcomes.

In evaluating proposals for reform of diplomacy some fundamental questions arise:

> How far does the world order influence diplomacy, and how far does diplomacy influence the world?
>
> How far is diplomatic progress impeded by an uneven process of global interaction, where a new consensus has to be built on each issue?
>
> Has diplomacy become lazy during a period of superpower dominance? Have we relied too long on the capacity of the United States to dictate outcomes and provide order in the world?
>
> If the United States is showing a declining capacity and inclination to guide international outcomes, how can the new powers contribute more effectively to the process of diplomacy?
>
> Does the world demonstrate more signs of convergence than divergence in an era of unprecedented economic globalization and revolutionary communication technologies?
>
> Where does the right interface lie between multiple economic powers and ever increasing resources and influence of nonstate actors?

We will first examine the priorities of the contemporary diplomatic agenda as seen by some of the most powerful countries in today's world. How do these countries view the important challenges, and how do they relate to the reform of diplomacy? Second, we will investigate how far the modern agenda of issues is moving diplomacy into new areas. And, third, we will look at current trends in diplomatic reform in some of the leading states in today's world.

DIPLOMATIC PRIORITIES

China

China's view on the priorities for the international diplomatic agenda is indispensable to any survey. The first illustration of thinking in Beijing is an extract from a Chinese foreign ministry document from 2004. Titled "China's Views on the Development of Multipolarization," it suggests a few continuing themes in China's role in the world.

> Currently, while complex and deep changes are taking place in the international situation, the trend towards world multipolarization has not changed. There are nearly 200 countries with a population of more than 6 billion in the world. A myriad of differences exists between these countries in ethnic traditions, religions and cultures, economic levels and political systems. It is hardly possible to imagine how to unify them with one model and one value or to "lead" them by one country. The basic norms governing international relations on equality of sovereignty and non-interference in each other's internal affairs between the member states as stipulated in the Charter of the United Nations are absolutely not outdated. The history and culture, social systems and development models of various countries should be respected. The multipolarization process may be zigzag, protracted and full of struggles, but this is a historical trend independent of human will. It is in conformity with the common aspirations and interests of the majority of countries and conducive to world peace and security.
>
> Our efforts to promote the development of the world towards multipolarization are not targeted at any particular country, nor are they aimed at re-staging the old play of contention for hegemony in history. Rather, these efforts are made to boost the democratization of international relations, help the various forces in the world on the basis of equality and mutual benefit, enhance coordination and dialogue, refrain from confrontation and preserve jointly world peace, stability and development.[3]

In a speech to a Chinese regional forum in April 2013, the then recently appointed president of China, Xi Jinping, described Chinese diplomatic priorities as follows:

> The world today is experiencing profound and complex changes. Countries have become increasingly inter-connected and interdependent. Several billion people in a large number of developing countries are embracing modernization. The trend of the times, namely, peace, development, cooperation and mutual benefit, is gaining momentum.
>
> On the other hand, our world is far from peaceful. Development remains a major challenge; the global economy has entered a period of profound readjustment, and its recovery remains elusive. . .
>
> Peace is the ever-lasting wish of our people. Peace, like air and sunshine, is hardly noticed when people are benefiting from it. But none of us can live without it. Without peace, development is out of

> the question. Countries, whether big or small, strong or weak, rich or poor, should all contribute their share to maintaining and enhancing peace. Rather than undercutting each other's efforts, countries should complement each other and work for joint progress. The international community should advocate the vision of comprehensive security, common security and cooperative security so as to turn our global village into a big stage for common development, rather than an arena where gladiators fight each other. And no one should be allowed to throw a region and even the whole world into chaos for selfish gains. With growing interaction among countries, it is inevitable that they encounter frictions here and there. What is important is that they should resolve differences through dialogue, consultation and peaceful negotiations in the larger interest of the sound growth of their relations.
>
> Promoting good neighborliness is a time-honored tradition of China. To enhance peaceful development and win-win cooperation in Asia and the world is a race that has one starting point after another and knows no finishing line.[4]

So, for China, the complexities of the interconnection of a multipolar world seem to be recognized. China sees profound changes in the world and includes China's own embracing of modernization as part of this. And it also sees major challenges to diplomacy. The stated objectives of China's views of the world are to promote common aspirations, a global village, and the continued validity of the Charter of the United Nations. Though the word diplomacy is not mentioned specifically, "dialogue, consultation and peaceful negotiations"[5] amplify the value that China's leadership attributes to it. Achievement of "win-win cooperation" is indeed a classic aspiration of diplomacy.

India

A recent statement of Indian priorities was set out by S. M. Krishna, Minister of External Affairs of India, speaking at Southern Methodist University in Dallas in October 2012.

> It was not so long ago that India was considered a mere idea! For over one and a half century, India was subjugated by colonial powers. Emerging independent in 1947, India transformed in diverse ways and in diverse sectors.
>
> In the past decade or so, the global interest in India has increased by leaps and bounds. This new mindset globally is borne out of a realization rooted in rapid economic transformation of India and the emerging role of India as a stabilizing power in the new global strategic architecture.

> This is further amplified by the fact that a large number of countries, including the Permanent members of the United Nations Security Council, have entered into strategic partnerships (with India) in the last decade. The most salient aspect of such partnerships is that they are not targeted against any country; the sole aim is to bring most optimal mutual benefit to the peoples of India and other countries in such partnership.
>
> Already the fast growing developing economies in Asia, Latin America and Africa account for over two thirds of the incremental global output. This relentless shift in the axis of economic power is also witnessing a fascinating transition in the global institutions of economic, security and political governance, of which India is a major part. The world, including the United States, wants to see India to play a substantive role in this seminal transition taking place in the institutions of global governance. India would be a focus of attention from this perspective also.
>
> India has inherent democratic checks and balances to tackle the various social and environmental spin-offs of consistently high economic growth. . . . It is not mere growth but an inclusive growth that is the objective of our developmental policies and programs. This requires a deepening of dialogue within India, and also with other countries as we live in the age of globalization.
>
> India as a nation of over a billion people, driven by the energy and enterprise of its youth, living in a democratic framework, celebrating its unparalleled diversity, pursuing sustainable and inclusive growth, and fulfilling its role as a responsible international citizen, will be a major factor of global peace, stability, development and prosperity in the 21st century.[6]

India then believes in a new strategic architecture and in diplomatic reform. It sees itself as a country whose status in the twenty-first century needs to be recognized, a status to match its strengths. The world is changing, its power centers are shifting, and global institutions are in transition. India is concerned that the institutional structure should reflect new realities, but they lament that there does not appear to be progress in this direction. India is keen to play a global role, but does not suggest how global consensus might be developed. The objective of Indian diplomacy is to ensure India plays a major part in how issues are discussed. And India shares with China the belief in a deepening of dialogue to promote global peace and stability.

Russia

Russia, like China, has one foot in the old world order, which created the United Nations and its five permanent members of the United Nations Security

Council (UNSC), and one foot in the multipolarism of the twenty-first century. Russia's view of the world in September 2012 was reflected in a speech at the United Nations General Assembly (UNGA) by the Russian foreign minister Sergei Lavrov.

> Let us not forget that the UN founding fathers in their wisdom agreed upon and endorsed the United Nations Charter that enshrined the principles for regulation of the multi-polar world order. Now, when the abnormal bipolar period of the Cold War is over, and when it has become obvious for everyone that there is no place for unipolarity in the modern world, and that the international reality can be only poly-centric, we have a unique chance to fully implement the original potential of the UN Charter.
>
> This is a hard challenge. International relations are clearly experiencing a lack of credibility. We regard this as the main obstacle to practical progress towards the establishment of universal foundations of equal and indivisible security—be it in the Euro-Atlantic area, the Asia-Pacific region or other parts of the world. Such a state of affairs clearly contradicts the concept of collective security embodied in the UN Charter, and the deep interdependence of the modern world where the majority of challenges and threats are common for all and have a cross-border dimension.
>
> Strengthening of confidence and collective principles in the international life with the emphasis on negotiating pursuit for compromise solutions would help substantially reduce the level of instability and move forward in the settlement of crisis situations not only in the Middle East, but also around Iran, Afghanistan, in the Korean peninsula and throughout the world.
>
> The final goal of the efforts to settle a conflict is to ensure the right to life and other fundamental human rights: political, economic and social. The events of the recent years confirm that without lasting peace and sustainable development, it is impossible to ensure human rights. In its turn, the protection of human rights should contribute to security and development of people rather than serve as a pretext for illegal interference in the domestic affairs of States.[7]

The Russian foreign minister sees the Cold War as a temporary aberration and argues there is a fundamental flaw in the modern system of international diplomacy. That is why it lacks credibility. It has failed to establish mechanisms for building consensus to produce an "equal and indivisible security." Russia calls for compromise solutions, universal rights, and a recognition of deep interdependence in the modern world where "threats are common for all." The need for creative diplomacy, compromises, and stability is central to Russian thinking, but there is again little in the way of specific proposals on how to achieve reform.

South Africa

South Africa is another emerging economy and a powerful force in Africa's diplomacy. Here is an extract from a statement made at the UNGA in September 2012 by Maite Nkoana-Mashabane, Minister of International Relations and Cooperation of South Africa, set in the context of the turbulent events of the Arab Spring.

> The complexities underlying these events underscore that no individual country or organization can address these developments on their own. The need for cooperation amongst states and international organizations when dealing with cross-cutting issues of peace, security and development is therefore paramount. Equally, the underlying causes of these uprisings, including long standing conflicts, have to be addressed in a coordinated manner.[8]

In May 2011, the government of South Africa summarized its foreign policy objectives in "Building a Better World: the Diplomacy of Ubuntu." South African policy is described as

> an approach to international relations that respects all nations, peoples, and cultures. It recognizes that it is in our national interest to promote and support the positive development of others. Similarly, national security would therefore depend on the centrality of human security as a universal goal, based on the principle of Batho Pele (putting people first). In the modern world of globalization, a constant element is and has to be our common humanity. We therefore champion collaboration, cooperation and building partnerships over conflict. This recognition of our interconnectedness and interdependency, and the infusion of Ubuntu—roughly translated as "human kindness"—into the South African identity, shapes our foreign policy.
>
> South Africa therefore accords central importance to our immediate African neighborhood and continent; working with countries of the South to address shared challenges of underdevelopment; promoting global equity and social justice; working with countries of the North to develop a true and effective partnership for a better world; and doing our part to strengthen the multilateral system, including its transformation, to reflect the diversity of our nations, and ensure its centrality in global governance.[9]

South Africa draws on its ethnic traditions and sees its influence as primarily in its own neighborhood. Yet it sees the need for a transformation of the multilateral system, and another shared objective in diplomacy with China, Russia, and India is a call for "collaboration, cooperation and building partnerships." Again, there are few specific proposals as to how global equity and social justice might be promoted. But working between North and South is central to their objectives.

Brazil

Dilma Roussef, President of Brazil and the final member of the BRICS (Brazil, Russia, India, China, and South Africa), presented her vision of diplomatic challenges at the UNGA in September 2012.

> Strengthening the United Nations is necessary at this stage when multipolarity opens a historic new perspective. We must work towards this end. We must work to ensure that in the multipolarity that comes to prevail, cooperation predominates over conflict, dialogue overcomes threats, and negotiated solutions are reached before and forestall interventions involving the use of force. I reiterate that in this necessarily collective effort, which presupposes the quest for consensus, the United Nations has a key role to play, particularly as the Organization and its various bodies become more representative and more legitimate and, therefore, more effective.[10]

Brazil sees the United Nations as the main source of inspiration for the future conduct of diplomacy and the strengthening of its own role in the organization so that it becomes more "representative and legitimate." Yet Brazil also sees serious flaws in the UN and international diplomacy. In 2013, as well as expressing indignation for U.S. surveillance of communications and calling for a new international governance of the Internet, President Roussef lamented the lack of

> a Security Council capable of fully exerting its responsibilities in today's world. The limited representation of the UN Security Council is an issue of grave concern, considering the challenges posed by the twenty-first century. The immense difficulty in offering a solution to the Syrian crisis and the paralysis in addressing the Israeli-Palestinian conflict exemplify this concern. In dealing with important issues, the recurring polarization between permanent members generates a dangerous paralysis.
>
> We must provide the Council with voices that are at once independent and constructive. Only the expansion of the number of permanent and nonpermanent members and the inclusion of developing countries in both categories will correct the Council's deficit of representation and legitimacy. We are guided by the defense of a multilateral world, ruled by international law, by the primacy of peaceful solutions to conflicts and by the quest for a more compassionate and just order—both economically and socially.[11]

Brazil, therefore, joins those who believe that the instruments and methods of diplomacy are inadequate to meet global challenges and that cooperation is essential in a multipolar world. But, from this evidence, there are few, if any, ideas on what diplomacy needs to do other than that more states should be elevated to permanent status in the UNSC. One common feature is the predominant wish to strengthen the sovereign state and little recognition of the impact of the nonstate sector.

Mexico

The Mexican government's foreign ministry, the Secretaría de Relaciones Exteriores, provided me with a summary of their approach to diplomatic reform:

> Regardless of the increasing influence of multinational corporations and other transnational organizations in international affairs, there is no reason to believe that the nation-state is likely to lose its central role in the near future. States will remain the most powerful and relevant actors in the global stage: they are a unique source of internal unity, order and legitimacy that provide the basis of social interaction, both domestically and internationally. Diplomacy, generally understood as the art and practice of representing the interests of a state, will therefore continue to play a prominent part in world affairs for the foreseeable future.
>
> Nevertheless, it is also clear that the international scene is in the midst of significant change. Nation-states will need to engage more closely with other organizations and bodies that are gradually gaining international relevance and influence. Indeed, a state's legitimacy is steadily becoming more closely linked to its engagement with non-state actors. Issues as far apart as financial regulation and human rights, trade and cultural exchanges, non-proliferation and the development agenda, are today driven not just or even primarily by the deliberation of elected assemblies or policy planning departments, but rather by the committed engagement of think-tanks, private firms, charitable foundations and other non-governmental organizations. Their role has been further enhanced by the vast amounts of information and the innovative communication tools that are readily available as a result of the spread of new technologies.
>
> Today, ministries of foreign affairs must endeavor to represent more closely the needs and aspirations of their constituents and, at the same time, seek the best possible accommodation with those put forward by other governments and organizations. This will demand adopting a more open, direct and active dialogue with other sectors, at home and abroad. Achieving a genuine engagement with a globalized non-state sector and embracing new technologies are necessary steps in this process.[12]

Mexico is recognizing that though the state will remain the main actor in diplomacy, it is essential to partner with other states and nonstate actors to achieve progress in the modern world. The ability of a state to do this is a new measure of its legitimacy.

The preceding extracts show that the process of reform is receiving much attention within many of the major states of the twenty-first century. The yearning for multipolarity poses challenges for diplomacy that mirror some of those of earlier eras. But the differences of perceptions and expectations from major countries suggest that the task of creating more productive diplomacy goes well beyond the formation of military alliances and the modern equivalent of dynastic marriages. All recognize that a permanent cooperative approach is required, but none is proposing any new ingredient that might stimulate progress in this direction.

The actors of the traditional diplomatic agenda, sovereign states, are in trouble. Not only must they recognize the first genuine multipolar world in the history of our planet but also a diminishing capacity of sovereign states to control developments. At the same time, the diplomatic agenda, rather than reflecting the ambitions and capabilities to solve issues of powerful sovereign states, increasingly concerns the failings of the states themselves. The state ceases to be an actor in diplomacy but becomes a problem for it. When states feel insecure, diplomacy is collectively undermined. These weaknesses are not just reflected in external threats or an inadequate or incompetent military. The inhabitants of states see them as a service provider to ensure the functioning of systems of health, education, security, and communications. Diplomatic failures reflect a wider frustration that states have a diminishing capability to deliver. Yet publics demand more of them, and in a world of interconnection, achievements of others accentuate perceived failures at home.

Two figures central to transnational efforts at improving mechanisms for peaceful resolution of problems expressed themselves in forceful terms in September 2014 about the effects of persistent failures in contemporary diplomacy. Pope Francis, speaking at a commemoration of the thousands of Italian soldiers killed in World War I, commented that "even today, after the second failure of another world war, perhaps one can speak of a third war, one fought piecemeal, with crimes, massacres, destruction."[13] Ban Ki Moon, the UN Secretary General, was equally despairing in a speech at UNGA. "Not since the end of the Second World War have there been so many refugees, displaced people and asylum seekers. . . . It may seem as if the world is falling apart, as crises pile up and disease spreads."[14] Ban called on leaders of diplomacy to find seeds of hope and nurture them into something bigger.

We will now examine how far diplomacy is facing new tasks that demand different approaches to make it work and how the currents diplomatic systems are responding.

THE NEW AGENDA: CORRUPTION

One activity that has been assisted by the development of a multipolar world is corruption. Corruption in a diplomatic system, as in any organization, undermines its collective ethos and heightens distrust. For governments, these risks are obvious, but there are others as well. Poor or dishonest governance suggests a distortion of purpose in the activity of diplomacy. States are no longer rational or even competent actors. The venal motive of those in power replaces the interests of the state and the pursuit of friendly international relations. Governments control such vast budgets in military expenditure, healthcare, education, and infrastructure contracts that proper accountability is tough to achieve. The revolving door of contractors, advisors, and cross-employment between senior procurement officers and the equipment makers become so dependent on the patronage of those they serve that internal whistle blowing is a rare phenomenon.

The World Bank has attempted to provide a nucleus of investigative capacity into corruption. And it has an active anticorruption unit, known as the Integrity Vice-Presidency. Between 1999 and 2012, the bank's Sanctions Board punished and sometimes banned more than 530 firms and individuals for corrupt practices in projects it funded. Though the bank has never sanctioned any government, it estimates that corruption can reduce a country's growth rate by 0.5 to 1.0 percent per year and that the annual cost of corruption amounts to more than 5 percent of global GDP with more than $1 trillion paid in bribes annually. The International Monetary Fund's (IMF) research has shown that investment in corrupt countries is almost 5 percent less than in countries that are relatively corruption free.

Corruption does not affect just the small-part players in diplomacy. Transparency International (TI) is an international civil society organization founded in 1993 by a former World Bank official and based in Berlin. It produces regular surveys of how states are viewed on various corruption measures. Many governments in the Group of Twenty (G20)—including Argentina, China, India, Indonesia, Italy, Russia, Saudi Arabia, and Turkey—are rated highly corrupt in surveys run for TI. In a 2013 TI survey of 114,000 people in 107 countries, more than one in four reported paying a bribe in the past year. And, perhaps ironically, corruption is often rampant in a system of representative democracy where political parties compete for power. Among group actors, parties were considered to be the most corrupt globally. Parties require vast funding to fight modern elections. New technologies such as blanket robocalls and online ads have sent costs spiraling. Barack Obama in 2012 spent over $870 million to get elected. In 1980 the two US presidential candidates spent under $100 million combined. India's 2014 elections cost more than $5 billion, which was estimated to be triple the cost of the elections of 2009. Bills have to be paid to fight elections, and the money is raised mainly from donors who expect rewards, which of course fuels corruption.

Corruption not only diverts diplomacy from its consensus-building functions but encourages appointments made on the basis of nepotism and cronyism rather than on merit. If the practitioners of diplomacy are not chosen because of their aptitude for it and their motives are more self-centered, then indeed the system is unlikely to deliver its intended results.

Such corruption affects all branches of government and economic activity. The state may be far from a unitary actor in diplomacy, but its disparate parts share the common malaise of corruption. Indeed, in some countries, the law enforcement branches themselves benefit most from the practice. In Venezuela, the minister for the interior in 2011 estimated that one in five crimes committed were by the police. In my posting in Venezuela during the 1990s, I was curious to attend a meeting with the then minister of the interior who played loud classical music throughout—obviously a sign that he suspected his own security were eavesdropping on him. In 2012, Kenyan members of Parliament earned the equivalent of over $10,000 a month and voted themselves a bonus of over $100,000 when the assembly adjourned for new elections. Average income in Kenya was around $750 a year and the proposal was vetoed by the Kenyan president. Greece, whose accounting appears to have deceived the EU's auditors to secure entry into the Euro mechanisms, was at the center of the euro crisis in 2008, and the gravity of its debts and profligate expenditure owed much to endemic corruption. Greek politicians and their allies had long ensured that none among the vastly profitable ship-owning community paid any income tax. The Greek government figured in the top five purchasers of military equipment in the world in the mid-2000s, a statistic fueled by the high kickback commissions involved in military deals. And the Greek railways, with an income of $100 million a year, had an annual payroll of over $400 million. The staff added to their sinecures by purchasing surplus railway equipment, receiving commissions from the manufacturers. It may seem a stretch to tie new Greek locomotives to a decline in diplomatic capacity of sovereign states and a cause of an existential crisis in the EU, but corruption and incompetence cast long shadows in international relations.

The UN itself has for obvious reasons never formalized an international approach to dealing with corruption. And it has been hard for the World Bank to make an impact when its own members and funders are part of the problem. State parties themselves are imperfect and devious actors. This is of course nothing new. The UN Office of Drugs and Crime, reporting in retrospect, estimated that between 1960 and 1999 over $400 billion was pilfered by political leaders in Nigeria. Yet if the opportunities a global economy and complex administration presents for corruption are great, other technology developments are increasingly allowing citizens to expose corruption through cell phone photos of abuses of power and "bridge to nowhere" projects for which money has been paid. Social media networks offer new avenues for those seeking accountability and greater participation. Corruption and cheating, international or national, carries a much greater risk.

In India, webcams are being used to ensure that teachers show up in rural schools. In Africa, text messaging technology is allowing citizens to check if the drugs they are buying in the pharmacies are genuine. In Latin America, Argentina ranks third in Facebook penetration worldwide, with over 62.1 percent of Internet users on the network in 2012, ahead of both the United States (59.1%) and Canada (61.0%). And in Brazil in 2011, a movement organized through social media produced a demonstration of 250,000 people on the streets to protest widespread corruption. They wore clowns' noses to reflect the "circus" that had become Brazilian politics. One protestor told the *Financial Times*, "Brazilians are always complaining but never leave their houses to do anything about it, so it's good to finally have a non-partisan movement to show our indignation."[15]

DECLINE OF SOVEREIGN STATES

The agenda of diplomacy increasingly reflects a decline of sovereign state power. Government resources now struggle to cover sufficient programs to produce social cohesion or deference. In 2012, the government budget deficit exceeded 8 percent of GDP in the United States, and 10 percent in the United Kingdom and Japan. In the seventeen countries of the eurozone, debt to GDP ratios and government budget deficits vary greatly, but bailouts and austerity programs undoubtedly divert attention from effective diplomacy. Governments who cannot pay their way will be cautious and unlikely to be equipped to take new diplomatic initiatives. At a time when government power is declining, global interconnection in business and in non-governmental organizations generates new problems for governments. These actors, outside the normal confines of state-centric diplomacy, increasingly set the agenda for diplomacy and cause the crises. The global financial contagion of 2008 and 2009 had its origins in both weak states and overconfident nonstate actors, many of whom felt few sovereign state constraints to their financial recklessness.

Even when states succeed in setting the diplomatic agenda, an extended period of diplomatic failure may result. Many sovereign states remain mired in decades-old territorial disputes despite diplomatic contacts. India and Pakistan cannot find a diplomacy that will escape memories of their painful separation, their disputes over small tracts of land in Jamu Kashmir, and the blows dealt by insurgent terror attacks. China and Japan, despite being major trading partners, have been diplomatically incapable of settling a dispute over uninhabited islands. After six decades, the division of the Korean peninsula is still based on a cease-fire rather than a postwar diplomatic agenda, and Israel and Palestine are not able or willing to sign a settlement despite repeated intensive efforts by the United States, EU, and the UN.

Historically, the diplomat as a negotiator has been adept and insistent in setting agendas. The limiting of issues to be discussed is as important as those that are included. And the diplomat has traditionally been good at framing issues so that states can discuss them in ways where mutually acceptable solutions may be possible. But modern diplomacy, because of the interconnectedness and enormous complexity of international relations, seldom has the opportunity to bundle issues that might unlock connected doors. The issues of diplomacy resemble a school timetable where students proceed from a class on history to one on music followed by physics. All are connected as each one is greatly influenced by the others. But in diplomacy, as in most systems of education, they are studied and graded separately.

The issue of Iran's nuclear ambitions has been on the diplomatic agenda for decades. It is complex and involves important national and international interests. Generally, only Iran's energy and weapons, together with its missile program, have been on the diplomatic agenda. The background is the NPT, the global nonproliferation treaty that Iran has joined as a nonnuclear weapon state. A history of regional conflicts and rivalries add to an already toxic mix of issues. Important economic partners of Iran like China and India have not been encouraged to develop key linkages. Diplomacy has perhaps been unduly constrained. In the case of North Korea, more imaginative solutions were tried. The Korean Energy Development Organization (KEDO)—an experiment in alternative development inducements for North Korea to wean the country from nuclear weapons ambitions—attracted widespread international support in the 1990s. But twenty years on, the same ambitions have resurfaced in unyielding forms. The tragedy of the Syrian Civil War proved beyond the capacity of diplomacy to prevent, though it did succeed in highlighting the humanitarian and refugee crises that in diplomatic agenda setting had to be treated separately from the civil conflict.

In many areas, diplomacy is reactive rather than proactive in setting the agenda. The Ottawa landmines treaty of 1997 owed almost everything to a coalition of NGOs led by an American, Jody Williams, whose country was seen as the major outlier in this exercise of arms control. Public diplomacy and uses of modern social media have developed in part because diplomacy wants to tap into and monitor what concerns global publics. The agenda now is increasingly set by actors and influences outside the control of the diplomacy of sovereign states. When the leaders of states see a multipolar world, they increasingly see a world not of rival sovereign states but one that appears impossible to categorize and to influence in a satisfactory or predictable manner. The struggle for the diplomatic agenda is increasingly the struggle for an amorphous area of international activity where diplomats are as much observers as setters of what are the priorities.

Agendas of course evolve over time. The durability of the Cold War, its seeming indefinite institutionalizing of hostility, economic incompatibility, and political standoffs produced a golden era for diplomacy. Diplomats played decisive roles because their authority reflected strong governments. With the end of the Cold War diplomacy lost its navigational aid. It had to address the aftermath of massive military spending on weapons of mass destruction that threatened global security because governments were no longer capable of securing them. And the world started worrying about a new issue—unipolarity—and the excessive power of one country, which many feared would undermine the classic balancing role of diplomacy.

At the same time as declining power blocs produced uncertainty in the direction of diplomacy, a vacuum of ideology was waiting to be filled. The rise of transnational religious-inspired militancy and extremist intolerance is a complex subject beyond the scope of this book. But the 1990s saw many newly independent states failing to consolidate their state-building powers and unable to deliver higher living standards. At the same time, the collapse of materialist ideologies such as Marxist-inspired socialism presented challenges to newly established sovereign states. By contrast, the power of Islam and evangelical Christianity derive from a transnational and otherworldly appeal. Simple rules appear to be available to control not only domestic issues—such as a sharia moral code and rules—but also to provide a road map for international initiatives. No state's diplomacy, however well executed or funded, can begin to rival the month of Ramadan in influencing the behavior of hundreds of millions of people across the globe.

Some have seen the rise of transnational religions promoting competitive world visions and rival interpretations of history as a lasting challenge to traditional sovereign state diplomacy. They suggest that the agenda of diplomacy has been changed to make consensus building an impossible mission. Samuel Huntington, for example, argued that diplomacy could no longer smooth all the edges. He wrote in 1993,

> Nation states will remain the most powerful actors in world affairs, but the principal conflicts of global politics will occur between nations and groups of different civilizations. The clash of civilizations will dominate global politics. The fault lines between civilizations will be the battle lines of the future.[16]

Some in the Islamic world fear that after the collapse of the Soviet Union the West has been in dire need of an enemy to help mobilize its forces and resources in service of its policies. Yet all states, including those with majority Islamic populations, are buffeted by the force of transnational movements, some of which promote radical solutions to the word's problems. Diplomacy is indeed facing new challenges to its intelligence and versatility.

THE NEW AGENDA? DIPLOMACY STEPS UP

When it has adopted a universal agenda, diplomacy has shown the capacity to make impressive progress. We have seen how the post-World War II years were extraordinarily productive. Yet, there have been few truly universal conventions along the lines of the UN Charter, the Vienna Convention on Diplomatic Relations (VCDR), and the NPT since the end of the Cold War. Fragmentation of power and the inability of leading states to frame issues in universal terms have slowed progress. In 2013, Moisés Naím wrote that "the twenty-first century will not belong to America, China, Asia or anyone else. It will be no one's world."[17] Diplomats are striving for new predictability. The à la carte nature of piecemeal diplomacy means that the separateness that diplomats feel implies the creation of a new relationship for each issue. The multidimensional power game makes diplomats suspicious and restless. Weakened states are nervous of their own ability to influence issues and distrustful of how other countries might be plotting to seize advantages. New technologies have opened up sinister new threats and opportunities for surveillance that is now an integral part of modern diplomacy. There are few lodestars in the new firmament.

Not all of the diplomatic agenda has changed. Indeed, its capacity to set an agenda is still a core diplomatic function. In May 2013, a conference to bolster the prospects of survival of a sovereign state, Somalia, was held in London. It was a diplomatic convention, attended by representatives of over forty governments and by the president of the country, who admitted he controlled only a fraction of what is recognized as Somali territory. Groups that claimed control of large breakaway sections of the territory, Somaliland and Puntland, boycotted the event. But at least the president of Somalia, Hassan Sheikh Mohamud, was able to boast that he had received mail in his office for the first time in over twenty years and his government was the first in more than two decades to be recognized by the United States and the IMF. The conference represented a new diplomatic coalition formed ad hoc to restore some parts of the state model. No other organization or provider of resources could have done this.

The good news for diplomacy is that most states are not complacent. They recognize that reform will be needed to make their efforts more productive. Leading states are revamping their diplomatic machinery. This is nothing new in the history of diplomatic practice, but in the early twenty-first century, the spirit of reform is in the air. Let us examine how the traditional systems are redirecting their resources to catch up with a world that is evolving in ways that diplomacy has never seen before.

DIPLOMATIC REFORM

This section examines current thinking about diplomatic reform in some leading states. Many ministries of foreign affairs are recognizing that traditional frameworks for diplomatic activity, training, and career expectations need to change.

The United States

The United States has long been one of the most self-critical of diplomatic actors. Few systems are so relentlessly quizzed by congressional hearings and scrutinized in a twenty-four hour news cycle. Few bring in academic expertise as frequently as the U.S. State Department or have combined political outreach with grand visions of how diplomacy can harness American military and economic power.

Two recent secretaries of state, Condoleezza Rice and Hillary Clinton, both came to the job with considerable experience. The first, a Sovietologist, had long worked as a security analyst and was formerly National Security Advisor. The second had seen U.S. diplomacy at close quarters, as First Lady, then as a U.S. senator and as a Democratic Party presidential candidate. Both have argued in public for a fundamental change in the objectives, working methods, and skills of the personnel employed in U.S. diplomacy.

Transformational diplomacy was a term used by Rice to describe how U.S. diplomats would use their diplomatic presence in countries to make a difference. Rice believed that it was only by this proactive diplomacy that major changes in governance, development, and security could be effected. This had implications for redeploying U.S. diplomatic assets to countries that were emerging powers like China, India, Brazil, and South Africa. And Rice believed that all career diplomats should be required to spend time in hardship posts like Iraq, Afghanistan, and Sudan. The concept of transformational diplomacy, Rice explained in 2006, was not about imposition of U.S. ideas but should be

> rooted in partnership; not in paternalism. In doing things with people, not for them; we seek to use America's diplomatic power to help foreign citizens better their own lives and to build their own nations and to transform their own futures.[18]

Clinton built on her predecessor's approach but saw more challenges for reform in the organization of the State Department machinery. She insisted on more coordination between the operational arms of U.S. foreign policy, particularly coordination between defense, development, and diplomacy. Both secretaries saw that the virtual embassy could be effective, where useful diplomacy could be accomplished from use of a laptop based in a hotel room in the receiving state or from a distance.

The concept of smart diplomacy was one further developed and defined by Secretary Clinton as the application of "the full range of tools at our disposal—diplomatic, economic, military, political, legal, and cultural—picking the right tool, or combination of tools, for each situation. 'Smart power' diplomacy will be the vanguard of foreign policy."[19]

The implications for American diplomatic training, as described in a document called *Forging a 21st-Century Diplomatic Service for the United States through Professional Education and Training*, produced by the American Academy of Diplomacy, were that every diplomat should have "the ability to think beyond the moment and tactical needs—to act strategically to plan and execute complex operations and policy initiatives, and to lead effectively in a vastly more varied foreign affairs environment than existed even a decade ago."[20]

Clinton saw that the State Department needed to improve its management and strategic planning. In 2009, she announced the first Quadrennial Diplomacy and Development Review (QDDR), which was intended to mirror how other departments of government operated. Nevertheless, Clinton saw that however great the resources the United States devoted to its diplomacy, something would be missing. This was the need to engage with overseas publics, not just in the sense of better public diplomacy but by getting to know and working with members of civil society. She recognized that governments involved in sending and receiving diplomats could not do everything. According to Clinton, this was recognition of the reality of "21st Century Statecraft."[21]

Central to Clinton's reform program was a belief that the influence that states and their activities can exert on diplomacy was declining relative to other actors. As Clinton's QDDR stated, "Power in the international system, once exercised more or less exclusively by a handful of great powers, is now shared by a wide array of states, institutions, and nonstate actors."[22] She translated this philosophy into how she saw her job. She told *Time* magazine in 2011,

> In a much more networked and multipolar world, we can't wave a magic wand and say to China or Brazil or India, "Quit growing. Quit using your economies to assert power." . . . It's up to us to figure out how we position ourselves to be as effective as possible at different times in the face of different threats and opportunities.[23]

The U.S. view, therefore, is that the threats to diplomacy from forces largely outside the control of states are more formidable than ever. Even economic power is ever more difficult to exert because the actors are global, more difficult to regulate because of the speed they can do business, and there are fewer state-owned companies. This imposes additional burdens on a state's diplomacy. As the QDDR states,

> Economic power is also becoming more diffuse—within two decades, nearly 60 percent of the world's GDP is projected to come from developing countries—even as markets are consolidating across national borders. And although these markets are global in reach and risk, they ultimately remain backstopped by national balance sheets, a gap that poses challenges for developed and developing countries alike.[24]

In this environment, Clinton suggests U.S. diplomacy should target intensification of civic engagement, working on water projects, health education, and experiencing the country alongside its nationals. U.S. diplomacy had to extend its partnering with different entities, making resources go further and ensuring proper coordination of diplomats with military and other personnel to produce better diplomatic results. Without local civil society commitment, diplomacy could not produce its consensus-building activities and solutions that would endure.

Clinton was particularly influenced with how she saw the role of diplomacy during the Arab Spring of 2011. She saw the randomness of the events but hoped that diplomacy, if applied in smart ways, could nudge events to produce peaceful progress. The Secretary of State told *Time*,

> As we look at how we manage the Arab Spring, we are trying to influence the direction, with full recognition that we don't have ownership and we don't have control. And there's a lot that's going to happen that is unpredictable. But we want to lead by our values and our interests in ways that, regardless of the trajectory over the next decade, people will know the United States was on the side of democracy, on the side of the rule of law. . . . And that will, I hope, be a strong antidote to the voices of either fatalism or extremism.[25]

The United States has supported a combined initiative to outreach to civil society, the Open Government Partnership (OGP). Launched in 2011 by Brazil, Indonesia, Mexico, Norway, the Philippines, South Africa, the United Kingdom, and the United States, it provides an international platform for domestic reformers committed to making their governments more open, accountable, and responsive to citizens. Since then, OGP has grown from eight to sixty-two participating countries. It aims to be an international standard setter for engagement with civic society.

The United States believes its diplomacy can influence events in a transforming world. But at the same time, it recognizes realistic limits of what it can achieve and the need to work beyond its traditional boundaries.

Russia

The diplomacy and government of Russia has been directed in recent years by a former professional in the intelligence services, Vladimir Putin. His old employer, the KGB, has been reformed into the Federal Security Service of the Russian Federation (FSB), but contribution of intelligence gathering to international affairs is one he values highly. Yet, in Russia as well, there have been some signs that the diplomatic component of overseas service is receiving more attention from the government. In 2002, President Putin inaugurated the National Diplomats' Day. Set in the context of the history of diplomacy, the holiday was established by a presidential decree to commemorate the foundation of the Russian diplomatic service in 1549. And Putin has also revived the celebration of Victory Day of Russia in World War II. He now stages a military parade on the day and in 2014 it was when he announced the annexation of Crimea.

The Russian diplomatic service faces new challenges. According to a study by Yelena Biberman of Brown University, who interviewed new entrants in the Russian foreign ministry in 2007 and 2008,[26] the problem in the ministry was not redefining strategy or declining resources but the loss of new recruits to other business sectors. She noted the ministry employed a total of 827 young diplomats thirty years old or younger out of a total of about 9,500. But, in the eighteen months leading up to July 2008, 107 young diplomats left, nearly half of the total number of the new admissions in 2007. As Deputy Minister of Foreign Affairs Andrey Denisov admitted in early 2008, "We cannot say that the personnel drain has completely ceased. Serious commercial structures remain a more attractive option."[27]

Russia too is adapting to an uncertain world. But the collapse of the Cold War brought not only diplomatic uncertainty for Russia and new overseas perspectives—in 2013, Russia started a security dialogue with U.S. ally Japan—but also promised new economic opportunities following the reconstruction of the formerly state-planned system. A booming Russian economy faces a problem with making its diplomatic career attractive to young professionals who see more lucrative opportunities elsewhere in government or in business. Serious reform may mean better salaries and also more real diplomatic influence. The relative recruitment statistics into the FSB are not available, but it would safe to assume that retention is not a serious issue.

Russia is now using public diplomacy in a much more sophisticated way than hitherto. Its state-owned television channel RT—formerly Russia Today—was founded only in 2005, but now broadcasts in several languages including English, Spanish, and Arabic. It is designed to promote a Russian view of the world and to change the image of Russia. RT is now widely viewed around the world and is one of the most popular news sites on YouTube. In addition, the Russian government employs staff to engage with opinion formers across the globe to explain Russia's domestic and international positions. Russian diplomacy organizes the annual Valdai Discussion Club that invites international scholars and journalists to Russia to discuss issues of concern. And scholarship programs such as the Alfa Fellowships bring young professionals from other countries to Russia for training programs.

Diplomatic reform is contagious, and Russia is not immune. Our analysis suggests that Russian interest in extending Russian influence in the territory of the former Soviet Union, including Ukraine, will be tempered by acknowledgment of the potential negative public diplomacy this will generate. Russia also recognizes that it operates in a newly interdependent world and has a strong interest in maintaining regional and global stability.

India

In India, the problem of reform of the diplomatic service is perceived differently. The Indian Foreign Service (IFS) is small, traditional, and fiercely defensive of its exclusivity. Created in 1947 out of the old British India Office, its system of recruitment has remained essentially unchanged since. The staff of the entire diplomatic service in 2013 was around 900. In 2008, Indian foreign secretary Shivshankar Menon proposed a doubling of the current diplomatic strength, increasing the annual intake from around fifteen to thirty. The government agreed to an increase of 520 personnel in total (320 in the main diplomatic category), but the service itself closed ranks to prevent any dramatic expansion. A bigger expansion would have required acceptance of external professional talent at all levels of the Ministry of External Affairs, including recruitment from the other services or even from the private sector. *The Economist* noted the anomaly in 2012. "As a measure of India's priorities, consider that the world's second-most-populous country has no more diplomats than tiny New Zealand."[28] India's diplomatic service is also similar in size to Singapore's, which has a population of just over five million people. In August of 2012 the IFS agreed to accept candidates applying from other government departments but not yet from the private sector. The examination to enter the IFS remains one of the most difficult in the world. Out of over 500,000 candidates, only 0.01 percent are admitted.

India has also been adjusting the tasks it sees itself assuming diplomatically. For long, India championed the principle of strict nonintervention in the affairs of others. As a post-colonial creation, and after a traumatic period of partition civil conflict, the Indian giant has been inward looking and reluctant even to play a role in issues close to its own identity like democratic values. Few Indian diplomatic statements were ever made about the long military rule in its neighbor Myanmar. Insiders to the ministry have suggested the aims of its diplomacy needed better definition. A former foreign secretary, Krishnan Srinivasan, argued in 2013 that "India did not display the independence to carve out a distinctive made-in-India foreign policy."[29] Economic diplomacy has been promoted more enthusiastically with trade and investment priorities. And Indian diplomats are now engaging fully in global issues like climate change, proliferation of weapons of mass destruction, terrorism, and public diplomacy. India is increasingly embracing membership in international groups like the G20 and participates in the meetings of BRICS countries. India, too, clearly has new tasks and objectives for its diplomacy.

The United Kingdom: British Foreign Office Reform

The United Kingdom's Foreign and Commonwealth Office (FCO) is an example of a traditional ministry of foreign affairs applying modern approaches to outcome delivery. One of the prime objectives of reform in London is to craft a diplomatic service more capable of producing results, to make things happen diplomatically by a target date. I reproduce from the Internet a detailed delivery plan for the month of May 2012. These are requested by the Prime Minister's Office to every department of government, and it gives an interesting insight into how the FCO manages its diplomatic efforts.

The measure of these tasks is of course enormous, and much of the language used to indicate progress is space filling. The trade targets for China, Qatar, and Turkey and the percentage of senior jobs in the EU's External Action Service (EAS) are specific, yet other language—"play a leading role in" and "ensure that the British perspective is reflected"—are attempts to look busy diplomatically to the prime minister's delivery unit. With his love of continuity, Cardinal Richelieu would probably have approved of the omnipresent status of work ongoing. The FCO is also recognizing it is in competition for resources

TABLE 9.1

Foreign and Commonwealth Office *Structural Reform Plan Monthly Implementation Update*		*May 2012*
Section	*Action*	*Status*
1.1(i)	Work with UK Trade and Investment (UKTI) to develop its new strategy, including: plans to double trade with India; increase trade with China to USD 100 billion per annum and increase exports to USD 30 billion per annum; double trade with Kuwait to £4 billion; double trade with Qatar to £4.4 billion and increase trade with UAE to £12 billion; double trade with South Africa to £16 billion; double trade with Turkey to £18 billion (end 2015)	Work ongoing
1.3 (i) (g)	Inward visits aimed at thickening our relationships with and increasing our engagement with emerging powers in South East Asia (end 2015)	Work ongoing
1.3 (i) (h)	Prime Minister to visit Brazil to reinforce bilateral relations and develop commercial opportunities (end 2012).	Work ongoing
1.3 (iii) (a)	Deliver immediate priorities and establish strategic relationships with all six Gulf States (end 2015)	Work ongoing
1.4 (iii)	Encourage greater Commonwealth trade flows resulting in increased opportunities for UK business (end May 2015)	Work ongoing
1.5 (i)	Support concerted international diplomatic efforts to build trust, confidence and consensus on non-proliferation and disarmament through existing international framework and conventions etc (end May 2015)	Work ongoing
1.5 (iv)	Play a leading role in an internationally-agreed twin-track diplomatic approach of pressure and engagement to stop Iran obtaining a nuclear weapon (end May 2015)	Work ongoing
1.5 (v)	Play a leading role in the international nuclear and biological security effort including through leading on the information security strand of the 2012 Nuclear Security Summit in 2012 (end Jun 2012)	Work ongoing
1.6 (iv)	Provide political and financial support for the Palestinian Authority programme to build the institutions of a future Palestinian state in order to prepare for a two state solution and create a conducive environment for peace (end May 2015)	Work ongoing
1.6 (vi)	Support the process of transition to democratic government in Egypt and Tunisia, including on electoral reform and the development of political parties, and offer assistance to support the stabilisation of the Egyptian and Tunisian economies (end Jun 2012)	Work ongoing

(Continued)

TABLE 9.1 **(Continued)**

Foreign and Commonwealth Office Structural Reform Plan Monthly Implementation Update		*May 2012*
Section	*Action*	*Status*
1.6 (vii)	Play a leading role in the development of a peaceful and more democratic Libya within existing international borders, including by working to ensure full implementation of all relevant UN Security Council resolutions and other international commitments (end Dec 2012)	Work ongoing
1.7 (vi)	Engage with US, Canada, Japan, African Union and Australia on national and global security risks of climate change, working with MOD and DECC (end May 2015)	Work ongoing
1.7 (vii)	Accelerate the global transition to a low carbon climate resilient economy	Work ongoing
1.9 (ii)	Contribute to the early expansion of the UN Security Council (end Dec 2012)	Work ongoing
2.1 (ii)	Work with international partners and the Afghan Government on the transition of security from ISAF to Afghan security forces by the end of 2014. Attend NATO Summit and commit to a way forward on transition, with the first phase beginning in early 2011 (end Dec 2014)	Work ongoing
2.1 (iii)	Work with ISAF partners to encourage all to stay the course, maintaining a force presence in Afghanistan during the transition process, and contributing to building the capacity of Afghan security forces (end Dec 2014)	Work ongoing
2.2 (i) (b)	Begin to provide monthly written updates to Parliament, including reports on progress in the implementation of Kabul and London commitments (end May 2015)	Work ongoing
2.3 (i) (b)	The British Pakistan Foundation helps to deliver stronger people to people links between the UK and Pakistan (end May 2015)	Work ongoing
2.3 (i) I	Set up and implement a programme of regular contacts, including visits, between the PM and other Ministers with their Pakistani counterparts (end May 2015)	Work ongoing
2.3 (i) (d)	Support Pakistan's efforts to implement a package of reforms agreed with the International Financial Institutions (end May 2015)	Work ongoing
2.3 (i) (e)	Enhance practical co-operation through the UK/Pakistan CT Joint Working Group (end May 2015)	Work ongoing
4.1 (i) (a)	Political and practical support to Croatia in fulfilling necessary accession criteria in 2011 to enable accession negotiations to close (end May 2015)	Work ongoing

Foreign and Commonwealth Office Structural Reform Plan Monthly Implementation Update		*May 2012*
Section	*Action*	*Status*
4.1 (i) I	Support steady progress in Iceland's EU accession negotiations, encourage the Icelandic authorities to develop and maintain necessary reforms end commercial whaling and resolve Icesave (end May 2015)	Work ongoing
4.1(i) (d)	Support an EU future for the Western Balkans region, once clear membership criteria are met. Support and encourage countries in the region to deliver reforms including through the EU accession process; focussing on stability, democracy, rule of law, reconciliation, continued resolution of conflict legacy (end May 2015)	Work ongoing
4.3 (i)	Seek tough and effective EU engagement on Iran (end May 2015)	Work ongoing
4.3 (iii)	Work to promote stability in the Western Balkans (end May 2015)	Work ongoing
4.3 (iv) (a)	Ensuring that 10% of EAS Assistant Director and above positions are filled by British nationals (end Dec 2013)	Work ongoing
4.3 (iv) (b)	Influence EAS policies to ensure they support UK security and prosperity and the EAS only acts where mandated to do so by Treaties (end Dec 2013)	Work ongoing
4.4 (i) (a)	Implement the EU Energy Third Package effectively (end May 2015)	Work ongoing
4.4 (ii)	Work with the Treasury to ensure that the next EU Financial Perspectives reflect Britain's views and take account of economic circumstances (end Dec 2012)	Work ongoing
4.4 (iv)	Ensure that the British perspective is reflected in EU institutions by increasing the number of British citizens entering EU institutions (end Jun 2012)	Work ongoing
5.1 (ii)	Align the work of the British Council and the BBC World Service with this programme	Work ongoing

Source: Foreign and Commonwealth Office, "Structural Reform Plan Monthly Implementation Update," May 2012, https://www.gov.uk/government/uploads/system/uploads/attachment_data/file/32856/business-plan-update-may-121.pdf.

with other departments like Defence and Overseas Development that have to produce similar plans. The UK government had already required that the UK Foreign Office's budget be reduced from £1.6 billion in 2011 and 2012 to £1.3 billion by 2014 and 2015, a cut of over 20 percent.

If delivery and accountability is a measure of British diplomatic reform, how is this reflected in the management of a modern diplomatic institution? Another example of how reform of diplomacy works in contemporary Britain is shown by a summary of an FCO Management Board meeting in October 2012. Here is an extract from the summary minutes of the meeting.

> The FCO Management Board met on 26 October 2012. Board members discussed a trio of papers under the heading "Improving the FCO." The first set out a vision for the FCO's IT in 2015; the second presented two options for delivery of a new Knowledge Excellence Programme; and the third provided an update on the work . . . to reduce bureaucracy and streamline FCO processes. Board members reviewed the Finance Key Performance Report for September 12 and discussed the outcome of the Quarter Two review. They received the first quarterly progress update from Corporate Procurement Group. Also on the agenda were: the quarterly review of FCO Security Key Performance Indicators on protecting staff, buildings and information; the monthly FCO priorities Dashboard and the summary of the Top Risk Register. The Board also noted decisions taken and issues considered by the Board's Sub Committees during October 2012.
>
> *Action Points*
>
> - To include in the Board's Forward Agenda a more substantive discussion of capital disposals and asset recycling. Action: Board Secretariat with ESD and Finance Directorate
> - To draft a follow up message from the PUS to all staff on security breaches. Action: ESD with Communications and Engagement Department
> - To revise the FCO IT Vision 2015 to reflect feedback from Board members; to develop the Terms of Reference for the new IT Customer Board; and to communicate both to staff. Action: I&TD with IFCO team
> - To develop a more detailed business case for the Knowledge Excellence programme pilot for consideration by Executive Committee in November 12. Action: IFCO team with input from I&TD and Corporate Procurement Group
> - To develop a proposal for a new e-diplomacy unit for consideration by Executive Committee in November. Action: IFCO team[30]

The British approach for encouraging better diplomacy is perhaps closest to a detailed business plan for a redirection of human and other resources. Set your objectives, and we will measure the results. The objective is refining the machinery of diplomacy, promoting discipline, and making diplomatic efforts go further.

The structural reform plan contains few items that are solely dependent on diplomatic action by the FCO. In every one, it needs partners and other actors to be able to deliver. Diplomacy's fundamental impotence as a sole actor is highlighted. In terms of results, some will speak for themselves—peace in Libya, Iceland's accession to the EU. But what of other measures of success—how, for example, does the FCO grade itself in the Pakistan outreach exercise?

To the business plan drafter, the FCO language may appear imprecise and comforting: "work with," "support," "begin to," "influence," "align the work." As EU activities, the UK objectives offer little on the vision of the EU as a more effective diplomatic actor. Rather, the FCO wants to make the EAS a new effective adjunct to UK diplomacy—to secure at least 10 percent of the senior appointments for UK nationals. As William Hague, the UK Foreign Secretary, has said,

> We cannot outsource parts of our foreign policy to the European External Action Service as some have suggested. There is not and will never be any substitute for a strong British diplomatic service that advances the interests of the United Kingdom. We can never rely on anyone else to do that for us.[31]

It is not only UK diplomats that recognize they work in a delivery system—a favorite word in central government—but they know their task is often intangible. The business of diplomacy senses it cannot always deliver as outsiders expect. That is its nature, and one of the themes of the later parts of this book is to explore why the present system is not delivering. In other activities of government targets are more measureable—schools built and exams passed in education; infant mortality and obesity levels in health. And the insistence that UK efforts, however determined and skillful, will count significantly toward achieving many of the results may be wishful thinking. Diplomacy is a team game, and the UK reforms might in addition look at how it might contribute to improving the functions of diplomacy collectively.

Germany

Germany is a state that has faced enormous challenges to reestablishing its reputation as a trusted and influential partner in modern diplomacy and has emerged with a prowess that is the envy of other countries. Without projecting military power, Germany has played a major part in building international institutions and in global issues.

The German foreign ministry, in a recent extract from its website, makes a strong case for the importance of diplomacy in the modern era.

> Germany's foreign policy is a policy for peace. All over the world we seek to promote democracy and human rights. We know, after all, that the challenges of our time cannot be tackled alone but only together.

> In an increasingly interconnected world, what we need is cooperation, not policies driven by national interests. This is precisely where Training for International Diplomats comes in.[32]

So one area where Germany is promoting its own distinctive imprint on diplomacy is through working with other diplomatic services and inviting young diplomats for training. Diplomacy is worth investing in because it serves the interests of all. This has produced a wide-ranging German outreach program, covering diplomats from countries such as Afghanistan, Iraq, China, Belarus, Ukraine, Egypt, Libya, and South Sudan. And with the lifting of EU sanctions on Myanmar, Germany in 2013 invited its young diplomats to participate.

Germany is an example of a successful country that believes that its rise is not due to diplomacy alone but that diplomacy has certainly played a part. Germany now sees that it is in its own interests to promote better diplomacy elsewhere.

France

In Chapter 3, we discussed how the French diplomatic system was held up by a British report as a model of success. France, of course, brought to diplomacy many of its early traditions, and its legacy can still be seen in the twenty-first century. But an announcement in 2010 suggested that the French did not think all was well. The then Foreign Minister, Bernard Kouchner, thought that France needed to raise its cultural impact through diplomacy. And so he instituted

> a sweeping reform of our "diplomacy of influence," the most important carried out in France for decades. (. . .)
>
> Why reform cultural diplomacy? I believe the answer is simple. We should have carried out this reform years ago! For years it had been called for by arts professionals and members of Parliament from both Left and Right! Everyone backed off in the face of the difficulty! Because it's always easier to make do with the inherited status quo than overturn it!
>
> A reform was necessary because, surely it's obvious, culture and knowledge play a more decisive role than ever in the globalized world! We mustn't close our eyes to what's happening: today there's a "soft-power"' battle. . . . In tomorrow's world they've got to be able to project their cultural content, influence the ideas agenda, promote their language and attract future elites to their schools and universities. They know that a great nation, as Hugo said, isn't just a powerful army and vast territory, but is capable of winning hearts and minds too. . . . So at the heart of the reform, there's the creation of an external

> cultural agency. . . . It's a more coherent instrument with a higher profile. The agency will draw on 143 French cultural centers abroad, which will . . . act under its name, i.e. "Institut français"; from now on, all French cultural diplomacy will operate in the world under one name, one label, which is essential in the globalization era.[33]

So France, for long the driving force in framing diplomatic practice and widely regarded as a premier diplomatic service, is also sensing that something is not working right. It believes it is underperforming in the battle for soft power.

China

"China is a big country and other countries are small countries, and that's just a fact,"[34] Chinese Foreign Minister Yang said at an ASEAN meeting in 2010, staring directly at Singapore's foreign minister, George Yeo.

China has reemerged as a giant on the diplomatic scene, and its approach to the new diplomatic agenda is important for any outcome in today's world. In the early nineteenth century, China was also an economic giant, accounting for up to one-third of world GDP. But by 1960, this had dropped to under 5 percent. Its Cultural Revolution caused turmoil internally and externally to Chinese diplomacy. Diplomats and Western-educated students were sent to work in rice fields. Yet China's engagement with the West predates its economic strength. The People's Republic of China assumed the Chinese seat at the UNSC in 1972, the United States and China established full diplomatic relations in 1979, and in the 1990s it espoused state-driven capitalism rather than egalitarian communism. In the 1990s, Deng Xiaoping quoted the watchwords of China's foreign policy in a twenty-four-character strategy: "Observe calmly; secure our position; cope with affairs calmly; hide our capacities and bide our time; be good at maintaining a low profile; and never claim the leadership."[35]

China's twenty-first century diplomacy is the starkest example of an activity driven by economic considerations and its requirement for resources. China has sent its state-controlled companies to make massive investments overseas, sweetening the deals with significant loans and military assistance. The strategy started in the late twentieth century. In 1996, with Western oil companies pulling out of Sudan, Chinese companies purchased a 40 percent majority share in the Greater Nile Petroleum Operating Company. In 2004, Iran, already a major source of oil for China, agreed to sell to China $20 billion worth of natural gas per year for twenty-five years, representing then the world's largest natural gas purchase. The discovery of a new gas field off the coast of Myanmar in 2004 heralded major new Chinese investment. By 2007, China had become the largest trading partner of Iran, North Korea, and Sudan and the second largest of Myanmar and Zimbabwe. In a world where the West agonized over human rights, proliferation, and other global issues, China talked money and resources.

China is now Africa's biggest trading partner. Enormous infrastructure projects, hospitals, mining, and military sales are intertwined with hundreds of billions of dollars of minerals and oil purchases by China. China is also investing in agriculture in countries like Mozambique and Uganda to promote food production that will supply China. China now has an obvious stake in ensuring the governments who receive these investments remain in power. China's relationships have become complicated. In 2008, the *New York Times* reported that dockworkers in South Africa refused to unload a Chinese cargo ship carrying three million rounds of ammunition and 1,500 rocket-propelled grenades bound for Zimbabwe. The China Development Bank had recently announced they would invest up to $10 billion dollars in Zimbabwe's mining and agricultural sectors. In 2012, President Mugabe opened a new $98 million military academy built by Chinese contractors with the project's cost being repaid in Zimbabwean diamonds. In some parts of the continent, these types of relationships have been viewed with concern. Speaking on a visit to Beijing in 2012, Jacob Zuma, President of South Africa, said

> Africa's commitment to China's development has been demonstrated by a supply of raw materials, other products, and technology transfer. This trade pattern is unsustainable in the long term. Africa's past economic experience with Europe dictates a need to be cautious when entering into partnerships with other economies.[36]

The Chinese presence has also created some bad public diplomacy. Zambian miners have protested against working conditions and their treatment by Chinese managers. Chinese-manufactured weapons were one of the main drivers of conflict in Darfur. And some Chinese projects have not been well executed. A Ghanaian highway, twelve months after construction, was riddled with craters; the Luanda general hospital in Angola had to be evacuated due to cracks in the walls; and the $200 million new headquarters for the African Union in Addis Ababa had a leaking roof. And despite all the attention, total Chinese investment in Africa, according to UN Conference on Trade and Development in 2013, was below that of the United States and France.

Because China's diplomacy has been economic driven, it undercut longstanding Western diplomatic practice in conditioning economic assistance on progress in areas like good governance and human rights. Several of China's partners were subject to international economic sanctions. And unlike most of the investment from the United States and EU, the resources were being deployed by the Chinese government itself. In the twenty-first century, China's principal Sovereign Wealth Fund, the China Investment Corporation, and China's state-owned companies such as Sinopec and China Mobile have shifted the diplomatic agenda.

In recent years, China has begun to respond to U.S. and European calls to become a responsible stakeholder in the international community. It has become more involved in diplomacy, sponsoring the six-party talks on the

North Korea nuclear and missile issue, and has voted with the West in the International Atomic Energy Agency (IAEA) Board expressing serious concern on Iran's nuclear program. As former U.S. Assistant Secretary of State Christopher Hill remarked, the six-party talks on North Korea's nuclear program have "done more to bring the U.S. and China together than any other process that I am aware of."[37]

The Chinese relationship with Myanmar is illustrative of another change in the diplomatic agenda. The Mysitone dam project on the Irrawaddy River became symbolic of the change in Myanmar's attitude to Chinese checkbook diplomacy. The $3.5 billion dam was funded by Chinese state-owned companies for hydroelectricity production for China, with the local population receiving little. The President of Myanmar, Thein Sein, suspended the project in an assertion of Myanmar's sovereignty. This had an effect. The Chinese National Petroleum Corporation that is building an oil pipeline across Myanmar to the border with China is now building schools in the villages near the pipeline.

Chinese diplomacy is evolving more widely, aiming to become a much more complete player in the field. Chinese government-funded Confucius institutes abound in different countries promoting a nonpolitical appreciation of Chinese culture. The hosting of the Beijing Olympics and Shanghai World Expo in close succession showed China's priority to win over some hearts and minds. China values a large diplomatic service. It currently has at least ten times the number of diplomats that India deploys. Energy and resource security dominate the objectives of contemporary Chinese diplomacy. Such diplomacy ties the destinies of the partner countries more systematically than treaties could ever do. A significant and lasting new factor has emerged on the diplomatic agenda.

Mexico

The Mexican Secretaría de Relaciones Exteriores provided a summary of how diplomatic reform is applied.

> Mexican diplomacy is looking for ways to enhance its dialogue with other countries and its presence in other regions. The following list provides a quick overview of current efforts:
>
> 1. We are increasing the number of our missions abroad. Admittedly, this is more of a traditional move, but it partly reflects Mexico's changing role as an emerging economy of considerable standing (a G20 member and Latin America's second biggest economy), and also as a middle power of growing influence in global affairs. In this process, we have sought to innovate, for example, by agreeing to share facilities with our partners from the Pacific Alliance (Chile, Colombia, and Peru), countries with which Mexico has fundamental values and goals in common.

2. We have developed closer links both with civil society through a division within Mexico's Ministry of Foreign Affairs that is wholly devoted to maintaining and strengthening our engagement with members of non-governmental organizations. And, along with other government agencies, such as ProMéxico (responsible for promoting trade and investment) we have fostered a closer dialogue with private firms, supporting their efforts to initiate or expand their international activities.
3. Mexico is widening its public diplomacy efforts, not only to update the country's image—which in some cases is the result of frivolous stereotypes or outdated notions—but also to increase its direct contacts with the general public of other countries. More frequent engagement with traditional media and the systematic use of social media tools are now part of our daily outreach efforts.
4. We are looking to increase our diplomatic presence in other regions, as well as our dialogue with other cultures, by enhancing our cultural diplomacy. Mexico is the most populated Spanish speaking country, it is heir to ancient civilizations, and it has a unique history that draws keen interest from other countries and cultures. Again, our aim is to reach the general public, not only our counterparts in government or business circles.
5. Educational exchanges are at the heart of our current strategy. Mexico is seeking to significantly expand the number of its nationals who travel abroad to undertake graduate studies, as well as the number of foreign nationals who come to Mexico to carry out similar studies.
6. We are widening our international cooperation for development. While we remain in a transitional stage, greater weight is increasingly given to the assistance we provide to other countries, especially in Central America and the Caribbean, whose development is of crucial importance for Mexico.
7. Through our diplomatic academy, we are availing ourselves of the new tools offered by information technology to carry out extensive online education and training courses that improve the skills and knowledge of our Foreign Service personnel and other officials from the Ministry of Foreign Affairs and from other ministries engaged in international activities.
8. We are seeking to develop closer links and coordination with like-minded countries. This was the reasoning behind the Pacific Alliance, which has created an area that will allow for the free movement of goods and people. It is also the motive behind our efforts to increase our dialogue and cooperation with other middle-powers that have a constructive outlook on world affairs, so as to coordinate our actions in international fora.

9. We have established the notion of responsibility as a global actor at the core of our foreign policy and, therefore, of our diplomatic engagement. We seek to ensure that our actions in the international stage not only respond to domestic interests, but also take into account the collective needs of the international community, particularly on global issues.[38]

Mexico is a good example of an emerging political and economic force using diplomacy to promote its development. Mexico clearly sees the opportunity to become a global actor and is deploying a full range of diplomatic techniques. Its strong regional presence is now being converted into global diplomatic activity. One element that receives little attention is whether the current global diplomatic institutional arrangements will enable Mexican objectives to be realized.

Sovereign Wealth Funds

Sovereign wealth funds are prominent in modern economic diplomacy. Unlike China's diplomacy, the Arab Gulf states are not in search of resources. Entities such as the Abu Dhabi Investment Authority and the Qatar Investment Authority are looking for long-term investment returns. Their investments are not just in developing countries but include many real estate and industrial projects in the developed world. When British Prime Minister David Cameron visited the United Arab Emirates (UAE) in 2012, he met with the UAE's largest sovereign funds, aiming to attract investment to the UK wind farm industry. The activities of these funds are not new. The oldest is the Kuwait fund, which was founded in 1961. Elsewhere, Norway operates what is one the largest funds, called the Government Pension Fund, with a global worth in 2013 of over $750 billion. It is derived largely from Norway's oil wealth and is reputed to own at least 2.5 percent of every publicly traded European company.

Our summary of the reform agendas of current major countries reveals different priorities, concerns, and approaches to achieving results. This poses obvious problems for diplomacy and also highlights some of the obstacles that prevent consensus on contentious issues. Diplomacy is seen as performing different functions within each system. Let us now turn to some common issues on the modern diplomatic agenda and whether they themselves are influencing how diplomacy operates and its plans for reform.

DEVELOPMENT ASSISTANCE IN THE DIPLOMATIC AGENDA

Economic assistance from one state to another—formerly known as aid—is a disturbing element of the diplomatic agenda. It is an indication that sovereign states wish to bolster other states and also recognition that the natural forces of trade and division of resources are unlikely to produce a stable or sustainable entity. The word *aid* has acquired a pejorative meaning and is now reformulated in the language of diplomacy as overseas development assistance (ODA) or development cooperation. Such funding is provided bilaterally and multilaterally. It has its origins in the post-World War II era where the Marshall Plan for post-war reconstruction was seen as vital to the reestablishment of a viable world economy. Economic assistance is provided with and without conditions, and it is also increasingly implemented by nonstate actors. Diplomats are usually central to the negotiations.

Set in the context of diplomacy, ODA raises important questions. What has development assistance achieved, and what lessons for diplomacy have been learned? Has development aid helped or hindered the consolidation of sovereign states? Is the world still divided between North and South, or are such distinctions now meaningless for today's diplomacy? Is the very activity of transferring funds from one sovereign state to another a pointless exercise, given concerns on other agenda issues like corruption? Might the objective of helping alleviate poverty and promoting better governance be better achieved through a renunciation of sovereignty? Or in the words of the historian Niall Ferguson in *Colossus*, "In many cases of economic backwardness a liberal empire can do better than a nation state."[39]

It is beyond the scope of this book to discuss fully the merits of such transfers of funds. Development has been called by U.S. Secretary of State Clinton as one of the three *D*s of modern U.S. foreign policy, alongside defense and diplomacy. As an integral part of diplomacy, it has been around for decades. And there have been global norms set as to what transfers are deemed as reasonable. In 1970, the UNGA passed Resolution 2626 titled "International Development Strategy for the Second United Nations Development Decade," which set targets for donors of development assistance.

> Each economically advanced country will progressively increase its official development assistance to the developing countries and will exert its best efforts to reach a minimum net amount of 0.7% of its gross national product at market prices by the middle of the decade.[40]

The original target date of 1975 is long gone, and diplomacy's efforts to set specific targets for overseas assistance have been shown to be ineffective and unrealistic. Table 9.2 shows ODA contributions in 2000, 2011, and 2012 given by members of the Development Assistance Committee (DAC) of the Organisation for Economic Co-operation and Development (OECD)—twenty-four of the richest countries in the world. Though all major countries are well below the 0.7 percent target, the total aid assistance given in 2012 was over $125 billion, representing more than double the total in 2000.

Development issues have been increasingly treated separately from classic diplomacy. Policy on ODA has had more to do with applying funds and delivery mechanisms overseas than it has with the business of handling wider international relations. Most major countries maintain separate departments for administering ODA from their foreign ministries.

TABLE 9.2 **Official Development Assistance Given by OECD Development Assistance Committee Members**

Country	*2012 Amount ($billion)*	*2012 ODA/GNI Percentage*	*2011 Amount ($billion)*	*2011 ODA/GNI Percentage*	*2000 Amount ($billion)*	*2000 ODA/GNI Percentage*
LUXEMBOURG	0.4	1.00	0.4	0.97	0.1	0.70
SWEDEN	5.2	0.99	5.6	1.02	1.8	0.81
NORWAY	4.8	0.93	4.8	0.96	1.3	0.80
DENMARK	2.7	0.84	2.9	0.85	1.7	1.06
NETHERLANDS	5.5	0.71	6.3	0.75	3.1	0.82
U.K.	13.7	0.56	13.8	0.56	4.5	0.31
FINLAND	1.3	0.53	1.4	0.53	0.4	0.31
IRELAND	0.8	0.48	0.9	0.51	0.2	0.30
BELGIUM	2.3	0.47	2.8	0.54	0.8	0.36
FRANCE	12.0	0.45	13.0	0.46	4.2	0.33
SWITZERLAND	3.0	0.45	3.1	0.45	0.9	0.34
GERMANY	13.1	0.38	14.1	0.39	5.0	0.27
AUSTRALIA	5.4	0.36	5.0	0.34	1.0	0.27

(Continued)

TABLE 9.2 **(Continued)**

Country	*2012 Amount ($billion)*	*2012 ODA/GNI Percentage*	*2011 Amount ($billion)*	*2011 ODA/GNI Percentage*	*2000 Amount ($billion)*	*2000 ODA/GNI Percentage*
CANADA	5.7	0.32	5.5	0.32	1.7	0.25
NEW ZEALAND	0.5	0.28	0.4	0.28	0.1	0.26
AUSTRIA	1.1	0.28	1.1	0.27	0.5	0.25
PORTUGAL	0.6	0.27	0.7	0.31	0.3	0.26
ICELAND	0.1	0.22	0.1	0.21		
U.S.A.	30.5	0.19	30.8	0.20	9.6	0.10
JAPAN	10.5	0.17	10.8	0.18	13.1	0.27
SPAIN	1.9	0.15	4.2	0.29	1.3	0.24
S. KOREA	1.6	0.14	1.3	0.12		
GREECE	0.3	0.13	0.4	0.15	0.2	0.19
ITALY	2.6	0.13	4.3	0.20	1.4	0.13
TOTAL	125.6	0.29	133.7	0.31	53.1	0.22

Source: Just1WORLD.org, "Overseas Aid (ODA)," http://www.just1world.org/development-aid.htm.

Most development aid is assessed by how the recipient country performs against measures of poverty. Thus the United Kingdom's Department for International Development (DFID) defines it mission as leading "the UK's work to end extreme poverty. We're ending the need for aid by creating jobs, unlocking the potential of girls and women and helping to save lives when humanitarian emergencies hit."[41] To fulfill this one international priority, DFID has an annual budget at over £6 billion, more than six times the budget of the FCO.

The U.S. agency for ODA, USAID, was created in 1961 and has a mission statement that breaks down development policy into several component areas of activity:

- Investing in agricultural productivity so countries can feed their people
- Combating maternal and child mortality and deadly diseases like HIV, malaria and tuberculosis
- Providing life-saving assistance in the wake of disaster
- Promoting democracy, human rights and good governance around the world
- Fostering private sector development and sustainable economic growth
- Helping communities adapt to a changing environment
- Elevating the role of women and girls throughout all our work[42]

These targets closely mirror many of the objectives of U.S. diplomacy. And the management of USAID has been increasingly integrated with the State Department. The Secretary of State and the Administrator of USAID submit joint budget priorities. There is also a wider diplomatic argument for why ODA is given. The donor recognizes that the prevention of collapse of states or the underpinning of development in others is in the donor state's interest. Its own security is linked with others. As President Obama said in a speech in May 2013, "Foreign assistance cannot be viewed as charity. It is fundamental to our national security. And it's fundamental to any sensible long-term strategy to battle extremism."[43]

Global ODA applied in 2012 was three times the size of Kenya's GDP and twenty times that of Rwanda. This indicates a significant interference in state sovereignty that goes well beyond the scope of normal diplomacy. A country is not just relating to another in negotiating, reporting, or protecting its nationals, but is transferring and investing funds to it. How far does ODA alter diplomatic relations, and what difference in calculations and influence has it made? And does the transfer of money weaken the long-term capability of the state to function by creating a permanent reliance on overseas sources?

ODA can take many different forms. The OECD defines ODA as grants and interest-free loans, and this is the most frequently cited measure. Yet China does not give much ODA by this measure; its ODA was estimated to be \$2 billion in 2010, which equates to 0.04 percent of its gross national income (GNI). Yet, as we saw above, China does give significant other assistance, such as export credits, lines of credit backed by natural resources, subsidies for private investment, and mixed credits that combine soft and market-rate loans. These are called Other Official Flows (OOF) by the OECD. China's OOF to Africa was at least three times what it gave in ODA. This contrasts to the United States, which gives far less OOF than ODA. The Export-Import Bank of the United States (Ex-Im Bank) authorized just under $10 billion in loans and other financing to Africa from 2004 to 2012, while in the same period its Chinese counterpart (EXIM) is reported to have authorized $38 billion for the continent.

Both approaches to overseas assistance claim successes. USAID quotes numerous statistical examples of what its ODA has achieved.

> More than 3 million lives are saved every year through USAID immunization programs. Since 1987, USAID has initiated HIV/AIDS prevention programs in 32 countries, and is the recognized technical leader in the design and development of these programs in the developing world.[44]

The Chinese, likewise, claim considerable overseas benefits from their donor activities. Writing in May 2013, a spokesperson for the Chinese embassy in Nairobi said that cumulative Chinese investment in Africa reached $20 billion by 2012 and

> out of the 2,000 Chinese companies in Africa, 85 percent of their workforce is comprised of local employees and with continuous training in highly technical areas. . . . By the end of 2012, it is estimated that China had facilitated the training of over 40,000 African professionals in various sectors.[45]

How far has this generation of spending in other countries brought diplomatic benefits to the donors and the recipients? In his book *Bottom Billion: Why the Poorest Countries Are Failing and What Can Be Done about It*, Paul Collier concentrates on the limits of what ODA can achieve in situations where countries are "trapped." No diplomacy can alleviate the viability of a sovereign state where important obstacles are in the way. The book argues that most countries in the developing world are getting richer at an unprecedented rate but some countries (mostly in Africa and Central Asia) are stuck and that development assistance should be focused heavily on them. But any ODA needs to take account of one or more development traps that prevent meaningful progress and limits to what can be achieved must be recognized. As Collier writes,

> We cannot rescue them. The societies of the bottom billion can only be rescued from within. In every society of the bottom billion there are people working for change, but usually they are defeated by the

> powerful internal forces stacked against them. We should be helping the heroes. So far, our efforts have been paltry: through inertia, ignorance, and incompetence, we have stood by and watched them lose.[46]

Collier identifies the following traps that stand in the way of ODA achieving its results:

a. A Conflict Trap: Civil wars (each of which he estimates has an average cost of $64 billion) and coups bring enormous economic costs to a country. Vested interests develop, and they seek to prolong conflict for their own ends.
b. A Natural Resource Trap: Surprisingly, countries that are rich in natural resources are usually worse off than countries that are not. Resources increase the likelihood of conflict; taxes are not levied, removing accountability leading to the survival of the "fattest"; the country's currency becomes inflated in value; and Dutch disease (or lack of competitiveness of other industries) develops.
c. Landlocked with Poor Neighbors: Switzerland is landlocked but has rich neighbors. Countries with coastlines trade with the world, while landlocked countries only trade with their neighbors. Collier sees few solutions for these unviable countries, and ODA will make little impact unless their neighbors help out.
d. Bad Governance in a Small Country: Small countries suffer most from bad governance—corruption, and their smallness discourages potential investors.

In Collier's view, ODA will be fruitless without wider diplomatic efforts and should increasingly be concentrated only in the most difficult environments. In some cases military interventions (such as the British in Sierra Leone) should be encouraged, especially to guarantee democratic governments against overthrow. Collier believes international charters are needed to encourage good governance and provide templates. Trade policy preference to the bottom billion can help, but concentrating just on poverty is too simplistic. "Poverty is not intrinsically a trap, otherwise we would all still be poor."[47]

Another prominent development economist, Jeffrey Sachs, argues that the long decades of ODA have achieved impressive results. Money does matter and has produced massive global improvement in living conditions. Sachs continues to believe that exhortations to donors and targeted global action are a vital part of the agenda of international relations and diplomacy. He was one of the leading advocates of a reassertion of global targets for ODA and reminding states of the 0.7% GDP target of 1970. In 2000, 193 member states of United Nations signed the UN Millennium Declaration promoting eight Millennium Development Goals (MDGs) to be achieved by 2015 or 2020. The MDGs represented the first time that a holistic strategy to meet the development needs of the world had been agreed, with measurable targets and defined indicators. They were aimed at

- eradicating extreme poverty and hunger,
- achieving universal primary education,
- promoting gender equality and empowering women,
- reducing child mortality rates,
- improving maternal health,
- combating HIV/AIDS, malaria, and other diseases,
- ensuring environmental sustainability, and
- developing a global partnership for development.

As a declaratory commitment, the MDGs are similar to the UN's 1948 Declaration of Human Rights. And modern advances in statistics have made it possible to track progress. The goals mean that every state has a set of obligations to the world community to meet and that other states, who have achieved these goals, have an obligation to help those who have not. The first seven MDGs are measurable goals, while the eighth lists a number of stepping stone goals—ways in which progress toward the first seven could be made. Sachs believes there is no mistaking their success. Writing in 2012, Sachs looked back to the world of 2000.

> In 2000, Africa was struggling with three major epidemics. AIDS was killing more than two million people each year, and spreading rapidly. Malaria was surging, owing to the parasite's growing resistance to the standard medicine at the time. Tuberculosis was also soaring, partly as a result of the AIDS epidemic and partly because of the emergence of drug-resistant TB. In addition, hundreds of thousands of women were dying in childbirth each year, because they had no access to safe deliveries in a clinic or hospital.[48]

By the end of the decade, diplomacy could claim to have contributed to major improvements in the battles against the three diseases. Nigeria hosted two summits, on malaria in 2000 and on AIDS in 2001, which were crucial spurs to action. The UN Secretary General Kofi Annan called for the creation of a Global Fund to Fight AIDS, Tuberculosis, and Malaria. This, too, was achieved. The Global Fund began operations in 2002, financing prevention, treatment, and remedial programs. Rich countries also agreed debt reduction programs, allowing developing countries to spend more on health care and less on crippling interest payments. This was ODA in partnership with the instruments of diplomacy. Ten years after the MDGs were set Sachs wrote,

> Around 12 million children under five years old died in 1990. By 2010, this number had declined to around 7.6 million. . . . Malaria deaths in children in Africa were cut from a peak of around 1 million

> in 2004 to around 700,000 by 2010, and, worldwide, deaths of pregnant women declined by almost half between 1990 and 2010.[49]

Sachs claimed the skeptics had been proved wrong. By mid-2013 programs supported by the Global Fund in more than 140 countries had provided 5.3 million people with antiretroviral therapy for AIDS, tested and treated eleven million people for TB, and distributed 340 million insecticide-treated nets to protect families against malaria.

A former research economist at the World Bank, William Easterly, has taken a position somewhere between Collier and Sachs. In his *White Man's Burden: Why the West's Efforts to Aid the Rest Have Done So Much Ill and So Little Good*, he argues that much aid is planned without sufficient thought. The real way to bring development is through stimulating the searchers for solutions. "In foreign aid, Planners announce good intentions but don't motivate anyone to carry them out; Searchers find things that work and get some reward. Planners raise expectations but take no responsibility for meeting them. Searchers accept responsibility for their actions."[50] So Easterly argues that ODA needs flexible entrepreneurs, not rigid bureaucrats, but it can produce results.

If the overall effect of ODA in sovereign states produces divided views, then what of the diplomatic relationship between the donor and recipient? How far should the assistance be tied and conditional? How far can the recipient be influenced to behave in a different way because of its dependence on ODA? And how does applying assistance funding contravene the noninterference in internal affairs provision of the VCDR?

Tied aid, or ODA conditional on it being spent in whole or in part in the donor country, is now illegal in the United Kingdom. But conditions on how the money is channeled to the recipient and what results are expected are now a standard feature of ODA accountability. The United States has long seen Egypt as an important strategic ally and has provided large sums in economic and military assistance. It has only recently sought to attach strings. Egypt in 2012 received $250 million in economic assistance and $1.3 billion in military aid. In 2012, the U.S. Congress passed bills requiring the U.S. Secretary of State to provide reports about how Egypt's aid is being used and on human rights compliance.

In 2013, UK members of Parliament overseeing the ODA budget for Pakistan noted that while Pakistan was the biggest recipient of the United Kingdom's ODA, and an increase of over 60 percent was proposed, over 70 percent of Pakistan's members of Parliament paid no income tax. Corruption was also rife, so why did the UK government not impose more conditions? A spokesperson for DFID acknowledged the problems.

> UK development assistance in Pakistan is predicated on a commitment to economic and tax reform and to helping lift the poorest out of poverty. We have made it clear to government and opposition politicians in Pakistan that it is not sustainable for British taxpayers to fund development spend if Pakistan is not building up its own stable tax take.[51]

Box 9-1 **Haiti's Global Assistance**

Paul Farmer, a founder of the NGO Partners in Health and subsequently Assistant to the UN Special Envoy to Haiti, estimated that in 2011 only 0.3 percent of the total global assistance pledged to Haiti after the earthquake went to the Haitian government. Just 1.3 percent of USAID funds applied went directly to Haitian companies. Sixty-seven percent of the $446 million disbursed went to U.S. contractors.

Recipient governments also use the noninterference provision of the VCDR to limit the activities of ODA agencies in their territories. In September 2012, Russia announced it was expelling officials of USAID, accusing it of meddling in politics because of its democracy promotion programs. This ended USAID's twenty-year presence in Russia. In May 2013, the President of Bolivia, Evo Morales, also expelled USAID personnel, alleging attempts to undermine his government.

ODA as part of diplomacy has broadened the diplomatic agenda, beyond the traditional confines of separateness. The funds applied in assistance raise other questions, particularly on implementation. Projects funded in education, medicine, and engineering require specialist implementers, not generalists. ODA has created a permanent and intricate interface between state providers of funds and nonstate implementers of development policies. Practical diplomacy has been outsourced beyond the state.

ODA is one of the areas of diplomacy where the partnership between states, NGOs, and other nonstate actors is essential to its implementation. The implications of such partnerships will be examined in detail in Chapter 10.

Case Study

Case Study of the New Agenda: Nation Building in Afghanistan

If ODA is part of the new diplomatic agenda that must take account of an array of powerful new players and new agenda issues, then the ultimate form of interventionism into the sovereign-state model is nation building or reconstruction. This goes beyond providing financial and technical expertise to prop up another state. It recognizes that no arm's length diplomatic efforts can succeed. We have already seen how transformative diplomacy and the delivery of results to influence how other countries behave are part of the reform agenda.

The failing state is a challenge for the whole diplomatic system. Many states are of recent creation, and have few, if any, roots in history. They may not even have clear or effective territorial boundaries. So the basic premise of diplomacy—that a state participates in international affairs because it controls some of the world's surface—may be absent. States sometimes disappear or break up. Syria and Egypt had a failed merger in the 1950s, and Czechoslovakia became two separate states in 1992. In other instances, states survive by help from others. The repairing or reconstruction of states is seen as both a national and international priority.

The longest exercise in reconstruction of a country in the twenty-first century is the U.S.-led operation in Afghanistan. The operation began as a response by the United States to an attack on it not by the government of Afghanistan but by nonstate actors. The reason why Afghanistan was targeted was because it had become a territory where nonstate actors had taken residence to create a transnational threat to disrupt and terrorize states of whose governance and actions they disapproved. They received support and shelter from, and indeed merged personnel with, a powerful internal political organization in Afghanistan, the Taliban. At the time of the U.S. response in 2001, the Taliban controlled the government of the country. The overriding priority of the U.S. action was retaliation and punishment. That then stimulated other aims, sometimes described in tabloid terms as "draining the swamp" that had produced the disease of terrorism.

Diplomacy came in at the start of the process after the Taliban had been removed from the government by U.S. military action. Under UN auspices and with the participation of leading Afghans, a conference was held in Bonn in December 2001 to discuss Afghanistan's future government. The Afghan Interim Authority (AIA) of thirty members was established with a six-month mandate to be followed by a two-year Transitional Authority. UNSC Resolution (UNSCR) 1386 in December 2001 established the International Security Assistance Force (ISAF) as a NATO-led security mission. Acting under Chapter VII of the UN Charter, ISAF was given an initial period of six months to assist the AIA with security. During this time it was charged with securing Kabul and surrounding areas from the Taliban, al-Qaeda, and factional warlords, so that the new Afghan Transitional Administration headed by Hamid Karzai could take shape. In October 2003, the UNSC authorized the expansion of the ISAF mission throughout Afghanistan.

The country was divided into provincial units. In Helmand Province, the name of the ISAF unit was not described as a consulate general or as the NATO headquarters but as the Provincial Reconstruction Team (PRT). This title went way beyond what a diplomatic presence is conceived as doing. It had echoes of former U.S. Secretary of State's Colin Powell's "Pottery Barn" principle of foreign policy—"If you break it, you own it."[52] The government of Afghanistan had been removed under international authority, and its main responsibilities were outsourced to other countries. They deployed a mixed team of diplomats, military, and civilians covering justice, security, development, and counternarcotics policy.

The personnel employed were diverse. Helmand was headed by a British diplomat with over one hundred civilian and military core staff, mainly from the United Kingdom, Afghanistan, Denmark, Estonia, and the United States. The funding was split between the United Kingdom, United States, Danish, and Estonian governments. The tasks evolved as the mission was extended . . . and extended. The PRT was headquartered in Lashkar Gah, with UK, U.S., and Danish district stabilization teams in ten of Helmand's fourteen districts. A stabilization team begat many acronyms with civilian Stabilization Advisers (STABADs), a UK Military Stabilization Support Team (MSST), and a United States or Danish Civil and Military Cooperation (CIMIC) Support Team.

With the totality of the PRT's responsibilities in Helmand, there was no longer any distinction between the sending and receiving state nor between the diplomat and the different reconstruction teams. Sovereignty took a back seat to making Afghanistan governable again, and the PRT's activities went well beyond security. One example was the Food Zone, aimed at the funding source for much of the insurgency—the drug trade from heroine poppies. The

(Continued)

(Continued)

United Kingdom provided support to the then Provincial Governor of Helmand, Gulab Mangal, to provide alternative livelihoods. The program provided wheat seed, fertilizer, and technical assistance to farmers to boost food income as an alternative to the poppy crop. The farmers were required to certify they renounced cultivation of heroine poppies, and the government then targeted its poppy eradication on these farms.

The first assessments of the tasks and the forecast of requirements of ISAF bore little relationship to what happened. As late as November 2003, the entire ISAF force, now formally under NATO command, consisted of only 5,000 troops and three helicopters. A study by CARE International in mid-2003 reported that Kosovo had had one peacekeeper to forty-eight people, East Timor one for every eighty-six, while Afghanistan had just one for every 5,380 people. By December 2010, the ISAF forces had risen to over 100,000 and the coalition had built over 700 bases in Afghanistan.

As the operation extended, so did the tasks. Planners were brought into all areas of reconstruction. A major emphasis was on training an Afghan security force. Yet, good as that looked in a strategy paper, Rory Stewart, a senior official in the UK team in Helmand has written that 92 percent of police recruits in Helmand province could not write their own names or recognize numbers from one to ten.[53] Tours of duty of military ranged from six months (the United Kingdom) to twelve months (United States). Diplomats seldom stayed longer than a year. Judges were also mostly illiterate. Some of the expectations took on a momentum of their own. Zalmay Khalilzad, an Afghan-American working for the RAND Corporation, was appointed special envoy and then U.S. ambassador to the country. Khalilzad understood the country, spoke the languages, and had billions of dollars of resources. At one point, he seemed to suggest that he would stand as a presidential candidate in succession to Hamid Karzai.

While in office, Khalilzad needed to sound optimistic for obvious reasons. Later, writing on the tenth anniversary of the invasion, he was circumspect.

> Ten years after the U.S. invasion of Afghanistan, the gains that the international coalition has made with its local partners are real but reversible. Afghanistan is no longer a global hub of terrorist activity, but a Taliban resurgence would threaten to make it one again. Reconstruction assistance has produced demonstrable progress in health, education, and economic well-being, but corruption and governance problems have undermined popular support for the government in Kabul and constrained the overall level of progress. Internationally, a coalition still backs the ISAF military mission. However, NATO's will is waning; China, Russia, and India are largely free riders; and Pakistan and Iran publicly say the right things, while destabilizing Afghanistan by privately meddling to their own ends.[54]

General David Richards, the UK commander and later Chief of Defense Staff, maintained his optimism to complete the task but warned of the terrible consequences of failure. "I'm convinced it is most certainly doable. We all know if we get this wrong there are all sort of implications not just for this generation but for our children's generation."[55]

Militarily, the Taliban could not be defeated. The world's most powerful sovereign state alliance could not subdue a group of unconventional fighters without air power or heavy armor.

NATO was forced regularly to revise its strength requirements and objectives. By January 2009, there were troops from twenty-six NATO members, ten Euro-Atlantic partners, and two other countries. From its contributors, ISAF represented a coalition of over 25 percent of the world's population. In 2010, President Obama sent an additional 33,000 U.S. troops. U.S. casualties grew with the growth of forces. In the first nine years, around 1,000 U.S. military lost their lives. The next twenty-seven months saw another 1,000 deaths. Security proved difficult to achieve even in Helmand province, one of thirty-four Afghan provinces that represented less than 5 percent of Afghanistan's 35 million population. By 2009, President Obama had defined U.S. commitments in Afghanistan in more limited terms to "promote a more capable and accountable Afghan government . . . and advance security, opportunity and justice."[56]

Had the world suddenly come together in a new mission that would show that diplomacy could perform unprecedented tasks? Had the international community shown diplomatic success or failure in this nation building? Was diplomacy evolving in a direction that renounced occupation but endorsed a collective commitment to improving governance and political processes? Afghanistan had become a threat to one quarter of the world not because the state was strong and capable of posing a military or economic threat but precisely because it was too weak to behave as a state. Some previous recent experiments in state reconstruction seemed to suggest a favorable approach was being reapplied. Khalilzad himself wrote approvingly of U.S. efforts post-World War II.

> Since World War II, U.S. statecraft has succeeded by sending American forces to regions of critical importance and working with partners—for decades if needed—to address mutual threats, build stability, and foster progress. This formula eliminated major power wars in Europe and East Asia for more than a half century and successfully concluded the Cold War—a historic triumph.[57]

And there were more recent precedents for Afghanistan. The conflict in Bosnia and the aftermath of the breakup of a sovereign state Yugoslavia initially saw world diplomacy avert its gaze. When the international intervention came in the region, it was the culmination of a concerted international reassessment of the issue of sovereignty. Despite horrifying reports of the failures of peacekeepers and monitors in Rwanda from April to July 1994 and in Srebrenica in July 1995, the U.S. Congress and public opinion had remained strongly opposed to deploying ground troops in Bosnia. The loss of eighteen American soldiers in Somalia in 1993 trying to act as peacemakers had left its mark. In fact, the Bosnia intervention was made possible not by a sudden shift in international opinion and its approach to diplomacy but by a change in the military balance of the fighting on the ground. This assisted the preparations for the Dayton peace process, and NATO bombing of Serbia reinforced that progress. By 1996, there were 6,000 international troops in a country of 4 million and over $5 billion had been raised at a donors' conference. The interventions in Bosnia and later Kosovo drew the highest number of soldiers per head of population of any peace enforcement missions in history. Optimism for future policy took hold. These interventions led the former Australian Foreign Minister Gareth Thomas to declare that it was within the power of the international community to "end mass atrocity

(Continued)

(Continued)

crimes once and for all."[58] Robert Cooper, a senior EU diplomat, called for postmodern imperialism. The RAND Corporation began work on systematic "Guides to Nation Building." Even the UN's long-standing reluctance to breach the principle of noninterference into the affairs of a sovereign state was eroding. In 1998, the UN Secretary General, Kofi Annan, reminded the world that states should not be complacent about their responsibilities: "Let me recall that in French law there is a crime called 'failure to assist a person in danger.'"[59]

If Bosnia and Kosovo were generally localized in diplomatic impact, the crisis that divided the world on intervention and nation building was Iraq. Saddam Hussein's actions had produced an impressively united diplomacy. A troublesome member of the international community had needed special treatment. Saddam Hussein had to be evicted from Kuwait because he had infringed the sovereignty of a member state. That was what the United Nations had been designed for. The credibility of the UN was at stake as described in the case study in Chapter 4. Iraq was held accountable to previous international treaties through an intrusive inspection regime. Yet, in the end, diplomacy did not smooth the edges, and even NATO allies like France and Germany disagreed profoundly with the justification for the U.S.-led invasion in March 2003. The United States, buoyed by its military success in Afghanistan, did not envisage much serious nation building in Iraq thereafter. How wrong can diplomats be?

Libya in 2011 appeared much more straightforward. Muammar Gaddafi, a despotic and brutal leader, had threatened the West with state-sponsored terrorism and sought to acquire nuclear and chemical weapons. He had been subjected to a wide-ranging sanctions regime, and in 2003 he had decided to change course. He accepted diplomatic negotiations with the agenda of renouncing weapons of mass destruction and support for terrorism in return for a lifting of sanctions. Yet, just as other sovereign states were embracing a new member and he was rewarding them with oil concessions, parts of the population turned on him and he was ousted after months of bloody fighting. NATO was uncomfortable. As the Afghanistan chapter was closing, did diplomacy really want to engineer another nation-building exercise? Yet the Libyan case did have some diplomatic advantages. The likely spectacle of thousands of rebels and their families being massacred was too much for many governments to ignore. And in Libya, the geographical features—clear visibility, open desert, the lop-sided military balance of heavy armament against rebels in pick-up trucks—were unusually favorable to a clear, clean intervention. NATO was duly authorized under UNSCR 1973 "to take all necessary measures . . . to protect civilians and civilian populated areas under threat of attack in the Libyan Arab Jamahiriya, including Benghazi, while excluding a foreign occupation force of any form on any part of Libyan territory."[60]

Libya now has had competitive elections, and has created new institutions, but also suffers from the aftermath of years of turmoil and unruly militias. In September 2012, Christopher Stevens, the first U.S. ambassador to be murdered in post since 1979, died in Benghazi. Yet overall, the lesson of Libya seemed to be that full interventions would in the future be shunned in favor of limited types of diplomatic and military nudging.

There are few repeats in diplomatic showpieces. The unique combination of circumstances of the power of the United States and the attack on the U.S. homeland made a response in Afghanistan inevitable. But the nonstate character of the attack raised unusual questions. The choice for diplomatic interventions is not always as clear as to build or not to build. In 1996, Anthony Lake, a future

U.S. National Security Advisor, had warned, "It is dangerous hubris to believe we can build other nations. But where our own interests are engaged we can help nations build themselves and give them time to make a start at it."[61] This suggests reconstruction will have limited, imperfect effects and sets the bar low for what can be achieved.

Box 9-2 **Benghazi**

Benghazi was a diplomatic tragedy for the United States. But it showed the limits of conventional diplomacy. There was no state capable of protecting Ambassador Stevens and the other Americans who died—neither Libya nor the United States. However much security is provided, short of a military occupation, diplomats are helpless in a hostile environment. Ambassador Stevens was best placed to see the turmoil of his receiving state, and he would have known that militia-controlled Benghazi would be no respecter of his status.

The important conclusion that diplomacy should draw is that each state intervention raises different problems. The size of a country is an obvious variable. Bosnia had a population of four million, Iraq thirty million, and Afghanistan thirty-five million. In the future, many will cite the results that Afghanistan has yielded and no doubt draw different conclusions. Two presidential and two parliamentary elections have been held. An opposition in Parliament has emerged and the media in Afghanistan are not fully censored. There has been impressive progress, admittedly from levels that hardly registered on conventional scales, in telecommunications, education, and health services. But in terms of having a functioning system of governance, a state fully built, an end to the economic cancer of drug dependency, the task is incomplete at best. Today's Afghanistan still makes its major decisions through a loyal *jirga*, an assembly of tribal leaders that dates back to the eighteenth century. Perhaps it was ironic that this group was convened in November 2013 to decide what future role the ISAF forces would have in the country. Most would agree that the full development of the state must await new generations of Afghan leaders who might be persuaded to stay in Afghanistan rather than emigrate to the West in search of a non-Afghan lifestyle.

Nation building is associated with another major problem. It is expensive. A study by a former Chief Financial Officer of the Department of Commerce published by Harvard University in March 2013 calculated that the wars in Iraq and Afghanistan had cost the United States between $4 and $6 trillion, including long-term care for the war's veterans. The two wars were the most expensive in U.S. history and "the largest portion of the bill is yet to be paid."[62] The consequences will be long lasting.

> The large sums borrowed to finance operations in Iraq and Afghanistan will also impose substantial long-term debt servicing costs. . . . The US will face constraints in funding investments in personnel and diplomacy, research and development and new military initiatives. The legacy of decisions taken during the Iraq and Afghanistan wars will dominate future federal budgets for decades to come.[63]

By March 2013, the U.S. government's cumulative debt had reached $16 trillion. It is obvious that nation building cannot be undertaken repeatedly, however powerful the state with such

(Continued)

(Continued)

building ambitions. In 2014, the income obtained by the Islamic State (IS) from black market oil sales amounted to over $2 million a day. In addition, they had seized millions of dollars from the banks they occupied in Mosul and elsewhere and in ransoms paid for hostage taking. IS showed that authority can be imposed on territory and a new state can be built if money is there to recruit and arm those keen to fight, and the states being replaced have serious flaws in their own construction.

CONCLUSION

The agenda-setting power of diplomacy is still one of its primary assets. Diplomats are interested in dialogue, in defining an issue and framing some consensual processes so this part of their activities remains central. Yet the national systems we have reviewed are all trying to make their diplomacy achieve more. Most seem convinced that the world would behave in a more predictable way, and their interests could be promoted more effectively, if their national diplomatic system could perform and deliver better. Our brief survey suggests states are still a long way apart in how they seek to achieve greater success. It also suggests that there is little consensus on how issues on the multilateral agenda like development and nation building should be handled. Diplomacy is still an activity conducted by a disparate set of actors from states with different agendas. It has plenty of mechanisms for settling crises and follow-up in an ad hoc way. But it's not yet a forum for a planning, anticipating, or producing an international dimension of thinking and action that can be drawn on as a necessary aide to the diplomatic process. Diplomacy is struggling to find a new framework to handle problems, many of which are caused by its weaker members.

We now turn to those who have long been active in diplomacy but who are increasingly making their voices heard and their influence felt—the nonstate actors.

SUGGESTIONS FOR FURTHER READING

1. U.S. Department of State. "The First Quadrennial Diplomacy and Development Review (QDDR): Leading through Civilian Power." 2010. http://www.state.gov/s/dmr/qddr.
2. Collier, Paul. *The Bottom Billion: Why the Poorest Countries Are Failing and What Can Be Done about It*. New York: Oxford University Press, 2008.
3. Sachs, Jeffrey. "Economic Solidarity for a Crowded Planet." The BBC Reith Lectures, 2007.
4. Stewart, Rory, and Gerald Knaus. *Can Intervention Work?* New York: W. W. Norton, 2012.

chapter 10

The Nonstate Actors

Global Citizens and Global Diplomacy

The Economist noted in 2012 that more people belonged to the Royal Society for the Protection of Birds in the United Kingdom than to all the three main British political parties combined. More young people voted on the show *American Idol*—many of them several times over!—than in recent U.S. federal elections. Trust in governments is also low. In her lecture "Saving America," Jessica Mathews says that polls in the United States show that "anyone under the age of forty has lived their entire life in a country the majority of whose citizens do not trust their own national government to do what is right."[1] Politicians in Lithuania have developed a novel solution to promote increased participation in elections—to give away drinks at polling stations. At a recent election, voting turnout increased from 23 percent to 65 percent as a result.

The signs that the inhabitants of the world are turning to other ideals and institutions outside government will have implications for diplomacy. The impact of the nonstate attraction is nothing new. We have discussed regional organizations and the search for global values and predictability. And we have also seen the decisive role that nonstate actors have played in establishing some of the key elements of current diplomacy and in setting the agenda for international fora.

This chapter analyzes how far new developments in the power and resources of nonstate actors are changing diplomacy in radical ways. It looks at the positive and negative influences and what responses state-directed diplomacy has made. It will examine how far the world is looking elsewhere for some of the traditional functions of diplomats, and whether the areas of activity are or might become complementary to traditional methods. The pace of the change in communication and in information gathering is also opening up new possibilities in diplomatic behavior for nonstate players. But, as we noted during our survey of public diplomacy, the increasingly chaotic nature of how information is obtained and how actions are taken on international issues has reinforced the view that outsourcing of diplomacy to global citizens or "netizens" may do more harm than good.

THE GLOBALIZATION OF IDENTITY: THE INTERNATIONAL COMMUNITY?

If individuals and nonstate actors such as companies and nongovernmental organizations (NGOs) do not see themselves as having a state identity, then the national boundary loses its characteristics for defining actions and motivations in international relations. And diplomacy in such circumstances moves into unaccustomed areas. Equally, the same developments mean that the services that state actors perform for citizens, such as in consular protection and in promoting exports of their country's business sector, also become blurred.

What implications does the growing fluidity of international identity and the decline in the influence of sovereign states have for the diplomacy? The media often suggest that views of the international community are frequently expressed, playing its part alongside other diplomatic platitudes such as space-filling descriptions of uneventful meetings as a productive dialogue. Yet for many who know the diplomatic process, an international community is an elusive quarry. Indeed, many see the situation as worse than ever. Richard Haass, a former Head of Policy Planning at the U.S. State Department and now President of the Council on Relations, wrote in 2012 that

> there is no international community. . . . Today's major powers do not agree on the rules that ought to govern the world, much less on the penalties for breaking them. Even where there is accord in principle, there is little agreement in practice. The result is a world that is messier and more dangerous than it should be.[2]

Let us assume that the modern era has brought new forces to bear. And let us also assume that sovereign states will remain the building blocks of the new system. We will examine how far the state will prove the bastion of stability and order amid the turmoil. But it is also possible that the decline of the state is an inevitable and accelerating process and that the rise of nonstate influences has much further to go. The optimists—or those who see the arc of progress ascending—would say that the state-centric system erects traditional barriers that ring fence problems and establish red lines. Solutions to contentious issues are only possible if the red lines are crossed. It may simply be that a messy world is getting messier, and to suggest diplomacy can do much better is naïve. What are the significant changes that make the modern era different in the number and variety of nonstate actors on the diplomatic stage? Which have the capacity or leadership to produce significant results? Commentators who travel the world and study modern interaction between states and nonstates believe watersheds are approaching. One view from a nonprofessional diplomat will give the flavor. "Traditional models of diplomacy hold only one lesson for how to manage the world: that they are themselves totally insufficient."[3]

THE NONSTATE ACTORS

Some of the trends we have examined in previous chapters are a reminder that we should not assume that just because most national boundaries have remained stable since World War II the principal actors have not changed. The number of countries has more than tripled. Forty major cities now account for more than two-thirds of the world's population. In 1946, forty-one NGOs held consultative status with the UN's Economic and Social Council (ECOSOC). Today that number is over 3,700. The world is a different place for both states and nonstates.

Some nonstate actors carry government responsibilities. Subnational divisions like California, Scotland, or Quebec appear to hanker after looser structures that would give them more diplomatic autonomy. Mayors of major cities conduct international meetings because their responsibilities and political exposure are now international. Mayor Bloomberg of New York used his office and personal wealth to promote global and national causes through an Office for International Affairs. A group of over sixty world cities, called C40, have formed a diplomatic alliance to discuss issues related to climate change. Cities hosting major international events like the Olympics are the focus of public diplomacy as much as the states themselves. And many national leaders—eight heads of world governments in May 2013—are former mayors of cities. Recep Tayyip Erdogan, the Prime Minster of Turkey, was mayor of Istanbul; Mahmoud Ahmedinejad, the former President of Iran was Mayor of Tehran. In 2012, the Supreme Court of Honduras struck down a plan to create some independent model cities—a scheme that had the support of President Porfirio Lobo—that would split off from the central government and run their own tax and justice systems. Cities offer lessons for states. Singapore is essentially a city-state of five million people, most of whom enjoy a high income. The Chinese government is known to be studying the success of the Singapore in maintaining one party control (the People's Action Party) alongside a competitive business environment, low corruption, and a tolerance of many ethnic backgrounds. Some states apply different economic regulations in zones within their territories. One is the Jebel Ali Free Zone in Dubai, one of the world's busiest ports. And in negotiations, some states may choose to have representatives of different parts of their state to ensure that the domestic reception to a diplomatic agreement is smooth. Thus, the Canadian delegation to free trade talks with the EU included representatives of all the provinces of Canada. Small may also be effective in diplomatic terms. Territories like Monaco, the Cayman Islands, and the British Virgin Islands have attracted some of the world's largest companies and funds because of their offshore tax regimes. Their unique status deprives larger states of enormous revenues.

If the boundaries of the units that participate in diplomacy are under constant discussion what of the coherence of those living within the boundaries? Weak domestic governments also mean fragile institutions, a diplomatic service without direction, and leaderships preoccupied with surviving both politically and physically. Political leaders may also seek to enhance their own status and power through partnering and synergy with those nonstate groups associated with global causes or individuals. Hybrid diplomacy—between state and nonstate actors—not only suits states and leaders with fewer resources, but it is essential to reinforce the agenda and secure acceptance of the outcomes.

Weak states and new divisions also open the possibilities for other actors to appeal to citizens for allegiance and to promote an agenda that is different from that of sovereign states. We have discussed the power of religions and ethnic identities. The Kurds have a strong cultural identity, but the geographic region of Kurdistan is governed from Iran, Iraq, Syria, and Turkey. Instability in Ukraine in 2014 was seized on by Russian-speaking minorities to urge the redrawing of Ukraine's boundaries. Beyond this blurring of state allegiance, citizen activism over global issues and global passions about social media, sport, music, or sustainable energy might create opportunities for diplomats to cultivate. The discussion of valence issues in domestic politics has relevance in diplomacy. For example, an international valence audience may share detestation of corruption and fiscally sound economic management without caring which state is advocating such policies.

GLOBAL CITIZENS?

The measure of these trends, as in many aspects of diplomacy, is difficult to establish. What evidence is there that growing use of social media and frequency of travel is opening eyes and minds to look beyond the state for solutions? Is there a correlation between those who travel and those who see merits in other countries' positions? A survey by World Public Opinion.org in 2009 of respondents from twenty-one countries asked if they had traveled outside the country in the last five years. Of those who had, they then asked how many

TABLE 10.1 **World Public Opinion.org Survey (In Percentages)**

In the last five years have you traveled to another country, or not?

	Yes	*No*	*Don't Know/Not Sure*
Mexico	24	76	0
US	30	70	0
France	61	39	0
Germany	70	30	1
Great Britain	77	23	1
Italy	53	47	0

	Yes	*No*	*Don't Know/Not Sure*
Russia	16	84	0
Ukraine	20	79	1
Azerbaijan	33	66	1
Egypt	19	79	3
Jordan	33	65	3
Palestinian ter.	24	74	2
Turkey	7	93	0
Kenya	5	95	0
Nigeria	13	86	0
China	5	96	0
India	8	76	16
Indonesia	1	99	0
South Korea	59	41	0
Thailand	16	75	9
Average	29	69	2

Do you consider yourself primarily a citizen of your own country, or of the world, or of both equally?

	Own Country	*The World*	*Both Equally*
Argentina	64	10	24
Mexico	56	9	35
US	72	5	22
France	48	14	37
Germany	59	19	18
Great Britain	59	9	29
Italy	51	21	27
Russia	79	5	13
Ukraine	81	6	10

(Continued)

TABLE 10.1 **(Continued)**

	Own Country	*The World*	*Both Equally*
Azerbaijan	89	4	5
Egypt	73	13	13
Jordan	80	8	7
Palestinian ter.	70	14	13
Turkey	80	9	10
Nigeria	69	11	19
China	35	6	44
India	40	14	32
Indonesia	68	2	27
South Korea	83	5	11
Thailand	48	15	23
Average	66	10	20

Source: WorldPublicOpinion.org, "World Public Opinion and Global Citizenship," May 19, 2009, http://www.worldpublicopinion.org/pipa/pdf/may09/WPO_GlobCit_May09_quaire.pdf.

considered themselves a citizen of one country or of the world as a whole, or of both one country and the world equally. Table 10.1 shows the results of this survey. A Pew Research survey in 2011 asked whether a citizen identified with a country or a global religion first. The results are set out in Figure 10.1.

These surveys suggest that global awareness does impact how citizens perceive their nationality. A surprisingly high percentage of Chinese and Indians, and of major EU countries, see themselves as citizens of both their own country and of the globe. The Pew Research figures suggest both weaknesses and strengths in sovereign states. The state of Israel's commitment to maintain a Jewish homeland is obviously reinforced by a figure of 57 percent identifying first as Jewish. But some of the survey's results for Muslim states pose problems for diplomacy. A lack of national identity in weak systems of government coupled with a preference for transnational allegiances such as adherence to Islam is a troubling phenomenon. It suggests that the country may struggle to conduct diplomacy on a genuinely independent basis with little inclination to engage with non-Islamic countries on issues even where there could be shared interests.

Figure 10.1 **What Do You Consider Yourself First?**

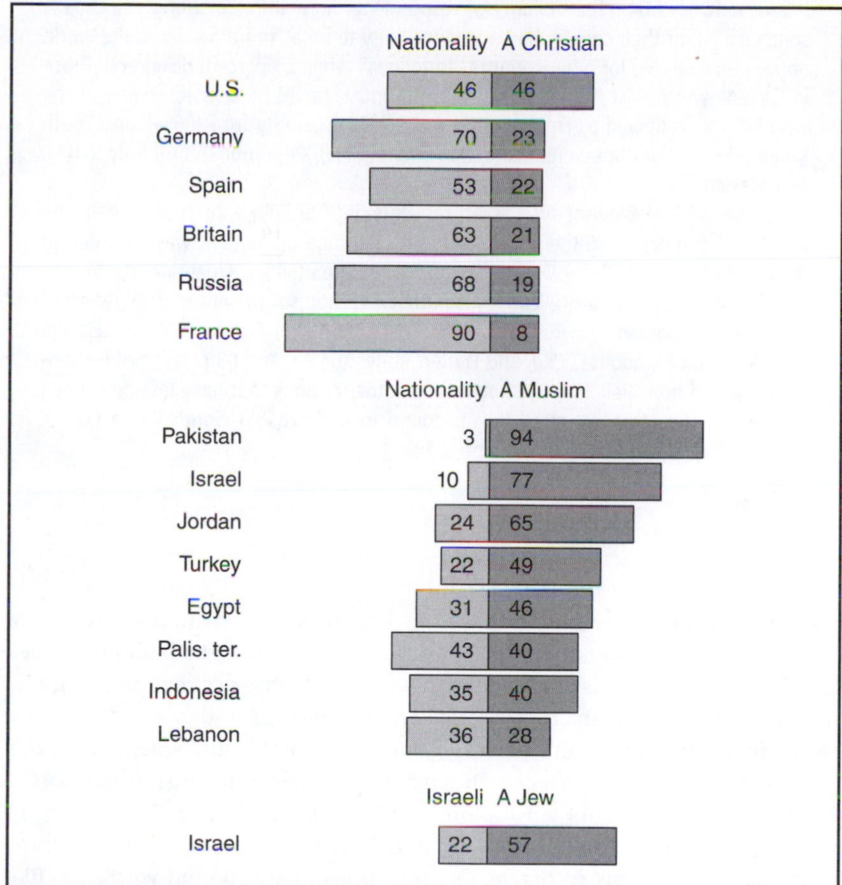

Source: Pew Research Center, "Muslim-Western Tensions Persist," July 21, 2011, http://www.pewglobal.org/2011/07/21/muslim-western-tensions-persist.

World Public Opinion in December 2009 also found a high enthusiasm in global publics for government to negotiate more constructively on issues than their governments had shown to date. Fifty-four percent of Russians and 54 percent of Americans agreed that their governments "should be more ready to act cooperatively to achieve mutual gains." So did 63 percent of Chinese, 76 percent of Egyptians and 81 percent of Turks. These findings have also been regularly confirmed.[4]

A survey by Ipsos Global @dvisor taken over several years has also confirmed that internationalist policies retain strong appeal even in time of economic troubles.

(Continued)

The survey has been conducted in twenty-four countries of over 17,000 adults aged between 18 and 64.[5] The majority of respondents agreed (34% strongly and 43% somewhat) that their country had a responsibility to be a "moral leader in the world and set an example for other countries to follow," while 23 percent disagreed. Those in Canada were most likely to agree their country should be a moral leader in the world (89%), followed by France (88%), India (87%), South Africa (86%), and South Korea (86%). Majorities were recorded in Spain (54%), Argentina (58%), Italy (64%), and Mexico (71%).

Ipsos Global @dvisor also asked respondents, "Should your country help the growth of democracy in the world?" High percentage agreement was recorded in India (88%), Mexico (86%), Turkey (85%), South Korea (84%), Argentina (82%), and Sweden (82%). Even those countries that were not so convinced still reflected majorities in agreement: Russia (69%), Hungary (69%), France (69%), Australia (71%), United Kingdom (71%), and United States (64%). And 63 percent of respondents agreed that their country should assist other nations that have less developed economies. The strongest support was found in India (85%), South Korea (78%), Japan (78%), Turkey (72%), and China (72%).[6]

Those who bother to respond to such a survey are naturally a receptive audience, but the results suggest that pure nationalism and a belief that one's country of citizenship is always right is not the only the driving force of international relations. Coupled with our earlier survey of leaders who see some misfiring of diplomacy and the urgent need for better dialogue, these polls indicate that there may be a constituency for an internationalist dimension to what citizens want from their diplomacy. And such diplomacy has worked in the past. The International Red Cross is living testament to a nineteenth-century global citizens' initiative. Organizations today abound with titles like Global Citizen, Global Citizens Initiative, and Global Citizens Network. The fund of goodwill rings out from their mission statements, and idealism still has its place. As the Global Citizens Network puts it, "The peoples of the world are *one people*, enriched by individual differences, united by the common bond of humanity. The diversity of the Global Community is its greatest strength; understanding and respect are its greatest gifts."[7] The question that might interest diplomats is whether this fund for internationalism is increasing. There may be evidence of this. Parag Khanna in his book *How to Run the World* cites a study that says that twenty years ago 18 percent of U.S. college graduates said they wanted to get out and change the world. Now 40 percent say they would.

Other nonstate actors show less concern with the world and arguably have more influence on diplomacy. In August 2013, the United States, the world's foremost diplomatic power, temporarily closed over twenty of its diplomatic missions in the Islamic world. The threat was real, detected by its sophisticated diplomatic reporting systems. It came not from a state but al-Qaeda, the group that had attacked the United States twelve years before. Al-Qaeda supports no sovereign state and is the enemy of most.

STATES AND NONSTATES IN DIPLOMACY

In global business, the calculations of many leading actors are not dependent on national identities. The global energy companies are among the world's largest. In 2013, Exxon Mobil was the most valuable corporation in the world, measured by market capitalization. Royal Dutch Shell was the most valuable company on the London Stock Exchange. Yet amid this evidence of private nonstate success, there were also the huge state-owned companies. In terms of oil production in 2013, the state-owned Aramco (Saudi Arabia), Gazprom (Russia), and NIOC (Iran) were the top three in the world. PetroChina, PetroBras (Brazil), Pemex (Mexico), and Petronas (Malaysia) are also giants in ultradeep oil exploration and research and development. So the power of the nonstates and states compete directly in globalized business. The workforces of these companies are unsurprisingly less and less nationally identified. A report by the U.S. Department of Commerce in 2012 showed that in 1989 79 percent of the workforce of major U.S. multinationals worked in the United States. By 2010, this figure had fallen to 67 percent.

It is one thing to describe opinion polls and market data. It is another to translate the sentiments and activities of nonstate actors into practical diplomacy. The diplomatic systems of states are deluged with proposals from NGOs, cities, businesses, individuals, and philanthropists who would love to change the world. The leaders of states have neither the time nor money to accommodate most of them. But internationalism now has many opportunities to gain a wider constituency. The information and communication revolution is producing a new cadre of netizens, those who use social media not to publicize their own lifestyles or views but as a way of interconnecting and energizing debate and action about issues of central concern to diplomats. We will examine this revolution and its implications for diplomacy in the next chapter.

One response to the decline of states and their angst about their roles in the world is to promote diplomatic consultancies to improve performance. This prompted the creation of The Independent Diplomat (ID), an organization to promote the benefits of diplomacy that does not represent a sovereign state. ID, headed by a former British diplomat Carne Ross, shows that some parts of the global map and state actors recognize a diplomatic deficit in their own capacities. ID's clients have included the government of Kosovo, the National Coalition Government of the Union of Burma, Somalia, the Turkish Republic of Northern Cyprus, and the region of Western Sahara. The complexities of the international diplomatic process pose formidable obstacles to the small, divided, and poorly resourced.

Whatever the merits of advice, buying diplomatic expertise and paying others to draft papers or mediate does not mean diplomacy can be created where it has few roots. If peace is to be promoted, diplomacy requires other elements than just negotiating advice. It involves the application of resources, a possibility of linkage with other issues, and a mechanism for implementation of agreed outcomes. No state can see a consultant as a permanent arrangement. An independent diplomatic partner able to deliver on whatever commitments it makes must be the objective. And it is a sad truth of today's world that some state units will not in the foreseeable future be equipped to play the role of full diplomatic actors.

Beyond the well-wishers, the underminers, and the moneymakers, who all interact with or try to outwit diplomacy, what value do nonstate actors bring to diplomacy? Is their effect temporary or sustainable, and how far can a nonstate partnership with states be developed? What expertise does the secretary general of an international organization have as a diplomatic negotiator? When the institutional means of conducting diplomacy fails, why might an individual, a nongovernmental organization, or a company achieve more?

A common circumstance where the nonstate diplomat might be enlisted is when devolving responsibility or passing the buck may suit the states. An outsourcing of the responsibility to a transnational representative such as the UN Secretary General or the EU High Representative is an obvious avenue. The ploy, used in the Syrian conflict, of appointing a UN and Arab League envoy showed that the international community was doing something. When the United Nations failed to produce either a cease-fire or negotiations, the United States and Russia returned to their own efforts to mediate a conference of the parties with the United Nations taking a back seat. The Egyptian government, after the removal of President Morsi in 2013, appeared to welcome the EU High Representative and two U.S. Republican senators—outside the U.S. administration—in an attempt to use nonstate diplomacy to broker an internal settlement. It also failed.

BEYOND STATES: THE NONSTATE ADVANTAGE?

The boundary between the state and nonstate is in many respects an illusion. The substance of diplomacy is never just confined to its effects on states. The state's role is as a representative of a system of organizing peoples, territories, and resources and as an entity that interacts with neighbors. States have never claimed that they would solve all problems because they were states. The state was created by people as a convenient instrument to achieve organization and provide security. Those not working directly for the state still have a stake in it. Perhaps President Kennedy had this in mind when he explained how problems needed to be addressed by everyone. "Our problems are man-made—therefore they can be solved by man."[8] The state is not them and us. It is all of us.

Throughout history, the nonstate business, campaigning, cultural, and religious actor has exerted a strong influence on the way states have developed their diplomacy. The pioneering trading companies such as the East India Company and the Hudson Bay Company lent money to the British government and operated with great independence and profit. They used the power of states to consolidate their involvement. The antislavery movement of the nineteenth century, the Suez Canal owners, the leaders of the modern Olympic Games, and inspirational leaders like Jesus Christ, the Prophet Mohammed, Mahatma Gandhi, and Martin Luther King are just some examples of important nonstate actors who have influenced both diplomatic agendas and outcomes. From the founding of the International Committee of the Red Cross (ICRC) of the nineteenth century to global campaigning technological hub Avaaz of the early twenty-first century, nonstate actors have partnered with states in running the world or in making their voices heard.

We have already noted that the range and number of nonstate actors is simply incalculable. We have also discussed some of the reasons for this growth and the issues on which nonstate actors have exerted their influence. NGOs enter the arena of international relations for different motives. Somali pirates have sought to raise funds by disrupting international maritime trade. Partners in Health, a Boston-based organization, offers international medical outreach to the poor because states have been unable to provide it. The global hackers Anonymous, who became universally recognizable through their V for Vendetta Guy Fawkes masks, were featured by *Time* magazine in 2012 as one of the 100 most influential people in the world. And there are innumerable groups formed specifically to influence states in their government and diplomacy—commonly known as lobbyists.

NGOs need an issue or issues to become an organization and to congregate a movement with people and resources. In this context, an NGO has the following advantages over states in diplomacy:

1. An issue coalition has more in common than a coalition of nations. Ownership of an issue draws attention to it and unites opinion across borders. National prejudices or cultural differences produce fewer problems.
2. The issue coalition can take nonpartisan stances, looking at arguments objectively.
3. Diverse and greater resources can be called upon. Netizens and philanthropists may prefer to make donations to NGOs rather than to governments.
4. NGOs are easier to wind up if they don't succeed and an alternative approach can be tried.
5. The creation of a new permanent bureaucracy can be avoided.
6. NGOs can build a reputation that can be applied to another issue. Such groups as Greenpeace or Human Rights Watch spread their influence across many issues.
7. An individual like Bill Gates or Mo Ibrahim may be sufficient to attract international attention. Because of their stature, they give credibility and resources to an issue. A formal NGO may be unnecessary.

Conversely, NGOs pose risks for diplomacy that may jeopardize their contribution to problem solving:

1. Coalition partners take on a life of their own. Their own jobs and budgets may depend on the issue continuing even when a solution is being achieved.
2. State institutions are usually necessary to monitor the implementation of solutions to diplomatic problems. Issue groups may distort their arguments about the issues for self-promotion and fund-raising.
3. Issues are linked. For example, climate change cannot be discussed without touching on sustainable development, poverty, and access to energy. Issue groups may be reluctant to link issues for fear of diluting their influence or enhancing that of their rivals.
4. Stakeholders in similar issues develop rivalries and may seek to develop economic advantage.
5. Only governments can administer laws that provide continuity of attention.
6. Governments look at the totality of their relations to achieve diplomatic results that contain areas of trust and distrust.
7. Issue groups may seek to undermine existing agreements that have worked among sovereign states. For example, some NGOs oppose the provisions of the Nuclear Nonproliferation Treaty because it has not produced nuclear disarmament.
8. The stateless diplomat is an oxymoron.

As the caliber of the diplomacy of states varies greatly, so does the capacity of nonstate actors. Their effectiveness may not be linked to the weight and relevance of their cause. Some leaders of successful NGOs have transferred their talents to government. Bernard Kouchner, the founder of *Médecins Sans Frontières,* has served as both French health and foreign ministers. Money may talk louder than ideas. Over 12,000 lobbyists in Washington, D.C., were active in 2012 and spent over $3.5 billion. Many employ former senior officials from the U.S. government. Many issue groups dedicate themselves purely to domestic policy such as gun laws (the National Rifle Association) or the interest of the retired (the AARP). Yet several significant groups engage the government in issues that directly impact U.S. diplomacy and foreign policy. The Cuban-American community has long been an influential actor in molding U.S.-Cuba policy through groups like the Cuban American National Foundation and The Cuba Study Group. The American Israel Public Affairs Committee (AIPAC), founded in 1951, has over 100,000 members in the United States and is recognized as the most powerful action group influencing U.S. foreign policy.

AIPAC's conventions regularly attract the attendance of over half of the members of the U.S. House of Representatives.

If the role of the nonstate actor can be useful and indispensable in contemporary diplomacy, then modern interconnection and instantaneous communication have greatly enhanced their capacity to disrupt and distort. The forces of globalization that create interdependence, freer markets, and open new avenues for nonstate voices and actions also foster social and political disintegration. Criminal activity is much easier to organize over the internet—the part of it dubbed the "dark net"—and its profits easier to conceal in false and offshore shell companies. Law enforcement authorities do not have the capacity to track all the transnational ingenuity of criminals. The state is forced to delegate and devolve responsibilities. Private security companies are increasingly being used by state and nonstate entities to supplement security services that used to be provided by states alone. Cheap, globally accessible technology with weaponry constructed from a YouTube video has shifted power to would-be nonstate disrupters. The Internet has opened ways of influencing opinion that no political or religious movement could have dreamed about in past eras. The suicide attacker has existed for centuries, but broadcasting the impact of such acts fuels imitation. Further implications of the information and communications technologies revolution for diplomacy will be discussed in the Chapter 11.

If communication is less and less impacted by state boundaries, so the globalized economy has produced stateless companies. The UK-headquartered bank HSBC employs over 300,000 people with 20,000 offices in eighty-three countries. This of course represents more than the combined diplomatic services of the all Group of Twenty countries. Companies develop different brands in different countries. They successfully avoid establishing a national identity and accountability to any state with expensively crafted tax domicile and registration provisions. Companies that used to identify with states like British Petroleum and American Telegraph and Telephone are now known by their initials. BP was an official sponsor of the U.S. Olympics team that competed in London in 2012.

Global products are nothing new, but the speed with which manufacturing now moves to different locations for incentives and low wage costs means that the transnational company has little allegiance to states. A company compares characteristics of states but is seldom limited in it decisions by state boundaries. Countries compete to attract and retain their investment. Global mobility means business calculations can impact states and their citizens as much as other threats to their security. The examples are many. Dell Computers moved a factory to Poland from Ireland. Ford shut a plant in Belgium to transfer work to Mexico.

The capacity of a small nonstate group to do immense damage means that the deployment of diplomatic resources needs to be diverted to counter their threat. Computer technology is not only used to transmit Instagram vacation photos across the world but also to keep the internet and GPS satellites in space. Drone and conventional military technology depends on a communications infrastructure creating interconnected vulnerability that the founders of the United Nations would have regarded as coming from the imagination of Arthur C. Clarke. And a nuclear dirty bomb will be as destructive if it comes from Peshawar as if it is stolen from a carefully primed and maintained weapons depot in Arizona. The commitment that diplomacy has to apply to counter the growing capacity of the nonstate actor has grown enormously.

Paradoxically, the effect of such threats has brought some new common ground to the agenda facing sovereign states. They have recognized that such threats cannot be combated by state-centric diplomacy. Diplomats share a common fear of the very act of engagement with some nonstate actors because physical closeness may give an opportunity to kill the messenger. A disguised suicide bomber may be the best way of attacking a diplomat who has agreed to a meeting rather than the indiscriminate car bomb in a public place of a few years ago. The system of discourse that is supposed to encourage convergence and smoothing of edges has now been challenged by nonstate actors deliberately disseminating information and motivational messages designed to make extremist converts and not to encourage discussion. The raw material of diplomatic exchanges can be easily poisoned. Such actors have the means to express their views in many states without governmental control. They will be wary of following Twitter hashtags but can respond immediately to events, organize meetings, and insult or praise anyone they choose. They can quote information that deliberately distorts what they know of the facts. The right to freedom of expression, so prized in the UN Declaration of Human Rights, has been achieved de facto in many parts of the world. It shows how united, concerned, bored, and fragmented the world is all at once. The diplomat absorbs all the chatter, tries to make sense of an information overload, but does not have a prescribed path to respond.

Yet the engagement of the nonstate citizen does offer some building blocks for diplomatic agendas. The reporting function of diplomacy is no longer confined to formal diplomatic contacts or the efforts that traditional diplomatic institutions like embassies make to engage in public diplomacy. Every diplomat now has a productive new source of information. No longer does the information conveyed to capitals reflect what the diplomat has been told by a politician leader, a mayor, or a president of a chamber of commerce. He or she can follow trending remarks by all elements of society. The diplomat may also find there is one new element that also offers a nondisruptive hope. The technology may helpfully uncover something of real interest to a diplomat—the true internationalist group or individual who does not just exercise thumbs texting from a smartphone but wants to contribute to diplomacy in its broadest meaning as a peaceful settler of problems.

THE BATTLE OF IDEAS: STATES VERSUS NONSTATES?

Cumulatively, the new information the diplomat has to survey will grow and grow. IBM estimates that 2.5 quintillion bytes are being created every day and that 90 percent of the world's stock of data is less than two years old.

This does not mean that the world is benefiting from thousands of new ideas every week. Many innovators in other fields, such as Einstein and Steve Jobs, borrowed from the ideas of others, some decades old. Nonstate actors have long had ideas and motivation that produced important diplomatic results. Actors like Cecil Rhodes and Rothschild's bank were the instigators of a strong British presence in Southern Africa. A. Q. Khan turned from state actor in running the Pakistan government's nuclear weapons program to a nonstate provider of nuclear weapons technology to any state that would pay for it. Edward Snowden decided after eight years in intelligence that some intelligence activities he had learned of and participated in were unacceptable. He turned nonstate actor and succeeded in redrawing the diplomatic dialogue between states. Is it possible that the business and NGO sectors will be the driving force for a fundamental overhaul of diplomacy in the twenty-first century? And if so, how will this be organized? Will states and nonstates become ever more embroiled in a battle of diplomatic ideas with conflict between the two protagonists more the norm than the exception?

Security has long been a responsibility and primary activity of sovereign states. Now the conventional heavy weaponry that only states could afford still projects power over territory, but there are few instances in modern history where a country can claim to have achieved its foreign policy goals simply through use of military power. Air forces and naval power of course remain an essential deterrent to a collapse of world order, but in terms of controlling an outcome on the ground where the survival of a state may be threatened they are less and less useful. As many analysts pointed out, air attacks by a coalition of states against the Islamic State (IS) in 2014 could not defeat it. Even the invention, use, and now intensive regulation of nuclear weapons have not readily enhanced the power of the great modern states to get their way in the world.

The world's security is now more analyzed in the wider context of stability and sustainability. States may not launch attacks on each other and seldom if ever declare war and wage conventional battles. But they do compete for resources, pollute the atmosphere, and seek out points of vulnerability in each other's capabilities to gain advantage. Those points of vulnerability are now more easily exploited because many of the new weapons such as cyber malware are developed and marketed to both governments and nongovernmental groups by nonstate actors. Drone manufacture and robotics, a vital new frontier for both military and civil technology, is being driven by private manufacturers. The technology is widespread and relatively cheap. A U.S. Government Accountability Office report in 2012 on unmanned aerial vehicles (UAVs)—or drones—stated that

> Currently, there are over 50 countries developing more than 900 different UAV systems. This growth is attributed to countries seeing the success of the United States with UAVs in Iraq and Afghanistan and deciding to invest resources into UAV development to compete economically and militarily in this emerging area.[9]

In late 2013, Iran claimed it had developed a drone with a range of 2,000 kilometers capable of delivering missiles to Israel. Drones are also comparatively cheap, have many civil uses, and are increasingly the weapons of choice for many human targets. A top-end Predator drone costs around $4 million, compared to a Stealth fighter with a price of hundreds of millions of dollars.

The Stuxnet virus that was introduced into the Iranian government's nuclear centrifuge computers combined government-developed exploits with some from the private sector. The pace of change, the need to develop antivirus and countermeasures often means that the small private sector developer is the best option to provide this technology. And of course the nonstate criminal gang or hackers for profit are also prized customers of these same developers.

State diplomacy may also be losing its traditional impact because success is not so easy to define. States that exert diplomatic influence do so for a variety of reasons, many with little to do with military prowess. Some are small and wealthy (Qatar); some have large populations and state-led commercial organizations (China, Russia); some like Norway engage in global initiatives not through military strength but use oil riches to fund constructive diplomacy. Megaphone diplomacy such as Venezuela's Hugo Chavez's against Western and U.S. influence in Latin America is augmented because of global interconnection. Diplomacy still reflects power, but power is increasingly fragmented. Joseph Nye sees diplomacy facing a three-dimensional puzzle in identifying power. First, military power remains, as it has long been, a reflection of those who direct strong militaries. Second, economic power now belongs to a range of countries, many of which, like Brazil and India, are not global military powers. And in the third dimension on global issues power is widely fragmented among many actors, both state and nonstate.[10]

A growing sense of confusion over what constitutes power has given an opening to the nonstate sector. International NGOs now have the capacity to choose their timing to raise the profiles of issues. They know that a 24/7 world media can give momentum to a report or film footage, and activate diverse action groups. News bulletins attract attention with phrases such as "Amnesty International reports," "International Crisis Group predicts," or "Save the Children warns." Such information is often portrayed as more authoritative and impartial than anything a state can provide. Such nonstate actors can also raise funds from donors who trust their governance and capacity to implement programs more than state actors.

Yet it is wrong to assume that states and nonstates are engaged in a zero-sum battle for diplomatic influence. Many aspects of the work of NGOs involve collaboration with governments. There is little that can be done on major global issues unless governments commit to the cause. NGOs need governments and generally are loath to usurp their roles. Many depend directly on governments for their operations. The World Bank estimates that over 15 percent of total states' overseas development assistance (ODA) is channeled through NGOs. Many, as we have seen, are officially accredited to the UN's ECOSOC. One example is the American Psychological Association (APA), which was granted special consultative status with the UN's ECOSOC in 2000. This gives the APA privileges to attend UN meetings, regional NGO conferences, and international congresses where it can submit written statements and make oral presentations to governments. In practical terms, such accreditation requires submitting quadrennial reports on the group's activities but also offers the possibility of collaboration in implementing UN agency programs—in APA's case, its relationship with UNICEF. And APA is also a member of the Conference of NGOs in Consultative Relationship with the United Nations (CONGO), which facilitates dialogue and cooperation between the UN and NGOs.

It is not just in the developed world that NGOs make an impact or raise funds. In Bangladesh, the economist Mohamed Yunus and the NGO BRAC have combined to make Bangladesh a pioneer in sources of microfinance. With a focus on reaching out to rural areas and the role of women, it has produced impressive results. Not only has the small loan bank provided seed corn capital to viable businesses, it has also worked to educate the population in family planning and birth control. The role of the government in this has been peripheral, but it has not stood in the way. Yunus's work won the Nobel Peace Prize, and his model has been transferred to other developing countries.

NGOs show the same diversity as states. Some are formed to influence policy through their writings and seminars and have little practical outreach. The Acronym Institute for Disarmament Diplomacy—comes into this category. Others are more concerned to raise funds to channel toward global issues. Private philanthropy is not new in international relations as the legacies of Peabody, Carnegie, Rockefeller, and now Gates testify. The Jimmy Fund in Boston does no cancer research itself but uses nonstate actors like the Boston Red Sox baseball team to promote its objectives. Other organizations are wider issue campaigners. Greenpeace is proud to be an actor and describes itself as "the largest independent direct-action environmental organization in the world."[11] Amid a jungle of overlapping environmental issues, most NGOs concentrate on one—such as The Rainforest Network Alliance. Multistakeholder organizations like the World Water Council grew out of the Rio Earth Summit to bring together NGOs, UN agencies, governments, and businesses to address freshwater issues. Another category of NGO is exploiting the Internet to campaign on any issue they feel needs global action. Such is Avaaz, a word meaning "voice" in several European, Middle Eastern, and Asian languages. Launched in 2007, it has the widest possible mission:

> to organize citizens of all nations to close the gap between the world we have and the world most people everywhere want. Avaaz empowers millions of people from all walks of life to take action on pressing global, regional and national issues, from corruption and poverty to conflict and climate change. Our model of internet organizing allows thousands of individual efforts, however small to be rapidly combined in a powerful collective force.[12]

The Global Fund to Fight AIDS, Tuberculosis and Malaria (The Global Fund) is an illustration of a major sustained collaboration between states and nonstates. We noted in Chapter 9 its diplomatic innovation and success in statistical terms. It is not an agency that concentrates on raising awareness or implementation of medical programs. But it had identified a new role that needed fulfilling. "The concept was simple: communities and countries already know what needs to be done. The role of the Global Fund is to provide the financial support needed to make it happen."[13] A public-private partnership, it has a secretariat based in Switzerland, and the Bill and Melinda Gates Foundation was one of the first private foundations among many individual donors to provide seed money for the project.

By mid-2012, The Global Fund had approved funding of $22.9 billion that supported more than 1,000 programs in 151 countries. It has financed the distribution of 270 million insecticide-treated nets to combat malaria, provided antituberculosis treatment for nine million people, and provided AIDS treatment for some 3.6 million people. In 2009, The Global Fund accounted for around 20 percent of international public funding for HIV, 65 percent for tuberculosis, and 65 percent for malaria.

While The Global Fund is not an implementing agency, it does monitor the programs it supports through a secretariat based in Geneva. Implementation is done by committees consisting of local stakeholder organizations in the program countries. Again, the model is mixed and includes governments, NGOs, the UN, and religious and private sector actors. This has kept the organization smaller than other international bureaucracies, and The Global Fund has set a high priority on efficient disbursement and eliminating corruption. It encourages whistle-blowers to raise issues of concern through its Office of the Inspector General.

Table 10.2 shows the origin of The Global Fund resources between 2001 and 2010 and highlights the significant contributions of major states, including the United States, United Kingdom, Germany, and France. The Gates Foundation has made a sustained commitment, and the business coalition of RED products is also a major donor. The popularity of a show like *American Idol* was exploited through direct dial-in calls. The model of partnership between state and nonstates also showed creative diplomacy. In return for strong U.S. support, President George W. Bush insisted on a new organizational framework with the UN agencies playing only a support role. As a result, UN bureaucracy is largely bypassed. Another innovation of diplomacy that Germany has pioneered is Debt2Health, part of The Global Fund that allows developing countries to free up debt and invest it in the programs. Germany has signed such agreements with Indonesia, Pakistan, Côte d'Ivoire, Egypt, and Ethiopia. One further impressive feature is that pledges have almost always matched contributions.

The Global Fund is a hybrid state-nonstate approach for fund-raising to address a global cause. It was designed as a customized diplomatic response to address a contemporary problem. In another area of diplomacy—agenda setting—former U.S. President Bill Clinton has offered a new avenue. Like Greenpeace and Avaaz, the Clinton Global Initiative (CGI) is an umbrella organization but one that

TABLE 10.2 **The Global Fund to Fight AIDS, Tuberculosis and Malaria Donors**

Countries	*2001–10 (in USD)*		*2011 (in USD)*
	Amount Pledged	*Amount Contributed*	*Amount Contributed*
Australia	171,027,145	171,027,145	42,150,000
Belgium	128,525,132	128,710,435	26,867,400
Brunei Darussalam	50,000	50,000	100,000
Canada	844,969,246	844,974,775	176,470,588
China	16,000,000	16,000,000	4,000,000
Denmark	209,934,225	209,934,225	30,723,315
European Commission	1,203,416,374	1,203,416,374	147,131,000
Finland	20,176,700	20,176,700	5,200,800
France	2,404,945,935	2,372,423,495	463,781,042
Germany	1,246,768,875	1,252,098,475	259,959,762
Greece	2,150,085	2,150,085	
Hungary	55,000	55,000	
Iceland	1,120,707	1,120,707	
India	11,000,000	10,000,000	
Ireland	194,119,527	187,862,209	
Italy	1,331,333,981	1,008,260,873	
Japan	1,287,415,754	1,287,816,091	114,229,085
Korea (Republic of)	13,000,000	13,000,000	2,000,000
Kuwait	3,000,000	2,000,000	500,000
Latvia	10,000	10,000	
Liechtenstein	771,660	771,660	105,369
Luxembourg	24,037,270	24,037,270	3,571,750
Malaysia	100,000	100,000	

(Continued)

TABLE 10.2 **(Continued)**

Monaco	132,000	132,000	
Namibia			250,000
Netherlands	637,476,225	619,784,017	88,406,540
New Zealand	2,840,840	2,840,840	
Nigeria	19,000,000	19,044,210	
Norway	352,247,049	352,247,049	75,700,227
Poland	150,000	150,000	
Portugal	15,500,000	15,533,866	
Romania	667,112	667,112	130,090
Russia	256,999,996	256,999,996	20,000,000
Rwanda			350,000
Saudi Arabia	28,000,000	28,000,000	
Singapore	1,000,000	1,000,000	
Slovenia	253,869	253,869	
South Africa	10,276,704	10,276,704	
Spain	828,447,085	687,359,548	
Generalitat de Catalunya/ Government of Catalonia	7,589,896	7,589,896	
Sweden	542,081,564	542,081,564	87,168,759
Switzerland	47,089,011	47,089,117	8,541,533
Thailand	8,000,000	8,000,000	1,000,000
Tunisia			2,000,000
United Kingdom	1,231,021,501	1,231,198,178	239,107,000
United States	5,455,952,435	5,455,952,435	992,419,312
Other Countries	3,967,635	3,444,990	
Total	18,562,620,539	18,045,640,913	2,791,863,571

Other			
Bill & Melinda Gates Foundation	650,000,000	650,000,000	150,000,000
Communitas Foundation	2,000,000	2,000,000	
Debt2Health			
Australia			
realized as restricted contribution from:			
Indonesia	1,849,875	1,849,875	3,965,437
Germany			
realized as restricted contribution from:			
Côte d'Ivoire	660,965	660,965	929,176
Egypt			4,807,118
Indonesia	21,538,187	21,538,187	7,169,194
Pakistan	13,067,454	13,067,454	7,137,089
UNITAID	38,691,956	38,691,956	
Anglo American plc.			1,000,000
Chevron Corporation	30,000,000	30,000,000	8,000,000
Comic Relief	3,294,240	3,294,240	
Exchange-Traded Funds (ETF)			9,208
(American) Idol Gives Back	16,600,000	16,600,000	
Gift From Africa			693,333
M·A·C AIDS Fund	875,000	875,000	500,000
(PRODUCT) RED™ and Partners: American Express, Apple, Bugaboo International, Converse, Dell + Windows, GAP, Giorgio Armani, Hallmark, Motorola Foundation, Motorola Inc. & Partners, Starbucks Coffee, Media Partners and (RED) Supporters		161,629,938	21,462,249
Takeda Pharmaceutical	1,083,265	1,083,265	1,152,361

(Continued)

TABLE 10.2 **(Continued)**

The United Nations Foundation and its donors:			
Hottokenai Campaign (G-CAP Coalition Japan)	250,000	250,000	
LMI (Lutheran Malaria Initiative)			338,944
United Methodist Church			1,590,000
Other UNF Donors	4,022,487	7,117,712	523,547
Other Donors		47,313	47,700
Total	783,933,429	948,705,906	209,325,357
Grand Total	19,346,553,968	18,994,346,819	3,001,188,928
Affordable Medicines Facility—Malaria (AMFm)			
Gates Foundation	19,365,000	19,365,000	
UNITAID	130,000,000	130,000,000	
United Kingdom	62,490,000	62,490,000	
AMFm—Total	211,855,000	211,855,000	

Source: The Global Fund to Fight AIDS, Tuberculosis and Malaria, "Pledges and Contributions," http://www.theglobalfund.org/en/partners/governments/.

focuses on enlisting wealthy and influential individuals from many countries, giving its high-profile meetings a distinctive theme, and exploiting the networking skills of its charismatic founder. The CGI acknowledges its link with conventional diplomacy by scheduling its annual meeting in New York to coincide with the UNGA. It is indeed global like the UN, but it makes no reliance on sovereign states for funding or participation. It brings together internationalists from politics, business, education, media, and NGOs. It is a hybrid between state and nonstate diplomacy and private sector brainstorming leading to projects effected within sovereign states. The theme of the 2012 meeting was "Designing for Impact," and Clinton described some of the initiatives that have borne fruit. Smartphone operators and banks had combined in Haiti to make money transfers and small loans feasible without a formal infrastructure. International business school students were combining their research and project skills to find solutions to global problems. And international hospitals were partnering with NGOs to provide health training in Africa.

The examples given are evidence that an agenda for new approaches for diplomacy exists outside state-to-state channels. Involvement of nonstate actors does not mean the issues themselves become less complex. The battle of ideas still exists, but in such a framework, it may be more about ideas than national prestige or entrenched positions. Issue campaigners tap into the global citizen, the business opportunist, and the nongovernmental organization survivor that needs a new cause. They can now craft solutions involving international actors to meet the needs of the moment. Many of these ad hoc alliances mean that solutions they promote will be transient depending on the continued cooperation of the stakeholders. Diverse project-specific partnerships are now common. One example is the Small-Scale Sustainable Infrastructure Development Fund, which provides villagers in India with modern lights, pressure cookers, and water purifiers. The partners have included the British Foreign Office, the Shell Foundation, the Blue Moon Fund, the Yahoo Employee Foundation, and Électricité de France.

The nonstate actor both opens new opportunities and absorbs scarce diplomatic resources because of the helpful and unhelpful attention they demand. The nonstate actor sees a world without state borders. In the words of Javad Zarif, the Iranian foreign minister talking to the BBC during the negotiations on the Iranian nuclear program, "Extremists know no boundaries; terrorists know no boundaries."[14] This suggests a key reason why a model of diplomacy based purely on states is limiting. The future crafting of solutions is likely to employ more variable geometry from governments, nonstate actors, businesses, and global citizens. Diplomacy now requires a range of skills that facilitate and manage the crossroads of interaction between the state and nonstate sector. Yet diplomacy as a whole has still to apply itself to promoting convergence between these new actors—what has been termed linking the dot.gov, dot.org, and dot.com sectors. How this variable geometry coalition might be developed is discussed further in the Chapter 11.

COMMON NEED: COMMON REFORM

The world's connectivity and increasingly borderless nature poses some common threats to states and nonstates. The state is wary of losing influence to others or compromising the security of its borders. Every nonstate actor is in some respects a rival with others who engage on similar issues. Al-Qaeda is wary of other jihadist groups, just as much as environmental lobbies need to watch the success of others. Thomas Rid has documented fissures in jihadism and how one of the most common ways terrorist groups dissolve is through internal strife.[15] Al-Qaeda rejected the rival IS, which had grown out of it in Iraq, as being too brutal. Likewise, commercial companies ebb and flow; some, like Kodak and Polaroid, disappear altogether. The world of internationalized business is fraught with struggles to fend off rivals or to find security in another corporate merger.

Both states and nonstates therefore share an anxiety about the future of diplomacy. Yet there is no forum where the modern clichés of reengineering or rebooting can be practiced. There is no Greenpeace for the cause of diplomacy. Global reform and innovation for diplomacy is missing from its own agenda. What passes as reform of diplomacy is essentially improving a state's efforts to achieve better results for its national interests. At its simplest, equip all diplomats with electronic tablets and that will improve their speed of delivery. Even though the processes of diplomacy have been impacted by the declining influence and resource of states and the nonstate sector has significant impacts on the handling global issues, diplomacy has yet to harness a reform lobby. Plenty of strategy papers and speeches at UNGA have addressed the inequities of permanent membership of the UN Security Council. But such institutional reform would still leave the activity of diplomacy itself largely unaffected and would not have any influence on the relationship between states and nonstate actors.

Diplomats admit that they now borrow ideas, organizational formats, and personnel from the nonstate sector. Innovators in health, business, and science come in and out of government service. A Nobel winning scientist, Steven Chu, served as the Secretary of Energy from 2009 to 2013 and was involved in discussing international energy policy as a diplomatic actor. David Miliband, a British politician and former Foreign Secretary, left politics to head a nonstate, nonprofit humanitarian agency in New York, the International Rescue Committee. Jim Yong Kim switched from a distinguished academic and NGO career to be president of the World Bank in 2012.

One area where both states and nonstates share an interest is education. The issue touches many global causes, is a key driver of economic development, constitutes a vast international business, and influences how extremists recruit and disrupt international relations. And education is an example in the modern world of the success of the nonstate sector in achieving results without the intervention of states. The digital age has seen vast advances in distance learning, international standards, and borderless education aids.

The virtual nonstate world is making some of its greatest advances in education. Take the example of one of the growing number of online learning programs. Students of the world can now be educated without state interventions. Udacity is one of many online community universities that is run as a business. It has enrolled 160,000 students from 190 countries. In 2012, it demonstrated its own interconnection capacity when its participants collectively fixed problems for a Pakistani girl who had access to her YouTube classes blocked by the Pakistani government after inflammatory anti-Islamic videos appeared. She received help in completing her classes from fellow students from Malaysia, Portugal, and the United Kingdom. Another educational pioneer, the Khan academy, offers courses free with the stated aim of a "world-class education for anyone anywhere."[16] In both formats—business and nonprofit educators—venture capitalists and students have achieved success and overcome barriers of bureaucracy and censorship of content. States also benefit from these initiatives by freeing up resources and having a better educated population. And Wikipedia is now a long-standing source of information for those who cannot access books or libraries.

If education is an example of cooperation bearing fruit for all types of actors, diplomacy faces many new dangerous and unforeseen challenges. The rise of the virtual—as opposed to the physical—world means game-changing elements for the operation of states and nonstates. They now exist in both worlds. This will be discussed further in Chapter 11.

Migration is a jolt to the operations of both states and nonstates. The boundaries of sovereign states are becoming more porous, and the identities of both state and nonstate actors are influenced not just by national characteristics and cultures but by globalization and migration flows. Migration is facilitated by better communications, better harmony between states, and economic opportunities. It is also the result of declining capacity of states to provide security to their populations and the rise of internal conflicts. Few families are now self-sufficient so once the state collapses, so does their capacity to survive. The UN Population Fund estimated that in 2010, some 214 million people—3 percent of the world's population—lived outside their country of origin. The magnitude and complexity of international migration make it an important force in development and a high-priority issue for both developing and developed countries. The fact that about half of all migrants are women, most of reproductive age, is another reason why the impact of population movements will grow. Migration often brings unexpected benefits to the receiving territory. Of the workforce that built the London Olympic facilities in 2012, 40 percent were self-employed immigrants from Romania.

Box 10-1 **#BringBackOurGirls**

In April 2014, over 200 girls were kidnapped in a boarding secondary school in Chibot, Nigeria. Their captors were the Islamist group Boko Haram, who said it would treat them as slaves as part of their "war booty."

The response was widespread horror from the world's media and growing frustration that weeks after the attack, the Nigerian army seemed incapable of staging a rescue mission.

Change.Org, an online petition site that earns revenues from major NGOs like Amnesty International, followed Twitter in using #BringBackOurGirls to accumulate one million signatures. This pressure on Nigeria and on leaders of major states resulted in contributions by states of equipment and expertise. YouTube videos were made, inter alia, by Michelle Obama and David Cameron. A former prime minister of the United Kingdom, Gordon Brown, and now UN Special Envoy for Education, backed the petition and traveled to Nigeria to deliver it.

(Continued)

(Continued)

The Bring Back Our Girls campaign shows another ad hoc diplomatic collaboration between the state and nonstate sector. Without the combination of media and online mobilization it is unlikely that none of this conventional diplomatic interaction would have happened.

Some argue that the forces at work will produce an "age of convergence." Jeffrey Sachs believes this is taking shape because "the measure of economic development, the methods, the institutions, the processes, the adaptation of advanced technologies, are becoming a worldwide phenomenon."[17] Sachs also argues that interconnection means the fate of states and nonstates are inextricably linked.

> The collapse of any single part of the world—even a place as isolated as Afghanistan—has implications for the entire world. Cooperation in an inter-connected world must therefore be comprehensive, something that our societies still do not appreciate or accept.[18]

Comprehensive means that the efforts of all matter.

States differ in their assessment of the role of nonstate actors in diplomacy. Not all states see they must accept a decline of influence. For some, the phenomenon of China's rise is a reminder that states can still control their own destiny. Others, like India and Russia, believe the state is strong and that nonstate actors have a subsidiary role. China's rise, despite criticism from many human rights and environmental groups, has won many admirers. Parag Khanna writes, "There is something to be said for a system that peacefully transitions more than one billion people from revolutionary communism to Confucian capitalism."[19] Yet China's success as a state does not necessarily suit everyone or reflect a trend that will encourage imitation. The educated young and those who have made money are showing an inclination to leave. One fifth of those sitting for the U.S. graduate exam for business school admission, the GMAT, are now Chinese.

Some states— over sixty by 2014—have embraced cooperation with the nonstate sector. They have committed themselves in the Open Government Partnership to work more closely with them in policy formation to promote "a shift in norms and culture to ensure genuine dialogue and collaboration between governments and civil society."[20] They themselves promise accountability and transparency in methods of government that will empower the nonstate sector. Yet many states have little inclination to systematize their links with the nonstate sector. This divergence in approach already causes international tensions. One illustration in 2013 was the arrest in Russia of twenty-six Greenpeace activists from seventeen different countries.

Some have argued that the size of the sovereign unit—in other words, the existing configuration of states is ill-conceived—is an impediment to diplomacy, and this flaw is itself a core element in the confusion and underachievement of diplomacy. Smaller units might make more sense in promoting better governance. A global citizen may identify with a global cause or religion but may have less patience and allegiance to a state entity. They argue that cultural and identity roots are local—tribal, religious, and regional. The success of Switzerland or Singapore suggests that smaller manageable units might make for a more stable international system. That is not the end of the debate because smaller governing units may not prevent the creation of a much larger diplomatic state actor. A modern federalist system like the United States where states retain many powers of governing has consciously nurtured traditions of patriotism in the wider entity. The singing of the "Star-Spangled Banner" or "God Bless America" is obligatory at most national sporting and cultural events.

The concept of multilateralism in diplomacy is important to both state and nonstate actors. Yet the universality and obligatory inclusiveness of diplomacy may be its downfall. Does the world need to tick all the boxes of every country and every region to secure a diplomatic outcome? In an overcrowded diplomatic arena of nearly 200 sovereign states and tens of thousands of globally operating NGOs, multilateralism may no longer be viable. Is the future of diplomacy, as Moisés Naím, a former editor of Foreign Policy, suggests, in minilateralism? If so, what mini groups should deal with tensions? How would diplomacy adapt to the exclusion of some sovereign parties? Do developments in today's world offer more flexible formulations than the mass inclusivity that lies at the heart of the UN? Will a more limited buy-in by countries promote a more effective way of dealing with contentious issues?

In the contemporary era, some of the answers to these questions can be facilitated by the communications revolution. We now move to a distinctive feature of the revolutionary nature of the modern diplomacy—the sweeping changes in communication and access to information and the effect they are having on diplomacy.

Case Study

Haiti and the Earthquake—State and Nonstate, the Republic of NGOs, the Alms Merchants

Haiti suffered a massive earthquake in January 2010. Over 225,000 people were killed and its capital city, Port-au-Prince, with over 3 million inhabitants, was devastated. Haiti had a long record of poor governance, foreign invasions, and little modern infrastructure. It had been a leader on major global issues of the nineteenth century—the first country to declare independence in the Caribbean and Latin America and the first to abolish slavery. More books were published from Haiti in the nineteenth century than from any other country in the Caribbean or

(Continued)

(Continued)

South America. Yet the twentieth century had been a disaster for Haiti's development—dictatorships, civil strife, and military and economic elites vying for power, both looting the country.

Haiti's latest catastrophe posed multiple simultaneous challenges to diplomacy and to the roles of states and nonstates. How could the relief and reconstruction be funded? At around $3 billion, the total government budget of Haiti was less than that of a small U.S. city. Of this, over 65 percent came from overseas assistance, loans, or from the Venezuelan-administered Petrocaribe oil fund. Would a response be organized effectively? What was there left of a government sector that could be used? What diplomatic interest did Haiti represent for the majority of the world? Could states with an antagonistic agenda like the United States and Cuba cooperate on an issue? And what role should the many competing NGOs play in a disaster relief operation where their donors would expect them to show results?

The story of Haiti's earthquake is still being written. But the insights Dr. Paul Farmer, a passionate nonstate actor who has become a semistate actor in his capacity as Deputy UN Special envoy for Haiti, are important lessons for cooperation between states and nonstates. Farmer's comments are also valuable because he had long experience in operating in Rwanda, another poor country with a tragic history. As one of the founders of the Boston-based health NGO Partners in Health, Farmer also had good contacts in U.S. government, the medical profession, and business. A close friend of Farmer's and cofounder of Partners in Health, Dr. Jim Yong Kim, moved from working in the health sector and the UN's World Health Organization to become president of the World Bank in 2012.

Since 1995, Haiti had had no army. It had endured external political intervention, the removal of the elected President Aristide and frequent elections, none of which seemed to have contributed to making a viable sovereign state. In 2009, half the school age children were not in school. Port-au-Prince, where over half the population lived, was dominated by steep hillsides with construction having largely been unregulated for decades. The NGOs had of course been present in Haiti for years—and their presence had been supplemented by UN agencies, Cuban doctors, and both UN and Organization of American States peacekeepers.

The key entity that was created to manage the complexities of the response to the earthquake was the Interim Haiti Recovery Commission (IHRC). This was conceived at a UN meeting on March 31, 2010, and approved by the Haitian government in April. It aimed to ensure the planning and implementation of the recovery efforts were Haitian-led; to involve and coordinate the donor, civil society, and private sector communities; and to promote Haiti's development goals. It committed itself to accountability and transparency for the Haitian people. In short, a model business plan for disaster relief.

The IHRC was co-chaired by the government of Haiti and the UN special envoy to Haiti. Its board of directors included voting members from Haiti's parliament, justice, labor, and business communities as well as the major donors—Brazil, Canada, Caribbean Community (CARICOM), the EU, France, Norway, Spain, United States, Venezuela, the Inter-American Development Bank, and the World Bank. There were also representatives from the Haitian diaspora, and Haitian and international civil society organizations. All major projects, those worth $10 million or more, had to be approved by the board.

The first official meeting of the commission's governing board took place in June 2010 in Port-au-Prince. This sounds orderly and logical, but the reality of Haiti was something very different. Twenty-eight of the twenty-nine Haitian federal ministry buildings had been destroyed by the earthquake and 40 percent of federal employees were injured. As Paul Farmer has described, there was plenty of goodwill offshore but what was needed was effective diplomacy, consensus building, and efficiency to produce an adequate response to the tragedy. Haiti was a three-hour flight from Boston and familiar to many key officials of UN agencies.

The response to the earthquake strained the workings of international diplomacy because the government of Haiti was incapable of coordinating it. The then Prime Minister Garry Conille resigned in February 2012 after just four months in office. The response from state and nonstate actors alike reflected a mosaic of efficiencies and motivations. There was no shortage of pledging of funds from a Washington conference of donors held in April 2010. But by the end of September 2010, less than 15 percent of all reconstruction pledges had arrived—$696 million compared to $10 billion in pledges. Humanitarian relief came from 140 countries, and fifty had contributed to reconstruction. In the 2004 Asian tsunami, the comparative figures for donor countries were eighty and twenty.

The UN attempted to bring order to their competing and overlapping agencies. The UN Humanitarian Coordinator, John Holmes, struggled to impose "lead clusters" on the agencies on the ground. The system of clusters should have been in working order. It had been established in 2005 along with a new emergency funding mechanism specifically designed to produce an efficient response. Yet in a leaked memo Holmes wrote in February 2010, he found the results unimpressive. "I am disappointed to find that despite my calls for the Global Cluster Lead Agencies to strengthen their cluster coordination capacity on the ground, very little progress has been made in this critical area."[21]

The United States deployed 22,000 military to restore order, and there were already over 9,000 UN peacekeepers, ninety-six of whom were killed in the earthquake. Yet two years after the earthquake, only 4,700 new houses had been built, while 520,000 people remained in squalid camps. Many more returned to wrecked homes rather than endure the camps' inhuman conditions. The NGOs had the money and were on the ground, but many acted as organizations bent on maintaining their funding and their own survival. The NGO personnel moved into Haiti in their thousands. Many had high housing allowances that drove up rents of those properties that were habitable. Haiti's prime minister claimed that 40 percent of aid money supported the foreigners handing it out. One local car dealer reported he had sold more than 250 Toyota Land Cruisers a month for some time, each costing over $60,000. An Irish aid worker commented, "You see traffic jams at Friday lunchtime of all the white NGO and UN four-wheel drives heading off early to the beaches for the weekend."[22]

(Continued)

(Continued)

In January 2012, the *New York Times* summarized the results of two years of relief efforts:

> The Interim Haiti Recovery Commission was one of Haiti's great hopes after the earthquake, a Haitian-led international partnership that would finally summon the money, will and organizational intelligence to build the country back better than before. But if you visit the commission's Web site today, on the eve of the second anniversary of the disaster, this is what you see: "Please kindly note that the mandate of the IHRC expired on October 21, 2011. Pending a decision of the Haitian Parliament regarding the future of the institution, a team is currently dealing with day-to-day business. The (re)submission of project proposals remains closed until further notice."[23]

By September 2012, a total of $2.79 billion in public sector pledges had been disbursed in Haiti since 2010 according to an analysis from the UN Office of the Special Envoy for Haiti. This represented a disbursement rate of 52.3 percent. Of a total of fifty-five pledge makers, only twenty-two disbursed 100 percent of their pledges for 2010 to 2011. The bulk of this funding, $1.94 billion, went to multilateral agencies, NGOs, and private contractors; $350 million went to direct budgetary support to Haiti's government; and $213 million in loans were made to Haiti's government.

All shapes and sizes of NGOs entered Haiti. Some like ATD Quart Monde had been working in the slums of Port-au-Prince for twenty-five years. The International Organization of Migration (IOM), which claims to be the "leading inter-governmental organization in the field of migration,"[24] was given the UN cluster lead on camp management. It became one of the many sources of often conflicting information on displaced persons and the conditions of the temporary camps. NGOs themselves recognized that the vast funding created a struggle between the nonstate actors for influence. The head of *Médecins Sans Frontières* in Haiti, Gaetan Drossart, said it was wrong for charities to raise more than they could spend. "Organizations want to be in front of the cameras in an emergency to attract attention since this gets the money. The humanitarian business is no different to any other business."[25] Drossart argued for limiting the numbers of groups allowed in to disaster zones given the chaos and poor coordination he witnessed in the earthquake's aftermath.

Bill Clinton, the UN special envoy, played the role of international coordinator and inspired many nonstate actors to come and help. Many college students were willing to volunteer for anything under the slogan "build back better." Clinton estimated that Haiti had the second highest number of NGOs per head in the world. And there were attempts at coordination. A logistical base—known as Log Base—was the center of the international recovery effort where aid agencies coordinated. Kathie Klarreich and Linda Polman, journalists of *The Nation*, reported on what happened at Log Base.

> There were more than seventy coordinating meetings each week among aid agencies and other interested parties—though not all interested parties. Few Haitians can cross from one side of the compound's walls to the other. To do so requires identification documents and an invitation from someone on the inside, two things very few Haitians have. And when they do, they find that most meetings are held in English, not Creole or even French. When a steering committee for NGO coordination was elected in July 2010 at Log Base, sixty international organizations cast their votes, but since there were no local NGOs present, no Haitians.[26]

And the contrast of the conditions in the Log Base to those being experienced by ordinary Haitians was stark.

> Here, it's a different world. Within the massive blue-and-white compound are revamped trailers, golf carts and more glistening public toilets than any other place in Haiti. . . . Flowers line the walkways, and machines blow a cool mist into an outdoor restaurant whose menu, on one random day, included sushi, jasmine rice, German potatoes, Brazilian cheese bread, halal shawarma and Häagen-Dazs ice cream. The American dollar, not the Haitian gourde, is the currency of choice.[27]

The NGOs agreed that funds were not arriving fast enough and progress was slow. Oxfam's director, Dame Barbara Stocking, urged donor nations to honor pledges for Haiti. Two years after the earthquake, Oxfam warned that reconstruction was moving ahead at a snail's pace and that 500,000 Haitians were still homeless. "Most Haitians do not have running water, a toilet or access to a doctor; cholera has claimed thousands of lives and remains a major threat to public health; and more than 70% of the workforce is under or unemployed."[28]

The second approach that both state and nonstate actors agreed on was that few funds should end up under the control of the Haitian government. Only 6 percent of bilateral aid for recovery projects, for example, was channeled through Haitian institutions. Less than 1 percent was given directly to the Haitian government for humanitarian aid. Cholera, widely believed to have originated from the UN Nepalese peacekeepers, exacerbated the problems of the displaced people. Again, the Haitian government was bypassed. UN figures showed that by August 2011, almost a year after cholera outbreak, only 12 percent of the tent camps equipped by NGOs had hand-washing stations. Of 12,000 latrines needed, only 38 percent were functional. There had of course been progress. UNICEF reported in 2012 that of the 4,000 schools destroyed or damaged, 653 had been repaired and 612 rebuilt. And Paul Farmer's Partners in Health insisted it worked closely with the Haitian Ministry of Health in its hospital building. Their hospital project at Mirebalais was intended to be a lasting benefit to the health sector and was designed specifically as a public hospital open to all.

(Continued)

(Continued)

One result of the general do-it-alone attitude of the NGOs and agencies was that their own priorities became the focus of their activities, rather than the preferences of Haitians and their governments. NGOs were pushing the construction of temporary homes not because survivors wanted them but because donors required visible signs of progress. One of these flagship communities was at Corail, about ten miles outside Port-au-Prince. Families arrived there with promises of clean water, medical care, education, and jobs in new garment factories. But the factories were not built, there were no hospitals, and the schools were poor. Those living there were charged twice the cost for water they paid in the camps.

A study by *The Guardian* in early 2013 found that from the total relief effort of around $9 billion about 94 percent of humanitarian funding went to the donors' own civilian and military entities, UN agencies, international NGOs, and private contractors.[29] They found few project evaluations and little published breakdown of who received the money donated by major governments. The caravan of the donor agencies and international appeals has long moved on.

Haiti and Rwanda

Paul Farmer of Partners in Health had also spent much time in another country that gave states a bad name—Rwanda. He has contrasted the fortunes of the two countries and drawn some conclusions. From the 1995 genocide, which happened in one of the world's poorest countries, a leader who served first in the Uganda army then in a Tutsi militia showed the capacity to revive Rwanda as a functioning state. Paul Kagame has proved that leaders can rebuild their countries with bold and firm direction. He launched a Vision 2020 program that gave priority to national economic and business development. By 2013, Rwanda's growth was one of the strongest in the world, foreign investment was flooding in, the service sector was booming, and corruption was low. According to the World Bank, the percentage of the Rwandan population living below the poverty line dropped from fifty-nine in 2001 to forty-five in 2011. And in 2012, the World Bank named Rwanda the eighth easiest place to start a business in the world. Transparency International ranked Rwanda the eighth least corrupt country in sub-Saharan Africa and the sixty-sixth in the world.

Rwanda has continued to receive substantial ODA and debt relief. Its results achieved meant that in 2010 the International Monetary Fund moved Rwanda to a Policy Support Instrument, which indicated that Rwanda would receive advice, not more loans. Rwanda joined the East African Community and is aligning its budget, trade, and immigration policies with its regional partners. It has also joined the Commonwealth and has a close economic relationship with China, despite being not rich in minerals. A state with few natural resources has proved that turnarounds are possible in governance and effective leadership will draw in the cooperation of nonstate actors like business. In Rwanda's case, the international actions of states and nonstates were incapable of preventing a man-made disaster in the 1990s. But international diplomacy and economic support have been shown to be available to help the state revive, and NGOs like Partners in Health have been able to contribute effectively to that process. Others like Human Rights Watch perform a useful nonstate function in holding states to common standards in areas where the UN, because of its sovereign state model, has largely proved ineffective. Rwanda may have impressed the financial and business community, but Transparency International and international media are now performing useful roles in ensuring that any excess of state power does not go unchallenged.

Conclusion

The story of Haiti, colored in tragedy, shows a diplomatic system without direction when a central government has abdicated its control or it has been negated. The earthquake was a scenario where there was a clear objective—the reconstruction of Haiti and providing relief to its people—and there was a lot of money donated very quickly. There were leaders and international agencies, all experienced in international diplomacy. In many respects, it was a perfect storm for nonstate diplomacy. Yet the results in terms of speed and efficiency of response, or a unifying of international project, were inadequate.

It proved impossible to dovetail the strengths and minimize the weaknesses of the state and nonstates involved. An ad hoc platform for cooperation was not up to the task. There was no model, no framework for synergy between the two. The result was that, despite the shared interests that were recognized on both sides, it was not possible to translate them into effective shared actions.

The UN was supposed to achieve this reconciliation of varied interests through its agencies and connections with NGOs. But the veneer of constructive multilateral diplomacy soon faded. Despite the hierarchy of control and preparation for diverse crises within the UN, it was unable to overcome overlapping bureaucracy and provide organizational focus. A charismatic non-Haitian leader, in the form of Bill Clinton, energized a response with his "Get Stuff Done" motto. But the task of ensuring a smooth coordinated state response was beyond him or the assorted 3,000 NGOs who were already in Haiti or joined this motley diplomatic response. Goodwill and good intentions are easily diverted when nonstate actors assume their delivery roles rather than concentrating on raising awareness and outreach.

The Haitian earthquake confirms that there is no substitute in diplomacy for a strong central government that is responsive to the needs of its people. Diplomacy seldom deals with ideal situations and must make the best of what it finds. The versatility of diplomacy is left groping for solutions when there is no unitary state. And, as always, diplomacy will try to learn the lesson for the next scenarios from the last. But these, by their nature, will never be exact repeats and will demand different responses.

SUGGESTIONS FOR FURTHER READING

1. Khanna, Parag. *How to Run the World: Charting a Course to the Next Renaissance.* New York: Random House, 2011.

2. Farmer, Paul. *Haiti: After the Earthquake.* New York: PublicAffairs, 2011.

3. Avant, Deborah D., Martha Finnemore, and Susan K. Sell, eds. *Who Governs the Globe?* New York: Cambridge University Press, 2010.

4. Clunan, Anne L., and Harold A. Trinkunas, eds. *Ungoverned Spaces: Alternatives to State Authority in an Era of Softened Sovereignty.* Stanford, CA: Stanford University Press, 2010.

chapter 11

The Continuing Information and Communication Revolution

Awaiting the Response of Diplomacy

One thing that is certain about the information and communication revolution (ICR) is that it has only just started. The International Telecommunications Union estimated that there were 545 million cell phone subscriptions in Africa in 2012, representing 63 percent of the population of the continent. This compared to only 12 million landlines that were in operation. In the first decade of the twenty-first century, Internet users in the world rose from 350 million to 2 billion. To call the information and communications age we live in a revolution is one of the understatements of history. And to compare the impact of the communication revolution that diplomacy faces today with what communications advances it has experienced over many centuries is again belittling its significance. In their book, Peter F. Cowhey and Jonathan D. Aronson describe the investment and construction of the infrastructure of the new information age as "the largest construction project in human history—dwarfing the money that built pyramids, and the Great Wall."[1]

THE ICR AND E-DIPLOMACY

The ICR has impacted virtually all aspects of diplomacy: obtaining and communicating information, setting an agenda, convening meetings, acting on information, seizing business opportunities, blocking the arguments of opponents, and negotiating diplomatic issues. It has also impacted the concept of national identity and sovereign states. Identities are now often cast to the wind of the Internet and data sharers. Physical borders are no barrier to theft. E-diplomacy has made great strides but is still in its infancy.

While these developments today seem indispensable to the lives states and nonstate actors lead, the commercial prospects of the uses of such technologies were long seen as uncertain. So what was to become the modern Internet and GPS depended on a government—that of the United States—playing the role of midwife of the revolution. The founding in 1958 of the Defense Department Advanced Research Projects Agency, commonly called DARPA, was a direct result of the rivalry between two sovereign states, the United States and the

Soviet Union. The launching of the Soviet Sputniks set alarm bells ringing in Washington. DARPA has since developed many of the mainstays of modern warfare—the cruise missile, unmanned drones, antiarmor weapons, the use of lasers in missile defense, and space-based defense techniques. U.S. government funding led to early investment in the Internet protocols as the key method of conveying data across computer network boundaries. In March 1982, the U.S. Department of Defense declared the TCP/IP protocols as the standard for all military computer networking and global positioning satellites, and they were first tested by DARPA for military use. So the greatest modern advances in creating stateless-based communications were themselves largely designed and developed by a state for its own use.

It is not only the speed and ease of communication internationally that has changed dramatically over the last half century. The cost has also plummeted. The explosion in use of smart phones and computers did not take off solely because of changes in technology, much of which had been available for years, but because the uses became affordable. With tumbling costs, the markets for all the products that have evolved from the ICR blossomed. And the pace at which all this happened explains the bottom-up architecture that has developed for global governance of communications. An ad hoc world and business coalition argued strongly for a world with minimal barriers. Access to vast new information does not of course imply new insights or depth of analysis. As Eric Schmidt and Jared Cohen have noted in *The New Digital Age*, "The strength of open, unregulated information-sharing platforms is their responsiveness, not their insight or depth."[2] The challenge to diplomacy is, therefore, to respond to a rapid technological revolution in the availability of communication and information. Both, as we have seen, are among its key activities.

One other complication for diplomacy is that several different forms of technology—telephone and wireless, broadcasting, data storage, and digital- and computer-based applications—have all been transforming themselves simultaneously. Many governments sought to control the development of new technologies such as railways and air travel by establishing national companies that would have large market share and would also allow governments to exert a degree of control. Now the interests of many governments, nonstate organizations, and individuals throughout the world converge. They depend on the use of the same satellites, cables, and common approaches to governance to make use of these cheap and, in some cases, virtually free technologies.

The ICR has reduced the cost of conventional diplomacy. Staff can be eliminated because diplomats now do their own word processing. Fewer people are needed to store and retrieve files, and diplomats can trace and disseminate material in a fraction of the time of old diplomacy. The cost of overseas phone calls now no longer embarrasses an embassy budget. The separation caused by distance in diplomacy has in many respects been reduced, and systems like Skype and videoconferencing are reducing the need for frequent travel. Nevertheless, more and cheaper does not always mean better and problem free. A priceless technology that transforms lives is not costless. The vulnerability of communications on which diplomacy has come to depend means that states share the risk of crippling attacks on their operations. Diplomacy has so far only started to consider the need for new diplomatic collaboration that, just as in the past, will attempt to ensure that states can protect their shared interests. Even if it caused little physical destruction or human casualties, an attack on satellites, data servers, and cables might in the worst case do as much collective damage to international and commercial relations as any world war or pandemic has in the past. Just as states are still grappling with the implications of the ICR for conventional diplomacy, the nonstate disrupters of diplomacy have only just begun to exploit vast new opportunities. By gaining access to hundreds of thousands of classified cables, Wikileaks served a warning that the new digital diplomacy has evolved too quickly for states to have absorbed the full implications. There is much catching up to do. And digital data, unlike paper files, cannot be shredded. Even if deleted, it can never truly be erased.

In a world where power is more diffused and interdependence is an economic and political reality, the global communications systems are a miracle, perhaps a fragile miracle, of adaptability, routers, and seamless innovation. Modularity is a key feature of the way the systems of voice, written, and data technologies have evolved. This breeds flexibility and vastly increased opportunities for innovation, reducing costs of entry, and accelerating the pace of development. Modularity, like a child's building blocks, produces standardized units or dimensions that make them easy to assemble and repair and flexible to use. Imagine if diplomacy were so simple to redesign!

Central to the new architecture of the ICR is the principle of interchangeability. Plug and play is not yet quite the rule, but the system is flexible and versatile with few proprietary barriers in hardware or software. The implementation by states of antitrust barriers has also been important to facilitate new entrants. The convergence of interests of all parties—suppliers and manufacturers on the one side and buyers and users of the products on the other—has been another happy coincidence. That said, the pace of change has meant that setting long-term guidelines seems foolhardy. The appetite of world consumers for new gadgets seems insatiable. To many, the old practices and rules of separation at the heart of diplomacy now have little application. As Larry Page, one of the founders of Google said in 2013, "Law can't be right if it's 50 years old—like it's before the Internet."[3]

Though much of the governance of the ICR appears to have evolved in the twenty-first century, a key date was 1984 when the United States began to break up the monopoly of the telephone company AT&T. From that time on, in the world's largest market, telecommunication development would be distinct from computer hardware and software. Indeed, for many years voice telephony outpaced the transmission of data for commercial use and information. But the break-up of the voice carrier monopolies throughout the world and the insistence of free use of the Internet paved the way for a system and business model that is transforming the way we communicate, receive, and store information and watch multimedia.

The following summary divides the implications of the ICR for diplomacy into two broad areas. The first category identifies what advanced national diplomatic systems can gain from the technology. The second looks at the wider implications of the ICR for diplomacy as a public good.

State-Owned Diplomacy

1. All states recognize that the benefits of the ICR are greatly diminished if the globality of the revolution is compromised. Sovereign states are faced, therefore, with a new global norm which gives some predictability to diplomacy. Yet states still control the servers and infrastructure and can influence access and monitor usage within their territories. In some respects the ICR has given states tools to strengthen their sovereignty. But interconnection across borders soon alerts the global consumer to what controls are being imposed. There is now a world ICR community that demands the products and services that others have.

2. The ICR puts out material that is instantaneous and free. It offers an opportunity for diplomats to gain a wider audience for their activities. And the technology also offers a mechanism for quick feedback.

3. The ICR has massive potential for consular work, particularly in the protection of nationals. Consular officials are now—and are required to be—always available. They must locate nationals in trouble and respond quickly to emergencies. They regularly face social media comment and photo evidence of their competence or otherwise. The U.S. State Department has used Twitter feeds to give newly created emergency numbers to U.S. citizens.

4. The technology offers new options to diplomacy to defuse crises. In 2010, after suspicions that crimes in Melbourne against Indian students were racially motivated, the number of university applications from India fell by half, cutting a big source of income for Australia. In 2012, when two Chinese students were attacked, Kevin Rudd, Australia's former foreign minister, went on Sina Weibo (the Chinese equivalent of Twitter) promising to investigate the matter—a small victory for diplomacy.

5. Digital sources of information prepare diplomats for developments that may require a response from governments. Diplomats can access Twitter feeds and social media traffic in all languages. This of course also amplifies the power of disrupters. The ICR gives everyone an outlet. Equally, diplomats no longer have to read the press or meet locals to gain a readout of current concerns and threats to their state's interests. Information on unrest can be received instantaneously, as well as the reaction to government measures. Diplomacy has never had such real-time information before. That adds to its tasks and requires a speedier response. Unlike in other professions, the ICR will not make many diplomats redundant.

6. It is now possible to create maps of online influencers by subject area, which allow diplomats on the ground to see who is driving discussion on specific issues and how they should be reacting. Diplomats can target their contacts more quickly and more systematically.

7. Specific methods of evolving new e-diplomacy are exaggerating the difference in skill level between the most developed countries and others. Those more poorly resourced are slipping further behind the best.

8. Administrative efficiency and internal management of information—such as digitalization of records, data, search, and other facilities—greatly enhances the capability of the central institutions of diplomacy—the ministries and missions—to coordinate receive feedback and brainstorm for ideas throughout their staff. Corridor is one digital forum developed internally in the U.S. State Department as an e-diplomacy hub.

9. Digital diplomacy also means that copying and stealing confidential information is far less challenging than in other eras. The disgruntled member of staff now can inflict devastating damage on the system of reporting and trust between the sending and the receiving state. Diplomacy collectively faces a massive new vulnerability based on the ICR. Control of information on a strict need-to-know basis is now more important than ever.

10. The ability to form groups serves multiple functions for diplomacy. Some are administrative to improve efficiency and are a feature of every office. Managers post meeting minutes, make action points for the week, and invite staff to report back to the group on their activities. They enable searches for colleagues with specific skill sets (e.g., language or science) who can then share knowledge and information, involving staff throughout the world. In old diplomacy, this would have taken days or weeks.

11. Innovative ideas in diplomacy tap into the expertise and enthusiasm of staff. It is possible to trawl all staff for new ideas to solve problems. Diplomatic systems are now in this real sense virtual because physical location in the world is no longer a barrier to contributing ideas. To encourage this, U.S. Secretary of State Hillary Clinton provided $2 million annually for a fund that rewarded innovation from staff. One idea that received an award from the fund was an air quality app to provide the U.S. community in Guangzhou with information on the real levels of air pollution in China.

12. States are obliged to make decisions on the ICR that highlight their national policies on information and freedom of expression. Different national laws on information, blasphemy, and antihate speech must now be reconciled. Controls imposed are noticed by foreign visitors and resident diplomats. Censorship is forced into the open and can no longer hide behind the printed page of a government-run newspaper. China's official Internet laws "prohibit the spread of information that contains contents subverting state power, undermining national

unity."[4] Internet-related international incidents now surface regularly in diplomatic problems. When the *New York Times* alleged the family of the then Prime Minister Wen Jiabao had become billionaires, their website was shut down. YouTube was blocked in Turkey for two years after the company refused to take down videos that criticized the country's founder. To control the ICR more widely, Iran is promoting an approved *halal* Internet. And Iran has launched its own version of YouTube—Mehr. In 2013, Vietnam enacted laws that prohibited the use of social media sites for disseminating political views. In response to the reports of U.S. and UK surveillance operations of Internet communications, Brazil, Russia, India, China, and South Africa announced they were considering installing their own Internet cable that would cut out U.S. server centers.

Diplomacy as a Public Good

The ICR is stimulating the following wider effects on diplomacy:

1. The ICR is seen by some countries as a threat to their cultures and religions. States may fear the loosening of values and their own social and economic cohesion. The West regards itself as having the most powerful communicable messages, but the emerging powers also wish to use the ICR for international outreach. The head of the Chinese government's Xinhua news agency, Li Congjun, wrote in China's People's Daily in 2013:

> Some hostile Western forces and media do not want to see a prospering socialist China. . . . They play up the "China threat theory" and the "China collapse theory," creating rumors to attack and vilify our country and party which harms our interests and national image. Overall, global opinions are still dominated by Western media outlets, and China's capacity to make its own voice heard fails to match its international standing.[5]

2. Technology will be increasingly be a cat and mouse game between those trying to evade national controls and those favoring repression. The advances will be countered by new restrictions, but business and public opinion will require constant upgrades of products and services. It is uncertain who will be the victors in this struggle.

3. The Internet may become fragmented in the world, with the former seamless access and identical technological formats no longer supported by major state actors. Such fragmentation will create new tensions, which will add to diplomacy's workload.

4. The global whistle-blower is taking on a new diplomatic importance. The ICR technology gives an individual an instant national and global audience. In Russia, Alexei Navalny started as a conventional politician but came to prominence through his use of blogs to expose corruption and organize protests.

5. There is evidence that instantaneous and free communication will not necessarily broaden international minds and promote convergence on the complex issues of diplomacy. On the contrary, it may be producing a narcissistic generation. The young who grow up in the post-Internet age are a generation weaned on new opportunities for selfies and changes of status. David McCullough, an English teacher at Wellesley High School in Massachusetts, achieved sudden fame in 2012 with his commencement speech. He told graduating students, "You're not special" nine times, and advised them to "climb [the mountain] so you can see the world: not so the world can see you."[6] According to Pew Research, in 2013 U.S. teenagers texted on average eighty-eight times a day. They are exposed daily to peer pressure on social media and seek instant gratification. The laborious process of building diplomatic progress may not interest them.

6. The ICR means that online surfing is easier than riding on waves in Hawaii and online dating means you don't need to meet at social gatherings. Equally, the ICR shows the world as accessible and travel as attainable. Curiosity is stimulated by clicks, and cross-cultural communication is a normal part of life. Again, no conclusions are possible, but diplomacy will not be unaffected.

7. There is a new, vast treasure trove of digital data available to states. Edward Snowden knew about data collection after eight years working in the CIA and NSA, but he decided to highlight for all what was well known to states and diplomats. Access to data is useful for diplomacy because it is now available in intimate detail because of the impact of the ICR. And the surveillance methods so far seem inevitably to involve collecting haystacks in the search of the proverbial needle. This vacuuming of information has created a new battleground between states and the nonstates who operate the platforms and websites where the data are obtained. Global users of digital devices feel they must communicate so diplomacy wants to know. Transnational conspiracies mean new elements of distrust have been created that undermine diplomacy.

8. Internet freedom seems likely to become a basic political and human right. Will repressive actions over the ICR stimulate a new class of refugees and new waves of migration? Will we see Internet asylum seekers?

9. The ICR has transformed the possibilities of public diplomacy. It has become more chaotic, massively crowded, but sometimes the new diplomatic virtuosity is exciting to see. Nevertheless, much of the often expensive wizardry now being applied will simply cancel out efforts of others. Every state and nonstate actor must be in the game.

10. The ICR has given the potential to everyone to influence diplomacy. We can all be activists on an issue. This may be undermining the concept of leadership. Do we all think we can do better than the politicians and the diplomats? There were no obvious leaders or indeed organizations behind the Occupy movement in 2011, the Turkish protests of 2013, or the anti-World

Cup movement in Brazil in 2014. Does the world now disrespect everyone, including the diplomats?

11. There are new nonstate actors that see the ICR as a major global issue like climate change or terrorism. The Electronic Frontier Foundation and others are trying to preserve the free environment of the ICR. They see Internet freedom as a new addition to the four freedoms of twentieth-century fame. Diplomacy is facing a new global issue with powerful international lobbyists.

12. The ICR is generating gigabyte profits, and the creation of new fortunes is, just as in the past, leading to big ideas and philanthropy to give back to the world. A group like Random Hacks of Kindness has partnered Microsoft, Yahoo, Google, NASA, and the World Bank with volunteer software developers to produce innovative open-source response mechanisms to disaster and crisis management.

INTERNATIONAL CHATTER

Dedicated platforms for international chatter are new to diplomacy. Social media are the newest arrival on the technology scene and for obvious reasons break down geographical and social barriers. The numerous platforms have opened up information that was previously inaccessible to a conventional diplomatic machine and enable international groups and individuals to communicate without use of an official interlocutor.

Experts in social media are at a premium in any organization and not least in diplomacy. No one knows the full potential or limits of social media. Obsolescence haunts the technology driver, and diplomatic systems are aware of the risks of investing in yesterday's fad. Netscape, Myspace, and others litter the cybergraveyard, and countless ambassadorial blogs that suggest diplomatic innovation still yearn for their first "like."

Yet the term *e-diplomacy* is already an active and well-resourced part of the cyberrevolution. Each bureau in the State Department now has an officer spending at least some time on work related to e-diplomacy, creating content in the form of blogs, Twitter or Facebook posts, videos, or pictures. Ministries and diplomats can now also report on their activities instantaneously so that press conferences may become stylized and negotiations can easily be influenced by judicious leaks of information rather than waiting for prime time TV or the morning newspapers. Hackers are now increasingly adept at creating false tweets and image-damaging posts that also demand a response. E-diplomacy is a new battleground where diplomats compete but also cooperate. The coming together to smooth edges can still work because the challenges and disruptions are common threats.

THE ICR AND A SHRINKING WORLD

We saw in Chapter 10 that the ICR has not only opened access to global learning materials, it has eased admission processes in education and offered new options. International education has also become big business with countries competing for the market of international students, the design of educational institutions, and materials. Diplomacy has and will continue to play a significant role in this process. Organisation for Economic Co-operation and Development (OECD) figures showed there were three and a half million international students in 2009, a fivefold increase since 1975 (see Figure 11.1). In 2012, there were over 800,000 international students in the United States alone, the world's biggest market, a 32 percent increase in the past decade. They spent $21 billion on tuition, fees, housing, and living expenses. Chinese students made up 22 percent of all international students in the United States followed by those from India, South Korea, and Canada.

If there is a benefit to diplomacy of a global baseline of information, then the creation of Wikipedia is a sign of progress, unthinkable without the ICR. The idea of a free source of reference, available throughout the world, was breathtakingly ambitious. And like other global activities, a united nations of knowledge shows bigotry, pedantry, and disputes over facts. Significantly, Wikipedia has developed an online dispute procedure, recognizes vandalism, and allows different national regulations. The project has proved the possibility

Figure 11.1 **International Student Numbers**

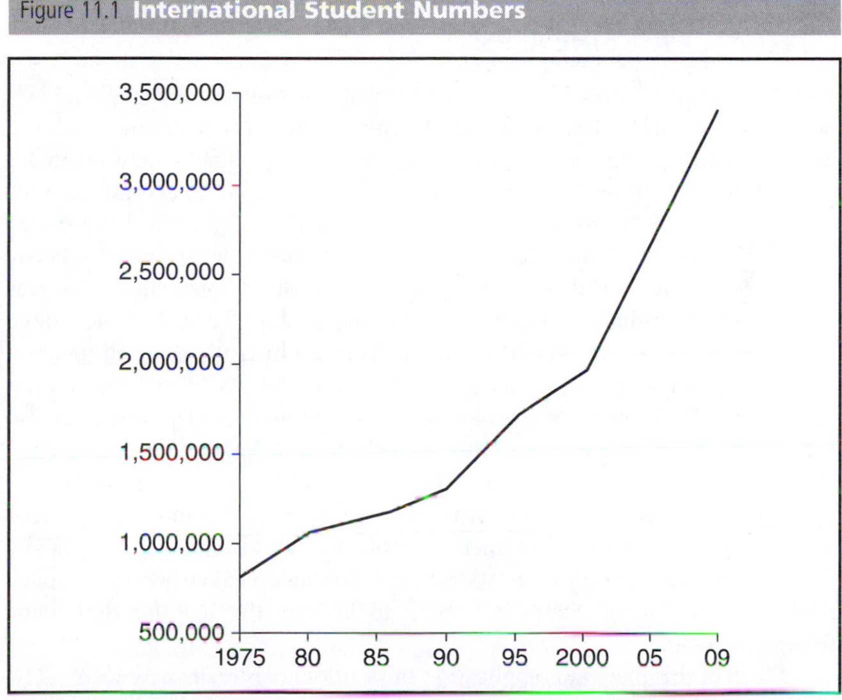

Source: OECD, *Education at a Glance*, 2011, http://www.oecd.org/education/skills-beyond-school/48631079.pdf, p. 320.

of a global community of knowledge run by volunteers. It has grown despite the flaws and inaccuracies, like the world. Students throughout the world have been warned that Wikipedia can damage their grades and health, but it works as an early baseline example of ICR interaction.

The ICR has also enabled inhabitants of the world to be more curious about their fellow inhabitants. The World Tourism Organization, a UN-affiliated group based in Madrid, defines tourism as the activities of people who travel outside their usual environment for less than a full year for leisure, business, and other purposes. The number of international tourists grew twenty-eight times between 1950 and 2000, and by 2011 there were 982 million tourists—nearly one-sixth of the world. Reservations, searching, access to photos and videos, ease of transfer of funds, and security checks for travel have all been revolutionized by the ICR. It all contributes to a massively increased diplomatic workload but also to a sharing of experiences. A survey by Isitour found that 26 percent of people in the United States used a mobile device to research a tourist attraction before they visit it. So the world is using the ICR not only for talking, texting, exercising its thumbs, and stretching a tablet screen. People are moving physically around the globe more than in any other era. But beyond these general trends, what specific responses have diplomatic planners made to the opportunities and threats involved in the ICR?

DIPLOMACY AND THE APPS

The ICR has given broadband power to transformational diplomacy. The U.S. State Department has developed with alacrity an array of ICR-stimulated aids to diplomacy that exploit the boundary-free technology that is now taken for granted. Some of them enter new ground for diplomatic interventions. One device is a mobile mesh network that can be carried around in a suitcase to allow activists to continue to communicate even when a government's security apparatus tries to shut down the Internet. It also funds projects by overseas NGOs in the techniques of news production in the digital age. And the United States has developed an app that allows activists to instantly erase all the contacts and messages on their phone if they are arrested. As Fergus Hanson has described in "E-Diplomacy: Revolution @State,"[7] the State Department is also using Tech Camps, Tech@State, and Virtual Student Foreign Service to reach out to civil society overseas. An Office of Verification and Transparency Technologies is setting up projects to encourage citizens to monitor activities and report movements of armaments, suspicious activity on weapons of mass destruction, human rights violations, and obstructions on access to social media. So the United States is hoping to harness the ICR for diplomatic whistle-blowing.

Much of this ingenious application of technology is really new-tech public diplomacy. U.S.-sponsored apps or convening of groups of young people to become tech savvy differs little from broadcasts of Voice of America or the State Department Arabic broadcasting services Alhurra and Radio Sawa. The

United States is applying its technology advances to further its national interests. The tech sector in the United States remains a unique asset that no diplomatic system can rival. All states recognize that diplomatic systems are now engaged in an ICR race and that diplomacy's traditional competition for influence is now moving to a new arena.

The United States is not alone. All major governments—China, Russia, and India—now have Twitter feeds on all their channels of information output to supplement their public diplomacy. Iran has not used its halal system to hermetically seal off Iran's websites from the outside world; rather, it has employed blocking measures such as very slow Internet speeds to discourage access to foreign websites. The restrictive actions of the authorities, however, do not just upset opposition activists. Cuba, for example, faces a current challenge as it seeks to modernize a state-owned economy with new foreign investment and a small private sector now approved for self-employment. The Cuban government has realized that Cuban Internet and censorship controls impact businesses' ability to interact with clients and the access of university students to sources of information. So the ICR is complicating the strategies of states designed to shackle its impact.

Communication and social media spending is a recognition that public diplomacy can potentially reach a borderless audience. Soft power now potentially has limitless new apps. In announcing its 2011 Rankings for Soft Power, the independent Institute for Government in the United Kingdom noted,

> International politics are undergoing a fundamental shift, driven by power diffusion, technological advances, networks, and an empowered global public. . . . Addressing the world's major foreign policy challenges . . . will require soft power approaches. Driving international affairs in the 21st century will rest on shaping narratives, setting international norms, mobilizing trans-national networks, and winning the battle for global public opinion.[8]

OH—AND WHAT ABOUT RADIO AND TELEVISION?

Television was the last big thing in communications. Indeed, *broadcasting* and *wireless* are very old words in the English language. The protocols developed for early broadcasting suited national states to perfection. The transmission governance for radio and TV was designed in every detail to follow the needs of the sovereign state. In some respects, the technological advances were similar to those of the twenty-first century ICR. Radio development originated from private citizens experimenting and recognizing a commercial opportunity. Radio manufacturers were indeed those who launched the fledgling broadcasting groups such as the Radio Corporation of America and the British Broadcasting Corporation. Governance models have since diverged, and the debate rages continuously over how far a government should regulate content and enter the political debate. The selection of ownership and funding models—commercial or taxpayer—determined how the organizations were managed and controlled. One lesson of radio and television for diplomacy is that countries imitate each other. Every country has them, and world standards in news presentation and graphics and some program content have converged. Sports, music, and entertainment, particularly game and reality TV shows, are now sold universally, vastly increasing revenues and offering new—sometimes indirect—public diplomacy opportunities.

In developing the governance of radio and TV, the state assumed its useful functions of consulting stakeholders, imposing order, and protecting nationally controlled territory, which in this case concerned ensuring radio and broadcasting frequencies were not overloaded. Regulation was obviously required, and antennas were needed to receive the signals. A pioneering international treaty like the UN Law of the Sea Convention expressly prohibited unauthorized broadcasting, by which it meant "the transmission of sound radio or television broadcasts from a ship or installation on the high seas intended for reception by the general public contrary to international regulations."[9] The advent of cable TV, satellite, and the Internet has in different but distinct ways eroded the powers of control of the sovereign state to regulate broadcasting.

The web has become a new battleground among international broadcasters vying to improve their nations' standing. Modern international broadcasting is a mainstay of public diplomacy. Major countries now have services operating in many languages. We have already mentioned the burgeoning roles of Al Jazeera, Russia Today (RT), and Iranian Press TV. Table 11.1, created by Aziz Douia of the University of Ontario, shows the major broadcasters from non-Arabic countries broadcasting in the Middle East at the time of the Arab Spring in 2011.

The direction of these technologies is unmistakable. Broadcasting is now being taken out of its national compartment. The computing power of modern wireless devices is such that receipt of live TV signals will soon become commonplace. Domestic control of broadcast media is fragmenting, and increasingly those who watch news do not do so on television sets at fixed times. A Pew survey from 2012 in the United States showed that only 34 percent of those younger than thirty said they watched TV news the day before; this is compared to 2006 when 49 percent of this group were TV watchers.

The high bandwidth that promises to be offered will enable a vast range of new services to be offered together with security and filtering. So governments will still have the capacity to control access. But equally, if they drive users off traceable systems, they lose access to highly valuable information that is directly relevant to managing security. States that have carefully crafted laws over what can be broadcast now have to explain why broadcast content is not freely available compared to other countries. Commercially as well, there is pressure on governments to give flexible access. Online broadcasters like Netflix of course offer enormous advertising opportunities, and they are all generating vast hauls of commercially relevant information. Honing and intruding into privacy over the Internet through AdSense and other programs has exposed international spending habits as never before.

TABLE 11.1 **International Broadcasters and Their Homepages**

Country	*Broadcaster*	*English website*	*Arabic website*
USA	Radio Sawa	http://www.radiosawa.com/ english.a spx	http://www.raqdiosawa.com/
United Kingdom	British Broadcasting Corporation (BBC)	http://www.bbc.co.uk	http://news.bbc.co.uk/hi/ara-bic/news/
Germany	Deutsche Welle	http://www.dw.world.de/ dw/0.2142.266.00.html	http://www.dw.word.de/ dw/0.2142.613.00.html
France	Radio Monte Carlo	http://www/rmc.mo.com/ar/ index. asp?PopUpLang=yes&PageUrl	http://www.rmc.mo.com/ar/ index. asp?PopUpLang=yes&PageUrl
Sweden	Radio Sweden. SR International	http://www.sr.se/international/ index.stm	http://www.sr.se/egi.bin/ International/programsidor/ index.asp?ProgramID=2494
Japan	NHK-Japan Broadcasting Corporation	http://www.nhk.or.jp/english/ index.html	http://www.nhk.or.jp/arabic. index.html
Canada	Radio Canada International	http://www.reinet.ca/rei/en/ index.shtml	http://www.reinet.ca/rei/ar
China	China International Broadcasting	http://en.chinabroadcast.en/	http://ar.chinabroadcast.en/
Russia	Voice of Russia	http://www.vor.ru/world.html	http://www.vor.ru/arabic
South Korea	KBS World Radio	http://world.kbs.co.kr/english/	http://rki.kbs.co.kr/arabic/ index.html

Source: Aziz Douai, "The Age of Web Diplomacy: An Exploration of International Broadcasting Online," First Monday, http://firstmonday.org/ojs/index.php/fm/article/view/3247/2768.

GLOBAL GOVERNANCE OF THE ICR

The future governance of new technologies generated by the ICR is a common issue facing all diplomatic systems. The advantages for diplomacy are clear—low costs of communication, crowd sourcing, and information gathering. But the risks and vulnerability posed for diplomacy are also far greater than the other global infrastructures that have been created such as global regimes covering air traffic control or maritime transportation rules.

Recognition of the effects of creating a practically and virtually smaller globe is not new. Adam Smith believed that the wealth of nations was interlinked. The belief that interconnection, knowledge, and cutting distances between different parts of the world is beneficial was fundamental to his argument that international well-being did not depend on one country's efforts. "By uniting, in some measure, the most distant parts of the world, by enabling them to relieve another's wants, to increase one another's enjoyments, and to encourage one another's industry, their general tendency would seem to be beneficial."[10]

Many of the forces of globalization were driven by private decisions rather than governments. The English Muscovy Company engaged Henry Hudson to explore northern trading routes, and the exploration of India and Asia owed much to pressure from spice merchants. Migration to the New World was pioneered by religious groups escaping intolerance. Private investment by railway companies and the industrial revolution transformed the lives of ordinary citizens and posed new challenges to diplomacy. Private sector inventions and technology applications have greatly enhanced the destructive power of war. Yet the ICR, also largely private sector driven, goes beyond any of these developments in its implications for governance. Without any center of gravity set by governments, business, or nonstate actors, the roles of each in the ICR face turbulent times.

Communication has, however, had international governance for well over a century. Since its foundation in 1865, the International Telecommunications Union (ITU) has supervised a system of international communications originally based on a small group of monopolistic telecommunications companies, each of which was supervised and championed by a sovereign state. The ITU administers the shared global use of the radio spectrum and promotes international cooperation in assigning satellite orbits. It also works to improve telecommunication infrastructure in the developing world and to harmonize global technical standards.

As we have seen, the 1980s and 1990s were a period of growing fragmentation of technologies and privatization of state telecommunication monopolies. Deadlock at the ITU over the reform of standards led to a rethink of governance methods—effectively a diplomatic revolution. The technical standards of wireless technologies evolved rapidly with 2G, 3G, and 4G following in quick succession, all producing such rapid improvements that governance could not catch up. Governments were dazzled by the business opportunities in selling off franchises and bandwidths. Global customers lapped up small gadgets, low-cost pieces of sophistication, which enabled them to spend less time in libraries, mailing letters, visiting stores, parking cars, or having face-to-face meetings. And interaction in a virtual world is spawning many new activities, most of which will have consequences for diplomacy. Some such as cyberbullying seem easy to combat by going offline. But the off key is no longer an option for many and, in any case, the damage may have been done.

The main growth of the Internet happened after the wireless revolution, and it required a new domain of governance simply to function. It could not wait for diplomatic rule drafters to assuage their sensitivities. As we have seen, Internet development was also driven by U.S. defense expenditure. But it was the U.S. private sector that recognized the new commercial opportunities of the medium that seemed to appear round every corner. Their proactivity led to new non-governmental arrangements for setting standards, the Internet Corporation for Assigned Names and Numbers (ICANN) and the Internet Engineering Task Force (IETF). These groups of experts assumed the task of Internet diplomacy and its agenda setting, and by the nature of their professions, they were brilliant networkers. Those who understood the technologies created something that worked, was virtually free, and seemed to require minimal government control. With this model of governance the ICR was de facto slipping away from the ITU.

As the ICR wrung its collective hands, the World Trade Organization (WTO) and its models, much more recent in creation, offered a way forward. In the WTO's Information Technology Agreement of 1996, the major trading countries simultaneously liberalized their tariffs on many new forms of network and computing services. This agreement was signed by fifty-two nations and marked a significant diplomatic shift away from the ITU tradition of universal consensus toward the WTO model of dispute settlement.

The Internet was also advancing at a pace far beyond the capacity of diplomacy to regulate. As broadband width expanded it offered vast scope for expanded applications, such as the use of video. The basis for the functioning of the Internet was set by the IETF group of experts and the IETF guidelines ensured that every computer using the Internet employed a unique protocol. Central to this was the TCP/IP protocol, which identifies a computer by its IP address.

All this was well established before the United States government gave the Internet much political attention. And the IETF has now morphed into a hybrid organism—part diplomatic, part expert. Many of the internal negotiating processes familiar to full-time diplomats have played their part in promoting consensus in the IETF. The second partner in the governance of the Internet is ICANN. This has provided the leadership and organization on the critical issue of domain names and top level domains (TLDs). These include the familiar suffixes like .edu, .com, .org, and all two letter country codes like .uk and .cn. The TLDs govern how IP addresses are organized on the Internet. An entry-free system for computer servers has been established, but the domain rules must be followed to make it workable. ICANN, like the IETF, now includes non-U.S. experts but still reports on its activities to and requires approval for changes from the U.S. Department of Commerce. Global governance has thus been achieved through de facto workability. The vast array of international stakeholders in software, hardware, commercial applications, data storage, and video and music streaming have made it impossible so far for sovereign of states to challenge a unique diplomatic achievement.

The implications for global governance of the creation of borderless virtual empires like Facebook, Twitter, Google, and Amazon are not yet clear. Apple, one of the most innovative manufacturers of the devices world consumers want, was in 2013 the most valuable company in the world, overtaking the big beasts of the oil jungle. But these companies themselves are already using the wealth they have generated to move in new directions. Google is just one example. The company was registered as a name in 1996, the same year as the crucial WTO agreement on information technology. By 2012, it had become the world's seventh-largest company in capitalization, employing over 53,000 people, significantly smaller number than other global giants. Google is developing driverless cars, artificial intelligence devices, and has its own think tank—Google Ideas. Its ability to access or partner with entities throughout the world has created a diplomatic actor that is hard to ignore in any global discussions. Its collection of raw data of what is going on in the world alone ensures this.

So far, so good. Governments, through combined pressure from innovation, commercial market opportunities, and global interconnection have been led to accept crucial elements of modern interaction as a de facto system of governance. Such expert-led diplomacy is not new—it has figured in international discussion on many issues such as disarmament, nutrition, development agendas, and climate change. But the participation of enthusiastic experts in the ICR turbo charges the ease of producing shared results. The involvement of multiple talented parties who share many common aspirations for the evolution of the ICR has given the process of diplomacy a priceless asset.

Ease of communication does not produce agreement, and sovereign states are suspicious of anything that seems to suggest growing dependence on factors outside their control. China already claims the highest number of Internet users in the world. But just because Internet technology has stimulated expert-driven consensus, the same is not true for the attitude of states to the control of the Internet's applications. As the U.S. Secretary of State's director of innovation, Alec Ross, said in March 2013,

> Many Middle Eastern countries, Russia, China and others I believe, are going to take an increasingly aggressive stand to try to control the Internet. In a world where countries like Russia China and others are in a completely different place than the United States and when there is a completely different vision for how the Internet should be governed, then I think it's going to be very difficult to get to the point of resolution on some of these issues.[11]

So far diplomacy has proved unable to resolve a new global approach to governance. The ITU sees its role eroding. In December 2012, it organized the World Conference on International Telecommunications 2012 (WCIT-12) in Dubai, a conference to address international telecommunications regulations. But it broke up without agreements, and the ITU is still figuring out ways to recover its lost domains.

The governance of the technological development and control of the Internet is an appetizer for the debate on far more delicate issues for diplomacy. One is the ownership and handling of the data obtained from Internet users. Most of the data being created is of no consequence for the big issues of international relations. One U.S. comedian joked that surveillance had confirmed that 90 percent of U.S.

cellphone calls were to order a pizza. But much data are of use to state and non-state actors and can of course be invaluable for security issues, commercial intelligence, and intrusion into what was thought to be private property. We are creating a global landfill where diplomatic treasure will be found, perhaps where the states as well as the originators least suspect. Surveillance is a major diplomatic tool and some, like Julian Assange, claim it is the new tyranny. German companies who provide email servers are now offering encryption to avoid U.S. surveillance. IBM called the new phenomenon "big data": "This data comes from everywhere: sensors used to gather climate information, posts to social media sites, digital pictures and videos, purchase transaction records, and cell phone GPS signals to name a few. This data is big data."[12] The U.S. CIA gave the provider of one cellphone number in Dubai a $200,000 sports car in the search for Osama bin Laden. The United States may have led the way, but diplomacy worldwide has followed and has sought to access digital data to improve its functions. Countries as diverse as Kenya, South Korea, the Netherlands, and South Africa have all admitted they are trawling digital material. Russia famously announced it had offered the U.S. eavesdropping material they had been acquiring on the families of the Boston Marathon bombing suspects living in Dagestan.

THE POSITIVES AND NEGATIVES FOR DIPLOMACY: COMMUNICATION UNLOCKS POTENTIAL AND PRODUCES NEW WEAPONS

The ICR, like diplomacy itself, is neither good nor evil. If diplomats are working to solve global problems like poverty, disease, and conflict, most normative systems would claim that better communication and information availability will help find solutions. But equally, diplomacy can be used to prevent such progress through blocking devices or moving the agenda elsewhere. The fascination of the ICR revolution is that it opens countless possibilities, but to make these opportunities benefit diplomacy, will require a new versatility and agility from the activity itself.

Social media open a gateway for global cooperation and exchange of ideas. Ideas are free and so is the medium. Jeffrey Sachs believes that such fora will enable the baton of new ideas to pass from governments to society. "Social entrepreneurs from every sector can step forward with proposed solutions. The main role of government is to stand prepared, with checkbook at hand and policy brief ready, to take working solutions to the needed scale."[13] The ICR has opened a new chapter for the possibilities of global cooperation. Partnerships between organizations like Rotary International, the Bill and Melinda Gates Foundation, and the UN's World Health Organization in the Global Polio Eradication Initiative would have been unthinkable as a practical alliance without the ICR. Communication—the ability to engage, activate, and deliver—has been made feasible and diplomatically efficient through technology. Donations for global causes can now be raised virtually and instantaneously through a text message or numerous other methods. The American Red Cross estimated that at least 50 percent of households in the United States gave something to the Haitian earthquake appeal.

The blogosphere in its widest sense is the diplomatic leap into the unknown of decentralization and crowd outsourcing. This is now so vast it is beyond diplomacy's capacity to monitor thoroughly, let alone police. The international police agency Interpol noted that the number of extremist jihadist-related websites had expanded from only twelve in 1998 to 4,500 in 2006. At the time of his death in 2011, Anwar al-Awlaki's sermons alone featured in more than 5,000 videos on YouTube.

In accepting the globalization of information, diplomacy has opened up a global area of vulnerability—the threat of cyberattack. In October 2012, the U.S. Secretary of Defense, Leon Panetta, warned that the United States was facing the possibility of a "cyber-Pearl Harbor"[14] and was increasingly vulnerable to foreign computer hackers who could dismantle the nation's power grid, transportation system, financial networks, and government. Satellites, with their military and communications functions and vital applications like GPS, could be vulnerable to antisatellite weaponry. GPS is owned and operated by the United States government as a national resource. But the EU, Russia, China, and India are recognizing that they cannot afford to rely on U.S. dominance, and competition is emerging for alternative positioning systems. For diplomacy as well, GPS has opened up vast amounts of new data. On some smart phones, the location of the owner is shown whenever a photo is taken or an app is used.

Cyberattacks vary in methods and objectives. Some can be simply more sophisticated and targeted forms of diplomatic reporting or gathering information. Yet sabotage, infiltration, and theft of trade secrets are more likely objectives. Some have a specific purpose—to produce Distributed Denial of Service (DDoS)—that does little lasting damage to the computer system but does harm an organization's or state's reputation. Cyberweaponry is developing fast in other areas. Some malware is able to act as a well-placed intelligence agent—capable of penetrating even protected and physically isolated systems and flexible enough to inflict direct harm. In its brief history, there are already some examples of interstate cybersanctions. The cyberattack on Estonia in 2007, following the Estonian government's decision to remove a Russian World War II memorial, showed the vulnerability of a highly wired country—the home of the inventors of Skype—to a DDoS attack by Russian hackers.

Diplomacy itself is vulnerable to attack because its means of communication depends on equipment outside national control. This was always the case with undersea cables, antennae, and the risk that diplomatic bags would be tampered with. But computers and the infrastructure that operates them—routers, antennae, and satellites—are especially vulnerable because they are part of a system that is also open to the nonstate sector. By partnering in this way, diplomacy has crossed the boundary that separated it from the rest of society. No amount of encryption of content will avert this risk.

Some see the very lifeblood of diplomacy—communicating and information gathering—as becoming a cause of future wars. A cyberattack may be a state's ideal weapon of choice. It can be powerful, customized, and conducted remotely and anonymously. It can be instantaneous or be embedded for months before being activated. To diplomacy's advantage, the threat is common to all states and therefore, as in the case of nuclear or chemical weapons, diplomats may have the capacity to create some global norms or taboos against cyberwarfare. NATO's summit in 2014 agreed that cyber defense is now part of the alliance's core task of collective preparation. And nonstate actors share the cyber vulnerability. Commercial organizations may be easier and more lucrative targets. In 2012, Saudi Arabia's national oil company Aramco said an attack had disabled over 30,000 computers. And the Stuxnet virus attack on the Iranian government's nuclear facilities affected thousands of non-governmental computers in the country as well.

States are responding to the threats. The U.S. government is requiring new standards be set at critical private-sector facilities like power and water treatment plants. Cyber and physical attacks are indeed likely to be combined. Such jamming attacks on radars and communications have been common for years. The range of weaponry now available is also far removed from the heavy armor, fighter jets, and aircraft carriers that used to be the power projection currency of international relations. Computer codes, known as exploits, allow hackers to infiltrate or even control computers running software with a design flaw. There is nothing right or wrong about a computer code so a diplomatic basis for dealing with the threat is problematic. And most exploits are only used once and some are never detected. The Stuxnet virus contained four such exploits, at least one of which was privately developed. The marketing of these exploits is also facilitated by online sites. Prices are high, and many governments are as a result now deciding to develop in-house exploits.

The global cyberthreat resembles terrorism and pandemics that respect no borders. But unlike some threats, the offensive and defensive capabilities of countries to respond are uneven. The United States has been open about its need for greater resources and has admitted that offensive cyber operations are part of their planning. Secretary Panetta described this capability:

> If we detect an imminent threat of attack that will cause significant physical destruction in the United States or kill American citizens, we need to have the option to take action against those who would attack us. . . . For these kinds of scenarios, the department has developed the capability to conduct effective operations to counter threats to our national interests in cyberspace.[15]

The U.S. cybersecurity budget for 2013 was $13 billion, over half that allocated for U.S. diplomacy to the State Department.

Diplomacy needs to address cyber threats, but difficulties abound, many of them new to diplomacy. Some doubt that wars will ever develop in the cybersphere because the effects would be so uncertain and states would not concede parts of sovereignty by blackmail, however sophisticated. So the cyberacts to be prevented by diplomatic regulation are as yet not fully defined.

There has already been extensive work at the United Nations in devising a coordinated approach. Consensus is not likely to be easy. The Shanghai Cooperation Organization (whose members include China and Russia) includes in its definition of cyberwar the dissemination of information "harmful to the spiritual, moral and cultural spheres of other states."[16] In September 2011, these countries proposed to the UN Secretary General a document called "An International Code of Conduct for Information Security." Western countries opposed the approach as amounting to political censorship of the Internet. A London conference on cyberspace in 2011, which was attended among others by the U.S. Vice President Joe Biden and the founder of Wikipedia, Jimmy Wales, discussed an approach that would be similar to that proposed by Russia and China but with a different objective—a global set of rules of the road.

According to a UK proposal, the following rules of the road in cyberspace would be applied by both states and nonstates:

- governments to act proportionately in cyberspace and in accordance with international law
- everyone to have the ability to access cyberspace, including the skills, technology, confidence, and opportunity to do so
- users of cyberspace to show tolerance and respect for diversity of language, culture, and ideas
- ensuring that cyberspace remains open to innovation and the free flow of ideas, information, and expression
- respect for individual rights of privacy and to provide proper protection to intellectual property
- all to work collectively to tackle the threat from criminals acting online
- the promotion of a competitive environment that ensures a fair return on investment in networks, services, and content

Box 11-1 **Degrees of Separation**

Not all experiments on social smallness date from the foundation of Google. In 1967, Stanley Milgram sent dozens of packages to random people in Omaha, Nebraska, asking that they pass them on to others who might get it to a final destination. A chain would take shape to get the packages closer to their intended final recipients. His famous result was that there were, on average, six degrees of separation between any two people. In 2011, Facebook analyzed the 721 million users of its social-networking site and found that an average of 4.7 hops could link any two of them via mutual friends.

Diplomacy will therefore face one of its greatest challenges in ensuring the regulation and nonregulation of the Internet continues in a way that brings maximum benefit but minimizes the risks for users and governments. It is interesting in retrospect to see these concerns were being widely debated well before Edward Snowden's revelations. Governments see more clearly what has been gained and lost from the ICR in terms of sovereignty and the objectives of diplomacy. But the driving forces of commercial advantage are common to many countries, and a fragmentation of services with complicated regional accesses would seemingly become a vote or power loser for many governments. Those who seek to limit these rights would be seen as swimming against the tide—perhaps akin to denying populations access to globally available vaccinations. What seems more likely is that Internet services will become compartmentalized and subject to national control. The costs to users may be driven up as those developing new advances in equipment and software may increasingly seek to guarantee their rewards and block the entrance of new competition.

The ICR is already causing tension between states and nonstates with neither sure of the power the other possesses. China attacked Google's intellectual property by accessing its Gmail accounts. Google responded by pulling operations out of China and redirecting searches to Hong Kong. But ultimately a state will balance the benefits of being part of a seamless global system against the domestic problems that may be caused. The original commercial advantages of modularity, freedom of entry, and innovation of the ICR have produced one of the greatest public goods in history. Diplomacy will now show its worth in how far it aligns itself with common shared benefits or allows state sovereignty to reassert its preference for national control.

COMMUNICATION: IT'S A SMALL WORLD—THE GLOBAL WHISTLE-BLOWER AND GLOBAL ACTIVISM

The ICR has made the world smaller. Size still matters in diplomacy, but the ability of a large and powerful state to resist threats purely through size have been greatly diminished. The ICR has given small states and nonstate actors vast opportunities to influence international events. A cybernetwork can attract a willing suicide bomber, or an individual social gadfly can use the ICR to make a mark. Mass movements such as political parties, religious groups, and issue groups can also make the world smaller through skillful use of social media. Equally they themselves are now much more vulnerable to the smallness of internal dissent and questioning of established leadership. A virtual world is taking shape because the ICR is closing the gaps in the physical world. The virtual won't replace the physical but will force it to function in different ways. Physical constraints are seen less and less as an excuse for diplomacy not to get involved. But the opportunities exposed by the virtual world require different diplomatic approaches where the state counts for less. The virtual world will increasingly influence the physical and both systems will need to adapt. The unique separateness of diplomats in their representation of physical sovereign states is becoming blurred by the ICR.

The ICR creates crowds of activism or simply friends who like to be associated. Over 20 million became followers of Barack Obama on Twitter, a medium that perhaps gives the small some feeling of contact with the big. This crowdsourcing of opinions has a certain use but does not make diplomacy. Diplomats can't take in every voice in the crowd, but global populations and groups can now be approached in different ways.

Nevertheless, activism can find a meeting of minds and sharing of knowledge within hours. One recent experiment seeking to prove this was the Red Balloon Challenge, staged in 2009 by DARPA, already renowned for its ventures into new technology. Its aim was to determine how quickly and efficiently information could be gathered using social media. Competitors were tasked to locate ten red weather balloons secured at random locations across the United States in return for a $40,000 prize. The winning team, from the Massachusetts Institute of Technology (MIT), found all the balloons in just nine hours by encouraging participation in a conventional way. The first person to send the correct coordinates of a balloon received $2,000, but whoever recruited that person received $1,000, and the recruiter's recruiter received $500, and so on. This depicts old-style incentives for a new type of treasure hunt. Ushahidi, a nonprofit website, gathers information in major crises such as the Haiti earthquake and the terrorist bombings in Mumbai. And the U.S. Department of Defense is now hoping to use social media platforms such as Instagram to encourage whistle-blowers around the world to report on proliferation of weapons of mass destruction and other threats to security.

Tina Rosenberg has examined the power of peer pressure and groups to produce social change. In her book *Join the Club*, she quotes examples in behavior, medical solutions, and social activism where a social wish to belong and imitate has facilitated progress toward solutions of group problems.[17] A social mobilization search app can then steer the query toward the people with the right information—another option revolutionized by the ICR. Social mobilization technology is available to promote any cause, good or bad, for international relations. So the possibilities are again there for diplomacy to seize the new feature of global smallness and use it for its collective advantage. Diplomacy could join the club with others in promoting group progress.

CONCLUSION

The ICR's implications for diplomacy are indeed transformational. It is already producing expected and unexpected new traffic on the highway of international relations, but so far diplomacy's collective reaction has largely been to stare into the headlights. The nonstate sector has benefited greatly from the ICR. But these often vast and richly resourced groups are generally not cooperating in a systematic way on how to build the functions of diplomacy in a multipolar world. When issues and global activities, harmful and positive, predominate rather than security and military power projection, then diplomacy has to come to the fore. Diplomacy has not been forced to adapt its fundamental operations since 1945. In the past, it has shown the capacity to adapt in remarkable ways. The next chapter looks at the prospects of it doing so again.

SUGGESTIONS FOR FURTHER READING

1. Schmidt, Eric, and Jared Cohen. *The New Digital Age: Reshaping the Future of People, Nations and Business*. New York: Alfred A. Knopf, 2013.
2. Hanson, Fergus. *Revolution @State: The Spread of Eduplomacy*. Lowy Institute for International Policy, 2012. http://lowyinstitute.richmedia-server.com/docs/Hanson_Revolution-at-State.pdf.
3. Rosenberg, Tina. *Join the Club: How Peer Pressure Can Transform the World*. New York: W.W. Norton, 2011.

chapter 12

Diplomacy in 2025

Diplomacy in the modern era displays many of the characteristics of its historic origins. However, the uniqueness of its practice as a conduit of international relations is a thing of the past. Much that happens in the world between and among countries is no longer controlled by governments. Much of the activity and agenda setting of diplomacy flies under the radar of governments, and they themselves are fending off challenges to many of their core activities. This chapter is titled "Diplomacy in 2025." It is intended not as a gaze into a diplomatic crystal ball but more as an assessment of how successfully will diplomacy influence the future of all states and inhabitants of the planet. How strong and wise will diplomacy be in 2025?

DIPLOMACY IN 1945

Let us begin with a look at some of the key ingredients diplomacy had in 1945. It had

- a major global issue to deal with—the aftermath of World War II;
- a large and munificent power to lead the effort—the United States—with a homeland largely untouched by the war;
- two power blocks that won the war but were destined to lock horns ideologically, economically, and strategically for many decades;
- powerful new resources to tap as stability and world trade were reestablished;
- new leadership movements made possible by a peace dividend;
- yearnings for self-determination, new state building, and new hopes to foster;
- the problem of nuclear weapons and the need for the arms control responses to an unprecedented collective threat;
- new mass media—radio and TV;
- the hope and innovation of the United Nations; and
- vast new industries such as the automobile sector and medical advances such as understanding DNA.

And no one doubted that diplomacy mattered. It set the agenda and was the first responder to any type of tension. It had power.

THE REASSERTION OF DIPLOMACY

The influence of diplomacy can be reasserted not because its own former monopolies can be revived but because there is no likelihood that any other system would aspire to assume its role. No one else rushes to try to solve destructive conflicts such as in Syria. Now, just as in the aftermath of Buchenwald and Hiroshima, it is diplomacy that must put the world together again. At its core, diplomacy can draw new strength from its traditional activities but there are as yet few signs that this will happen. The public good of diplomacy is still valid, but it has not redefined its essential characteristics for decades. The other actors in international affairs, growing more prominent every year, have different roles and different objectives. They are issue driven, they wish to grow their own organizations, differentiate themselves from the competition, or they wish to exploit the facility of global interconnection and interdependence for ends that do not necessarily include friendly international relations. The future of diplomacy, therefore, will continue to depend on the common interest of states in cooperating and perpetuating its functions and institutions. So that gives reformers something important to build on. But its collective power is declining as a problem solver and the power of disrupters is consequently growing.

In terms of multinational institutions, diplomacy has resources in abundance. Many have impressive achievements and still provide unique functions. They are well funded by the states who support them. Yet faced with comparatively small convulsions of the world order, key agencies like the UN Peacebuilding Commission and the World Bank underperform. The United Nations was set up to stop wars, the World Bank to provide a lifeline to poor countries. But the president of the World Bank, Jim Yong Kim, said the best that could be said about their cooperation in the Democratic Republic of the Congo in 2013 was that "sometimes they didn't hate each other."[1] The multiple failures of diplomacy have repeatedly allowed other influences to assert their power. Diplomacy has been pushed aside as others rush in to exploit its weakness.

Today's diplomacy as a skill and an activity has many unprecedented advantages compared to 1945. In our world, there is more tourism, more international education, and more netizens than ever in history. But there is no international community. As Richard Haass, President of the Council on Foreign Relations, has written,

> Those looking to the international community to deal with the world's problems will be disappointed. This is not reason for despair or grounds for acting unilaterally. But so long as "international community" is more hope than reality, multilateralism will have to become more varied.[2]

Diplomacy has of course not stood still since 1945. Every state's diplomatic system participates in the United Nations and many other regional organizations, has regular contacts with nonstate actors, and has invested heavily in new technologies. All states, large and small, are battling for influence in the arena of public diplomacy. It is in the area of collective diplomacy where the world has largely been treading water. Even when we sense some innovation in collective diplomacy, such as the launching of regular Group of Twenty (G20) summits, their thirty-page communiqués show little sign of real consensus building. Few citizens of the world, however interested in the subject matter, would be reading the results of their deliberations a week after they have been printed—thankfully, on recycled paper.

The essence of diplomacy remains a mutual benefit. The Vienna Convention on Diplomatic Relations (VCDR) is a universal convention that establishes the framework so that diplomacy can operate in optimal conditions. The VCDR treats the world as one of states where decisions are made by actors that have the capacity to govern. The issue of diplomacy in its purest sense has received little attention since. It is indeed hard to see what type of revised convention might meet with universal approval in the early decades of the twenty-first century.

In the modern era, international relations lack commonality on guiding principles in areas such as ideology, economic systems, or military power. They also lack agreements on what functions diplomacy should perform. Trade and investment promotion, public diplomacy, and digital outreach and surveillance have all redrawn its parameters. Yet diplomacy is not revamping its own design so that technology and nonstate actors become full partners in the elusive search for an intelligent and productive diplomacy for the digital era. Diplomacy is so far not showing an appetite to regain its decisively beneficial role. Its traditional qualities of versatility and resourcefulness are currently evident only sporadically.

DIPLOMACY STILL VALID FOR 2025

Perhaps we have exaggerated the role of diplomacy. Perhaps it would serve our planet better in 2025 for it to have a more limited role. If diplomacy merits less attention, which of its activities, pared to essentials, will continue to have value in the first decades of the twenty-first century and which cannot be replicated by other activities and actors?

First, diplomacy has the capacity to link issues in international affairs. Few international issues can now be viewed in isolation. For example, education affects business, religion, travel, human rights, and intellectual property rights. Diplomacy cares about the overall outcome of a negotiation, not the result of one deal. In one scenario, if there is success on reducing the damage caused by climate change but a catastrophic failure to halt nuclear proliferation, then diplomacy overall has failed.

Second, social media and global technology surges impact many aspects of international relations. International contacts and interaction now often fly under the radar of official communications. Much of what diplomacy seeks to influence in official exchanges is increasingly governed by the pace the world outside diplomacy is setting. Daily mountains of data are being accumulated that add to our knowledge of what is happening in the world but diminishing our capacity to influence it.

Third, diplomacy offers the only forum for countries to plan for the future. International relations are increasingly complex with areas of consensus and mutual advantage but others where tensions and rivalry predominate. Territorial, commercial, and other ambitions dictate an official agenda where nationalism is inevitably used to build support with domestic electorates and audiences. Diplomacy remains the only international antidote to allowing short-termism to dominate calculations.

Fourth, the world is increasingly spawning ungoverned spaces with no clear state authority but frenetic virtual interaction in activities ranging from humanitarian relief and medical research to transnational crime and untraceable money transfers. Much of the Internet is itself an ungoverned or unregulated space. Diplomacy may try to rebuild the authority of states in the hope that they will live up to their supposed roles. But some states themselves show signs of being ungovernable. Diplomacy again must be central to building coalitions to regain influence where erosion of control by states will cause collective harm.

Fifth, diplomacy is the only activity that can confront existential struggles for the collective survival of the planet. The battles for resources, water, food, and energy are challenging the states and organizations that need and procure them. Diplomacy has been unable to set new norms of behavior in a range of areas. Technology, for example, is being harnessed to produce new food and energy sources. But it will need diplomacy to manage the struggles that will increasingly threaten our way of life.

Diplomacy now faces fewer barriers to entry than ever before. The world is no longer deferential to diplomacy or to big powers. A multipolar world reflects a world where every issue is potentially everyone's business. It is a world more open to outside influence but one where the business of careful consensus building and interest in peaceful resolution of issues has little immediate attraction. Diplomacy must reassert its value and demonstrate again the reasons why it is indispensable.

LOOKING AT THE FUTURE: THE ISSUE OF STOVEPIPES

Many hybrid public-private studies are addressing the response of global governance and diplomacy to the challenges identified. A notable example is the Global Governance 2025 (GG 2025) survey commissioned by the American National Intelligence Council (NIC) and the European Union's Institute for Security Studies (EUISS). Conducted in 2010, it drew in experts from over a dozen countries to assess how robust and flexible governance and diplomatic systems were to address critical current and future issues. Though none of those participating were state employees, it is one of the most comprehensive, recent, and publicly available examples of a multilateral report on global diplomatic reform. GG 2025 identified several key gaps in governance that needed to be filled to ensure that diplomacy adapted to both the new features of a multipolar world and developing global threats. Many of the threats they identified related to struggles for scarce resources. Others highlighted the multiplicity of issues that were in danger of overwhelming the capacity of diplomacy to respond. Diplomacy's effectiveness in addressing these issues was reduced because "the problems of 'span of control', increasing 'stovepipes', and 'lack of strategic oversight' have come increasingly to the fore as major challenges to ensuring effectiveness in the [governance] system."[3]

Stovepiping, the separate consideration of issues and the discouragement of lateral thinking, means that diplomacy is fragmented and not holistic. Diplomacy has no machinery to build consensus on connected but not identical crises. An example of the results of stovepiping approaches to diplomacy occurs in international health policy. One beneficial side effect of global advances in medicine and vaccination is that populations are booming with GG 2025 forecasting another 700 million people in the world by 2025. But even with existing populations, many countries face resources crises. "In 2010, 21 countries, accounting for about 600 million people, are assessed as either cropland or freshwater scarce, according to internationally accepted benchmarks. Current technology and input costs put these countries well beyond the realm of food self-sufficiency."[4] Successful policy in one area has produced problems in another. The massive impact of hydraulic fracturing—or fracking—of oil and gas reserves is making the United States largely self-sufficient and independent of sources in the Middle East. But if those producers lose their markets then greater instability in the region may increase pressure on the United States to intervene militarily.

One instance of resource tensions surfaced in June 2013 when the Egyptian government reacted to plans of Ethiopia to divert part of the Blue Nile to build a massive hydroelectric dam to provide power for industrial expansion, much of which was required for Chinese-funded investment. Egypt claimed the project violated its rights under a 1959 agreement to receive water from the river. The resource issue was still unsettled in early 2014 despite each interested country's agreeing to set up a panel of experts. Egypt's irrigation minister said, "We need 80 billion cubic meters. We will not let go of one drop of water."[5]

GG 2025 recognizes that while states are increasingly interdependent, there is a growing fragility of state governance. At the same time, the capacity of the disrupter or those who oppose rather than support a cause has soared. Calls for instantaneous action, reforms, and changes, which seem feasible in the virtually connected world, cannot be delivered. The world takes the pictures, creates the hashtags, and a momentum for which there is seldom adequate machinery to respond. States resort to dealing only with issues that can be settled, and they are tackled in isolation. The intractable issues get ignored. Though the world's major countries may have some strong convergence in economic and trade issues—General Motors now sells more cars in China than in the United States—on others there is no diplomatic mechanism for the world to resolve its current impasses.

Just as national governments increasingly recognize the ineffectiveness of their bilateral diplomacy, GG 2025 sees transnational discontent as more easily propelled in the future. An armed group or a powerful non-governmental organization (NGO) that seizes attention can appeal to the populace's wish for clear solutions, even if imposed by violence or direct action. Globalized financial mechanisms are continuing to make funding such groups or facilitating arms for resource swaps ever easier. Elections now no longer always offer the chance for renewal and new hope they once did. Few elections are seen as fair and free, and the era of the good loser in democracies seems increasingly a feature of the past. Communications stir protests and reveal manipulation, undermining the legitimacy that diplomacy requires to function. Governments are frequently reluctant to renounce political power because it means loss of material patronage. The absence of lasting coalitions on issues will encourage more states to resort to authoritarian measures to control their territories. Diplomacy is sidelined.

More optimistically, GG 2025 noted the capacity of the world to come together on issues has been facilitated by the emergence of well-funded, well-organized, and technology-savvy NGOs. These do not, as we have seen, see their operations as limited by national boundaries. In civil society, and as faith-based, commercial, and issue-based organizations, they have shown their capacity to reframe issues to command international support and to mobilize publics. International exchanges between groups show them discussing issues outside the confines of national positions. And few, if any, come together on a platform based on violence. Yet the capacity of all countries, as in diplomacy, is not equal in NGOs. Those from developing countries often have limited influence and few resources. And the proliferation of NGOs from the developed world increasingly makes meaningful cooperation impossible. The Doha meeting of Parties to the Intergovernmental Committee on Climate Change in 2012 was attended by some 17,000 delegates including 7,000 members of NGOs, 1,500 from the media, and ninety television stations, all massively denting carbon footprints.

The future may hold sterner challenges to diplomacy than have been confronted in the past. We have noted that the collapse of countries with around thirty million people have stretched global resources in the current era. In Pakistan or Nigeria, the populations well exceed 100 million and a collapse of governance would draw the world into problems of a magnitude it has yet to face. Many see migration to another region or country as the only option. Syria was the world's refugee crisis from 2011 to 2014, but it was itself a haven for over one million refugees from the earlier Iraq crises. The involvement of major states in receiving immigrants and in addressing its associated problems is also uneven. GG 2025 notes,

> Ten countries host over half of the world's migrants. One in five lives in the United States, with Canada also featuring in the top ten. Europe

> has four countries on the list, namely Germany, France, the United Kingdom and Spain. Russia and Ukraine feature on the list as well as Saudi Arabia and India, reflecting the growing importance of rising powers as receivers of migrants. China is an outlier.[6]

China does not yet view the issue as impacting it as other major countries. Beijing's foreign population is less than 1 percent of the total. By contrast, in New York City, some 35 percent of the population is foreign born.

GG 2025 is not hopeful for the prospects of institutional reform. The sovereign state model does not readily lend itself to solving competition for resources, and free trade has already produced all its likely benefits for some. Technology will benefit from interconnection and business opportunities, but diplomacy has not created a forum for over-the-horizon preparation of future analysis and responses. The report suggests that resource competition is likely to hit poor states the hardest, leading in the worst case to internal or interstate conflict and regional destabilization. GG 2025 sees a list of issues where diplomacy cannot forecast the results—these include migration, the potential opening of the Arctic, and risks associated with the biotechnology revolution. These

> are likely to rise in importance and demand a higher level of cooperation. These issues are difficult ones for multilateral cooperation because they involve more preventive action. Under current circumstances, greater cooperation on those issues in which the risks are not clear-cut will be especially difficult to achieve.[7]

COMPLEX ISSUES OR INADEQUATE DIPLOMACY?

GG 2025 shows the diversity of forward thinking among international experts. What they and others agree on is that there is currently no mechanism where the future of diplomacy is being examined—nowhere to analyze the differences between its current activities and what it must do in future. Diplomacy has been up to task before. The responses it made after 1945 were because many of the looming issues had been identified in diplomatic thinking—the need to reconstruct devastated economies to give lasting peace a chance, the disarming of aggressor states, the problem of nuclear proliferation, and the process of decolonization and self-determination. Diplomacy looked ahead and was unusually creative and determined in refashioning multilateral diplomacy.

Since then, the shortcomings of diplomacy have been obscured by the Cold War and the dominant capabilities, both militarily and diplomatically, of a few powers. The U.S. role in the world has veered between aggressive reactions to threats to its own security as perceived in Vietnam, Iraq, and Afghanistan or responding to international 911 calls to intervene in cases like Bosnia, Kosovo, and Libya. The United States is now, and is likely to remain, reluctant and less capable to play either role. Diplomacy in its core functions will need to exert a stronger influence though analysts like Robert Kagan insist that a world order cannot function properly without such non-diplomatic interventions. In their view, fundamental cleavages still exist between liberalism and autocracy, modernity and traditionalism. The liberal order that exists and the development and survival of democracy and open markets depend on U.S. military power. As Kagan has written, "International order is not an evolution; it is an imposition."[8] If the United States is the world's indispensable power, it increasingly finds too many problems laid in its inbox. Bruce Jones has characterized the United States as no longer the CEO of the world but as a major stakeholder on all global issues.[9] It is inconceivable that a solution will be found without U.S. agreement. The United States remains indispensable to diplomacy but is calling on others to take their share of responsibility. Ben Rhodes, Deputy National Security Advisor to President Obama, described the objective in 2013: "We want to galvanize collective action, to underpin global norms. We don't want to do these things alone: we welcome others to be involved."[10]

In a multipolar world, where power has slipped from all governments, leaders are reluctant to change a system that, whatever faults it may have, does exalt the status of each individual sovereign state. The model of the United Nations—where Palau, the Marshall Islands, and Micronesia have an equal vote to the United States and China—is obviously appealing. But the capacity of many states to engage in diplomatic exchanges on the global issues of the time is limited or nonexistent. Many of the stakeholders and actors capable of deploying resources are not even governments themselves. But the application of change or innovation to diplomacy still depends on the leaders of these states. And, as Henry Kissinger noted in 2014, "World order cannot be achieved by any one country acting alone." To achieve a new stability, "global, structural and juridical" issues must be aligned in "a concept of order that transcends the perspective and ideals of any one region or nation."[11]

Diplomacy has never been planned or designed for the job. We have seen some recent examples such as the evolution of Internet governance or the hybrid Global Fund for AIDS as illustrating the resourcefulness of international actors. As former President Clinton used to say in the Haiti context, what diplomacy needs to show is its capacity to get stuff done. It has a framework for action in the VCDR and Vienna Convention on Consular Relations (VCCR), but the collective mechanism for reform or unlocking new potential does not exist. For leaders of states, the status quo seems the safest option. They take comfort in low-risk, photo opportunity diplomacy that runs on autopilot. Satow would recognize little diplomatic intelligence[12] being applied to planning for 2025 or highlighting the mutual benefit of international relations that lies at the heart of the VCDR.

If we are to advance the agenda of diplomatic reform, then we need to take account of realities. An arcane paper, a communiqué, a multistakeholder seminar with carefully crafted agenda and conclusions, or the many elegant diplomatic dinners staged in Paris and other capitals will be comfortable for all concerned but will not produce innovation. The diplomatic community will soon move on. What, therefore, might be doable in the modern era of frenetic, tense, and media-scrutinized politicians? We must examine what might appeal as a starting point taking account of the priorities of leaders. What structure might supplement and replace in part what we have today, and how might it tap into some of the positive new developments that offer fruitful opportunities for diplomacy? Is this wishful thinking or, as Barack Obama told the Nobel Peace Prize ceremony in Oslo, is there still an international yearning to "reach for the world that ought to be"?[13]

THE FORUMS FOR DISCUSSION

Diplomacy continues to function on the basis of shared interests. It is only the nature and scope of these interests that have changed over centuries. Wars, exploration, technologies, travel, the types of weaponry in conflicts, and global financial collapses all receive diplomatic attention according to the forum convened—the G20, the UN Security Council (UNSC), the International Monetary Fund, the Arctic Council, and so on. States send different representatives to each meeting.

The forum for discussion and analysis in diplomacy is often the most important influence on the outcome. Those currently invited to such fora are suspicious of ideas for change or of the fear of exclusion. They are wary that the commitments they make will reduce their sovereignty. The United Nations has now developed such a mature bureaucracy with predictable diplomatic maneuvers that the conventional array of agencies usually produces responses designed for the last and perhaps greatly different crisis. Are there new possibilities for diplomatic discussions that might serve to make diplomacy more productive in 2025?

PERMANENT CRISES

In present diplomacy, a crisis shapes the diplomacy, not the reverse. UN intervention in the Ivory Coast in 2012 took place when mediation and peacekeeping had failed. Major powers such as China, Brazil, and India all voted in the UNSC for use of force in a decision that represented a substantial interference in the Ivory Coast's sovereignty. Yet, in the case of Libya in 2011, the UN-authorized NATO intervention suggested a specific bloc of interests. The African Union (AU) in particular had attempted to play an active diplomatic role. The exclusion of the AU from the Libya Contact Group and the omission of any invitation to the BRICS countries (Brazil, Russia, India, China, and South Africa) to participate in the action bred suspicion about the diplomatic objectives. There has been little inclination by the AU or the BRICS to engage in postmilitary diplomacy and the subsequent efforts to reconstruct Libya.

If a crisis blows up, diplomacy will do its best. A massing of Indian troops on its border with Pakistan will send diplomacy into overdrive. Naval exercises close to disputed islands in the South China Sea will have encrypted emails flying around capitals and embassies demanding immediate access to senior officials. Diplomacy will apply all its efforts to encourage, cajole, convene meetings, and make frenetic contacts. If force is used by sovereign states, others generally react against it. But the crisis is seldom preceded by a period of diplomacy. A recent New York University (NYU) study of crisis management titled *The Use of Force, Crisis Diplomacy and the Responsibilities of States* concluded there was a need for permanent discussion fora.

> It should be a long-term strategic goal of the major powers to pull together and consolidate . . . contact groups to address future crises—preferably initiating discussions before a crisis comes to a head, so that all sides have some grasp of the interests and positions involved. Such groups can be initiated informally around the UN . . . or potentially as offshoots of the G20 . . . for some high level inputs.[14]

The permanence of such discussions, says the NYU report, will bring added diplomatic benefits.

> Groups of this type can take on many confidence-building and strategic coordination tasks . . . addressing unintended economic consequences . . . or ironing out clashes between mediation, the use of force or other forms of coercion. . . . Above all, groups of this type can ensure that diplomacy . . . is not crushed under the weight of military operations, sanctions regimes and vicious rhetoric.[15]

The tools of crisis management have not been advanced in a multilateral context, and conventional mediation has not enjoyed conspicuous success. Repressive governments, by their nature, do not engage in domestic dialogue, let alone international. But the embedded power structure of the United Nations and its bodies, with its attendant overlapping management centers, setting of precedents, and concerns about status, puts a premium on caution. The twenty-first century offers the chance to build additional rooms in the diplomatic house. The information and communication revolution and the first thoroughly multipolar and interdependent world in diplomatic history make significant diplomatic innovation feasible and possible. The cause of diplomacy needs a new forum existing in both the virtual and physical worlds. Dovetailing nonstate actors—from business and non-governmental groups—into the discussions would add new options to diplomacy. Diplomacy knows sufficiently how to maintain its core activities to ensure this modest innovation would not lead to a slippery slope of diplomatic chaos.

FUTURE CRISES

"Don't wait for the crisis" is one message diplomacy should absorb. Diplomacy has never been good at forecasting future crises, and the sovereign states are likely to be marginalized when the crisis originates from the nonstate sector. Thus, few active in contemporary diplomacy foresaw, let alone prepared for, the financial collapse in 2008 and 2009. A crisis in the future governance of the Internet would likely produce a similar unprepared, hastily assembled group of stakeholders.

The multiplicity of actors with a modern capacity to influence diplomacy exacerbates the risk of unexpected challenges from unanticipated events. If policy planners had thought it through, it would not be a crisis. Not only are the crises more unpredictable—few forecast the Arab Spring—but the course they take thereafter defies the experts. Syria's crisis started as a civil unrest in 2011, and it appeared to conventional diplomacy that the actors and their objectives were clear. Leaders would be established and diplomacy would build a stalemate-based negotiation in which the positions of each party would take shape. Yet the ingredients of the crisis outpaced conventional diplomacy—the ability to finance purchases of arms, transport fighters from different locations, and exploit weak neighboring states all produced an amorphous crisis, which diplomacy could not fathom. Playing catch-up has led to collective onlooking rather than diplomatic effectiveness. Syria was a very modern civil war that also reminded the world of an issue that used to preoccupy diplomacy—the use of chemical weapons.

All states see their diplomacy increasingly being overtaken by events. The United Kingdom said in 2010 that it would prioritize the forging of a strategic partnership with Turkey. That sounded reasonable enough since Turkey had heralded its wish to join the EU and of becoming an important global actor in diplomacy. Other countries had already signed such partnerships. Yet complex alignments and the unexpected soon highlighted different UK and Turkish priorities. In the Syrian crisis in 2012, Turkey took a strong line against Bashar al-Assad, who had been an important supporter of Hamas in Palestine and Hezbollah in Lebanon. But Turkey also called Israel a terrorist state for its conflict with Hamas. Turkey had no wish to see Iran a nuclear power but depended heavily on oil and gas supplies from Iran. Just a few years on from the United Kingdom's wish to prioritize relations with Turkey, much changed in the perception of each country. Though Turkey may still be interested in joining the EU, there was doubt about the United Kingdom's own intention of remaining a member state. Meanwhile, the Kurdish minority was becoming a major factor in the Syrian conflict, Turkey was hosting hundreds of thousands of Syrian refugees, Iran was negotiating with the United States, and the Turkish government had been under regular domestic pressure and had little time for new diplomatic initiatives.

The speed with which global opinion and movements impact the world also sweeps up states in a hurry. The issue of same-sex marriage engulfed opinion in many countries because it had been tabled in a few. The forum of debate rapidly became global, outpacing government discussions. Only a decade after the Netherlands stood alone at the turn of the twenty-first century in legalizing same-sex marriage, by 2013, over twenty countries with collective populations of over one billion had recognized in whole or part of their territory the right to marry of same-sex couples. Again, this is testament to the wildfire speed of diplomatic adjustments.

The world may be more globalized in culture, economic habits, and the way it connects, but the crisis scenarios seldom reflect globalized visions. In the same week in November 2013 that the United States, EU, Russia, and China were working together on a deal to limit Iran's nuclear program, Russia was agitating against EU links with Ukraine and the United States was challenging China's assertion of controlled airspace over the East China Sea.

INTELLIGENT, VERSATILE, RESOURCEFUL: THE DIPLOMAT IN 2025

If diplomacy should acknowledge its declining influence, it should also recognize that its role and versatility are unique. A diplomat in 2025 will still be deployed as a facilitator, a conceptualizer, and a symbol of cooperation who has the capacity and mind-set to link complex issues. The diplomat will also likely still be a fund-raiser internally and outside his or her system, a softener of workplace rivalries, an intermediary between members of his or her own state's government. The diplomat will harness communication and information tools to maximize diplomacy's effectiveness. To speculate what technological advances, resources, or environmental challenges will confront diplomacy in 2025 has limited utility. But it does suggest that diplomacy should not assume that much will continue just as the same. Diplomacy will be impacted by a more virtually interactive world, crises exploding and sometimes disappearing at speed. The media, NGOs, and business entities will all give intense temporary scrutiny to their implications. But diplomacy must be in a position to react to and wrestle with complex problems where no clear national interest will be vindicated and where compromise and internationalism will form part of the solution. Diplomacy may take comfort from the likelihood that the planet will not be vastly different. There will be no colonies on Mars, most people will drive cars to a workplace, and most students will attend classes within walls of bricks and mortar. Inventions will have suggested new medical cures, new ways of producing food and energy, and one of the largest twenty companies in the world had probably not been founded when this book was published. Diplomacy can do little to alter the course of world events and technological innovation, but it must nevertheless update and modify its own capacity to play its traditional role in the world of intelligent international problem solvers.

The future of diplomacy in 2025 will still be rooted in the state. But it will require states to show intelligence and a capacity to see collective forces at work in the world. States need to develop new mechanisms for the survival of the planet and mechanisms that promote global and collective solutions. As we have seen, all major powers recognize that their own capacity to influence outcomes alone is limited. So the search is on for something else. This would be something groundbreaking, but so were the ideas of the founders of the United Nations and the drafters of the VCDR. It is a task where minds need to be applied in ways that Satow would have applauded. Diplomacy as a cause needs to come together to find ways it can reassert its influence. Diplomatic reform also needs to take account of what is practicable and what, given the circumstances of the time and the motivations of political leaders, might be achievable. States are not going to put their weight behind innovations that will further weaken their influence on outcomes. The final chapter attempts to identify what steps might meet these objectives.

SUGGESTIONS FOR FURTHER READING

1. European Union Institute for Security Studies and United States National Intelligence Council. *Global Governance 2025: At a Critical Juncture*. 2010. http://www.iss.europa.eu/uploads/media/Global__Governance_2025.pdf.

2. Kagan, Robert. *The World America Made*. New York: Alfred A. Knopf, 2012.

chapter 13

Diplomacy for the Ages

Intelligent Innovation for the Modern World

This chapter is not about writing. It is about identifying some new diplomacy that is doable, deliverable, and, occasionally, daring. What can we suggest in improvements to diplomacy that could make a practicable difference in today's world?

The practical aspects of diplomacy are what justify its existence. International relations theory and projections about future world orders are of little use to thousands huddled in refugee camps or civilians faced with daily artillery barrages from their own governments. We have seen how pragmatism has driven diplomacy's development and the services that all countries offer. But diplomacy has not evolved accidentally. Its institutions and versatility have been molded by leadership that saw the value of international communication and institutional reform. Diplomacy did not stop with the convening of a conference or a confidential negotiation. It put into effect mechanisms that would solve problems and thereafter monitor the implementation of those solutions. Unfortunately, the efforts of the postwar years were not sustained as Cold War divisions and the power of the few gave diplomacy a diminishing role. For a while after 1990, the few became the power of one and the indispensable power of the United States. Now the world order is without much of the order. Diplomacy is consequently required to perform more effectively and in more versatile ways than ever before.

Diplomacy has been underachieving for many reasons, but some of the main ones are

- the decline of the power of the state,
- the information and communications technologies revolution that has blurred the lines between states as the principal actors in diplomacy,
- the growth of the resources, cross border activities, and the international appeal of the nonstate actor,
- random events within states impacting other countries,
- the interconnection of complex global issues that highlights the necessity of multipolar diplomacy,

- corruption and lack of accountability of those who govern, and
- the rise of the influence of smallness, so diplomatic clout no longer is simply a reflection of size.

As in the past, diplomacy needs to be applied in areas where it can be most effective. Without refreshment, it has fallen back on its ritualistic and competitive forms of behavior. At its most absurd, every country attempts to talk to the same contacts and arranges innumerable visits of officials to that country, many of whom will never visit again. Diplomacy tries to work in a world where the old currency of power and foreign policy is no longer sufficient. Each state is recognizing that the old rules don't produce the same results. Some are doing better, some worse, in the new order.

The survey in the previous chapters has identified many achievements of our diplomatic ancestors. It has also suggested that frameworks conceived for the work of bilateral and multilateral diplomatic institutions in a different era cannot be assumed to be the only possibilities available for today's world. We have seen that in diplomatic practice, states mimic others, and each is engaged in a restless search for better diplomatic delivery. We have also seen that major countries agree on the need for more cooperation, more sharing of the burdens of diplomacy, and a reaching out to involve and tap the resources of nonstate actors. Fundamental functions and responsibilities of states are unlikely to change. Diplomacy's protection duties, the promotion of trade and investment, and public functions are widely accepted as worthwhile uses of taxpayers' money.

The world, meanwhile, has evolved toward a much more loosely assembled unit in which problems are exposed faster, and what works in new business or governance has often bypassed traditional methods of diplomacy. No one approach, whether it is through the United Nations or private philanthropy, is contributing to a new paradigm. In the words of the 2014 session of the Davos World Economic Forum, itself a rare example of a permanent experiment in new diplomacy,

> Profound political, economic, social and, above all, technological forces are transforming our lives, communities and institutions. Rapidly crossing geographic, gender and generational boundaries, they are shifting power from traditional hierarchies to networked heterarchies. Yet the international community remains crisis-driven rather than strategic in the face of the trends, drivers and opportunities pushing global, regional and industry transformation.[1]

The future narrative of diplomacy, as currently conceived, is more akin to fire extinguishing than reforming fire-prevention materials or regulations. Publics are receiving less and less in free services from governments and see a free Internet and other benefits as unrelated to their state's responsibilities. They view state diplomacy as less and less relevant to their lives. Yet diplomacy's continuity means it is impossible to stop, get off, and remount. There are no fresh starting points. Many diplomats are trying to do things better, create new groups, use the digital era in a savvy way, and bolster the states that fail. The world has spawned new shared activities that suggest a widening discussion. Groups such as the Davos Forum and the Clinton Global Initiative at least talk about issues with diverse stakeholders and differing views without the straitjacket of debates on voting rights or squabbles over status. But they themselves have not so far tackled the topic of innovation in diplomacy itself.

How can diplomacy make sense of a world with few leaders, weak states, and where international interaction is productive and can be profitable for diplomacy but can also be readily derailed by a disrupter's actions? Diplomacy can no longer take shelter behind the big power enforcers or drawing of boundaries. A multipolar and multiactor world needs to find a consensus-building mechanism that can offer new diplomatic options. Failure should not become the norm of diplomacy in the twenty-first century. The dangers of that go beyond disillusionment. Complacency has caught diplomacy out before. Writing in 1910, Norman Angell argued in *The Great Illusion* that "wars between great powers would be the height of irrationality" and "neither the people nor the bankers would allow it."[2] Angell had rightly recognized the power of the nonstate actor before World War I. He drew the wrong conclusion but did subsequently win the Nobel Peace Prize. There are plenty of more recent examples of diplomacy getting it wrong. As Robert Kagan has cautioned, "The difficulties in shaping the international environment in any way are immense. . . . Foreign Policy is like hitting a baseball; if you fail 70% of the time you get into the Hall of Fame."[3]

The question for diplomacy is whether it can reasonably raise its batting average. What could it do to avoid failures in crises and collaborative planning that give the activity a bad name? Can it move forward from fragmentation, short-termism, or even the inevitability of defeat? Diplomacy's unique role in translating shared interests into shared actions is stalling, and the internationalism that all diplomacy requires in some measure is being squeezed out. On its current path, nothing is on its agenda to reempower diplomacy. There is no appetite to try new approaches. The world is too busy looking elsewhere. So if there is a desire to add a new option or create a new path for diplomacy, some initiative will have to be taken. This is not being a diplomatic Pollyanna, but it is recognizing, as David Miliband, the former UK Foreign Secretary said, that "patriotism requires internationalism."[4]

A humble diplomacy would acknowledge that it has a capacity to try new approaches. An agile, recharged diplomacy that is demanding of itself would establish an appropriate performance measure where the contribution of creative ideas to shared solutions would be a collective project. Many other activities combine elements of competition with collective efforts to promote the main endeavor. In the world's most global sport—football, or soccer—all countries compete vigorously for success and lobby for the right to stage international tournaments. But they also contribute funds and staff to a governing body, FIFA, whose business is to grow and manage the sport in the interest of all. This is a different model from the United Nations where individual states often have little stake in the success of collective outcomes. In the business world, such combinations of competition and cooperation exist in bodies representing world commodity producers such as the International Coffee Organization and even among major global operators such as airlines groups, which support the International Air Transport Association.

A new look at diplomacy's methods and institutions would be a modern application of Satow's intelligence[5] to the greater good of functioning diplomacy. Moisés Naím had defined the four elements that produce power. Diplomacy knows that two—carrots and sticks or muscle and reward—sometimes work. But diplomacy is usually missing two. These are the code of behavior that produces international norms and the ability to persuade states to perceive their actions differently.[6] In other words, perhaps powerful diplomacy is missing spaces where diplomats would be welcomed if they sometimes proposed simply international ideas. In the past, states have responded to calls for innovation with wry smiles, voted to spend a few million dollars, and acquiesced in some healthy steam venting or hand-wringing by well-meaning non-state actors. It has often been convenient to call meetings to show governments have reacted. But the blurring of such responsibility for diplomacy has seldom been productive. In contrast to previous eras, governments need now to take the lead. Diplomacy must be made to work, and it is the states themselves that must, as baseball would say again, step up to the plate.

Diplomatic start-up ideas and investments in new ventures will be regarded with suspicion in a world of many formal procedures and status-conscious states and individuals. In order to stimulate a wider debate, I have sought to look behind these formal features and to identify some doable steps for diplomacy. We are fortunate that our collective power of creativity is great, and no one has a monopoly of good ideas in this the most internationalist of pursuits. So for this final chapter, I have contacted individuals and foreign ministries from over a dozen countries to begin a debate to brainstorm innovation in diplomacy. Some of the following fifteen ideas are mine, and the rest are from specialists around the world.

FIFTEEN IDEAS TO RAISE DIPLOMACY'S BATTING AVERAGE

1. A New Forum for Some Practical Consensus Building: An International Peace Corps

To address the dysfunctional multilateralism of today, a new forum might be convened—virtually as well as physically—with its tasks defined by governments to think creatively rather than argue over national interest. It would address issues collectively, apply preventive diplomacy to anticipate problems, and suggest ways that might make the attainment of shared actions for shared interests more within reach.

Who would be the fortunate members of such a group, and what would be the basis that might maximize its chances of success? What existing functioning institution might be a model for it?

One model that has a strong pedigree and ensures true commitment to the internationalist cause is the U.S. Peace Corps (USPC). This is innovative because it appoints volunteers for two years who are funded by the U.S. government. The volunteers are assigned to projects agreed between the United States and the government receiving the volunteers. Over 200,000 have served in 139 countries since its foundation, and the projects now include technology assistance such as developing computer apps for use in language translations in multiethnic countries like Zambia.

A small international peace corps would draw on an established diplomatic instrument modified to meet the circumstances of today's world. Like the U.S. model, those participating would serve full-time for a fixed term and then return to the world outside. The volunteers would not be experts in the complex issues of poverty, economic development, religious tolerance, or migration. So the forum would need to be able to call on varied experts who would be available virtually to assist. The conclusions of the endeavors would of course not be binding on governments, so that is one reason it might appeal to them. But it would be an avenue for thought and for breaking impasses. In practice, how might it be established?

Diplomacy suggests that any new group should start small but promise diversity and inclusivity. That is nothing new in diplomacy. States are attracted to join something that works and attracts attention and will gain momentum. The Group of Twenty (G20) would be a candidate to launch it. They would provide the funding and a small secretariat with diplomatic experience to guide and focus the efforts. Both physical and virtual projects would be tackled. Each participating country might nominate ten participants who are interested in international issues and committed to brainstorm solutions, made up as follows:

- At least half from the non-governmental sector, including applicants from the business sector, NGOs, and those with technology and science skills
- No pay but, as in the Peace Corps, living expenses would be paid
- Maximum two years term
- No maximum age—but the average for the USPC is twenty-seven
- Some demonstrated commitment to internationalism

To ensure some structure, the participants from each G20 country would assume the lead role in project work on one global issue. Thus, Turkey might address migration, China the environment, and so on. Obviously, the wider work of the G20 might also evolve so that each country would drive discussions on a particular topic. In time, other states could participate in the group and the United Nations, European Union (EU), and other regional organizations might also be invited to second some of their staff. A strict upper limit of size will need to be enforced since smallness and rotation of intake should guard against bureaucratic fiefdoms and infighting.

The important advantage of such a new forum would be its visibility and unashamed capacity to innovate. A big symbolic gain would be the image of governments reaching out for external ideas, collaboratively addressing global issues without commitment to any outcome but with a commitment to conversation. The issues would, for a while at least, be discussed not only in diplomatic institutions. If it doesn't work, there will be no institution fatigue, no pointless summits and dreary communiqués. It would be wound up and something else could be tried.

2. Use of Embassies in Capitals

A second proposal would be to assign new productive tasks to established institutions. Diplomats now know more about the world than ever in history. But so do nonstate actors frustrated by the boundaries of states. Here then is a self-interest rationale for closer coordination between the diplomatic missions of countries. Diplomacy should not just be convened in a crisis.

States would instruct their resident embassies to devote part of their time and resources to brainstorm policy approaches among themselves and with their host country. Where can diplomacy add value? Where can it eliminate wasteful duplication? Embassies would devote part of their time to continuous discussion of global issues of particular relevance to the host country—a useful innovation away from ritualistic and competitive diplomacy.

3. A "Greenpeace" for Diplomacy

The gap in the diplomatic firmament that contrasts with other important global issues is that there is no "Greenpeace" for the activity. The third idea is to create one. If it works, this could be funded by any state or nonstate foundation interested in the outcomes of diplomatic decisions. It would look at the mechanisms of diplomacy, how they could be improved by tapping into nonstate activism and consensus building. There would be no need for any offices—virtually all could be virtual.

4. A Diplomacy Message Board

Diplomacy should receive comments about how to do diplomacy. Of course it would mix the sane with the profane and inane. This could be run by the brainstorming "Greenpeace" described above. The BBC has a "World Have Your Say" blog. It is, therefore, possible to administer and maintain some decorum while reaching out to the world.

5. A Nobel Prize for Diplomatic Innovation, Not Just for Peace

Peace is important for diplomacy. But this separate prize would honor innovation, research, and new discoveries that advance the cause of diplomacy such as those awarded for the natural and social sciences.

6. Global TV Discussion: Leaders Encouraged to Step Up

It is remarkable how reluctant global leaders are to discuss issues in public that all recognize no state can solve alone. It seems extraordinary when live debates are now common in national politics that there has never been a live televised discussion between heads of major governments dealing with the same international questions. An example could be set by a smaller group of countries, perhaps starting with the Group of Seven or Group of Eight. It might start with nothing too contentious and would encourage leaders to produce convincing arguments on global issues for publics beyond each state. To be world leaders in diplomacy today, they need to be capable of that. Who knows? It might catch on.

7. State Representatives for Diplomatic Innovation

Each G20 government would appoint a point of contact on diplomatic innovation. If J. P. Morgan could tell potential investors in 2013, "It's not an overstatement to say that we are living through the largest policy experiments of the last 300 years,"[7] then each major state participating in diplomacy needs the capacity to think beyond its own performance. It makes sense to have at least one mind in a large organization employed to look at diplomacy as a public good and to accept responsibility for improving collective diplomacy. This would create a small internationalist dimension and perhaps an element of competition for the best ideas, which would do diplomacy no harm.

8. Updating the Key Agreements of Diplomacy

A conference of all parties to the Vienna Convention on Diplomatic Relations and the Vienna Convention on Consular Relations could be held to update the provisions. These conventions have served diplomacy and consular relations well for over half a century but were negotiated in a world with less than a third of the number of sovereign states that exist now, and before the development of new major diplomatic activities—commercial and investment promotion functions of diplomats, modern public diplomacy techniques, and the Internet. Such a conference would remind all states of the value of diplomacy and reinforce its role in international relations. It won't be easy to achieve results, but few worthwhile outcomes are.

9. A UN Rebirth

Member states should accept that the United Nations can be made more effective and flexible for the twenty-first century. How this might be done is part of the debate—perhaps a conference or perhaps a commission of the wise and the young. Yes, of course, it will be hard to avoid the struggles over status in the UN Security Council. But the exercise might also shine a light on why the United Nations still has some vital functions and why it can coexist with some of the other innovations that diplomacy will hopefully be applying. The objective would be to inaugurate a rebirth, reassessment, and rebooting of the United Nations. Even the U.S. Constitution has been revised more often than the UN Charter. No document that influences diplomacy so profoundly should be too sacrosanct or too difficult to modernize. As Thomas Jefferson wisely noted about the need to update all institutions, "Our children will be as wise as we are and will establish in the fullness of time those things not yet ripe for establishment."[8]

10. Management of International Public Goods through a G5

Sir Paul Collier, CBE, is Professor of Economics and Public Policy at the Blavatnik School of Government, Director for the Centre for the Study of African Economies at the University of Oxford, and Fellow of St Antony's College. He is the author of *The Bottom Billion: Why the Poorest Countries Are Failing and What Can Be Done about It*; *The Plundered Planet: Why We Must, and How We Can, Manage Nature for Global Prosperity*; and *Exodus: How Migration Is Changing Our World*. He writes on the critical need in the future for better diplomatic management of important public goods.

> Diplomacy at its best enables countries to reap mutual benefits from long term cooperation. The 20th Century had less need for such diplomacy than the 21st. The milestones of the 20th Century were the provision of a range of public goods such as education, health care and pensions: these could be achieved by *national* actions and *annual* budgeting. In the 21st Century, as rising populations and incomes come up against limited global resources, and as technology creates new unregulated global arenas, many of the key public goods will be international, and they will require long-term perspectives. We will need institutions equivalent to national, annual budgets that work *internationally* and *inter-temporally*. Tackling global warming; conserving fish stocks, exploiting the polar regions, and managing the web; are evident examples of the international public goods that require such institutions. There is no prospect of them being generated by a centralized global government. Instead, they will have to be achieved piecemeal through cooperation between key countries.
>
> In *The Plundered Planet* I sketched a possible route to such cooperation, using the concept of the "G5." As with any public good, the key problem is free-riding. The G5 is a notional grouping of those polities which are manifestly too big to think that they could free ride: unless they participate in a solution the problem will not be solved by others. These five are the USA, China, the European Union (to the extent that it can act in a unified fashion on global issues), India and Japan. A pressing task for diplomacy is for these five countries to recognize that they face the same problem: they cannot free-ride on solutions to global problems whereas smaller countries can. The task of getting these five to cooperate is difficult because they have historic

rivalries and no tradition of cooperation. Yet it is far easier than getting global cooperation through the UN: 200 radically different countries can barely agree on anything.

The G5 jointly have the responsibility for building the institutions the world will need. Through a mixture of carrots, sticks and flattery they will jointly have to induce as many other countries as possible not to free-ride. I predict a preference for sticks over carrots: sticks are usually cheaper. The global public goods agenda thus calls for two new tasks of diplomacy. One is that the G5 have to learn how to cooperate with each other, starting from positions of deep distrust. The other is that collectively, they will have to coax and cajole other countries into supporting rather than undermining the institutions that are now needed.[9]

11. International Stakeholder Structures in Diplomacy

Parag Khanna is Director of the Hybrid Reality Institute, Senior Fellow at the New America Foundation, Adjunct Professor in the Lee Kuan Yew School of Public Policy at the National University of Singapore, Visiting Fellow at LSE IDEAS, Senior Fellow at the European Council on Foreign Relations, and Senior Fellow at the Singapore Institute of International Affairs. He is the author of *The Second World: Empires and Influence in the New Global Order; How to Run the World: Charting a Course to the Next Renaissance*; and co-author of *Hybrid Reality: Thriving in the Emerging Human-Technology Civilization*. The criteria for establishing membership for new diplomatic institutions should contain key ingredients.

Any new institutions of diplomacy must have three features:

- Stakeholder inclusive: Is there a structural role given to governments/governmental agencies, the private sector, and civil society?
- Bottom-up/subsidiarity: Are maximal resources allocated to actors closest to the problem, empowered to develop their own solutions?
- Mutual accountability: Are stakeholder relations structured to make coalition members accountable to each other and the collective agreed goals?

The resulting institutional selection would favor initiatives such as the Extractive Industries Transparency Initiative (EITI), while de-emphasizing proposals such as a "World Environment Organization," and regional peacekeeping bodies/operations over Western-led ones.[10]

12. New Education for Diplomats

Paul Sharp is Professor and Head of Political Science at the University of Minnesota Duluth, coeditor of the *Hague Journal of Diplomacy*, and author of

Diplomatic Theory of International Relations. He suggests focusing reform on how diplomatic education is framed.

> Most education in social studies, history and civics focuses on developing students' abilities to discover their own position on a particular issue, problem or topic, and to make the case for why others should regard their position as right. Diplomatic education, as I understand it, would shift their focus to creating and developing workable/liveable solutions, as well as valuing coexistence and simply rubbing along together. For example, the questions "who is right?" and "what is the correct solution?" are not particularly useful questions to ask regarding Syria at the moment, but those are the question that our students are taught to ask and answer. More diplomatic education would result in a citizenry which would be more tolerant of ambiguous, imperfect and incomplete answers, in making sense both of disputes around the world and those which they get into in their own lives.[11]

13. Parties to a Dispute at the United Nations May Brief in Person

Carne Ross is the founder of Independent Diplomat, which is based in New York City, and provides confidential advice and practical assistance in diplomatic strategy and technique to governments, political groups, international organizations, and non-governmental organizations. He proposes reforming a practice of dispute settlement at the UN Security Council.

> The idea is a simple one. All parties to a dispute should be given the chance to air their views in any diplomatic discussion of that dispute. At present, at the UN Security Council for instance, it is usual practice for Council members to invite UN officials to brief them on an agenda item. Only rarely are the actual parties consulted directly. Occasionally, the Council may use its so-called "Arria formula" meetings to invite a non-state party to address them in an informal meeting, but this tool is infrequently used, and when it is, it is invariably to introduce the views of a party to whom one Council member—usually a P5 member—is sympathetic. More often, the Council may hold an open meeting at which other UN member states may speak, including those most directly involved. But there is no routine practice whereby the parties are consulted, either during informal or formal meetings. This makes no sense. At a minimum, diplomatic decisions, for instance at the UN, would be better informed if those making them knew the views of those most concerned from them directly (and not mediated by others). Resulting decisions, or diplomatic agreements, would be more likely to endure if they accounted for such views. Finally, simple justice is better served by such inclusion. Such a practice is easily introduced

and requires no formal vote or General Assembly decision. There are no formal rules of procedure at the Security Council. Council members could simply agree to allow the parties to put their views to them. Ideally, this would take place in person in order to allow an exchange which would also help the party concerned understand the Security Council's own views. But if not possible, for instance if a visa is denied, this might take place by video link (something the Council has started to use, a little) or, at a minimum, on paper. One typical objection is that the invitation to such parties may "legitimize" them by giving them status at the world body. But this might be avoided by treating such discussion as purely informal, or by denying the party the possibility to attend in person. Of course, the objection would be minimized if the practice were routinely instituted.[12]

14. Examples of Innovative Methods of Diplomatic Consultation

Alan K. Henrikson is the Lee E. Dirks Professor of Diplomatic History at The Fletcher School, Tufts University. He is the author of, inter alia, *The Future of Diplomacy? Five Projective Visions*; *What Can Public Diplomacy Achieve?* and "United States Contemporary Diplomacy: Implementing a Foreign Policy of 'Engagement,'" in *Diplomacy in a Globalizing World*. He focuses on innovative diplomatic groupings and their memberships.

Three examples of innovative approaches to inclusiveness and new alliances in diplomatic processes are evident in The Arctic Council, The Global Compact and in the UN Alliance of Civilizations. They show international groupings of states or multilateral groups engaging in diplomacy on international issues not simply from the standpoint of one national interest.

(a) The Arctic Council provides for the full participation of Arctic Indigenous Peoples. They are known as Permanent Participants and representatives of six Arctic Indigenous Peoples' Organizations work side by side with the eight Arctic Member Countries. The Council's mandate includes incorporating the traditional and cultural needs, values, rights and practices of Arctic Indigenous Peoples in its programs and policies.

(b) The Global Compact is a UN initiative to encourage acceptance by international business and professional bodies of sustainable and universal social principles. It covers human and labor rights, the environment and anti-corruption measures. The Compact is not a regulatory instrument but an innovative forum for discussion combining two non-state actors—the UN and business groups—to promote global norms.

(c) The Alliance of Civilizations. The United Nations Alliance of Civilizations (UNAOC) is an initiative proposed at UNGA in 2005. It was co-sponsored by the Spanish and Turkish Prime Ministers. It is a transnational alliance to promote access to education and online resources which promote international, intercultural and interreligious dialogue and cooperation. It has staged a series of fora aimed at defusing tensions between the Western and Islamic worlds.[13]

15. Training for Nonstate Actors

Dr. Peter Howarth, Director Political & Strategic Issues at the Government of Australia, Department of Foreign Affairs and Trade. He proposes a diplomatic initiative to improve the capacity of nonstate actors to participate in diplomacy.

> While there are a number of initiatives for building understanding and practical capabilities for state actors in international diplomacy, as far as I am aware there are few (if any) similar initiatives for non-state actors. Yet it is a commonplace in commentary on contemporary diplomacy that non-state actors play an increasingly important and influential role. In the early 1990s Australia included representatives from Greenpeace and the Australian Coal Association on our delegation to the negotiating committee for the Framework Convention on Climate Change. In those days, this was regarded as a fairly radical innovation. Nowadays, it is unremarkable. So, would there be some value in developing activities—such as conferences or training courses—to improve the understanding and the capacity of non-state actors to engage in diplomacy?[14]

FINAL THOUGHTS

Diplomacy has a distinguished history. It has been brave and compassionate and produced remarkable results. The four freedoms of Franklin Roosevelt still provide simple focuses for its core activities. The drive to rescue our fellow humans from poverty and disease, as well as ensure freedom from want, has been a noble, if messy and incomplete, process. Modern technology has also given many freedom of expression. But the freedom of religion that depends on tolerance of others and the freedom from fear are still far from realized. And it is a salutary thought that the divisions of the world would perhaps be seen as more trivial if diplomats got out more—out into space.

Three citizens of different states who have traveled in space have offered similar perspectives on the shared interests we all have.

> "I felt like I was almost looking at a secret . . . that humans weren't supposed to see this. It's too beautiful."—Michael Massimino, a U.S. astronaut who worked at the Hubble Space Telescope[15]

> "The world looks marvelous from up here, so peaceful, so wonderful and so fragile. Everybody, all of us down there, not only in Israel, have to keep it clean and good."—Israeli Air Force Colonel Ilan Ramon, the first Israeli astronaut[16]

> "We were flying over America and suddenly I saw snow, the first snow we ever saw from orbit. I have never visited America, but I imagined that the arrival of autumn and winter is the same there as in other places, and the process of getting ready for them is the same. And then it struck me that we are all children of our Earth."—Russian cosmonaut and flight engineer Aleksandr Aleksandrov[17]

If just a few of the ideas outlined attracted support and funding, then diplomacy would have ticked a box of progress. If more ideas were added, and unsuccessful ones discarded, then diplomacy would indeed be advancing. Sovereign states would not be threatened, and collectively they would be recognizing their shared interests. By questioning its operations, diplomacy will suggest to the global public it believes in its functions and is determined to fix its collective problems. As Elon Musk, a versatile South African/Canadian/U.S. entrepreneur and engineer, has said, "If something's important enough you should try. Even if . . . the probable outcome is failure."[18] If diplomacy is trying, then disillusioned youth in Peshawar, Peoria, or Phnom Penh might just notice. Some of them might be inspired by a similar exhortation as President Kennedy gave in March 1961 to nondiplomats, the first men and women to apply to the U.S. Peace Corps. He called on them "to sacrifice their energies and time and toil to the cause of world peace and human progress."[19]

As it stands, diplomacy is a cause without a rebel. It has little agenda for reform, little capacity for continuous and constructive dialogue outside the framework of the sovereign states, and no broad vision of collective existence on the planet. Diplomacy's contribution to human development has been substantial. Now that the power of many has replaced the power of few, diplomacy must be made to work better. Ultimately, its failures lead to actors' choosing alternative courses, many of which involve repression, violence, and greed. All who detest such activities have an interest in diplomacy reasserting itself.

Notes and References

Introduction Notes

1. Sir Ivor Roberts, ed., *Satow's Diplomatic Practice,* 6th ed. (New York: Oxford University Press, 2009), xxv.
2. Ibid.
3. Sir Harold Nicolson, *Diplomacy* (Washington, DC: The Institute for the Study of Diplomacy, School of Foreign Service, Georgetown University, 1988), 4.
4. Henry A. Kissinger, *A World Restored: Metternich, Castlereagh and the Problems of Peace 1812–1822* (Brattleboro, VT: Echo Point Books & Media, 2013), 326.
5. Paul Sharp, *Diplomatic Theory of International Relations* (New York: Cambridge University Press, 2009).
6. John S. Dryzek, *Foundations and Frontiers of Deliberative Democracy* (New York: Oxford University Press, 2010).

Chapter 1 Notes

1. Sir Harold Nicolson, *The Evolution of Diplomacy: Being the Chichele—Lectures Delivered at the University of Oxford in November 1953* (New York: Collier Books, 1962), xxv.
2. Niccolo Machiavelli, *The Prince,* ed. Quentin Skinner and Russell Price (Cambridge, UK: Cambridge University Press, 1988).
3. Armand Jean du Plessis Richelieu, duc de, *The Political Testament of Cardinal Richelieu,* trans. Henry Bertram Hill (Madison: University of Wisconsin Press, 1961).
4. Emer de Vattel, *The Law of Nations: Or, Principles of the Law of Nature, Applied to the Conduct and Affairs of Nations and Sovereigns,* 6th ed., ed. Joseph Chitty (Philadelphia: T. & J. W. Johnson, 1844), chap. VI, para. 57.
5. Emer de Vattel, *The Law of Nations: Or, Principles of the Law of Nature, Applied to the Conduct and Affairs of Nations and Sovereigns,* (Washington, DC: Carnegie Institute of Washington, 1916), 362.
6. Sir Ivor Roberts, ed., *Satow's Diplomatic Practice,* 6th ed. (New York: Oxford University Press, 2009), 15.
7. Woodrow Wilson, "Analyzing German and Austrian Peace Utterances," address to Congress, February 11, 1918, http://www.gwpda.org/1918/wilpeace.html.
8. United Nations, "Trade and Development Report, 2011," United Nations Conference on Trade and Development, http://unctad.org/en/docs/tdr2011_en.pdf, I.
9. United Nations, "World Economic Situation and Prospects 2012," United Nations, http://www.un.org/en/development/desa/policy/wesp/wesp_archive/2012chap2.pdf.
10. William Hague, "The Foreign Office, One of the Great Offices of State," speech on December 18, 2012, https://www.gov.uk/government/speeches/the-foreign-office-one-of-the-great-offices-of-state.
11. Anne-Marie Slaughter, "Remarks, the Big Picture: Beyond Hot Spots & Crises in Our Interconnected World," *Journal of Law & International Affairs* 1, no. 2 (2012), http://elibrary.law.psu.edu/jlia/v011/iss2/5.

12. Henry Kissinger, *Diplomacy* (New York: Simon & Schuster, 1994), 27.
13. Woodrow Wilson, "Peace Without Victory," January 22, 1917, Mount Holyoke College, https://www.mtholyoke.edu/acad/intrel/ww15.htm.

Chapter 2 Notes

1. H. M. A. Keens-Soper & Karl W. Schweizer, eds., *François de Callières: The Art of Diplomacy* (Leicester, UK: Leicester University Press, 1983), 50–1.
2. Ibid.
3. Ibid.
4. From Documents Diplomatiques Français, 1871–1914, quoted in Keith Hamilton and Richard Langhorne, *The Practice of Diplomacy: Its Evolution, Theory, and Administration* (London, UK: Routledge, 2011), 191.
5. Christopher Meyer, "Getting Our Way: 500 Years of Adventure and Intrigue, the Inside Story of British Diplomacy" (London: Weidenfeld & Nicolson, 2009), 17.
6. Jeremy Greenstock, "The Rules of the Game: Does the Diplomat's Guidebook Need an Update?" October 28, 2009, *The Times Literary Supplement*, http://www.the-tls.co.uk/tls/.
7. From *Vienna Convention on Diplomatic Relations and Optimal Protocol*, © 1961, United Nations. Reprinted with the permission of the United Nations.
8. Ibid.
9. Ibid, Article 8.
10. Ibid, Article 13.
11. Ibid.
12. Ibid.
13. Ibid.
14. Ibid.
15. Ibid, Article 9.
16. Ibid.
17. United Kingdom Foreign & Commonwealth Office, "Written Ministerial Statement: Diplomatic Missions and International Organisations in the United Kingdom with unpaid London Congestion Charge and Fines: 2011," http://www.publications.parliament.uk/pa/cm201213/cmhansrd/cm120705/wmstext/120705m0001.htm.
18. Lynn Berry, "Russia Accuses USAID of Trying to Sway Elections," September 19, 2012, http://bigstory.ap.org/article/russia-accuses-usaid-trying-sway-elections.
19. From *Vienna Convention on Diplomatic Relations*, © United Nations. Reprinted with the permission of the United Nations.
20. Lydia Polgreen, "Malawi Leader's Death Is Reported Unofficially, and U.S. Worries about Succession," *New York Times*, April 6, 2012, http://www.nytimes.com/2012/04/07/world/africa/questions-swirl-around-malawis-president-after-heart-attack.html?_r=1&.
21. From *Vienna Convention on Consular Relations*, © 1963, United Nations. Reprinted with the permission of the United Nations.
22. Ibid.
23. Ibid.
24. Ibid.
25. Atle Grahl-Madsen, *Territorial Asylum* (Stockholm, Sweden: Almqvist & Wicksel International, 1980), 57.

26. From *Vienna Convention on Diplomatic Relations*, Preamble, © United Nations. Reprinted with the permission of the United Nations.
27. UN General Assembly, Declaration on Territorial Asylum, 14 December 1967, A/RES/2312(XXII), Article 1.
28. From *Vienna Convention on Diplomatic Relations*, Preamble, © United Nations. Reprinted with the permission of the United Nations.
29. Ibid.
30. Ibid.
31. Organization of American States, Department of International Law, "Convention on Diplomatic Asylum," 1954, http://www.oas.org/juridico/english/treaties/a-46.html.
32. Kevin Rawlinson, "Exclusive: 'Incredible strain' in Relations between Ecuador and Wikileaks Founder Julian Assange over His Involvement in Edward Snowden NSA Whistleblower Affair," *The Independent,* July 1, 2013, http://www.independent.co.uk/news/world/politics/exclusive-incredible-strain-in-relations-between-ecuador-and-wikileaks-founder-julian-assange-over-his-involvement-in-edward-snowden-nsa-whistleblower-affair-8681776.html.

Chapter 3 Notes

1. G. R. Berridge, *Diplomacy: Theory and Practice,* 3rd ed. (Basingstoke, UK: Palgrave Macmillan, 2005), 5.
2. Sir Harold Nicolson, *Diplomacy* (London: Oxford University Press, 1945), 33.
3. François de Callières, *The Practice of Diplomacy,* trans. A. F. Whyte (London: Constable & Co. Ltd., 1919), 31.
4. From *Vienna Convention on Diplomatic Relations and Optimal Protocol,* © 1961, http://www.state.gov/documents/organization/17843.pdf, United Nations. Reprinted with the permission of the United Nations.
5. Ministry of Foreign Affairs, Dhaka, "Foreign Service Academy: About Academy," http://www.mofa.gov.bd/index.php?option=com_content&view=article&id=114&Itemid=106.
6. Anna Codrea-Rado, "Foreign Office Beefs up Diplomats' Language Training," *Guardian,* September 30, 2013, http://www.theguardian.com/education/2013/sep/30/foreign-office-opens-language-centre.
7. "The Effect of the Spending Review on the Performance of the FCO," February 11, 2011, http://www.publications.parliament.uk/pa/cm201011/cmselect/cmfaff/572/57206.htm.
8. "Examination of Witnesses (Questions 1–47)," January 20, 2011, http://www.publications.parliament.uk/pa/cm201011/cmselect/cmfaff/438/10090802.htm.
9. Jonathan Fenby, "Does China Have a Foreign Policy? Domestic Pressures and China's Strategy," LSE Ideas, *China's Geoeconomic Strategy: Special report,* June 2012, http://www.lse.ac.uk/IDEAS/publications/reports/pdf/SR012/fenby.pdf, 1.
10. William Hague, "Speech: The Foreign Office, One of the Great Offices of State," December 18, 2012, https://www.gov.uk/government/speeches/the-foreign-office-one-of-the-great-offices-of-state.
11. Kathyrn Blaze Carlson, "Opposition Outrage Aside, Joint Embassies with U.K. Are 'a No-Brainer,' Experts Say," *National Post,* September 24, 2012, http://news.nationalpost.com/2012/09/24/opposition-outrage-aside-joint-embassies-with-u-k-are-a-no-brainer-experts-say.

12. Parliament of Canada, "41st Parliament, 1st Session, Edited Hansard, Number 151," September 24, 2012, http://www.parl.gc.ca/HousePublications/Publication.aspx?DocId=5716754&Language=E&Mode=1.
13. United Kingdom Foreign & Commonwealth Office, *Active Diplomacy for a Changing World: The UK's International Priorities,* March 2006, https://www.gov.uk/government/uploads/system/uploads/attachment_data/file/272260/6762.pdf, 20.
14. Dan Roberts, "Obama Tries to Ease NSA Tensions and Insists: Europe Spies on US Too," *The Guardian,* July 1, 2013, http://www.theguardian.com/world/2013/jul/01/obama-europe-monitoring-data-surveillance.
15. Kayte Rath, "French Diplomatic Service is the World's Best, U.K. Says," BBC News, November 8, 2012, http://www.bbc.com/news/uk-politics-20218377.
16. Ibid.
17. Ibid.
18. United Kingdom Foreign & Commonwealth Office, "Foreign Secretary Launches New FCO Crisis Centre," October 16, 2012, https://www.gov.uk/government/news/foreign-secretary-launches-new-fco-crisis-centre.
19. Sherard Cowper-Coles, *Cables from Kabul: The Inside Story of the West's Afghanistan Campaign* (London: HarperCollins, 2011), 94.
20. Ibid, 93.

Chapter 4 Notes

1. Charles Seignobos, *1815–1915, From the Congress of Vienna to the War of 1914,* trans. P. E. Matheson (Paris: A. Colin, 1915). Accessed via https://archive.org/details/cong18151915from00seigrich.
2. Oscar Wilde, *The Soul of Man under Socialism* (Boston: J. W. Luce, 1910), 27.
3. From *Charter of the United Nations, Chapter I: Purposes and Principles,* © 2014, United Nations. Reprinted with the permission of the United Nations.
4. From *The United Nations: An Introduction for Students,* © 2000, http://www.un.org/pubs/cyberschoolbus/unintro/unintr03.htm, United Nations. Reprinted with the permission of the United Nations.
5. From *Charter of the United Nations, Chapter V: The Security Council,* © 2014, http://www.un.org/en/documents/charter/chapter5.shtml, United Nations. Reprinted with the permission of the United Nations.
6. From *General Assembly—Fifth Session,* © 1950, http://www.un.org/en/sc/repertoire/otherdocs/GAres377A(v), p. 1, United Nations. Reprinted with the permission of the United Nations.
7. From *United Nations General Assembly, Sixty-Sixth Session Third Committee Agenda Item 69,* © November 17, 2011, http://www.un.org/ga/search/view_doc.asp?symbol=A/C.3/66/L.57/Rev.1, United Nations. Reprinted with the permission of the United Nations.
8. From *Charter of the United Nations, Chapter XVIII: Amendments,* © 2014, www.un.org/en/documents/charter/chapter18.shtml United Nations. Reprinted with the permission of the United Nations.
9. From *Charter of the United Nations, Chapter VII: Action with Respect to Threats to the Peace, Breaches of the Peace, and Acts of Aggression,* © 2014, www.un.org/en/documents/charter/chapter7.shtml, United Nations. Reprinted with the permission of the United Nations.
10. Ibid.
11. Ibid.

12. United Nations, "Charter of the United Nations, Chapter X: The Economic and Social Council," 2014, http://www.un.org/en/documents/charter/chapter10.shtml. Reprinted with the permission of the United Nations.
13. United Nations, "Charter of the United Nations, Chapter IX: International Economic and Social Co-Operation," 2014, http://www.un.org/en/documents/charter/chapter9.shtml. Reprinted with the permission of the United Nations.
14. United Nations, "Charter of the United Nations, Chapter X: The Economic and Social Council," 2014, http://www.un.org/en/documents/charter/chapter10.shtml. Reprinted with the permission of the United Nations.
15. Ibid.
16. Sir Ivor Roberts, ed., *Satow's Diplomatic Practice,* 6th ed. (New York: Oxford University Press, 2009).
17. United Nations, "The Role of the Secretary-General," 2014, http://www.un.org/sg/sg_role.shtml?fb_action_ids=639360066126169&fb_action_types=og.recommends&fb_source=aggregation&fb_aggregation_id=288381481237582. Reprinted with the permission of the United Nations.
18. United Nations, "Charter of the United Nations, Chapter XV: The Secretariat," 2014, http://www.un.org/en/documents/charter/chapter15.shtml.
19. Associated Press, "Samantha Power: United Nations 'has lost its way,'" *Politico,* August 11, 2013, http://www.politico.com/story/2013/08/samantha-power-united-nations-lost-its-way-95422.html.
20. Samantha Power, "Force Full," *New Republic,* March 3, 2003, http://www.newrepublic.com/article/srebenica-liberalism-balkan-united%20nations.
21. United Nations, "Charter of the United Nations, Preamble," 2014, http://www.un.org/en/documents/charter/preamble.shtml. Reprinted with the permission of the United Nations.
22. "UN Security Council Resolution 1973 (2011) on Libya—Full Text," *The Guardian,* March 17, 2011, http://www.theguardian.com/world/2011/mar/17/un-security-council-resolution.
23. Aljazeera, "UN's Pillay slams Security Council 'failure,'" August 22, 2014, http://www.aljazeera.com/news/middleeast/2014/08/un-pillay-slams-security-council-failure-2014821223555682253.html.
24. United Nations, *An Agenda for Peace: Preventive Diplomacy, Peacemaking and Peace-keeping,* June 17, 1992. http://www.unrol.org/files/A_47_277.pdf.
25. United Nations, "Global Issues: Health," 2014, http://www.un.org/en/globalissues/health. Reprinted with the permission of the United Nations.
26. United Nations, Mandating and Delivering: Analysis and Recommendations to Facilitate the Review of Mandates, March 30, 2006. http://www.securitycouncilreport.org/atf/cf/%7B65BFCF9B-6D27–4E9C-8CD3-CF6E4FF96FF9%7D/A60733.pdf. Reprinted with the permission of the United Nations.
27. Ibid.
28. Ibid.
29. Ibid.
30. Associated Press, "U.S. Statement on UNESCO," *New York Times,* December 30, 1983, http://www.nytimes.com/1983/12/30/world/us-statement-on-unesco.html.
31. United Nations High Commissioner for Refugees, "About Refugees," 2014, http://unhcr.org.au/unhcr/index.php?option=com_content&view=article&id=179&Itemid=54. Reprinted with the permission of the United Nations.

32. International Commission on Intervention and State Sovereignty, *The Responsibility to Protect,* 2001, http://responsibilitytoprotect.org/ICISS%20Report.pdf, vii.
33. *The Contitutive Act of the African Union,* http://www.au.int/en/sites/default/files/ConstitutiveAct_EN.pdf.
34. United Nations, *Resolution Adopted by the General Assembly: 60/1. 2005 World Summit Outcome,* October 24, 2005, http://www.un.org/womenwatch/ods/A-RES-60-1-E.pdf. Reprinted with the permission of the United Nations.
35. Statement by H. E. Ambassador Antonio de Aguiar Patriota, February 21, 2012, http://www.un.int/brazil/speech/12d-agp-RESPONSIBILITY-WHILE-PROTECTING.html. Reprinted with the permission of the United Nations.
36. United Nations. *Annex to the Letter Dated 9 November 2011 from the Permanent Representative of Brazil to the United Nations Addressed to the Secretary-General,* November 11, 2011, http://www.un.int/brazil/speech/Concept-Paper-%20RwP.pdf. Reprinted with the permission of the United Nations.
37. World Commission on Environment and Development. *Our Common Future.* (Oxford: Oxford University Press, 1987), 43.
38. United Nations Framework Convention on Climate Change, "Article 2: Objective," 1997, http://unfccc.int/essential_background/convention/background/items/1353.php.
39. United Nations, "About the Ethics Office," 2014, http://www.un.org/en/ethics/what.shtml. Reprinted with the permission of the United Nations.
40. United Nations, "The Millennium Goals: Eight Goals for 2015," 2014, http://www.undp.org/content/undp/en/home/mdgoverview.html. Reprinted with the permission of the United Nations.
41. Matthew Saltmarsh, "A Bloated U.N. Bureaucracy Causes Bewilderment," *New York Times,* January 5 2011, http://www.nytimes.com/2011/01/06/world/europe/06iht-nations06.html?pagewanted=all.
42. George W. Bush, "Summary of National Security Strategy 2002," http://georgewbush-whitehouse.archives.gov/nsc/nss/2006/sectionV.html.
43. Ibid.
44. Hans Blix, "All Eyes on the Inspector: An Interview with the U.N. Diplomat," *Time,* March 3, 2003, 2.
45. United Nations, "Iraq Cooperating with Disarmament Procedures, but Many Banned Weapons Remain Unaccounted for, Inspectors Tell Security Council," February 14, 2003, http://www.un.org/News/Press/docs/2003/sc7664.doc.htm.
46. Organisation for the Prohibition of Chemical Weapons, "Update on Chemical Demilitarization," April 21, 2009, http://www.opcw.org/news/article/status-of-chemical-demilitarisation-as-at-21-april-2009.

Chapter 5 Notes

1. The Churchill Society, "Mr. Winston Churchill Speaking in Zurich, 19th September 1946," http://www.churchill-society-london.org.uk/astonish.html.
2. Robert Schuman, "The Coming Century of Supranational Communities," May 16, 1949, http://www.schuman.info/Strasbourg549.htm.
3. "The Schuman Declaration—9 May 1950," European Union, http://europa.eu/about-eu/basic-information/symbols/europe-day/schuman-declaration/index_en.htm.

4. Strobe Talbott, "What Would Jean Monnet Have Done?" *New York Times,* February 7, 2014, http://www.nytimes.com/2014/02/08/opinion/what-would-jean-monnet-have-done.html?_r=0.
5. BBC News, "UK Risks 'Turning Inwards' over EU Referendum—US Official," January 9, 2013, http://www.bbc.com/news/uk-politics-20961651.
6. Maxine James and Matthew Purvis, "The European Union," House of Lords Library Note, April 23, 2014; The European Citizens' Initiative, "FAQ on the EU Competences and the European Commission Powers," http://ec.europa.eu/citizens-initiative/public/competences/faq#q1.
7. Robert Schuman, "Speech at the United Nations General Assembly, 3rd Session, 28 September 1948," http://www.schuman.info/UN4849.htm.
8. "European Union Is 'Too Big and Too Bossy,'" Sky News, May 28, 2014, http://news.sky.com/story/1270238/european-union-is-too-big-and-too-bossy.
9. "EU election: France's Hollande Calls for Reform of 'Remote' EU," BBC News, May 27, 2014, http://www.bbc.com/news/world-europe-27579235.
10. The Lisbon Treaty, "Article 17," 2007, http://www.lisbon-treaty.org/wcm/the-lisbon-treaty/treaty-on-european-union-and-comments/title-3-provisions-on-the-institutions/86-article-17.html.
11. Vivien A. Schmidt, "The European Union's Eurozone Crisis and What (Not) to Do about It," *Brown Journal of World Affairs* XVII, no. 1 (2010), http://fmwww.bc.edu/ec-j/SemF2011/Schmidt.pdf.
12. European Commission, "Economic and Financial Affairs," http://ec.europa.eu/economy_finance/international/enlargement/criteria/index_en.htm.
13. Vivien A. Schmidt, "The European Union's Eurozone Crisis."
14. "The High Representative of the Union for Foreign Affairs and Security Policy," European Union External Action, http://eeas.europa.eu/ashton/index_en.htm.
15. Pew Research Global Attitudes Project, "European Unity on the Rocks: Greeks and Germans at Polar Opposites," May 29, 2012, http://www.pewglobal.org/2012/05/29/european-unity-on-the-rocks.
16. Andrew Osborn, "Britain Asks Germany to Help Lead Reform of EU," Reuters, May 31, 2013, http://www.reuters.com/article/2013/05/31/us-britain-europe-germany-idUSBRE94U0MI20130531.
17. "38th Assembly of Heads of State and Government of the OAU, 8 July 2002: Address by UN Secretary-General Kofi Annan," African Union Summit, http://www.au2002.gov.za/docs/speeches/anna087a.htm5.
18. African Union, "Synthesis Paper on Boosting Intra-African Trade and Fast Tracking the Continental Free Trade Area," http://pages.au.int/sites/default/files/Synthesis%20Paper%200n%20Boosting%20Intra-African%20Trade%20Jan%202012_0.pdf.
19. Republic of the Philippines Department of Foreign Affairs, "The Founding of ASEAN," http://www.jakartapm.dfa.gov.ph/index.php/asean-history.
20. Joshua Kurlantzik, "ASEAN's Future and Asia Integration," Council on Foreign Relations, November 2012, http://www.cfr.org/asia-and-pacific/aseans-future-asian-integration/p29247.
21. Ben Bland, "ASEAN Chief: South China Sea Risks Becoming 'Asia's Palestine,'" CNN, http://edition.cnn.com/2012/11/28/business/south-china-sea-asia-palestine/index.html.
22. Organization of American States, Department of International Law, "Charter of the Organization of American States (A-41)," 1948, http://oas.org/dil/treaties_A-41_Charter_of_the_Organization_of_American_States.htm.

23. Yale Law School, The Avalon Project, "Pact of the League of Arab States, March 22, 1945," http://avalon.law.yale.edu/20th_century/arableag.asp.
24. "The Empire Strikes Back: Some British Eurosceptics See the Commonwealth as an Alternative to Europe. It isn't," *The Economist,* http://www.economist.com/news/britain/21567071-some-british-eurosceptics-see-commonwealth-alterna tive-europe-it-isnt-empire.
25. David H. Dunn, ed., *Diplomacy at the Highest Level: The Evolution of International Summitry* (New York: Palgrave Macmillan, 1996), 17.
26. The White House Office of the Press Secretary, "Press Conference by the President: U.S. Press Filing Center, L'Aquila, Italy," July 10, 2009, http://www.whitehouse.gov/the-press-office/press-conference-president-laquila-italy-7–10–09.
27. Manfred Ertel, "Norway Takes Aim at G-20: 'One of the Greatest Setbacks Since World War II,'" *Der Spiegel,* June 22, 2010, http://www.spiegel.de/international/europe/norway-takes-aim-at-g-20-one-of-the-greatest-setbacks-since-world-war-ii-a-702104.html.

Chapter 6 Notes

1. Aljazeera, "Syria envoy says UN Council 'last appeal'" February 2, 2013, http://www.aljazeera.com/news/middleeast/2013/02/2013227334225520.html.
2. Ibid.
3. United Nations, "Charter of the United Nations, Preamble," 2014, http://www.un.org/en/documents/charter/preamble.shtml. Reprinted with the permission of the United Nations.
4. G. R. Berridge, *Diplomacy: Theory and Practice,* 4th ed. (New York: Palgrave Macmillan, 2010).
5. Raymond Cohen, *Negotiating across Cultures: International Communication in an Interdependent World,* rev. ed. (Washington, DC: United States Institute of Peace, 1997).
6. Ibid, 201.
7. I. William Zartman, ed., *The Negotiation Process: Theories and Applications,* (Beverly Hills: Sage, 1978).
8. Todd Hall and Keren Yarhi-Milo, "The Personal Touch, Leaders' Impressions, Costly Signaling, and Assessment of Sincerity in International Affairs." *International Studies Quarterly* 56 (September 2012): 560–73.
9. Nicholas Cull, "Public Diplomacy: Taxonomies and Histories," *Annals of the American Academy of Political and Social Sciences* 616, no. 1 (2008): p. 31–34.

Chapter 7 Notes

1. The Fletcher School, Tufts University, "What Is Public Diplomacy?" http://fletcher.tufts.edu/Murrow/Diplomacy.
2. Nicholas J. Cull, *Public Diplomacy: Lessons from the Past,* (Los Angeles: Figueroa Press, 2009), 6.
3. Kirk Johnson, "For the Vice President of China, Tea Time in Iowa," *New York Times,* February 15, 2012, http://www.nytimes.com/2012/02/16/world/asia/xi-jin-ping-of-china-makes-a-return-trip-to-iowa.html?_r=0.
4. Howard Somerville, "Oliver Franks," http://www.hsomerville.com/meccano/Articles/Franks.htm.

5. G. R. Berridge, *Diplomacy: Theory and Practice,* 4th ed. (New York: Palgrave Macmillan, 2010), 179.
6. Nicholas J. Cull, "Public Diplomacy: Seven Lessons for Its Future from Its Past," *Place Branding and Public Diplomacy* 6 (2010): 11–17.
7. *The Writings of Thomas Jefferson, Memorial Edition,* ed. Andrew A. Lipscomb and Albert Ellery Bergh, vol. 10 (Washington, DC: Thomas Jefferson Memorial Association of the United States, 1903), 341.
8. Joseph S. Nye Jr., *Soft Power: The Means to Success in World Politics* (New York: Public Affairs, 2004).
9. Lord Carter of Coles, *Public Diplomacy Review,* December 2005, http://www.britishcouncil.org/home-carter-report.
10. Robin Brown, *The Four Paradigms of Public Diplomacy: Building a Framework for Comparative Government External Communications Research,* 2012, http://pdnetworks.files.wordpress.com/2012/04/isa-2012-v4.pdf.
11. United Kingdom Foreign & Commonwealth Office, quoted in Harriet Straughen, "Image is everything: The Importance of Public Diplomacy in the Israeli-Palestinian Conflict," 2011, http://www.miftah.org/Doc/SpecialStudies/2011/Image_is_everything.pdf.
12. United Kingdom Foreign & Commonwealth Office, *Business Plan 2012–2015: Foreign & Commonwealth Office,* May 31, 2012, https://www.gov.uk/government/uploads/system/uploads/attachment_data/file/32853/business-plan-12.pdf.
13. Ibid.
14. United States Information Agency, Office of Public Liaison, "USIA: An Overview," August 1998, accessed October 19, 2012, http://dosfan.lib.uic.edu/usia/usiahome/oldoview.htm#overview.
15. National Commission on Terrorist Attacks upon the United States, "9/11 Commission Report," July 22, 2004, http://www.9-11commission.gov/report/911Report.pdf.
16. Judith A. McHale, "Strengthening U.S. Engagement with the World: A Review of U.S. Public Diplomacy," June 21, 2011, http://www.state.gov/r/remarks/2011/166596.htm.
17. Tara Sonenshine, "The State of American Public Diplomacy," June 28, 2012, http://www.state.gov/r/remarks/2012/195947.htm.
18. Aamer Madhani, "Cleric al-Awlaki Dubbed 'bin Laden of the Internet,'" *USA Today,* August 24, 2010, http://usatoday30.usatoday.com/news/nation/2010-08-25-1A_Awlaki25_CV_N.htm.
19. Encyclopaedia Britannica, "Beijing 2008 Olympic Games: Mount Olympus Meets the Middle Kingdom," Retrieved from https://www.britannica.com/olympics/reflections/article-277303.
20. Robert Bound, "Art Attack," *Monocle,* September 2009, 85–89, http://images.monocle.com/magazine/issues/26/art-attack.
21. Pew Research Global Attitudes Project, "Global Opinion of Obama Slips, International Policies Faulted," June 13, 2012, http://www.pewglobal.org/2012/06/13/global-opinion-of-obama-slips-international-policies-faulted.
22. People's Daily Online, "Shanghai Expo Gives Big Boost to UK University," April 15, 2011, http://english.peopledaily.com.cn/90001/90782/90873/7351449.html.
23. Ibid.
24. Visit Britain, "Inbound Tourism," http://www.visitbritain.org/insightsandstatistics/inboundtourismfacts.

25. "Anyone for Cocktails?" *The Economist,* June 26, 2008, http://www.economist.com/node/11632877.
25. Africa Files, "No Mo Ibrahim Prize for African Leadership," http://www.africafiles.org/article.asp?ID=22089.
26. Sir Ivor Roberts, ed., *Satow's Diplomatic Practice,* 6th ed. (New York: Oxford University Press, 2009).

Chapter 8 Notes

1. *Vienna Convention on the Law of Treaties,* 1969, http://legal.un.org/ilc/texts/instruments/english/conventions/1_1_1969.pdf, Article 2. Reprinted with the permission of the United Nations.
2. *Vienna Convention on the Law of Treaties between States and International Organizations or between International Organizations,* 1986, http://legal.un.org/ilc/texts/instruments/english/conventions/1_2_1986.pdf. Reprinted with the permission of the United Nations.
3. *Treaty on the Non-Proliferation of Nuclear Weapons,* 1968, http://www.iaea.org/Publications/Magazines/Bulletin/Bu11104/10403501117.pdf.
4. United Nations, "174 (II). Establishment of an International Law Commission," November 21, 1947, http://www.un.org/ga/search/view_doc.asp?symbol=A/RES/174(II). Reprinted with the permission of the United Nations.
5. International Committee of the Red Cross, *Increasing Respect for International Humanitarian Law in Non-international Armed Conflicts,* 2008, https://www.icrc.org/eng/assets/files/other/icrc_002_0923.pdf.
6. United Nations, "Charter of the United Nations: Chapter XVI: Miscellaneous Provisions," 2014, http://www.un.org/en/documents/charter/chapter16.shtml. Reprinted with the permission of the United Nations.
7. Historical Resources about the Second World War, "Declaration Regarding the Defeat of Germany and the Assumption of Supreme Authority by Allied Powers," August 19, 2008, http://historicalresources.wordpress.com/2008/08/19/declaration-regarding-the-defeat-of-germany-and-the-assumption-of-supreme-authority-by-allied-powers.
8. Robert Jackson, "Opening Statement before the International Military Tribunal," November 21, 1945, http://www.roberthjackson.org/the-man/speeches-articles/speeches/speeches-by-robert-h-jackson/opening-statement-before-the-international-military-tribunal.
9. United Nations, *1948 Convention on the Prevention and Punishment of the Crime of Genocide,* 1948, http://www.un.org/en/ga/search/view_doc.asp?symbol=A/RES/260(iii). Reprinted with the permission of the United Nations.
10. United Nations General Assembly, *Convention on the Prevention and Punishment of the Crime of Genocide,* December 9, 1948, Article VI.
11. Jack Cloherty and Pierre Thomas, "Attorney General's Blunt Warning on Terror Attacks," ABC News, December 21, 2010, http://abcnews.go.com/Politics/attorney-general-eric-holders-blunt-warning-terror-attacks/story?id=12444727.
12. United Nations, "Charter of the United Nations, Preamble," 2014, http://www.un.org/en/documents/charter/preamble.shtml. Reprinted with the permission of the United Nations.
13. *The Universal Declaration of Human Rights,* 1948, http://www.un.org/en/documents/udhr/index.shtml. Reprinted with the permission of the United Nations.

14. Franklin D. Roosevelt, "Annual Message to Congress (Four Freedoms)," January 6, 1941, Records of the United States Senate, SEN 77A-H1, Record Group 46, National Archives. http://www.ourdocuments.gov/doc.php?flash=true&doc=70.
15. Organization of Islamic Conference, *Cairo Declaration on Human Rights in Islam,* 1990, http://www.bahaistudies.net/neurelitism/library/Cairo_Declaration_on_Human_Rights_in_Islam.pdf, Article 24.
16. Ibid, Article 1.
17. "Declaration on Atomic Bomb by President Truman and Prime Ministers Attlee and King," November 15, 1945, http://www.nuclearfiles.org/menu/key-issues/nuclear-energy/history/dec-truma-atlee-king_1945-11-15.htm.
18. U.S. Congress, Office of Technology Assessment, *Nuclear Safeguards and the International Atomic Energy Agency,* OTA-ISS-615 (Washington, DC: U.S. Government Printing Office, June 1995), 25. Accessed via http://www.princeton.edu/~ota/disk1/1995/9530/953004.pdf.
19. U.S. Department of State, *A Report on the International Control of Atomic Energy,* March 16, 1946, http://www.foia.cia.gov/sites/default/files/document_conversions/50/Report_on_the_International_Control_of_Atomic_Energy_16_Mar_1946.pdf.
20. Dwight D. Eisenhower, "Atoms for Peace," December 8, 1953, http://voicesofdemocracy.umd.edu/eisenhower-atoms-for-peace-speech-text.
21. Ibid.
22. *Treaty on the Non-Proliferation of Nuclear Weapons.*
23. Adam Smith, *The Wealth of Nations,* Book IV:2, Modern Library ed. (New York: Random House, 1994).
24. Cordell Hull, *The Memoirs of Cordell Hull* (New York: Macmillan, 1948), 81.
25. Cordell Hull Institute, "Who Was Cordell Hull?" http://www.cordellhullinstitute.org/role/who.html.
26. Jide Nzelibe, "Symposium: Public International Law and Economics: The Case against Reforming the WTO Enforcement Mechanism," *University of Illinois Law Review* 319 (2008), https://litigation-essentials.lexisnexis.com/webcd/app?action=DocumentDisplay&crawlid=1&doctype=cite&docid=2008+U.+Ill.+L.+Rev.+319&srctype=smi&srcid=3B15&key=4522d3c205e8b257c0b14ded201996dc.
27. International Monetary Fund, "About the International Monetary System: What is the International Monetary System, and Why Does It Need Reforming?" February 10, 2011, http://www.imsreform.org/about.html.
28. International Court of Justice, *Accordance with International Law of the Unilateral Declaration of Independence in Respect of Kosovo,* July 22, 2010, http://www.icj-cij.org/docket/files/141/15987.pdf.
29. United Nations, "Resolution 1214," December 8, 1998, http://www.treasury.gov/resource-center/sanctions/Documents/1214.pdf. Reprinted with the permission of the United Nations.
30. United Nations, "Report on the Question of International Criminal Jurisdiction by Emil Sandström, Special Rapporteur," *Yearbook of the International Law Commission* II (1950), http://legal.un.org/ilc/documentation/english/a_cn4_20.pdf. Reprinted with the permission of the United Nations.
31. United Nations Security Council, "Resolution 242 (1967)," November 22, 1967, http://unispal.un.org/unispal.nsf/0/7D35E1F729DF491C85256EE700686136. Reprinted with the permission of the United Nations.
32. Ibid.

33. United Nations Security Council, "Resolution 1737 (2006)," http://www.iaea.org/newscenter/focus/iaeairan/unsc_res1737-2006.pdf. Reprinted with the permission of the United Nations.

Chapter 9 Notes

1. Keith Hamilton and Richard Langhorne, *The Practice of Diplomacy,* 2nd ed. (New York: Routledge, 2010), 271.
2. Paul Sharp, *The Diplomatic Theory of International Relations* (New York: Cambridge University Press, 2009), 310.
3. Government of China, "China's Views on the Development of Multipolarization," May 17, 2004, http://ee.china-embassy.org/eng/zggk/xzgwjjs/t110330.htm.
4. Xi Jinping, "Working Together toward a Better Future for Asia and the World," April 7, 2013, http://news.xinhuanet.com/english/china/2013-04/07/c_132290684.htm.
5. Ibid.
6. S. M. Krishna, "Address on 'India Now' at the Carrington Endowed Lecture Series Event, Hosted by the Southern Methodist University, Dallas," October 3, 2012, http://mea.gov.in/in-focus-article.htm?20646/External+Affairs+Ministers+address+on+quotIndia+Nowquot+at+the+Carrington+Endowed+Lecture+Series+event+hosted+by+the+Southern+Methodist+University+Dallas.
7. Sergey Lavrov, "Statement at the 67th Session of the UN General Assembly," September 28, 2012, http://gadebate.un.org/sites/default/files/gastatements/67/RU_en.pdf. Reprinted with the permission of the United Nations.
8. Republic of South Africa, International Relations & Cooperation, "Statement by H. E. Minister Maite Nkoana Mashabane, Minister of International Relations and Cooperation of the Republic of South Africa at the Debate of the United Nations Security Council on the Situation in the Middle East, 26 September 2012," http://www.dirco.gov.za/docs/speeches/2012/mash0926.html.
9. South African Foreign Policy Institute, "White paper on South African Foreign Policy—Building a Better World: The Diplomacy of Ubuntu," 2011, http://www.safpi.org/publications/white-paper-south-african-foreign-policy-building-better-world-diplomacy-ubuntu.
10. Dilma Roussef, "Statement at the 67th Session of the United Nations General Assembly," September 25, 2012, http://gadebate.un.org/sites/default/files/gastatements/67/BR_en.pdf. Reprinted with the permission of the United Nations.
11. Dilma Roussef, "Statement at the 68th Session of the United Nations General Assembly," September 24, 2013, http://www.un.int/brazil/speech/13d-PR-DR-68-AG-Abertura-Ing.html. Reprinted with the permission of the United Nations.
12. Personal correspondence with Dr. Gonzalo Canseco, Director General of Policy Planning at Secretaría de Relaciones Exteriores, March 10, 2014.
13. "Pope Warns of a 'Third World War,'" *Telegraph,* September 13, 2014, http://www.telegraph.co.uk/news/worldnews/europe/italy/11094114/Pope-warns-of-a-Third-World-War.html.
14. "Opening General Assembly Debate, Ban Urges Leadership to Move from 'Turbulence' to Peace," *Irish Sun,* September 25, 2014, http://www.irishsun.com/index.php/sid/226040005/scat/b8de8e630faf3631.
15. Iona Teixeira Stevens, "Brazil: Taking a Stand against Corruption," *Financial Times,* September 8, 2011, http://blogs.ft.com/beyond-brics/2011/09/08/brazil-taking-a-stand-against-corruption.

16. Samuel Huntington, "The Clash of Civilizations?" *Foreign Affairs,* Summer 1993, http://www.foreignaffairs.com/articles/48950/samuel-p-huntington/the-clash-of-civilizations.
17. Moisés Naím, *The End of Power: From Boardrooms to Battlefields and Churches to States, Why Being in Charge Isn't What It Used to Be* (New York: Basic Books, 2013).
18. U.S. Department of State, "Secretary of State Condoleezza Rice," http://2001–2009.state.gov/secretary.
19. CBS News, "Clinton: Use 'Smart Power' in Diplomacy," January 13, 2009, http://www.cbsnews.com/news/clinton-use-smart-power-in-diplomacy.
20. The Henry L. Stimson Center, American Foreign Service Association, and American Academy of Diplomacy, *Forging a 21st-Century Diplomatic Service for the United States through Professional Education and Training,* 2011, http://communicationleadership.usc.edu/forging_a_21st-century_diplomatic_service_for_the_united_states_through_professional_education_and_t.html.
21. U.S. Department of State, *Leading through Civilian Power: The First Quadrennial Diplomacy and Development Review,* 2010, http://www.state.gov/s/dmr/qddr/2010.
22. Richard Stengal, "Q&A: Hillary Clinton on Libya, China, the Middle East and Barack Obama," *Time,* Oct. 27, 2011, http://swampland.time.com/2011/10/27/qa-hillary-clinton-on-libya-china-the-middle-east-and-barack-obama.
23. Ibid.
24. U.S. Department of State, *Leading Through Civilian Power.*
25. Richard Stengal, "Q&A: Hillary Clinton."
26. Yelena Biberman, "The First Post-Communist Generation of Russian Diplomats and Prospects for Change in Russian Foreign Policy," 2008. In *Political Science Quarterly* 126, no. 4: 670.
27. Ibid, 671.
28. "The Elephant in the Region," *The Economist,* February 18, 2012, http://www.economist.com/node/21547795.
29. Krishnan Srinivaran, "India at the UN Security Council: A Retrospect," *The Telegraph Calcutta,* January 23, 2013, http://www.telegraphindia.com/1130123/jsp/opinion/story_16467700.jsp#.U8Q605RdWPY.
30. FCO Minutes of Management Board, from fco.gov.uk, accessed October 26, 2012 (no longer available).
31. Nicholas Watt, "UK Will Not 'Outsource' Foreign Policy, Says William Hague," *The Guardian,* September 8, 2011, http://www.theguardian.com/politics/2011/sep/08/not-outsource-foreign-policy-william-hague.
32. Government of Germany Federal Foreign Office, "Training for International Diplomats," http://www.auswaertiges-amt.de/EN/AusbildungKarriere/InternationDiplAusbildung/Uebersicht_node.html.
33. France in the United Kingdom, "Statement by Bernard Kouchner, Minister of Foreign and European Affairs, During His Joint Press Conference with Frédéric Mitterrand, Minister for Culture and Communication, and Xavier Darcos, Ambassador for External Cultural Action (Excerpts)," July 30, 2010, http://www.ambafrance-uk.org/Bernard-Kouchner-on-new-Institut.
34. John Pomfret, "U.S. Takes a Tougher Tone with China," *Washington Post,* July 30, 2010, http://www.washingtonpost.com/wp-dyn/content/article/2010/07/29/AR2010072906416.html.

35. "Deng Xiaoping's '24-Character Strategy,'" GlobalSecurity.org, http://www.globalsecurity.org/military/world/china/24-character.htm.
36. Leslie Hook, "Zuma Warns on Africa's Ties to China," *Financial Times,* July 19, 2012, http://www.ft.com/intl/cms/s/0/33686fc4-d171-11e1-bbbc-00144feabdc0.html#axzz3F69LddvA.
37. Christopher Hill, "Update on the Six-Party Talks," February 22, 2007 http://2001–2009.state.gov/p/eap/rls/rm/2007/81050.htm.
38. Personal correspondence with Dr. Gonzalo Canseco, March 10, 2014.
39. Niall Ferguson, *Colossus: The Rise and Fall of the American Empire* (New York, Penguin Books, 2005).
40. Integrated Implementation Framework, "UN Target for ODA—Global," http://iif.un.org/content/un-target-oda-global.
41. United Kingdom, Department for International Development, "What We Do," https://www.gov.uk/government/organisations/department-for-international-development.
42. U.S. Agency for International Development, "What We Do," http://www.usaid.gov/what-we-do.
43. The White House Office of the Press Secretary, "Remarks by the President at the National Defense University," May 23, 2013, http://www.whitehouse.gov/the-press-office/2013/05/23/remarks-president-national-defense-university.
44. USAID, "Progress," last updated March 17, 2014, http://www.usaid.gov/results-and-data/progress.
45. "Africa a Beneficiary of Chinese Cooperation," Capital FM News, May 14, 2013, http://www.capitalfm.co.ke/eblog/2013/05/14/africa-a-beneficiary-of-chinese-cooperation.
46. Paul Collier, *Bottom Billion: Why the Poorest Countries Are Failing and What Can Be Done about It* (New York: Oxford University Press, 2008), 96.
47. Ibid., 5.
48. Jeffrey Sachs, "Foreign Aid Works—It Saves Lives," *The Guardian,* May 30, 2012, http://www.theguardian.com/business/economics-blog/2012/may/30/foreign-aid-works-saves-lives.
49. Ibid.
50. William Easterly, "Planners vs. Searchers in African Agricultural Aid," A Living from Livestock: Pro-Poor Livestock Policy Initiative, April 12, 2008, http://www.fao.org/ag/AGAInfo/programmes/en/pplpi/docarc/pplpi_planners.pdf.
51. "Stop UK Aid To Pakistan Unless Taxes Increase, Urge MPs," Malaysan Digest, April 4, 2013, http://www.malaysiandigest.com/news/36-loca12/121512-mahathir-receives-2012-rafik-hariri-un-habitat-memorial-award-.html.
52. Robert Siegel, "Powell's Cautious on Iraq," NPR, April 20, 2004, http://www.npr.org/templates/story/story.php?storyId=1844476.
53. Rory Stewart and Gerald Knaus, *Can Intervention Work?* (New York: W. W. Norton, 2012).
54. Zalmay Khalilzad, "The Three Futures for Afghanistan: Why the Country Needs a Long-Term Commitment from the United States," *Foreign Affairs,* December 16, 2011, http://www.foreignaffairs.com/articles/136870/zalmay-khalilzad/the-three-futures-for-afghanistan.
55. Sean Rayment, "Army Chief Warns of 'Terrifying Prospect' of Failure in Afghanistan," *The Telegraph,* October 3, 2009, http://www.telegraph.co.uk/news/newstopics/onthefrontline/6258028/Army-chief-warns-of-terrifying-prospect-of-failure-in-Afghanistan.html.

56. Rory Stewart, "What Can Afghanistan and Bosnia Teach Us about Libya?" *The Guardian,* October 7, 2011, http://www.theguardian.com/world/2011/oct/08/libya-intervention-rory-stewart.
57. "The Three Futures for Afghanistan—Zalmay Khalilzad," JK Alternative Viewpoint, December 16, 2011, http://jkalternativeviewpoint.com/jkalternate/?p=1716.
58. "The Responsibility to Protect: Ending Mass Atrocity Crimes Once and for All," Brookings Institution, September 1, 2008, http://www.brookings.edu/research/books/2008/responsibilitytoprotect.
59. Kofi Annan, "Intervention," June 26, 1998, http://www.ditchley.co.uk/conferences/past-programme/1990–1999/1998/lecture-xxxv.
60. "UN Security Council Resolution 1973 (2011) on Libya—Full Text," *The Guardian,* March 17, 2011, http://www.theguardian.com/world/2011/mar/17/un-security-council-resolution.
61. Anthony Lake, "Defining Missions, Setting Deadlines: Meeting New Security Challenges in the Post War World," March 6, 1996, http://clinton4.nara.gov/textonly/WH/EOP/NSC/html/speeches/tlgwu.html.
62. Linda J. Blimes, "The Financial Legacy of Iraq and Afghanistan: How Wartime Spending Decisions Will Constrain Future National Security Budgets," Harvard Kennedy School, 2013, http://www.hks.harvard.edu/var/ezp_site/storage/fckeditor/file/pdfs/centers-programs/centers/mrcbg/publications/fwp/MRCBG_fwp_2013-01_Bilmes_financial_legacy.pdf.
63. Ibid.

Chapter 10 Notes

1. Jessica Tuchman Mathews, "Saving America," Thomas Jefferson Foundation Medal Lecture In Citizen Leadership, April 13, 2012.
2. Richard N. Haass, "What International Community?" Project Syndicate, July 24, 2013, http://www.project-syndicate.org/commentary/the-broken-tools-of-global-cooperation-by-richard-n-haass.
3. Parag Khanna, *How to Run the World: Charting a Course to the Next Renaissance* (New York: Random House, 2011), 209.
4. World Public Opinion: Global Public Opinion on International Affairs, "Poll Finds Most Publics around the World Want Their Governments to Be More Cooperative," December 9, 2009, http://www.worldpublicopinion.org/pipa/articles/views_on_countriesregions_bt/650.php?lb.
5. Ipsos Global @dvisor, "Methodology," http://ipsosglobaladvisor.com/methodology.aspx.
6. Ipsos, "Global Citizens Express Broad Support for Involvement in World Affairs: Less So During Difficult Economic Times," November 18, 2011, http://www.ipsos-na.com/news-polls/pressrelease.aspx?id=5417.
7. Global Citizens Network, accessed October 15, 2014, https://www.globalcitizens.org/missionvision.
8. John F. Kennedy, "Commencement Address at American University," June 10, 1963, John F. Kennedy Presidential Library and Museum, http://www.jfklibrary.org/Asset-Viewer/BWC7I4C9QUmLG9J6I80y8w.aspx.
9. U.S. Government Accountability Office, "Nonproliferation: Agencies Could Improve Information Sharing and End-Use Monitoring on Unmanned Aerial Vehicle Exports," July 2012, http://www.gao.gov/assets/600/593131.pdf.

10. Joseph Nye, "Get Smart: Combining Hard and Soft Power," *Foreign Affairs* (July/August 2009), http://www.foreignaffairs.com/articles/65163/joseph-s-nye-jr/get-smart.
11. Greenpeace, "What We Do," http://www.greenpeace.org/usa/en/campaigns.
12. Avaaz.org, "About Us," http://www.avaaz.org/en/about.php.
13. The Global Fund to Fight AIDS, Tuberculosis and Malaria, "Fighting AIDS, Tuberculosis and Malaria," http://www.theglobalfund.org/en/about/diseases.
14. ABC News, "Iranian Foreign Minister Javad Zarif in an Exclusive Interview with ABC," September 29, 2013, http://wn.com/iranian_foreign_minister_javad_zarif_in_an_exclusive_interview_with_abc.
15. Thomas Rid, "Cracks in the Jihad," *Wilson Quarterly* (Winter 2010): 40–7.
16. Khan Academy, "Our Mission," https://www.khanacademy.org/about.
17. Jeffrey Sachs, "Lecture 2: Survival in the Anthropocene," BBC Reith Lecture at Peking University, 2007, http://www.bbc.co.uk/radi04/reith2007/lecture2.shtml.
18. Jeffrey Sachs, "Lecture 3: The Great Convergence," BBC Reith Lecture at Columbia University, 2007, http://www.bbc.co.uk/radi04/reith2007/lecture3.shtml.
19. Parag Khanna, *How to Run the World: Charting a Course to the Next Renaissance* (New York: Random House, 2011), 57.
20. Open Government Partnership, "About: Mission and Goals," http://www.opengovpartnership.org/about/mission-and-goals.
21. Paul Farmer, *Haiti: After the Earthquake* (New York: PublicAffairs, 2011),145.
22. Ian Birrell, "Haiti and the Shaming of the Aid Zealots: How Donated Billions Have Increased Poverty and Corruption," January 27, 2012, http://www.dailymail.co.uk/news/article-2092425/Haiti-earthquake-How-donated-billions-INCREASED-poverty-corruption.html.
23. "Haiti's Slow Recovery," *New York Times,* January 8, 2012, http://www.nytimes.com/2012/01/09/opinion/haitis-slow-recovery.html.
24. International Organization for Migration, "About IOM," http://www.iom.int/cms/about-iom.
25. Ian Birrell, "Haiti and the Shaming of the Aid Zealots: How Donated Billions Have Increased Poverty and Corruption," *Daily Mail,* January 27, 2012, http://www.dailymail.co.uk/news/article-2092425/Haiti-earthquake-How-donated-billions-INCREASED-poverty-corruption.html.
26. Kathie Klarreich and Linda Polman, "The NGO Republic of Haiti," *The Nation,* November 19, 2012, http://www.thenation.com/article/170929/ngo-republic-haiti.
27. Ibid.
28. Tom Phillips and Claire Provost, "Haiti Earthquake: Two Years on, and Just Half of Promised Aid Has Been Delivered," January 11, 2012, *The Guardian,* http://www.theguardian.com/world/2012/jan/11/haiti-earthquake-promised-aid-not-delivered.
29. Ibid.

Chapter 11 Notes

1. Peter F. Cowhey and Jonathan D. Aronson, *Transforming Global Information and Communication Markets: The Political Economy of Innovation* (Cambridge, MA: MIT Press, 2012), 7.
2. Eric Schmidt and Jared Cohen, *The New Digital Age: Reshaping the Future of People, Nations and Business* (New York: Alfred A. Knopf, 2013), 49.

3. Jay Yarow, "Google CEO Larry Page Wants a Totally Separate World Where Tech Companies Can Conduct Experiments on People," *Business Insider,* May 16, 2013, http://www.businessinsider.com/google-ceo-larry-page-wants-a-place-for-experiments-2013–5.
4. Eric Schmidt and Jared Cohen, "Web Censorship: The Net Is Closing In," April 23, 2013, *The Guardian,* http://www.theguardian.com/technology/2013/apr/23/web-censorship-net-closing-in.
5. Ben Blanchard, "Head of Xinhua Says Western Media Pushing Revolution in China," September 5, 2013, Reuters, http://whatsupic.com/news-politics-world/2551-head-of-xinhua-says-western-media-pushing-revolution-in-china.html.
6. Valerie Strauss, "Commencement Speaker Blasts Students," *Washington Post,* June 8, 2012, http://www.washingtonpost.com/blogs/answer-sheet/post/commencement-speaker-blasts-students/2012/06/08/gJQATvF1MV_blog.html.
7. Fergus Hanson, "Revolution @State: The Spread of Ediplomacy," Lowy Institute for International Policy, March 2012, http://lowyinstitute.richmedia-server.com/docs/Hanson_Revolution-at-State.pdf.
8. Jonathan McClory, "The New Persuaders II: A 2011 Global Ranking of Soft Power," Institute for Government, http://www.instituteforgovernment.org.uk/sites/default/files/publications/The%20New%20PersuadersII_0.pdf.
9. The United Nations Law of the Sea Treaty Information Center, "The Law of the Sea Treaty: Background," http://unlawoftheseatreaty.org.
10. Adam Smith, *An Inquiry into the Nature and Causes of the Wealth of Nations,* 2 vols., ed. R. H. Campbell and A. S. Skinner, textual ed. W. B. Todd (Indianapolis, IN: Liberty Fund, 1981; Oxford, UK: Clarendon, 1976), IV.vii.c.80: 626.
11. Stephanie Nebehay, "China, Russia Seek Greater Control of Internet: U.S.," March 7, 2013, Reuters, http://www.reuters.com/article/2013/03/07/net-us-internet-usa-idUSBRE92617220130307.
12. IBM, "What Is Big Data?" http://www-01.ibm.com/software/data/bigdata/what-is-big-data.html.
13. Jeffrey Sachs, "Lecture 5: Global Politics in a Complex Age," BBC Reith Lecture Series, 2007, http://www.bbc.co.uk/radi04/reith2007/lecture5.shtml.
14. CBS News, "Leon Panetta Warns of 'Cyber Pearl Harbor,'" October 13, 2012, http://www.washingtonpost.com/posttv/leon-panetta-warns-of-cyber-pearl-harbor/2012/10/13/6cdcbd6e-14c9–11e2–9a39–1f5a7f6fe945_video.html.
15. Elisabeth Bumiller and Thom Shanker, "Panetta Warns of Dire Threat of Cyberattack on U.S.," *New York Times,* October 11, 2012, http://www.nytimes.com/2012/10/12/world/panetta-warns-of-dire-threat-of-cyberattack.html?pagewanted=all&_r=0.
16. Asif Ahmed, "Cyber Warfare and Information Security for India," February 16, 2014, http://www.eurasiareview.com/16022014-cyber-warfare-information-security-india.
17. Tina Rosenberg, *Join the Club: How Peer Pressure Can Transform the World,* New York: W. W. Norton & Co., 2011.

Chapter 12 Notes

1. Daniel Howden, "World Bank Chief Jim Yong Kim: 'They Said Poverty Would Always Be with Us. Well, Maybe Not,'" July 7, 2013, *The Independent,* http://

www.independent.co.uk/news/people/profiles/world-bank-chief-jim-yong-kim-they-said-poverty-would-always-be-with-us-well-maybe-not-8693880.html.

2. Richard Haass, "What International Community?" Project Syndicate, July 24, 2013, http://www.project-syndicate.org/commentary/the-broken-tools-of-global-cooperation-by-richard-n-haass.
3. European Union Institute for Security Studies and United States National Intelligence Council, *Global Governance 2025: At a Critical Juncture,* 2010, http://www.iss.europa.eu/uploads/media/Global__Governance_2025.pdf
4. Ibid.
5. William Davison and Ahmed Feteha, "Ethiopia Rejects Egypt Proposal on Nile as Dam Talks Falter," Bloomberg, January 8, 2014, http://www.bloomberg.com/news/2014–01–08/ethiopia-rejects-egyptian-proposal-on-nile-as-dam-talks-fal ter.html.
6. Institute for Security Studies, *Global Governance 2025.*
7. Ibid.
8. Robert Kagan, "America Has Made the World Freer, Safer and Wealthier," CNN, March 14, 2012, http://www.cnn.com/2012/03/14/opinion/kagan-world-america-made.
9. Bruce Jones, "Managing a Changing World: How the United States Has Become the Largest Minority Shareholder in an Expanding Global Order," *Foreign Policy,* March 14, 2011, http://www.foreignpolicy.com/articles/2011/03/14/building_the_new_world_order.
10. "Making Up: In the Bush Years America Seemed Overmighty. It Is Now Pulling Back," *The Economist,* November 23, 2013, http://www.economist.com/news/special-report/21590109-bush-years-america-seemed-overmighty-it-now-pulling-back-making-up.
11. Henry Kissinger, *World Order,* (New York: Penguin Press, 2014), 372–3.
12. Sir Ivor Roberts, ed., *Satow's Diplomatic Practice,* 6th ed. (New York: Oxford University Press, 2009).
13. The White House Office of the Press Secretary, "Remarks by the President at the Acceptance of the Nobel Peace Prize," December 10, 2009, http://www.whitehouse.gov/the-press-office/remarks-president-acceptance-nobel-peace-prize.
14. New York University, Center on Global Cooperation, *The Use of Force, Crisis Diplomacy and the Responsibilities of States,* May 2012, http://cic.es.its.nyu.edu/sites/default/files/abu_dhabi_conference_2012.pdf.
15. Ibid.

Chapter 13 Notes

1. World Economic Forum, "World Economic Forum Annual Meeting 2014: Executive Summary," http://www3.weforum.org/docs/AM14/WEF_AM14_ExecutiveSummary.pdf.
2. Norman Angell, *The Great Illusion,* quoted in Robert Kagan, *The World America Made* (New York: Vintage Books, 2013).
3. Robert Kagan, "The Myth of American Decline," *New Republic,* January 11, 2012, http://www.newrepublic.com/article/politics/magazine/99521/america-world-power-declinism.
4. David Miliband, "Responsible Sovreignty," Speech at Peking University, Beijing, February 29, 2008, http://collections.europarchive.org/tna/20080205132101/

www.fco.gov.uk/servlet/Front%3fpagename=OpenMarket/Xcelerate/ShowPage&c=Page&cid=1007029391647&a=KArticle&aid=1203946851345.

5. Sir Ivor Roberts, ed., *Satow's Diplomatic Practice,* 6th ed. (New York: Oxford University Press, 2009).
6. Moisés Naím, *The End of Power: From Boardrooms to Battlefields and Churches to States, Why Being in Charge Isn't What It Used to Be* (New York: Basic Books, 2013).
7. J. P. Morgan, "Eye on the Market: Outlook 2013," http://www.zerohedge.com/news/2013-01-02/96-charts-have-be-seen-believed-2013.
8. University of Groningen, "Thomas Jefferson letter to John Tyler, May 26, 1810," http://www.let.rug.nl/usa/presidents/thomas-jefferson/letters-of-thomas-jefferson/jef1205.php.
9. Personal email correspondence with Sir Paul Collier, December 28, 2013.
10. Personal email correspondence with Parag Khanna, September 26, 2013.
11. Personal email correspondence with Paul Sharp, December 30, 2013.
12. Personal email correspondence with Carne Ross, January 2, 2014.
13. Personal email correspondence with Alan K. Henrikson, February 9, 2014.
14. Personal email correspondence with Dr. Peter Howarth, March 17, 2014.
15. Tariq Malik, "Astronaut Looks at Earth: 'It's Too Beautiful,'" Space.com, May 18, 2009, http://www.space.com/6715-astronaut-earth-beautiful.html.
16. "Media Brings Disaster Home," *Union-Tribune San Diego,* February 3, 2003, http://legacy.utsandiego.com/news/science/columbia/20030203-9999_1c3tvspace.html
17. Donella Meadows, "Astronauts and Cosmonauts Tell Us about Home," October 20, 1988, http://www.donellameadows.org/archives/astronauts-and-cosmonauts-tell-us-about-home.
18. 60 Minutes, "Tesla and SpaceX: Elon Musk's Industrial Empire," March 30, 2014, http://www.cbsnews.com/news/tesla-and-spacex-elon-musks-industrial-empire.
19. John F. Kennedy, "Establishment of the Peace Corps," March 1, 1961, http://millercenter.org/president/speeches/speech-3366.

CQ Press, an imprint of SAGE, is the leading publisher of books, periodicals, and electronic products on American government and international affairs. CQ Press consistently ranks among the top commercial publishers in terms of quality, as evidenced by the numerous awards its products have won over the years. CQ Press owes its existence to Nelson Poynter, former publisher of the *St. Petersburg Times,* and his wife Henrietta, with whom he founded *Congressional Quarterly* in 1945. Poynter established CQ with the mission of promoting democracy through education and in 1975 founded the Modern Media Institute, renamed The Poynter Institute for Media Studies after his death. The Poynter Institute (www.poynter.org) is a nonprofit organization dedicated to training journalists and media leaders.

In 2008, CQ Press was acquired by SAGE, a leading international publisher of journals, books, and electronic media for academic, educational, and professional markets. Since 1965, SAGE has helped inform and educate a global community of scholars, practitioners, researchers, and students spanning a wide range of subject areas, including business, humanities, social sciences, and science, technology, and medicine. A privately owned corporation, SAGE has offices in Los Angeles, London, New Delhi, and Singapore, in addition to the Washington, D.C., office of CQ Press.

Index